Ken Murray is an award-winning journalist and presents *The Agenda* on LMFM Radio.

From 2016 to 2025, he covered Ireland for Euronews TV in Brussels.

A *Jacobs Radio Award* winner in 1990, he has been a former Dublin correspondent for BBC Northern Ireland.

He was also a political correspondent with INN Radio News.

In 2008, he won an *Irish World* Humanitarian Award in London when a radio appeal he reported helped to find the last missing next-of-kin from the 1974 Dublin-Monaghan bombings.

In 2021, he was presented with a *Diplomacy Ireland* Award for his reporting on the Irish dimension of Brexit for Euronews TV.

Ken ghost-wrote *All Kinds of Everything*, the autobiography of former MEP and Irish presidential candidate Dana Rosemary Scallon, published in 2007 by Gill and Macmillan, Dublin.

He holds a Master's Degree in Journalism from Dublin City University.

Dedication

This book is dedicated to my Father and Mother, Jimmy and Sadie Reavey, and the families of all those who died in The Troubles and are still seeking truth and justice.

The Killing of the Reavey Brothers

British murder and cover-up in Northern Ireland

My story of British collusion and cover-up

Eugene Reavey

with

Ken Murray

MERCIER PRESS

MERCIER PRESS
Cork
www.mercierpress.ie

© Eugene Reavey & Ken Murray, 2024.
First published in June 2025.

ISBN 978-1-78117-875-1
978-1-78117-876-8 eBook

Cover design: Sarah O'Flaherty

Acknowledgements

The author and publisher would like to thank Aaron Stephen Fanning and Proper Octopus Records for permission to quote from A.S. Fanning, 'Never Been Gone'. Thanks also to Walton Music Ltd for permission to quote from 'The Boys of the old Brigade', words and music by Patrick McGuigan.

This book is sold subject to the condition that it shall not, by way of trade or otherwise, be lent, resold, hired out or otherwise circulated without the publisher's prior consent in any form of binding or cover other than that in which it is published and without a similar condition including this condition being imposed on the subsequent purchaser.

No part of this publication may be reproduced or transmitted in any form or by any means, electronic or mechanical, including photocopying, recording or any information or retrieval system, without the prior permission of the publisher in writing.

Printed in the EU.

Contents

Preface	7
Introduction	9
A Wild Child	13
Sectarian Tensions start to Boil	21
Crouzon's Syndrome comes to our door	35
Mystery Surrounds Local Killings	47
Bloodbath	57
Hell on Earth	72
The Village of Black Flags	89
From Hope to Heartbreak	97
Step Out of the Car Please	118
Welcome to South Armagh	124
British Brutality in Ballymoyer	136
Building an Empire	151
Cover-up Starts to Emerge	154
The Slaughter Continues	165
Better to Let Sleeping Dogs Lie	167
The Hunger Strikes hit Home	182
Pay up or Pay the Price	194

Jimmy Craig, 'An Innocent Man', so to speak	211
The Collusion Intensifies	222
He calls himself 'Doctor Death'	234
Porridge	241
Brits Signal Desire to Leave	250
Talks about Talks	255
King Rat	258
Paisley puts our Lives in Danger	261
The Collusion Cat Escapes from the Bag	272
Un-Fair, Fair	282
There's a New Sheriff in Town	283
Garda File goes Missing	289
The Cover-up Continues	292
Paisley says 'No, No'	311
Raised Hopes amid Family Loss	317
Glenanne Gang Names Revealed	326
The Long Search for Truth Continues	332
The Quest for Truth and Justice still Goes On	338
Endnotes	365
Bibliography	368
Index	369

Preface

'On some other plane
Nothing is wrong
I can see you walking in
Smiling like you'd never been gone.'
AS Fanning, 'Never Been Gone'

We are surrounded by the ghosts of loved ones. Eugene Reavey is haunted by them.

On 4 January 1976 around teatime, gunmen walked through the always open front door of the Reavey family home. On any other Sunday, they would all have been there, bar Kathleen who lived in London, the eight boys, three girls and Eugene's parents. But on that evening, they had gone to visit their Aunt Rose-Ellen in Camlough, except for John Martin, Brian and Anthony, who had stayed at home to watch *Celebrity Squares*.

The first gunman opened up with a Sterling submachine gun, killing John Martin in a hail of bullets. He was twenty-four years old. Brian tried to run but was shot through the heart and died on the bedroom floor. He was twenty-two. Anthony, who was only seventeen, dived under the bed and despite being riddled with bullets, he survived, and crawled 200 metres to Pat and Angela O'Hanlon's house. When the O'Hanlon's opened their door, the blood-soaked boy told them, 'they're all dead'. Within a month, Anthony was dead too. The murders were carried out by the Glenanne gang, a secretive alliance of loyalist paramilitaries, British soldiers and police officers from the Royal Ulster Constabulary who murdered Catholics with impunity – no point calling the police when the police are doing the killing.

I have seen and felt Eugene Reavey's pain too often. The Bloody Sunday families. Ballymurphy. Springhill. My good friend John Finucane whose father Pat was murdered in front of him. In our part of the world, the list is endless. As a barrister, I have watched the grieving parents of murdered sons and daughters sit at the back of court through long trials and inquests. I have seen the Stardust nightclub families suffering as though their loved ones died yesterday, not half a century ago.

Like Eugene Reavey, they are tied to the stake. They suffer because they must. Because deep down, there is something in human beings that demands justice, some- thing that demands respect and honesty. Something that screams, 'I deserve to be seen and heard. I will not be treated with contempt. I will not be lied to.'

I hope that this book helps to bring Eugene the justice and peace he deserves. That some day, on that other plane where nothing is wrong, he will see his brothers walking in. Smiling like they've never been gone.

JOE BROLLY

Introduction

On Sunday 4 January 1976, British paramilitary group, the UVF, shot dead two members of the Reavey family in Whitecross, Armagh. Ten minutes later, twenty miles away, three members of the O'Dowd family in Ballydougan near Lurgan were also shot dead. A third member of the Reavey family who sustained injuries in the first shooting, died three weeks later from a so-called, 'brain haemorrhage'.

As events emerged, it became apparent that these killings were outstanding for a variety of reasons. In the case of the Reavey brothers, UVF gunmen were able to move in and out of Whitecross village in South Armagh, carry out their fatal shootings and disappear in minutes without fear of arrest, prosecution or conviction. The subsequent management of the investigation by the RUC police force was also suspicious, unorthodox, shoddy and incomplete, raising concerns that a more sinister agenda was at play.

A number of high profile, but highly suspicious, atrocities had occurred in the mid-Ulster region in the previous two years raising additional questions. As events and developments evolved in subsequent years, the resistant behaviour of the British political system and the revelation that a local protected paramilitary gang was allowed to run amok, cast ever further suspicion on the nature and motives behind the six Reavey and O'Dowd murders.

For Eugene Reavey, the slaughter of his three brothers for being nothing other than Catholics/nationalists and the constant rebuttals of co-operation from the British state, has led him on a lifetime journey of relentless search-after-search in pursuit of justice and above all else, the truth. Like so many other families in Northern Ireland, he has engaged in a personal odyssey of discovery to establish who exactly murdered his three brothers, but in the process found himself threatened, harassed, humiliated and blamed in the British parliament for a separate massacre that he had no hand, act or part of. His determined quest for answers has dominated his entire adult life since 1976 only to be met with a British agenda that fails to own up to its own malevolent conduct in Northern Ireland which cost innocent lives on both sides of the religious and political divide.

The Reavey quest for answers has been driven by a conflict where discriminated Catholics/nationalists said 'enough was enough'. By the early 1970s, the 'Troubles' in Northern Ireland were at their peak. What had started out in the late 1960s as peaceful demands for civil and equal rights by oppressed nationalists/Catholics against a culture of blatant discrimination by pro-British unionists, supported by a London government, had deteriorated to a state of almost civil war.

Almost all British security services agencies engaged in appalling activities that amounted to state-backed murder and atrocities. The list is as lengthy as it is shocking. They included the British army and its numerous regiments, the unionist-dominated RUC police force, the Ulster Defence Regiment, MI5, MI6, the Secret Air Service (SAS), Special Branch, the Forces Research Unit (FRU) the Mobile Reaction Force (MRF) and finally, certain individuals who later continued their careers with the Police Service of Northern Ireland to name some.

In predominantly nationalist South Armagh, families got on with life in the early 1970s. However, as killings and sectarian assassinations mounted across, what will be referred to in this story as, Northern Ireland, a number of families in the South Armagh area found themselves targeted by a ruthless loyalist gang for simply being Catholic and Irish nationalists. The same loyalist gang had the assistance of certain elements within the British security apparatus which meant the UK government was effectively complicit in murder.

This is the story of extraordinary events in South Armagh as recalled by Eugene Reavey, a committed GAA football fan and dedicated family man who believes in a united Ireland by peaceful means. In his own words, he tells the story of his ongoing battle with a stubborn British establishment which has put every conceivable legal obstacle in the way of the Reavey family in an effort to cover up who attacked his family home and robbed them of their three brothers in the prime of their young lives in horrific circumstances.

His story of endless personal threats and brutal intimidation by British security units is not an isolated one by any means in the long bloody history of Northern Ireland. It reveals how a rural farming community was deliberately besieged and abused by British security forces whose outrageous activities helped to prolong the Troubles.

Despite a concerted malicious campaign by a local British loyalist to wrongly label him a member of the IRA, with devastating consequences for being nothing more than a GAA enthusiast, Eugene Reavey is emphatic that he was never a member of any republican group.

This story highlights the extraordinary pressure put on his innocent family because of blatant lies told in the House of Commons. It should be stressed that Eugene Reavey and his family are *not* anti-British but his story is highly critical of British policy and conduct in Northern Ireland.

This shocking personal account on the horrendous events of that time in South Armagh also reveal how an exclusive select group of local ruthless unionist paramilitaries were all but given free rein to operate undercover with the support and encouragement of elements within the UK Ministry of Defence. Most of the same local paramilitaries were allowed to avoid prosecution and convictions in the courts as competing units within the UK security structure engaged in cunning cover-ups to protect their sectarian hitmen.

This book also reveals, for the first time, an extraordinary British army policy to execute innocent nationalists in a ruthless plan to provoke the IRA into a full-scale war with loyalists and the security forces during a time of ceasefire.

The Killing of the Reavey Brothers: British murder and cover-up in Northern Ireland is a stark reminder that while the Troubles are over since the late 1990s, many families, on both sides of the political and religious divide, are still seeking truth and justice. Their determined quests are made more difficult by an unhelpful and stubborn British state which is determined to bury all records of its sinister military past in Ireland.

This is Eugene's story.

Ken Murray

A Wild Child

> As we knelt down to say our prayers last night and prayed for my sons who died and the son who was injured, we prayed also for the men who had shot them because they will have more to suffer as the years go on. I hope there will be no retaliation either on my Protestant neighbours or indeed Protestants anywhere. My feeling is that if my sons' deaths help to stop the killings then they will have not died in vain.
>
> JIMMY REAVEY, 5 JANUARY 1976

MENTION THE WORDS 'SOUTH Armagh' to anybody outside the area and the most familiar response is, 'Bandit Country'. Everybody in the area has heard this before and, in most cases, it has been amplified by the media in Belfast, Dublin and London who are completely ignorant of the culture, history and nuances of everyday life in border communities. The outside view has been exaggerated to give the impression that this is a hostile place for anybody who doesn't support Irish unity.

In reality, South Armagh is an extraordinary place. It is an area with a vibrant cultural identity, rich in traditional music, Irish dance and Gaelic games. It is a place of outstanding natural beauty with a proud and welcoming people and has played an important part in the history of Ireland.

For me, South Armagh and in particular, the village of Whitecross, is home for the Reavey family. It's where I was born, educated, married and raised my seven children. It's also where our three innocent brothers on one horrible Sunday night of terror back in 1976 were shot. But what were the controversial circumstances by which John Martin (24), Brian (22) and Anthony (17) were gunned down in a one-minute bloody blitz at our family home and what have their horrible deaths done to lead me on a continuing crusade to seek the truth all these decades later?

My mission is not a lone one as so many families in Northern Ireland and some in the Republic continue to seek answers from the British as to why their innocent loved ones were killed by UK loyalists and agents of the crown to ensure that the six counties remain under London rule.

In order to know where I come from, one needs to know where my family fit into the everyday life of Whitecross in rural South Armagh, a small village surrounded by rolling green hills of farmland, eight miles from the Co. Monaghan border, six miles from Newry, five from Markethill, three from Bessbrook, four from Newtownhamilton and forty miles from Belfast.

The Reaveys have a long association with Whitecross, Armagh. My grandfather Patsy, a council worker, was born outside Newtownhamilton in 1882 on the Monaghan-Armagh border while my grandmother Catherine Conlon, was born in Ballinarea, Co. Armagh in 1888, four miles away.

The penniless nationalist Ireland they lived in was under harsh British rule where the ruling unionist class controlled wealth-creation and lived in the luxury of the day.

The shocking legacy of the British penal laws on the nationalists in Ireland was still being felt as access to full education and owning assets or accumulating anything that might be classed as 'wealth', was unthinkable.

When my grandparents got married in 1910, they moved to Whitecross and lived in a labourer's cottage, a move that firmly planted the Reavey roots in the area. Patsy Reavey, my uncle, was the first born in 1912 followed by Laura, John, Philomena who died aged four in 1927, Frank who died aged nineteen in 1935 and my Father James, known locally as Jimmy, came along in 1923.

My Father Jimmy, just like my uncle Patsy, left school at fourteen and went to work at Patton's Flax Mill in nearby Carrickananney. They could only get bouts of work in three and four-month blocks. Pattons, it should be stressed, were good honest unionist employers and long after the Mill had ceased to function in the early 1960s following a fire, my Father remained close friends with them. My uncle John, just like my Father, was also a 'scutcher' with Pattons, a job that separated the impurities from flax to prepare it for spinning into cotton cloth.

If one was to draw a line south of nearby Markethill, it revealed that the British government never invested in industry around where we lived. Pattons aside, one made a hard-earned living of very modest means from farming and that was the way my Father and his siblings endured things throughout their working lives.

On and off, my Father worked for Pattons for about thirty years and along the way he met Sadie Loughran from Tullyah townland, two miles up from where we lived and they married in Carrickananney chapel in October 1942. They rented a wee house nearby where their first three children, Kathleen (1943), Seamus (1945) and Frank (1946) were born. By 1947, Mum and Dad moved to the Forrester's Hall in Greyhilla on the Priest Bush Road in Whitecross where they set up home in very unusual circumstances.

The wee hall, at one time a dancing venue for céilí bands and practice centre for St Theresa's pipe band, became vacant and somebody made it known locally that it could double up as accommodation for an expanding family. My Father enquired and before long, he, Sadie and clan ended up living in the hall with the Reaveys occupying the upper end of the building which doubled up as a meeting room for the committee of Drumherriff Gaelic football club. Unorthodox it was, but for the newly married couple with three noisy children, it was home.

I came along in April 1948. The night I was born was remembered locally for good and bad news. As I came into the world, a GAA football match was taking place in O'Hanlon's ten-acre field across the road from the Forrester's Hall. During the match, word came through that young Frank Cunningham was found drowned near his home in Ballymoyer. Frank was an uncle of the great Pat Jennings who went on to play in goal for Tottenham Hotspur, Arsenal and Northern Ireland. It was a week of mixed emotions for Mum and Dad as I had been born and they both knew Frank well.

My brother, John Martin, was born in the hall in 1951 and shortly afterwards, we moved to Drumherriff townland to a semi-detached two-storey council house. Oliver was born in 1953. Towards the end of 1954, my grandfather and my uncle John bought a farm in Drumhoney, Whitecross and when the cottage where my Father was born became vacant, we moved from Drumherriff to Greyhilla, Whitecross, to the house where it all began for my Father.

Eileen was born there in 1955, followed by Brian in 1957, Anthony in 1958, Paul in 1963, Una in 1965 and Colleen in 1968. The Reavey family was then complete. As a child I was something of a rambler, running here and there as curious energetic little boys do. When I was five years old, I used to run away from Drumherriff to my grandmother's house on the Tullyah Road. My grandmother had a habit of opening the curtains early in the morning before the Mill lorry for the linen factory in Bessbrook would pass to pick up workers. When she opened her blinds in the morning, sometimes as early as 7.15 a.m., she would see me sitting on the big stone at the end of her wall. My grandmother had no way of contacting my Mother to let her know where I was. If she saw someone she knew coming along the road on a bicycle, she'd say 'will you run down to Sadie Reavey and tell her this little skitter is here'.

Shortly after returning to live in Greyhilla in 1953, Dad built a shed adjacent to the house. My uncle, Peter John Loughran, who lived locally, put in trojan work in helping him get the job done. It was constructed of second-hand timber and tin. At the rear of the cottage, we had half an acre of land where my Father planted potatoes and vegetables every spring.

WHEN I WAS FIVE years old, I was sent to St Malachy's primary school in nearby Ballymoyer which is about three miles up the road from our house. There were no buses at the time which meant a lengthy walk to and from there every day. I can remember the first day I went to school. It was a very wet morning. I had a wee cap and a coat on me. My older brothers Seamus and Frank took a hand each as they walked me out the gate. From what I recall, I was an energetic child at school and was regularly up to mischief meaning that every so often, I was called before the Head Mistress Mrs Kennon to explain my actions.

As I came to the end of my time in primary school, one day Mrs Kennon handed me an envelope addressed to my Mother. 'Oh no,' I thought, 'I'm in trouble again!'

My Mother opened the envelope as my legs shook from nervousness. As her eyes worked their way down through the page, I could slowly see the expression on her face change from one of worry to delight. She informed me that Mrs Kennon had recommended me for a place at the Abbey Christian Brothers primary school in Newry with a view to sitting the 11-plus exam. At the time, it was rare for somebody in Ballymoyer school to get the opportunity to sit the 11-plus and in 1958, my recommendation was a big deal – I entered Abbey Primary School in April of that year.

When I sat my 11-plus exam, I failed it. I returned the following year and did the Review Exam and having been successful this time, I received a scholarship to attend the Abbey Grammar School in Newry. Going from a country primary school to one in a town was a big adjustment for me to make but I couldn't wait to get started in secondary school, in particular, I couldn't wait to get on the school GAA teams.

The GAA continued to be a major part of my life throughout my teenage years. I was playing for the local St Killian's Under-16 and Under-18 teams in Whitecross and played regularly for their senior team. This was mainly because many of our players had emigrated in the early 1960s rather than me being a gifted footballer. Gaelic football was very tough in South Armagh at the time. The old heavy brown ball didn't favour young light players.

IT WAS AROUND THIS time in 1966, Gusty Spence of the UVF

shot dead eighteen-year-old Catholic barman Peter Ward in the Shankill area in Belfast. Ward had been drinking with friends in the Malvern Arms off the Shankill Road when Catholics could do such a thing in that part of the city. While it got a mention on the radio news, we all presumed it was over some local dispute that got out of hand. Little did we know that this one killing and events elsewhere were to be the start of an endless murder cycle that was to destroy thousands of families, including our own.

Around that time, as I made my way through Abbey Grammar school, I became acquainted on the school bus with Noel Kilpatrick from outside Glenanne village which is two miles north of where we lived at Whitecross. Noel went to the Newry Model School for Protestant boys. We nodded for the first few weeks and as time passed, we got to know each other well. We found that we had a lot in common. In those days, Catholics and Protestants mixed freely in rural areas, unlike some other parts of Northern Ireland. He also had a great interest in rugby and played every Saturday for Newry High and later was a first-team player with Portadown Rugby Club. I would regularly regale him with our exploits on the GAA fields of South Armagh. Most of the topics covered on a Monday were outshone by tales of rows held on the Gaelic football fields the day before.

By the mid-1960s, I was doing well. I had passed my 'O' or Ordinary-Levels and was back at Abbey Grammar in Newry studying for my 'A' or Advanced-Level exams. I was studying English, Irish and Geography for my 'A'-Levels with no idea in my head what career path I wished to pursue.

One day shortly after returning to school following the summer break, I was talking to my Geography teacher, Jimmy Haffey, who asked if I had any career ambitions. I told him 'no' and he replied that someone like me who had experience of working on a farm, would be better off going to Loughry College in Cookstown, Co. Tyrone and studying agriculture. Jimmy contacted the principal at Loughry College and they agreed to accept me. It was all done quickly and one month later in October 1966, I was a new entrant, courtesy of a generous scholarship, learning everything from when to pull a calf, the scourge of mastitis, when not to plough a field and trying to sort out that great poultry conundrum of all time namely, which came first, the chicken or the egg? I was a lucky man!

Living in Cookstown meant that I had to be up early every morning and cycle to the dairy complex in Loughry to commence milking at 6 a.m.

We all learned over the year to be proficient at milking dairy cows and the science that went with it such as feeding, nutrition, identifying ailments, how to treat them, good general dairy practice and so on. We learned how to make butter and cheese as well as learning about the ingredients that went into their creation. It was in the poultry section that I excelled. I took to it like a duck to water. There's a pun in there somewhere! I had some idea of how the poultry industry operated, having helped out at Magee's family farm at Kingsmills, not far from our family home in Whitecross.

By mid-September 1967, I completed my studies in Loughry and had moved on to Glasgow University, specialising in agriculture and Poultry Husbandry. Instead of spending my free time in bars and hanging out with my new-found friends in Glasgow, the potential disappointed feelings of my Mother and Father and how they would react if I returned home empty-handed, made me determined to succeed. I studied morning, noon and night and filled my head with as much knowledge as I could. By the end of year one which was the following Easter, I nervously sat my exams. If I didn't pass, it was goodbye Glasgow and back to the green fields and rolling hills of South Armagh and in all likelihood, a life of slog on a building site carrying blocks and bricks which wasn't the route I wanted to take.

But I managed to pass all my first-year subjects including physics and chemistry. For me, it was a personal miracle. Even to this day, I still can't believe I managed to get myself over the line. I knew that whatever came after that in relative terms, would be easy. Meanwhile as I basked in my own studious abilities, I kept fit by running round the back streets of Glasgow every morning. Fitness was hugely important to me at the time as I wanted to ensure that when I returned home during the summer, I would be up to standard for matches with Whitecross GFC.

When I completed my studies in Glasgow, I moved down to Harper Adams college in Shropshire to sit for my National Diploma in Poultry Husbandry. When the exams were over and eventually the results were posted on the board on a Thursday evening, I feared I had failed because of a self-perceived poor performance in other exams, in particular the area of genetics. My fears were unnecessary because when I checked the board, I saw the words 'Reavey E.K. – PASS.' Brilliant. I ran to the nearest phone box and rang Mrs O'Hanlon who lived next to my Mother in Whitecross. I told her the good news and asked her to pass on the word. This was a huge personal result not only for me but to all those around me who helped along the way, my Mum and Dad for all their prayers and my brother Frank who supported me financially when I was stone broke.

It was July 1969. I had a national and internationally-recognised diploma, a company car, a new career with Newtown Hatcheries in Newtownhamilton, South Armagh, owned by the McKee family, a good income and a full working life to look forward to.

As I looked forward to a comfortable life that my parents could only dream of, political events were about to get out of control and would change my life forever.

Sectarian Tensions start to Boil

Working for the McKee family was a delight. They had close on twenty full-time employees and were the smallest commercial hatchery in Northern Ireland when they started out in 1967. The company imported grandparent stock in the form of fertilised hatching eggs from Babcock Incorporated based at Ithaca in upstate New York. These eggs were then placed in incubators where chicks were born twenty-one days later.

My job as a technical poultry advisor was to support the sales reps out on the road who sold day-old chicks and point – of lay pullets – a name given to chickens more than eighteen weeks old. This meant driving up and down every rural bumpy twisty road, side lane, back street and townland right across the six counties in Northern Ireland and most counties in the Republic.

Driving around the highways and by-ways in Northern Ireland proved to be an extraordinary education in itself and made me quickly realise that while I lived in the quiet and close-knit hamlet of Whitecross in South Armagh, others elsewhere were revealing their dislike of Catholics.

As sectarian politics were starting to heat up in Co. Tyrone, in the Quaker village of Caledon not far from Dungannon, civil rights organisers were telling Catholic families with young children on the housing list to squat in newly-built council homes in Kinnard Park.

The local authority evicted the squatters, including the grandparents of former Sinn Féin MP Michelle Gildernew and gave one of the houses to a nineteen-year-old single Protestant girl called Emily Beattie who happened to be the secretary of a local unionist politician. To add to the local anti-Catholic conspiracy of the time, the policeman who assisted in the evictions just happened to be Emily Beattie's brother.

'VIP Emily' was allowed to jump the queue of 269 people,

many of whom were older, married with children and desperately in need of new homes Many on the list already lived in dilapidated houses, several of which were unfit for human habitation. A young Stormont MP and member of the Nationalist Party at the time, Austin Currie, pushed and pushed to ensure the isolated Catholic families at the time got housing but his success was not without a determined fight. One could say with some degree of understatement that Catholic families who were crying out for council houses were furious at this blatant form of bias and sectarianism, but as events unfolded, what happened in Caledon was the tip of the proverbial iceberg that was coming around the corner.

Such was the anger over the Caledon affair, the Civil Rights Association held a march in Derry over discrimination against Catholics in education, housing, employment and voting. It should be remembered that Catholics were the majority population in the city but partisan unionists in 1924 had structured the voting arrangements in such a way that *they* held the majority of seats on the City Council.

In 1967, over 60 per cent of the adult population in Derry City was Catholic/nationalist yet 60 per cent of the seats in the council were occupied by unionists. The voting system [called gerrymandering] created a result at each election whereby twelve British unionists won seats with only eight going to Irish nationalists!

The allocation of housing was no different.[1] Unlike elsewhere in the UK, where houses were allocated on a 'points system' whereby those who were longest on the waiting list and most in need, were given priority, in Northern Ireland, unionist-controlled local authorities gave out houses along religious/political lines.

If you were Protestant and working with no children, you were top of the queue. However, if you were an unemployed Catholic with nine children, then that was just tough even though it was blatant discrimination along sectarian lines. The system was also designed to maximise unionist votes. When it came to voting, one needed to own a property to vote. Those who

Sectarian Tensions start to Boil

owned business premises of a rateable value of over ten pounds could vote for every ten pounds that their respective property was designated, up to a maximum of six votes. What this all meant was that as the vast majority of businesses were owned by Protestants, they could secure extra votes above the traditional head count on polling day! If one was Catholic and poor, you just didn't exist as far as local democracy was concerned. By the mid to late 1960s, some 10,000 married couples living with others were without a vote, and three-quarters of that figure were Catholics.

Looking back, it's hard to believe that since Ireland was divided in 1921, unionist politicians had over forty years to create an all-inclusive society in Northern Ireland but instead treated Catholics as an inferior class This stone-age policy turned out to be a breeding ground for sectarian trouble.

Former SDLP MP Seamus Mallon recalled the story many times of one Catholic family in the 1960s who lived in a dilapidated house in Markethill, six miles up the road from where we live. Having no luck in securing a house for many years, the family approached Seamus who in turn raised their plight with a unionist councillor to see if anything could be done for their cause. When Seamus pitched the case for the desperate family, the response he got from the bigoted councillor was, 'No Catholic pig and his litter will ever get a house in Markethill while I am here'. This horrific response was not an isolated one and summed up the horrible attitude that some hardline Protestants had towards Catholics.

With protests over racial discrimination happening in the US and similar events cropping up all over the six counties over the appalling treatment of Catholics by Protestant politicians, it was decided to hold a major march across Northern Ireland to voice opposition and perhaps put some pressure on the political class in Stormont to bring about positive change. 'One man, one vote' was the main rallying call.

In January of 1969, a People's Democracy march was planned from Belfast to Derry. After a number of days on the road, the marchers reached Burntollet Bridge in Co. Derry, where they were ambushed and stoned by supporters of Ian Paisley, aided by the RUC and B-Specials. While we didn't realise it at the time, the flame that lit the fuse had now released the genie of warfare from the bottle, resulting in a sectarian conflict that lasted for over twenty-five years. The violence at Burntollet was so bad that when it was screened on TV news that night, rioting broke out in Derry City.

News coverage showed us that rioting day after day was out of control in Belfast and Derry. As the months rolled on, the arrival of 400 British soldiers, from the Yorkshire Regiment, on 14 August 1969 to quell the Battle of the Bogside in the Maiden City, was a development many thought would be short-term.

Among those marching from Belfast to Derry in support of Catholics was the surprising figure of Protestant political activist Ivan Cooper. Very much ahead of his time, he believed that the real issue in Northern Ireland was not just fair treatment for those on the green side but those on the orange one as well. He didn't believe that one class of people should have dominance over others but that all communities regardless of their colour, faith and status should be treated the same. This was a simple, workable and understandable philosophy in other democratic countries but unfortunately this was not the way of life in Northern Ireland.

On 9 January, I went to Newry where a similar march was taking place. 5,000 took part, including political figures John Hume, Frank McManus, Paddy O'Hanlon, Austin Currie, Paddy Devlin, Gerry Fitt, Ivan Cooper and solicitor Rory McShane who, with fifty others, were charged by the RUC for taking part in an 'illegal civil rights march'. The turnout was significant and while there were scuffles with the RUC, the event, overall, passed off relatively peacefully. But the involvement of so many local people radicalised some of them for the first time. I wasn't fired up like others as I was primarily there out of curiosity, but I became more alert to a political system that was blatantly biased against nationalists/Catholics.

Sectarian Tensions start to Boil

Looking back, nationalist people in Northern Ireland were hugely disappointed with the ruling Fianna Fáil Party in the south of Ireland. For all their rhetoric on being opposed to the 1921 Anglo-Irish Treaty which divided Ireland and left Catholics in Northern Ireland to fend for themselves, the so-called 'Republican Party' seemed to turn a blind eye to what was happening in the six counties of Northern Ireland. Had Fianna Fáil been more persuasive with London, the blatant unionist discrimination against Catholics in the 1940s and 1950s, the carnage that followed might never have happened at all.

When Irish-American John F. Kennedy became US President in 1960, a golden opportunity was missed for Dublin to persuade Washington to apply pressure on the British to sort out civil rights in Northern Ireland once and for all.

Nationalists/Catholics in Northern Ireland had nobody to speak up for them at international or diplomatic level and the lack of commitment shown by Fianna Fáil leaders Éamon de Valera, Seán Lemass and Jack Lynch cost us all very dearly in the end. When things got out of control following the Bogside riots in August 1969, Jack Lynch went on RTÉ TV and said, 'We can no longer stand by'. Unfortunately, that's exactly what he did.[2]

MEANWHILE, FOR US IN South Armagh, the political divisions that were causing so much strife in Belfast and Derry were happening 'up there' which was a world away from the sleepy peaceful green hills around Whitecross. This will sort itself out in a matter of weeks, we thought. This wouldn't darken our doorsteps, or so we thought! After all, the GAA season at local level was warming up and dedicated families like the Moleys, the Toners, the Malones and the Reaveys to name some of many, were busy getting on with life.

By the summer of 1969, John Martin was seventeen and was in his second year as an apprentice bricklayer working mainly in the Newry area. He always had great stories every night when he came home. Brian (15) was at St Paul's comprehensive school in nearby Bessbrook. Like Oliver (16), he was on the way to an apprenticeship in carpentry and joinery. He was also making quite a name for himself on the sports field and was, at this stage, on the winning team that won the Armagh schools' championship in Gaelic football for the first time.

Anthony was ten years of age by 1969 and had started to show an interest in writing poetry at primary school in St Brigid's, Drumilly, about two miles away from our family home at Greyhilla, Whitecross. My older sister Kathleen (26) was now a trained nurse at the Whittington Hospital in north London while Seamus (24) and Frank (22) were busy working as plastering contractors in the South Armagh/South Down area. Eileen was fourteen and at the Sacred Heart school in Newry, Paul (9) and Una (6) were still in Drumilly while Colleen was just one-year-old. Our Dad Jimmy (47) was working as a labourer with Frank and Seamus at this stage. Our Mother (46) was up to her eyes looking after all of us like a proud swan guarding its young while continuing to bake her award-winning soda farls.

Normal life was trundling along and the horrible violence that had gripped Belfast and Derry in August 1969 hadn't, thank God, reached South Armagh. This was someone else's problem and unfortunately people on both sides were losing their lives. Surely the politicians would see sense and sort it all out, yes? Well as it happened, no!

Catholics came under sustained attack from Protestant mobs for simply asking to be treated fairly. The violence that was dominating the news and the resistance to change, shown by firebrand Protestants such as Ian Paisley, forced the resignation in 1969 of Terence O'Neill, the prime minister of Northern Ireland, after six years in office. Terence O'Neill's modest offers of a better deal for Catholics were met with severe hostility by hard-line pro-British unionists, who, if only they showed some vision and a sense of Christian thinking, could have prevented so many deaths in the subsequent years.

By the end of 1969, sixteen people were dead. That figure had jumped to twenty-six by the end of 1970, with casualties on both sides. The rioting seemed to be getting worse by the week, but it was still happening 'up there' in Belfast, forty-odd miles away and in Derry City, almost 100 miles from South Armagh.

In August 1970, RUC Constables Sam Donaldson and Roy Millar were killed at Crossmaglen when IRA activists booby-trapped their Ford Cortina car, a tragedy that was condemned locally. According to the brilliant book *Lost Lives*, ten wreaths were sent by local Catholic families who were horrified by the killings.[3] Most people in the area hoped their deaths would not draw the locality into the chaos that was engulfing Derry and Belfast. Despite these killings, by the summer of 1971, there was practically no IRA activity in South Armagh. The British army was nowhere to be seen. The RUC and the UDR, while visible, were not seen to be as intimidating and sinister as they later became.

The modest way of life we enjoyed though in rural peaceful South Armagh was about to change dramatically when the British badly messed up and completely misread the mood of angry nationalists. Riflemen in the British army continued to treat Belfast and Derry Catholics as though they were casual target practice. Its trigger-happy attitude was to result in one single incident that would have horrifying consequences for almost every family in South Armagh. The episode, unfortunately, escalated, and spread the geographical impact of the evolving war with horrific ramifications for Ireland, Britain and its people in the decades that followed.

Twenty-eight-year-old Dundalk-born Harry Thornton was a married father and a labourer from Tullydonnell, Silverbridge, South Armagh which was not too far from where we lived. He worked in Carryduff, outside Belfast, and due to the nature of his work, opted to stay in the city during the week, returning home at weekends. On the morning of 7 August 1971, he was driving his van down the Falls Road in west Belfast and stopped in the traffic queue outside the RUC police station adjacent to Springfield Road. The exhaust on his van backfired twice in quick succession and when those at the RUC building heard the two loud bangs, a British soldier rushed out and shot Harry dead.

According to *Lost Lives*, which records every single death of The Troubles, 'Harry Thornton's companion, Arthur Murphy was arrested and taken into the barracks'.[4] An angry crowd gathered outside, demanding the man's release and jeered at police and troops. 'When the man was finally released some hours later, his face was swollen and bandaged. By early afternoon, local republicans in the district were handing out leaflets headed 'murder, murder, murder'.

The first army statement on the incident said 'two shots were fired from a passing car and sentries returned two rounds'. Later, army chief of staff, Brigadier Marston Tickell told a press conference 'in the army's view, the soldiers concerned in the incident had good grounds for believing their Post had been fired on from a van and acted correctly in accordance with their instructions.'

Harry had no involvement in politics or paramilitary activity and left behind a broken-hearted widow and six young children without any financial income whatsoever. It was bad enough that Harry Thornton was brutally shot dead but the dismissive comments and condescending tone on the TV news that evening of Brigadier Tickell in his posh English accent saying the army was justified in responding to the 'two shots' sparked fury and rage locally. Later that night, Crossmaglen RUC station came under attack by angry locals who fired stones and attempted to burn it down. Four buses were attacked and one was hijacked and driven into the gates of the RUC station.

Anecdotal evidence suggests that on that very day and subsequent weeks, the IRA in South Armagh was formally re-established with scores of locals lining up to join its ranks. In the days following Harry Thornton's death, loyalists and IRA gunmen went into overdrive against each other as 'revenge for revenge' became the new normal.

One would have thought the arrival of the British army to

Sectarian Tensions start to Boil

'protect' Catholics from violent loyalist mobs would have calmed the situation. As events from August 1969 onwards showed, the presence of her majesty's military and more significantly, its appalling aggressive tactics angered so many in the Catholic community, it turned out to be an unlikely recruiting agency for the then poorly organised IRA. The great irony of the time was that by the mid-1960s, the old IRA had all but disappeared off the political pitch.

The televised scenes of the Royal Ulster Constabulary beating defenceless women and young children and how they badly handled the Battle of the Bogside in Derry in August 1969, forcing the British government to send in the army, saw IRA numbers swell. When the British army imposed the Falls Road curfew in July 1970 killing four Catholics and the subsequent imposition of internment without trial one year later, when over 342 nationalist arrests were made on 9 August, IRA recruits increased again.

The British army then went and killed eleven innocent Catholics in Ballymurphy, west Belfast, between 9–11 August 1971, two days after the killing of Harry Thornton. This saw even more angry people sign up to join the IRA. The British army had killed twelve innocent people in the space of four days. They adopted the same brutal tactics of Belfast-based military Brigadier Frank Kitson which he developed to quash the KLFA/Mau-Mau revolt in Kenya in the 1950s and killed tens of thousands of natives who wanted nothing more than to end Britain's colonial rule.

In Yemen during the period of 1963–1967, the port of Aden was crucial for the flow of British trade to and from India.[5.] When the locals wanted their port back for themselves, there were stories of locals being subjected to electric shocks, anal rape and sleep deprivation, itself a common British torture technique. A damning investigation by Amnesty International was rejected by the British PM of the time Harold Wilson. As usual, the British 'never' did anything immoral. Even the most brutal of terrorists would have been shocked at some of the things the

British got up to in their 'civilising' foreign wars. A dangerous precedent but well-established formula had been normal and as we were to learn, the British would break every rule in the military handbook in a desperate attempt to achieve victory.

Northern Ireland though was not east Africa or the middle east, even though Frank Kitson and his British military pals behaved as if it was. They seemed to overlook the fact that Northern Ireland was politically part of the United Kingdom. The Irish were not like the Mau Mau in that they were white, had access to European media, had the support of a large diaspora, especially in America where most of the famine emigrants fled and had handed down the stories of British oppression in Ireland.

What's more, the British failed to understand that the cruel Penal Laws, Oliver Cromwell, the Famine, 1916, the infamous Black and Tans period – the list goes on and on – were prominent infamous milestones of our troubled history but hardly registered in theirs. Oppressed Irish nationalists hadn't forgotten the horrible legacy of British colonisation. The British viewed us as being a complete underclass of un-educated folk. The Irish were seen as being expendable and the British were prepared to do whatever it took, legal or otherwise, to crush local opposition to their unionist control.

Kitson had similar form in other places where the hostile behaviour of the British military towards local rebels saw mass killings. The British have a long track-record in this type of ruthless conduct and as my family later found out, it didn't stop when they stepped off the navy ships in Belfast docks on to Irish soil for their next call of duty!

In Kitson's first book, he had the brazen hard neck to write that 'the British behaved honourably in Kenya'. In fact they behaved so 'honourably', that when they were eventually found out by the wider world, the government in London was forced to pay out £19.9 million in compensation to 5,228 Kenyan survivors in 2013![5]

Kitson, who later misled the Bloody Sunday Inquiry, was

not the only Brit with murder on his agenda. His number two at the time, Col Derek Wilford who headed up 1 Para, the infamous British army regiment which massacred eleven innocents in Ballymurphy Belfast in 1971 and fourteen in the Bogside Derry in 1972, was equally as ruthless and economical with the truth.

WE DIDN'T KNOW IT then but Harry Thornton's killing was a significant development. Where once a peaceful and mainly farming community existed in South Armagh with nothing on its mind but making a decent living, now its people were under attack and would see themselves going into defensive mode to have and hold what was theirs.

Two weeks after the Thornton killing, the IRA ambushed a British army armoured vehicle on the Armagh/Louth border at Courtbane near Hackballscross and shot dead Cpl Ian Armstrong. British Prime Minister Edward Heath was furious as was the Taoiseach Jack Lynch in Dublin who accused the 'occupying' British army of repeatedly crossing in to the Republic. Tension was mounting, although it would be some time before any more killings happened in South Armagh.

Thirty-four people had been killed in Northern Ireland by August 1971. Nineteen of those were civilians, four were RUC and eleven were British soldiers. From August to December that figure jumped to 139 dead, ninety-five were civilians.

Locally, Newry Town was, bit by bit, being burned to the ground. On Wednesday 26 January 1972, four major business outlets in the town were burned down when IRA activists in the area firebombed 'Toners' Electrical Supplies' on Hill Street, Sands Mill on Canal Quay, the Inland Revenue building on Merchant's Quay and the Rowland and Harris car sales outlet on Railway Avenue. Next day, the UVF struck back in Newry and Etams' drapery store as well as the Pearl Assurance office were bombed.

Newry was crumbling before our very eyes and the destruction was adding to the already growing unemployment figures in the South Down/South Armagh area. Businesses were struggling as daily spend declined and numerous retail outlets closed.

The IRA also stepped up their campaign against the British army, the RUC and the Ulster Defence Regiment making the lives of decent local unionists miserable. The harassment of local nationalist youths by the British army was now more frequent and visible. Every corner you went around, somebody had just been dragged from a car and was verbally abused and threatened.

If one thought things couldn't get any worse, well they did and guess what? The British made an already bad situation worse when they messed up again although knowing the tactics of Frank Kitson, it was all part of their military strategic plan.

A public march protesting for Civil Rights was planned in Derry for 30 January 1972. The march passed off peacefully until people began to gather close to army barriers adjacent to Rossville Street flats in the city. When stone-throwing commenced and the army attempted to stage arrests, a full-scale riot developed.

The 1st Battalion of the Parachute Regiment began to fire shots, having claimed it came under attack. It seems there are many different versions of what happened but one thing is clear, thirteen innocent nationalists were shot dead on the day many in the back and a fourteenth died later. The anger amongst the nationalist community over what happened in Derry was everywhere. It spread to the south resulting in the British embassy on Merrion Square Dublin being burned down on 2 February. Relations between Dublin and London were at their worst since the War of Independence.

If the events in Derry weren't enough to infuriate nationalists in Northern Ireland, tensions increased further when British establishment figure Lord Chief Justice Widgery, who could hardly be described as being independent, was appointed by her majesty's government in Whitehall London to hold an 'Inquiry' into the killings. Then there was further outrage when Widgery's flawed Inquiry ruled in April 1972 that the Parachute Regiment had been fired upon first and that there was no reason to suppose it would have opened fire otherwise.

Widgery's findings were at variance to the Derry City coroner, Hubert O'Neill, whose inquest in to the killings in 1973 said, 'It strikes me that the army ran amok that day and they shot without thinking of what they were doing. They were shooting innocent people. These people may have been taking part in a parade that was banned-but I don't think that justifies the firing of live rounds indiscriminately. I say it without reservation – it was sheer unadulterated murder'.[6]

After Widgery's fabrication of the truth, nationalist distrust and loathing of the crooked UK state reached a new high while the western world looked on in horror at the way the British army was blatantly killing unarmed innocent Irish people. The events in Derry were probably the biggest game changer of all in the history of the Troubles.

My thinking at the time was that the British were deliberately provoking nationalists to engage in an all-out civil war. Why would that be the case? Well if one looks back on the time, the British army was brought in to be peace-keepers but that was not something they were trained to do. They were military men, amongst the best trained and equipped in the world and being stuck in the middle between warring Irish nationalists and British unionists must have been very frustrating. I'm in no doubt that the managers in the army, having already crushed empire opposition in Africa and elsewhere, wanted to engage in direct warfare to satisfy and impress their political masters in London.

With acts of terrorism already out of control and the findings of the Widgery Tribunal amounting to blatant lies, the rage in the nationalist community was understandable. With paramilitary activity now beyond a peaceful solution and unionists refusing to hand over the management of security to Whitehall, London lost patience. As far as unionists were concerned, they knew what was best to keep law and order in the six counties of Ulster. As far as London was concerned, they had made a mess of things since 1921. Ted Heath's Conservative government indicated it was time to put manners on unionists and the collapse of the Stormont government saw the introduction of direct rule from London.

Unionists saw it as a sell-out while Irish nationalists were delighted. It formally ended local unionist control over oppressed nationalists for the first time since partition. Hopes were high that London would end the unionist culture of treating nationalists as second-class citizens but as events unfolded, all of us on the green side would be left waiting.

CROUZON'S SYNDROME COMES TO OUR DOOR

WHILE NORTHERN IRELAND WAS falling further and further in to the political abyss, life went on and the biggest thing on my agenda was my wedding. I had met an attractive young Róisín Quinn from nearby Belleeks village at a céilí in Whitecross parochial hall. I had spotted her earlier in my life at mass when I used to be an altar boy at Carrickananney chapel. The céilí sessions took place once a month and for many of us at that time, it was the highlight of our life.

Nobody had a car and if you had a bicycle, you were deemed a 'good catch' as you owned something. The *céilí* nights were all harmless craic. There was no alcohol in the dance halls and a bottle of 7-Up was as far as it went when it came to drink. It cost sixpence each to get in and it was a rural Irish scene. Men lined up on one side and women on the other. Fr Pat Smith acted like a security man and walked around the floor throughout the night with a blackthorn stick in his right hand. If he observed a young man dancing too close to a female friend, he would give them a tap on the shoulder to ensure they kept their distance and didn't develop any impure thoughts. It was a time of pure innocence. I had my eye on Róisín for a long time but the circumstances never presented themselves whereby we could have a chat.

One particular Saturday night in 1965, I said to myself, 'Tonight's the night. It's now or never' and having plucked up the courage, I walked across the floor and asked her out for a dance. She must have thought I was a 'fine thing' as to my surprise, she willingly said 'yes'. We hit it off straight away and have been inseparable ever since.

After seven years of love and romance, Róisín and I got married on 5 April 1972 in St Laurence O'Toole Catholic church in nearby Belleeks, two miles up the road from Whitecross. I was twenty-four, Róisín was twenty-two. Frank, my brother, was my best man while John Martin was groomsman. Róisín's sister, Mary, was her bridesmaid as was her other sister, Briege. The weather was wet and windy but despite this, we all headed across the border to the Fairways Hotel in Dundalk where we had a great day.

Our honeymoon was spent in Killarney. I was somewhat nervous heading to the Kingdom of Kerry as I had some news for Róisín that I knew she would not want to hear. There was a GAA game I needed to attend. I'm sure if the game was in Killarney or Tralee, she wouldn't have blinked an eye but it wasn't. The game was in the very location we had left to make our way to Killarney – South Armagh.

Brave as it may read, I drove home on my own five days after our wedding on the following Friday to play football for Whitecross against Keady in the 'exciting' confines of Division 3 of the Armagh Junior League. I'm sure if I rang ahead and said, 'Lads, I'm on my honeymoon and I can't make it this Friday', the sky would not have fallen in but it highlights, if perhaps somewhat selfishly, my dedication to my club.

I should add that Róisín had been warned many times by my Father before we tied the knot, that if she ever married me, she would instantly become a GAA widow. We were married less than a week and she now knew exactly what my Father meant. I'm glad to report that the power of love overcame a personal crisis. Any other woman would probably have given me my marching orders.

Back in South Armagh, our new home for the first year of our married life was spent in Campbell's House in nearby Drumhoney. We rented for the first twelve months while we explored building a house of our own. I'd been searching high and low in the locality for a suitable site on which to build. I approached a family friend, Arthur Markey, who lived at Drumherriff. His quarter acre site of land cost me £600. It was a huge sum of money. I now had to go and get planning permission and before I knew it, we turned the sod to build our new house in March 1974.

On 9 July 1973, forty-one-year-old single Protestant man Isaac Scott from Benagh, Co. Down visited Tully's Bar in Belleeks, two miles away from Whitecross. He had been a regular visitor to the pub in recent weeks. On the night in question, he sat in the pub with a female companion and as they got into their car to head home, he was shot through the windscreen and killed on the spot. It emerged some time afterwards that he was a former member of the Ulster Defence Regiment, a local part-time wing of the British army.

Whether anybody in Belleeks or beyond in the republican movement knew that he was no longer in the UDR is unknown. There was revulsion locally but this was yet another killing on the conveyor belt of slaughter that we had become used to.

On Wednesday 22 August 1973, the madness came firmly knocking on our door. Our first cousin, twenty-year-old single man Seán McDonnell from Belleeks, a heavy plant driver, went to bingo in Newry with his eighteen-year-old girlfriend Agnes O'Hare from Mayobridge. The couple got engaged the previous Christmas and were inseparable. On the night in question, they had come home from the bingo and turned down the Ryan Road where Agnes lived.

Having stopped at Agnes' driveway, they chatted about their wedding plans. Unknown to them, two people had climbed a tree adjacent to the house and waited for the car to arrive. As it did, the two shone a light from a torch as the signal for the hit. As Seán and Agnes chatted, two vehicles, which had been driving around in the locality earlier, pulled up from behind and Seán was dragged from the car. Just as he was abducted, one of the gunmen said to Agnes, 'This is for Isaac Scott'.

Seán was driven further along the Ryan Road in Mayobridge for about a mile close to where Isaac Scott lived. The car pulled in to a gateway and Seán was dragged from the back seat and put standing at a gate post at Heslop's farm before being shot eleven times by a Sterling nine-millimetre sub-machine gun, a standard British army weapon. A Ford Escort car, which had been stolen in Banbridge on the night of the killing, was found burned out at Heslop's Lane.

Seán's brother Gerard told me many years later that his teeth were removed before he was shot dead, leading one to wonder what was to be gained by that horrible act of brutal torture. They were obviously seeking information about the local IRA but Seán was the wrong man to be asking. He and his family were never involved in criminality or paramilitary activity and found the evolving conflict scary.

Dr Michael McVerry from Newry told Seán's inquest at the inappropriate location of Banbridge Orange Hall that 'the death appeared to be of five to seven hours duration'. A horrific killing for a young man in the prime of his life. For a grieving family from nationalist South Armagh to attend an inquest into the death of their loved one in an Orange Hall in the 1970s added to the sense of intimidation, insensitivity and insult.

Seán McDonnell was the most innocent young man one could ever meet. He was a quiet but hard worker and helped his father Charlie on the family farm. He lived for the GAA, his work and his girlfriend. He was a diligent young man making his way in life with not a care or political thought on his mind. His killing caused disbelief in South Armagh. His mother Laura, my auntie, just could not believe that her son could be targeted. The level of fear in the community was extraordinary with everyone in the locality wondering at the time if this was perhaps, a case of mistaken identity or, if it was a taste of more to come?

The sense of anger in our wider family was hard to grasp. The word 'revenge' was not in our dictionary and laying Seán to rest became our immediate priority. In fact looking back on it now and the sense of drama that hit us with Seán's killing, it took about three months for his death to fully sink in.

The results of the ballistic analysis on Seán's murder suggested that the weapon used to kill him was linked to four other recent loyalist paramilitary shootings. Many years passed for us to learn that a murky force combining of loyalist paramilitaries and sinister elements of the British state were hard at work in mid-Ulster. They not only targeted Seán but eventually the

Reaveys and a host of other innocent individuals and families.

One of the men sent out to investigate Seán's killing was RUC officer John Lindsay. Constable Billy McBride, who died some years back, accompanied him. McBride was later described in an Irish Government Report by Judge Henry Barron as being a gunsmith. He, with others, supplied weapons to the UVF in Portadown. We didn't know it then but McBride lived in Benagh close to where Isaac Scott was from. Some years later, local ballad singer Tommy Sands, originally from Mayobridge, wrote a poignant song called 'There were Roses'. It connected the killings of Isaac Scott and Seán McDonnell and focused on the futility of sectarian murder.

ELSEWHERE, RÓISÍN AND I were buoyed up by the impending arrival of baby number one and on 17 September 1973, Catriona arrived into the world at Daisy Hill Hospital in Newry. She was ten days overdue and born by caesarean section. After she was delivered, I went into the ward to see Róisín but she was still asleep from the anaesthetic. Looking so pale and worn out, I hadn't the heart to wake her up and I went home. The next morning when I went in to the Ward, Róisín was having tea and toast.

'I haven't seen the baby yet,' she said. 'Who is she like?'

No doctors or nurses had told Róisín anything at this stage. I said I would go to the nursery and carry Catriona in to the ward. When I placed Catriona in Róisín's arms, I could see the expression on her face change instantly. We both knew instinctively that something was not right about her appearance. Her head was oval-shaped, abnormal somewhat and despite our concerns, the nurses assured us that after a few days, it would return to a normal appearance. Catriona also appeared to have protruding eyes. We sensed something was not as it should be.

They told us the abnormality was due to Róisín's lengthy labour. I didn't know if they were trying to pacify us until they established the real diagnosis of her condition. Catriona was baptised in Daisy Hill Hospital Newry by Fr Peter Hughes our local parish priest in Whitecross with Mary Quinn, Róisín's sister and my brother Frank as her godparents. She was then taken to the Royal Victoria Hospital in Belfast several days after for further assessment.

Then we got the news we didn't want to hear. Consultants at the RVH told us that Catriona had been diagnosed with Crouzon's Syndrome. Crouzon's is a malformation of the bone structure in the face and is a one in two hundred million occurrence. She was also diagnosed with Craniostenosis which sees separate bones in the skull fuse together creating an unusual head shape.

The first of many surgeries went ahead when Catriona was six weeks old. Surgery involved opening her head from ear to ear and splitting all the bones. Apart from a breathing and hearing problem, Catriona is in good health otherwise and as the years rolled by, her positive personality has lit up our life and those around her. Catriona had numerous operations in all to correct the Craniostenosis and spent much of the first three years of her life in the Royal Victoria Hospital, Belfast.

One day Róisín was fortunate to pick up a copy of *Reader's Digest* magazine. It contained an article about a girl from France whose face was so disfigured, her parents hid her in a chicken coop so as to be hidden from the neighbours. Róisín turned the pages slowly and as she did, her attention was caught by a line that read, 'Surgeon with the magic touch'. The article was about a Dr Paul Tessier, a French plastic and reconstructive surgeon who operated on people with facial deformities. He had also perfected a technique to operate on people with Crouzon's Syndrome. The article said he believed that 'the earlier a sufferer was operated on, the better.'

She didn't have Dr Tessier's address but took a chance and wrote to him care of the hospital mentioned in the *Reader's Digest* article. Róisín posted the letter and prayed that the French postal service was up to standard. Months passed and no reply. We were gradually giving up hope when one day, out of the blue, a letter arrived with a Paris postmark. Dr Tessier had received our letter, understood our plight and was willing to help. His letter had promising news. Even though he was a busy man, he was prepared to see us for a consultation in the summer of 1982. Dr Tessier's letter gave us great hope. Could he be the man we had searched for so long?

After much correspondence, numerous phone calls and raised hopes, we now had an appointment for our Catriona in Paris with Dr Paul Tessier. Catriona would be his first ever Irish patient. We decided to take the whole family and travelled with caravan in tow to the French capital. Needless to say, I got lost over and over trying to find our way around Paris with a bulky caravan behind me. Yes, you can take the man out of South Armagh …..!

We believed that Dr Tessier was the right man to perform the much-needed surgery on Catriona who was by now seven months away from celebrating her tenth birthday. A date for the surgery was set for April 1983. The Whitecross community raised £2,500, itself an extraordinary figure for the time considering the small number of people that live in the locality. Róisín, Catriona and myself headed off to Paris.

By 1990, the corrective bone surgery was complete and by coincidence, Dr Tessier retired. In the same year, Catriona got some very uplifting news. In November, she was invited to The Savoy Hotel in London for a special event organised by the famous children's charity Barnardos and she was presented with a 'Triumph over Adversity' Award which is given to individuals 'who have shown courage, perseverance or accomplishment in the face of illness, handicap or adverse circumstances.' The exclusive Scroll was presented to her by HRH, the Princess of Wales, Lady Diana Spencer. Catriona was over the moon with this recognition and described it as 'the highlight of her life.' She was most grateful to her teacher Mrs Ann McKeown, who nominated her.

After all these years, Catriona still has many milestones to overcome. As the years rolled on, she has lived as normal a life as she possibly could, going to discos, cinemas, concerts and even shouting for Armagh in the Ulster Championship!

Despite setbacks though, we know that if Dr Tessier hadn't

performed his magic in Paris, life could have even been tougher for Catriona and we will be eternally grateful to him and his team. After all these years, brave Catriona lives independently in her own apartment outside Bessbrook.

SHORTLY AFTER CATRIONA WAS born, in late October 1973, a dispute between two men in Banbridge, Co. Down resulted in the next sectarian killing. To the outside world, it was just another statistic in the evolving horror that had taken over Northern Ireland but as subsequent events would reveal, the killing was highly significant as it saw one name in particular enter the public domain for the first time. Robin Jackson, a native of Donaghmore, Co. Down, had worked in 'Down Shoes' in Banbridge. One of his work colleagues was Patrick Campbell, a thirty-four-year-old-Catholic, amateur boxing activist and president of the Northern Ireland division of the National Union of Footwear, Leather and Allied Trades. A father of three and totally non-political, he had made a number of objections to the British military using the staff canteen at Down Shoes for meals. As he saw it, it would make the company a possible target for the IRA and would, likewise, be viewed as being supportive of the British army.

On the night of 28 October, a knock came to the front door of the Campbell home at Clive Walk in Banbridge and when Patrick's wife Margaret opened the door, two men asked if they could speak to her husband. Thinking the request was to discuss something sporting or work related, Margaret called her husband who came to the door to talk to his unexpected 'guests'. A struggle ensued at the front door, at least nine shots were fired and shortly afterwards Patrick Campbell was dead.

The Ulster Freedom Fighters (UFF), a name regularly used by the Ulster Defence Association, said they carried out the killing claiming that Patrick Campbell was in the IRA. The RUC investigated and two names emerged – Wesley Somerville, a native of Moygashel, County Tyrone and Robin Jackson. Robin Jackson was charged. He was a member of the Ulster Defence

Regiment, a position that gave him legal right to carry a weapon.

Sometime later, Mrs Campbell received an unexpected visit from the RUC who told her to put her coat on in a hurry and attend a hastily arranged identity parade – without allowing access to her solicitor. Somewhat distressed by the conduct of the RUC officers, she attended Banbridge station. At the identity parade, the suspects were lined up. Mrs Campbell was asked to identify the individual that showed up at her door and fired the shots. She pointed her hand at Robin Jackson and said, 'that's him'. She was asked to place her hand on the suspect's shoulder but froze and couldn't pluck up the courage to do that. The suspects were asked to leave the room and returned several minutes later and put in a different standing order. Once again, she was asked to identify the suspect. She identified Robin Jackson but again was too intimidated to place her hand on his shoulder.

Jackson was charged and held in custody for some weeks. However, the RUC released him on 4 January 1974 when the charges against him were inexplicably dropped. Why would the RUC let a man clearly identified by Mrs Campbell as being at her front door when her husband was shot dead be allowed to get off scot-free? The RUC, the British army, Security Service, MI5, Secret Service, MI6, the part-time UDR and other related 'security' agencies of the UK state, who we all thought in 1969 were here to keep the peace, were now suspected of dirty tricks and all that before you even mention the UVF, UFF, UDA, Red Hand Commando and like-minded groups.

Shortly afterwards, little coverage or notice was given to two killings that occurred a couple of miles up the road from our house, just outside the village of Glenanne on 20 March 1974. Two British soldiers in plain clothes, Michael Francis Herbert (31) and Michael John Cotton (36) of the Kings Hussars Regiment, who were 'keeping an eye' on a 'house of interest', were killed by members of the RUC who incorrectly assumed they were IRA men on reconnaissance. The deceptive British line at the time to prevent political embarrassment – for secrecy and security reasons – was that the two soldiers were killed in 'tragic accidents' at separate locations, Herbert at Shaw's Lake in Glenanne and Cotton at the nearby village of Mowhan.

For two British soldiers from the same regiment to be killed at separate locations one mile or so apart on the same day on their own is stretching credibility but when you're dealing with the British establishment, truth, honesty, openness and transparency do *not* go in the same sentence.

Local anecdotal evidence however told a different story It turns out that the 'house of interest' at Ballylane Road in Glenanne was situated in what could be described as a 'no-go area' at certain times of the week for Catholics. It was even a no-go area for most members of the British security forces who were 'not in the know'. The security at Ballylane Road at certain times was actually tighter than would be the case every day at Downing Street! Designated units of the military would seal off the road at pre-determined times to ensure that only certain people entered and left, leading one to ask why would a modest, unassuming farmhouse surrounded by rolling green fields at the end of a muddy driveway be of such interest to secretive people within the British security services? What was going on in the locality that the British army was so determined to protect?

This 'house of interest' turned out to be central to some sinister activity which claimed many innocent lives in later years. According to the writers of *Lost Lives*, the two plain clothes British soldiers that were killed, were members of the SAS who were based at Gosford Castle near Markethill. They had strayed into territory where their colleagues mistook them for republicans and that cost them their lives.

THE SUNNINGDALE AGREEMENT OF December 1973 between the British and Irish governments proposed to give Dublin a greater say in the running of affairs in Northern Ireland for the first time since partition. Unionists were furious as they felt they were being sold out by London. Unionists and loyalists were out on the streets protesting over what they felt was a slippery slope to Irish unity. With fear of all-out war looming, to the dismay of everybody on the nationalist side, the British government decided on 14 May 1974 to make paramilitary group the UVF a legal organisation – just think about that for a moment.[1] The UVF, some of whose members doubled up as members of the legal UDA (Ulster Defence Association), as well as the British security forces and had been on a killing spree since the start of the Troubles, were a legal organisation. What that meant in everyday speak was that the secretary of state for Northern Ireland, Merlyn Rees and the British state made it clear to the UVF, that they could do whatever they wanted to as long as they didn't get caught.

Three days later on 17 May, the UVF took full advantage of its new freedom and carried out four bombings. In ninety minutes on a damp grey Friday evening, three car bombs exploded in Parnell Street, Talbot Street and South Leinster Street in Dublin, killing twenty-seven people – followed ninety minutes later by one in Monaghan Town which claimed seven lives.

Thirty-four people including an unborn child, were killed. As the dust settled in the coming days, one of the big questions being asked was 'Who would bomb Dublin and Monaghan with the severity of an attack that hadn't even been seen in Northern Ireland up to then? Subsequent forensics revealed that the expertise and materials used by the UVF in making these explosives was way superior to any of the crude home-made devices they used up to, and after, that date.

One of the greatest mysteries relating to these atrocities was that crucial garda files on the worst day of violence ever to happen on the island of Ireland, went missing. Those all-important files were never to be seen again. Maybe the late former garda commissioner, Larry Wren, who was one of the senior police investigators in to the bombings and was well acquainted with MI5/6 operators in Ireland at the time, knew exactly what happened? In the meantime, requests by the families of those who died for the outstanding files to be released have been rejected by the gardaí. Why?

Despite repeated calls for a public inquiry into the Dublin-Monaghan bombings, the government of the day, led by Taoiseach Liam Cosgrave of Fine Gael, said 'no'. Why? We can only assume that certain individuals in the employ of the Irish state knew exactly what happened to the mysterious files that went missing and did not want their engagement with the British security services to be fully revealed.

On 15 December 1974 in Church Street, Newry, a separate UVF gang also bombed Hughes' Bar fatally injuring twenty-one-year-old engineer John Mallon and reportedly celebrated their 'hit' later in Harry's Bar in Banbridge. Nobody was held to account for these killings. Despite the fear caused by these attacks, there was some good news on the political front. The Provisional IRA announced a ceasefire on 20 December. It lasted until 2 January 1975 and gave the British government an opportunity to assess a number of proposals offered by Republicans at a secret meeting in Feakle, Co. Clare to sort out the impasse.

A Christmas without violence was something we hadn't seen in five years and hopefully the Troubles would be over once and for all. We waited and prayed.

Mystery Surrounds Local Killings

DESPITE OUR HOPES FOR the year ahead, 1975 got underway and life in Northern Ireland basically continued where it left off in 1974. In fact, things got worse and a lot murkier. Although the IRA ceasefire was extended, it ended at midnight 2 January 1975 after the British failed to respond positively to the demands sought at the Feakle meeting. These included the treatment of prisoners and of course the ultimate objective namely, a timetable and commitment on British withdrawal from Northern Ireland. There was no talk of ceasefire on the loyalist side where it was business as usual.

Domestically I was now working for Ross Poultry in Portadown. Róisín had been busy teaching at St Malachy's in Camlough and was now in the final stages of her pregnancy with our second child. Aisling was born on 13 June 1975 and I'm glad to report was in perfect health, much to our delight.

ON THE NIGHT OF Wednesday 30 July/Thursday 31 July 1975, the popular Dublin-based Miami Showband had been playing in The Castle Ballroom in Banbridge, Co. Down. Shortly before 2 a.m., the six members of the band packed their equipment into their Volkswagen mini-bus to head back to Dublin. Drummer Ray Millar opted stay at his parents' house in Antrim leaving his five colleagues to make the ninety-minute trip to Dublin, which they made every other week for the previous ten years or so. Halfway between Banbridge and Newry at a junction called Buskhill, the band's mini-bus was waved down by a man dressed in army uniform with a red-lit torch. The lads presumed it was a routine military check-point, an all-too regular feature of driving around Northern Ireland at the time. According to a book on Robert Nairac called *Secret Hero*, eight soldiers were present at the checkpoint.[1]

The musicians were asked to vacate the mini-bus for the customary check to see if they had any weapons on board. They were lined up at the side of the road facing the hedge. The chat between the band members and 'the soldiers' was jovial at the outset until guitarist Stephen Travers saw a member of the army move his precious bass guitar. From nowhere, a car pulled up. A man immaculately dressed in a uniform, with an Oxbridge English accent, took charge and the mood changed. Stephen, who had worked for Lloyds in London, quickly realised that this guy was well educated and spoke with a tone of great authority. Stephen moved from his position in the line-up to query what was going on and as words were exchanged, things got a little bit heated. Unknown to the lads in the band, one of the 'army' was busy planting a bomb in the mini bus under the driver's seat.

Their plan was simple. Place the bomb in the bus and send the band on its way. Once the bus crossed the border, the bomb would explode and the security forces would issue a press statement saying nobody claimed responsibility but this would be proof that bands were carrying explosives for the IRA. The band would look bad in the eyes of the public, politicians and the media. Unionist and British politicians would then call for the border to be sealed, effectively cutting off Northern Ireland from the Republic. Pressure would then come on the Dublin government from London to go along with that proposal and increase security along their frontier.

The plot with the bomb didn't go to plan. As the device was placed in to position on the bus, it exploded prematurely, killing Harris Boyle and Wesley Somerville, prominent members of the UVF. Such was the force of the blast; Somerville was blown 100 yards away. Harris Boyle's severed arm was found nearby with the words 'Harris' and 'UVF' tattooed on it. The force of the blast threw the band members into the adjoining field resulting in 'the soldiers' opening fire on them to try to ensure they didn't live to reveal what happened. Stephen Travers was hit with a dum-dum bullet in mid-air as he was blown off his feet and survived. The bullet entered Stephen's body at his hip and exploded within, causing sixteen fragments to disperse. The impact expanded his stomach giving him the look of a man who was pregnant.

Mystery Surrounds Local Killings

According to Stephen Travers in the book *The Miami Showband Massacre*, the UVF described the musical group as being 'ruthless gun runners for the IRA'.[2] The book quotes the UVF as saying the killings were 'justifiable homicide'. It said an organisation called the Ulster Central Intelligence Agency (UCIA) – which nobody ever heard of before or since – claimed that Boyle and Somerville were on border patrol duty when they came across an ambush and as they investigated the mini-bus, a bomb exploded. The UVF even claimed that its members came under attack from the musicians in the band.

The atrocity claimed the lives of talented musicians Fran O'Toole, Brian McCoy and Tony Geraghty. Fellow musicians Des Lee and Stephen Travers miraculously survived the massacre while drummer Ray Millar drove home that night to his parents' house in Antrim Town. The killings shocked every civilised person on the island of Ireland and beyond.

Next day, 1 August, journalist Conor O'Clery of the *Irish Times* formally revealed what we all suspected. Members of the UVF dressed as British soldiers carried out the killings. The mis-information put out by the UCIA showed that the UVF were not only telling blatant lies but were probably protecting one or more individuals operating undercover. The passing of time revealed that the members of the Ulster Volunteer Force who lost their lives were actually assisted by other dark forces when they showed up at Buskhill that night. Information emerged sometime later that Robin Jackson was present at the Miami Showband massacre working with Somerville, Boyle and of course, certain members of the British security forces.

The subsequent media coverage saw three words enter the daily speak of what was happening around us – 'The Murder Triangle'. They were written to describe the wider area from South Down to Dungannon in Tyrone on towards Portadown and back through South Armagh to Newry. The UVF had become a deadly force in mid-Ulster during the previous two years killing innocent Catholics and curiously, there seemed to be a remarkable low conviction rate of loyalists from this area in the courts. The scary thing for us was, Whitecross, South Armagh was in 'The Murder Triangle' so there was now even more reason to be worried.

The sense of rage in South Armagh and South Down over the Miami killings was palpable. You could feel the tension in the air. We sensed it wouldn't be long before the UVF struck again and those in the nationalist community felt that it would only be a matter of days if not weeks before the IRA hit back.

Two weeks after the Miami murders on 15 August, the local IRA struck when they abducted twenty-nine-year-old married Protestant William Meaklim near Crossmaglen. He operated a local mobile shop, and would drive his van from house to house selling everything from potatoes to sugar and bread. The IRA believed that Willie, a former member of the RUC reserve force, was collecting intelligence for the British. Anecdotal evidence suggests he was subjected to severe torture to expose what he knew but when he wouldn't reveal what the IRA was looking for, he was killed two miles from his home at Newtownhamilton South Armagh on the Castleblayney Road. His killing commenced a chain of murders on both sides in the locality. Protestants and Catholics in the area were living in awful fear.

Retaliation was swift. On 24 August, Colm McCartney (22) from Bellaghy, Co. Derry, a cousin of the poet Seamus Heaney and John P. Farmer (32) from Moy, Co. Tyrone, were both Catholic workmates at an engineering company in Newry. They had attended the Derry *v* Dublin match in the All-Ireland football semi-final and were returning home from Croke Park in Dublin. A questionable 'diversion' on the road forced them to take an alternative route, resulting in their car being stopped at a checkpoint at Cortamlet, Newtownhamilton, on the Monaghan-Armagh border at 11.45 p.m. When they stopped, a conversation ensued. What was said is not clear.

According to Anne Cadwallader's *Lethal Allies*, an RUC patrol of three officers in the area led by Frederick Bartholomew had earlier come upon a fake checkpoint of soldiers dressed in army uniforms.[3] Unsure if the soldiers were UDR or had

Mystery Surrounds Local Killings

accidentally strayed from Keady, the RUC patrol continued on its journey. Despite subsequently notifying his superiors and the British army in Newtownhamilton about the suspicious checkpoint, nobody followed up on Bartholomew's information. The checkpoint was unofficial and had one objective namely, to ambush a Catholic or two. In this case, Colm McCartney was shot four times and John P. Farmer had six bullets pumped into his head for being nothing more than GAA supporters. The ruthless killers poured petrol on Colm McCartney's new Ford Cortina car and set it on fire to destroy evidence. This led the fuel tank to explode.

Subsequent GAA fans travelling back to Co. Derry who arrived on the scene of the fire, smoke and death were horrified at the sight of two blood-covered bodies lying on the road. Two drivers and their passengers, shocked at what they saw, drove on to Keady to inform the RUC. They were never interviewed about what they saw in the subsequent investigation!

Within hours of the killings, we all knew that this was a double murder. Although we didn't know the two innocent men, everybody in the GAA community was traumatised. Not only was it the killing of two innocent men but was seen across the country as a sectarian attack on the GAA itself. Such was the fear at this time, the players and supporters of GAA clubs in the area would always travel to local games in a convoy of twenty to thirty cars. Whatever suspicions and fears we had up until then, it was becoming clear that a loyalist gang or unit was operating locally that appeared to be able to move around freely without fear of arrest or prosecution from the British state.

These killings provoked a quick response. Six days later on 30 August, the IRA hit back. Forty-nine-year-old Robert 'Bertie' Frazer, a member of the Ulster Defence Regiment, a former resident of Whitecross, then living in Dungormley, Newtownhamilton, was a council employee and worked weekends on Joe Watson's farm a mile up the road from our house in Whitecross. As Bertie reversed his car out of Watson's farm on the Ballymoyer Road, two gunmen lay in wait for him. He was taken from the car, shot and died at the scene. Joe Watson heard the commotion and as he ran out through his front door, the IRA told him to get back into the house and made their getaway in Bertie Frazer's car, heading towards the border. Before they abandoned the car, they took Bertie's UDR uniform and state-issue pistol with them.[4] According to the book *Bear in Mind These Dead*, his son Willie told author Susan McKay that his father Bertie worked on covert operations for the British SAS or Special Air Service.[5]

Four decades later, the Historical Enquiries Team (HET) which was set up in 2005 to investigate unsolved killings before being mysteriously wound down in 2014, stated in a report that UDR man Bertie Frazer, RUC officer and UVF bomber Laurence McClure, Robert McConnell of the UDR and Phillip 'Shilly' Silcock were involved in the killings of Colm McCartney and John Farmer.

Some republicans in a suspected splinter group weren't satisfied in killing Bertie Frazer. Next day, 1 September, they struck again. Tullyvallen is a townland about seven miles from our house, close to the Armagh-Monaghan border. An entirely agricultural area dotted with farms, the majority of the population living there at the time was Protestant and the Orange Order in the area had an active membership.

A meeting of the Guiding Star Temperance Orange Lodge was taking place on the Monday evening at the hall on the Altnamackin Road. As the meeting progressed, two gunmen burst in and sprayed the place with bullets. Four people died instantly and a fifth man passed away two days later. Six people were injured.

The dead were William McKee (70), his son James (40), Nevin McConnell (40), John Johnson (80) and William Herron (67). The British army later found a metal container with two pounds of explosive mix at the entrance to the hall. Eleven families were left to suffer because of this shocking attack. Just like every other family who had death visit at their door, they should not be forgotten.

Mystery Surrounds Local Killings

The Provisional IRA said that this attack was not approved by its leadership. A new organisation that called itself 'The South Armagh Republican Action Force' claimed responsibility, a development that left everyone outside the region wondering who are these people? Other republican sources added that further actions could not be ruled out as a reaction to the activities of loyalist paramilitary groups. We all knew it wouldn't be long before some sort of revenge would result, as had now become the routine cycle of events.

In Tyrone, Denis Mullen was chairman of the Moy branch of the SDLP and an election agent for former Northern Ireland Assembly member Austin Currie. Denis had recently been promoted to the position of ambulance controller at Dungannon Hospital. However, the local Orange Order had written to the hospital objecting to the position being given to a Catholic.

In September 1975, Denis, Olive and their two children, three-year-old Denise and Edward, thirteen months, were at home in their isolated farm house when they heard the sound of two sods of clay being thrown at their front window. Not suspecting anything sinister, Denis opened the front door and was killed instantly by seventeen bullets fired from a Sterling sub-machine gun. Olive fled to her kitchen where she miraculously dodged thirteen bullets.

Ambulance staff from all across Northern Ireland formed a guard of honour at Denis Mullen's funeral. Garfield Beattie aged nineteen, barely out of his school uniform and on his first mission for the UVF, was one of two men convicted for his murder. William John Parr, his fellow gunman, also received a life sentence. Their pal, William Corrigan, who was alleged to have also been involved in the killing but not jailed, was subsequently shot dead by the IRA in October 1976 suggesting his name was passed on by someone to the Provos.

THE TIT-FOR-TAT VIOLENCE that was now happening on an almost hourly basis came our way again on 7 November. Johnny Bell (57) from Ballymoyer, about a mile up the road from our house, was a lance corporal in the UDR and a brother-in law of Bertie Frazer. That evening Johnny was on his way home from work and as he turned into his laneway, IRA gunmen, who had been lying in wait, opened fire killing him. I always found Johnny Bell to be a good neighbour. He regularly gave us lifts home from dances in Newry and we'd have a laugh and a bit of craic in the car. The Reaveys and the Bell family were always close.

Fr Con Malone, a Whitecross man who was home from missionary work in Tanzania, accompanied me to Johnny Bell's wake. We were well received by the Bell family and as we made our way down the stairs to head home, we met Rev. Ian Paisley working his way up the stairs accompanied by a young Willie Frazer. Courtesies were exchanged and we went home.

By this time, somebody in London had got the message. The decision to effectively make the UVF a legal organisation one year before was an unmitigated disaster. The British approach, thinking that the UVF might see sense and convert to democratic politics, was clearly miscalculated, itself a reflection of how out of touch London was with the reality on the ground in Northern Ireland. With twelve killings comitted in Northern Ireland since they were made a legal organisation in May 1974, London decided to declare the UVF illegal again on 3 October 1975.

AROUND THIS TIME, MY day job as a technical adviser with Ross Poultry took me all over the six counties. Among the local farms I called to was that of Protestant man James Mitchell who ran a poultry and beef operation on the Ballylane Road in nearby Glenanne, two miles from Whitecross. Once a month I would call to Mitchells' to advise James on developing his poultry business and the chat would be very cordial. His farm looked like a normal place of work with nothing outstanding to catch my attention. I didn't know it then, but the very place I was calling to was to play a major role in some of the most horrific crimes ever committed in the history of Ireland, unimaginable atrocities that continue to reverberate to this very day.

On 19 December 1975 with everyone preparing for Christmas, the loyalist killing machine struck twice within a few hours on both sides of the border about ten miles or so apart. Shortly after 6 p.m., a car bomb exploded outside Kay's Tavern in Crowe Street, Dundalk, Co. Louth. It cost the lives of Hugh Waters, a tailor, who just happened to be in the bar delivering clothes and Jack Rooney who was walking on the opposite side of the street. He died after being struck by shrapnel. The fact that the bombers came south of the border again and to Dundalk, perceived by many as a safe place for those on-the run, was worrying at the time. The feeling that circulated on the ground and in Dublin was a fear that British loyalists were upping hostilities to push for a civil war.

Three hours later in Silverbridge South Armagh, not far from Dundalk, the Red Hand Commando, as they called themselves, targeted the popular Donnelly's Bar where the main topic of conversation in the pub was the earlier attack on Kay's Tavern. Despite the awful news from Dundalk, spirits were high in the pub as many were anticipating finishing work for the Christmas break. Fourteen-year-old Michael Donnelly, a son of the owner, was pumping petrol into a car owned by Patrick Donnelly (24) – no relation – outside the pub when loyalist gunmen pulled up and opened fire.[6] Patrick Donnelly, a local farmer, died instantly. Young Michael ran inside to alert those in the pub. A bomb was then thrown inside the door while another gunman opened fire.

In the pub that night was thirty-two-year-old Trevor Brecknell who had moved to Silverbridge from England, having married his wife Ann from nearby Cullyhanna. He had a special reason to be there as his wife had just given birth to their third child and first daughter, Róisín, at Daisy Hill Hospital in Newry two days earlier. The happiness that birth brought led him to meet up with some friends that night for a celebratory drink.[7] Trevor's celebration was short-lived. The Red Hand Commando blitzed the place with bullets before the bomb exploded. Young Michael Donnelly and Trevor Brecknell became the second and third fatalities at the pub. At least five others were injured.

According to *Lethal Allies*, the RUC had raided the pub six weeks previously in a rare visit for what many felt later was a scouting mission to check the place out.[8] RUC Detective Sergeant Gerry McCann later revealed that there was no record of the raid in the Day Book at Forkhill Station for the visit to Donnelly's Pub. For such a visit to take place in that area, the British army would have been told. The entire circumstances of the RUC raid added to the suspicious nature of what happened.

Horrific and all as these killings were, the UVF and their pals in the UDA, UFF and so-called Red Hand Commando were clearly intent on stepping up their malicious activity. 1975 was ending and 266 people had died in the previous twelve months. In South Armagh we sensed that maybe a covert UVF unit or gang was in our midst that appeared to be getting more blood-thirsty with each passing week. Yet, in the vast majority of killings that had happened locally in the previous twenty-four months, the number of people arrested, charged, prosecuted and convicted for these murders was so low, it barely made the news. The low prosecution rate was remarkable considering the place was over-run with British soldiers and security personnel at the time.

With over twenty people per month dying on both sides and what felt like a more concentrated attack on Catholics in our particular area, we thought, surely, things couldn't get any worse? But things did get worse, unimaginably worse and in the coming weeks and months, our lives were about to be turned upside down.

Bloodbath

CHRISTMAS 1975 WAS A good one for the Reaveys. The IRA had been on ceasefire for almost a year even though a number of killings had been claimed by 'republicans'. We all hoped and prayed that the recent upsurge in loyalist violence was finished. I can recall us all thinking that if only the politicians could get their act together, it would be all over in a few weeks and we could get back to living normal lives.

As we talked about the possible political manoeuvrings of the time over the Christmas period, I recall a great sense of unity in the Reavey family. Our Mother was never so happy in her life and we were all making our way nicely with our respective working careers. I was busy with Ross Poultry in Portadown and we had two young mouths to feed. Dad was painting and decorating; my brothers Seamus and Frank were well established as plastering contractors; John Martin was a brick layer and before Christmas, had just completed building a fireplace for Noel Dalzell, a respected Protestant businessman from nearby Markethill. Oliver was a joiner with Cole's of Warrenpoint, so too was Brian who was with Campbells in Newry, Eileen was a student nurse in the Royal Victoria Hospital in Belfast while Una, Paul and Colleen were still at school. Anthony was waiting to start an apprenticeship as an electrician while Kathleen, the eldest, was working as a nurse at the Whittington hospital in north London.

Five days later on Tuesday 30 December 1975, some strange activity happened close to our house which didn't fully register with us at the time. A mile down the road from our house on the Whitecross to Bessbrook Road near Kingsmills, an unidentified man approached the farmhouses of neighbouring large Catholic families adjacent to each other. The Magee and McGuinness families operated sizeable dairy and poultry farms while the McKeown family ran a dairy operation. The unidentified man told the McGuinness and Magee families to vacate their farm houses and sleep somewhere else at night. Later, Mrs Magee sent her brother Hughie over to McKeowns to alert them of possible danger. The Magees, McKeowns and McGuinness families took the warnings seriously in light of all that was happening in the vicinity.

The McGuinness family left their house and stayed overnight with Robbie McGuinness' sister Alice O'Hare up at Newtowncloghoge, ten miles away. For the following days, they would milk their cows as usual, leave the houses no later than 7 p.m. and sleep with relatives. I became aware of this two days later on Thursday 1 January, having been being told by Robbie McGuinness. The Magees stayed in Newry with the Connolly family. The McKeown family lived down a long lane at Tullywinney near Whitecross. Peter McKeown and his wife Frances moved out of their new bungalow and went to live with his parents further down the lane.

A worried Robbie McGuinness enquired, in confidence, on Thursday 1 January, if the Reaveys had received a similar request from this mysterious man? The answer was 'no'. Two other families, one Catholic, the other Protestant, were also asked to leave their homes in the locality but opted not to. While I was surprised, I passed it off as nothing more than a security procedure. It was common at the time for either the IRA to temporarily take over a house to target security personnel or the British army might raid houses searching for weapons. I learned years later that the man who called to the doors advising people to seek night-time accommodation elsewhere, was an English man.

This type of activity was not unusual in nationalist areas, particularly in Belfast and Derry, so I just assumed that maybe it went with the political and military climate of the time in South Armagh. I said nothing as Robbie had spoken to me in confidence and gave it no further thought.

New Year's Eve came along and we rang in 1976 hoping for a peaceful twelve months ahead. That night, 31 December, my younger brother Anthony and his girlfriend Lillian had been out socialising in Jackie Murphy's pub in Dundalk on the old Dublin Road. While in the pub, Lillian happened to meet her friend Imelda Cunningham who lived in Camlough. She introduced her boyfriend Barry O'Dowd from Ballydougan near Gilford. Barry had been home from working on an oil rig in the North Sea off the coast of the Orkney islands and was scheduled to return on Monday 5 January.

We woke up on the morning of 1 January and switched on the radio to hear that a bomb had exploded the night before at the Central Bar in Gilford, North Armagh. Three Protestants were killed in the explosion which left us all wondering, who was responsible? After all, the IRA had officially been on cease-fire since February 1975 though some elements were still active using cover names. Next day, Friday 2 January, my brother Brian and Phelim McGuinness whose family had to vacate their farmhouse at night time, were in my Mother's house at around 7.30 p.m. The two lads were chatting away, smoking cigarettes and having a laugh. Our parents were in Newry shopping. Afraid that our Mother might reprimand them for filling the kitchen/living room with smoke when she returned, they opted to open the front door to let some fresh air in.

Suddenly, three armed men, in military outfits, walked in and ordered them out into the garden. Three other armed men stood outside on watch. According to Phelim, one of the men present had an English accent. Brian and Phelim were told to lie face down while the armed men chatted amongst themselves before leaving. Brian was asked where the rest of the family were and obviously gave them an answer that they didn't want to hear.

Before they departed, they warned Brian that they were returning to England next week and would shoot him before they left. This comment wasn't taken seriously because a number of people in the locality were told this by the British military from time to time. Phelim and Brian didn't tell anybody what happened as they feared relaying the story might cause unnecessary distress to the McGuinness and Reavey families.

On the evening of Saturday 3 January, a number of strange events happened which, with the benefit of hindsight, subsequently turned out to be extraordinary. Our Brian had earlier in the day played a game of soccer with the local team in Bessbrook and arranged to meet Reggie and Walter Chapman, in The Lough Inn pub in nearby Camlough which was owned by the Boyle family. John Martin went along as well. The lads had a few drinks, a laugh or two, played a game of pool, discussed their performance earlier and the outstanding results of the English League Division 1 earlier that day. Whilst they were playing one of their many games of pool, a small explosion occurred at the front door. A number of people were injured, though not seriously. Several were rushed to Daisy Hill Hospital in Newry and fortunately were not detained long. It was assumed the bomb was placed at the door by loyalists.

When the RUC came to the pub, those inside were told to vacate the premises. Brian, John Martin, Reggie and Walter went outside, had a cigarette each and discussed what had happened until the bomb disposal experts checked the place before giving the all clear. The lads went back inside, gathered up their coats and went across the road to Doyle's pub. Waiting for them in Doyle's was Barry O'Dowd and his girlfriend Imelda. Brian's girlfriend, Alice Campbell, my cousin Nora Barbour and her husband Davy were there also. Alice and Brian didn't stay long as she had to start her shift in Daisy Hill Hospital at 8.30 p.m. Brian drove Alice to the hospital and returned to Doyle's Bar where he spent the rest of the evening socialising with John Martin, the Chapman brothers, Barry, Imelda, Nora and Davy. Within days, most of the above would make world news!

Sunday 4 January started off as a normal day. Our Father had everybody in the house up early and in time for 10 a.m. mass in St Brigid's church in Carrickananney. Every Sunday, we met up outside the chapel afterwards with locals for a friendly chat. Normally on a Sunday afternoon, we would all congregate at my parents' house. It was a chance to catch up and see how the rest of the clan were doing. However that morning, our Mother told us all that there was no need to call that evening as she was visiting her sister Rose Ellen Sheeran who lived at Camlough Lake five miles away. Mammy, Daddy, Colleen and Una got ready around 6.00 p.m. to head to Sheeran's. John Martin offered to drive them in his car when Oliver popped up and said he would take them. When John Martin realised that his favourite TV programme at the time, *Celebrity Squares*, was about to be on UTV, he opted to let Oliver do the driving. They left the house at 6.05 p.m. approximately and headed off for Camlough Lake. Brian, Anthony and John Martin remained at home to mind the house and watch TV.

It was not unusual for twenty or more people to be in our house on a Sunday evening. Ours was a céilí house and we always had friends in for a bit of music, food, craic and general chit-chat. The key was always in the door and everybody was welcome. At approximately 6.10 p.m. as the lads sipped tea, munched their biscuits and laughed at the answers on the telly, from nowhere, the barrel of an automatic machine gun appeared through the top of the front door into the kitchen. The lads spotted it but didn't move as they thought it was the British army carrying out a regular house check.

Then the door burst opened and four big burly men wearing army jackets stormed in firing a salvo of shots at John Martin who fell out of his chair and collapsed on to the floor, bleeding heavily in the process. As he squirmed and screamed for his life, they pumped another magazine of shots into his body. With noisy rapid gunfire filling the house, Brian and Anthony, in a state of sudden panic, desperately attempted to escape into the big bedroom. Brian ran through the door but was shot in the back. A bullet went through his heart forcing him to fall into the bedroom fireplace.

Anthony ran into the big bedroom and dived under the bed. The gunman followed him and fired thirty shots through the mattress, striking him seventeen times. Assuming he was dead, the gunman went back into the kitchen and continued shooting. He fired through all the doors leading off the kitchen, thinking the rest of us were in the house.

Miraculously, Anthony was still alive under the bed while pretending to be dead. He listened attentively and when the shooting stopped, he could hear the sound of heavy boots running quickly out the garden path to the road. A waiting car revved up and drove off at screeching speed, then Anthony crawled out on his hands and knees from under the bed, dripping in blood. He came across Brian sitting lifeless in the bedroom fireplace. He felt his pulse but knew in an instant that he was dead. He then crawled from the bedroom into the kitchen where John Martin lay dead in a pool of blood. Such was the velocity of the gunfire, John Martin's clothes had been ripped to shreds.

Getting weaker by the minute, Anthony, who was bleeding heavily, crawled on his hands and knees across the road. He somehow managed to drag himself for 200 yards along the wet mucky margin on the side of the road and up the steep hill to Pat and Angela O'Hanlon's house. As he struggled, along the way, a Volkswagen car passed him and despite his bloody desperate state, Patsy McKeown, the driver from Ballymoyer, opted not to stop and revealed to me some time later that he thought Anthony was acting the fool.

When Anthony eventually dragged himself to O'Hanlon's house, he lifted himself up by clinging on to the steel bars on the garden gate. He then made a lunge towards the front door where he banged as loud as he could. Angela and her son Patrick junior heard the commotion at the door and when they opened it, Anthony fell into their arms shouting 'I've been shot and they've all been shot'. He then passed out and Mrs O'Hanlon fetched a couple of pillows, a blanket and tended to him before ringing the RUC, doctor and the local priest, Fr Hughes.

IN THE MEANTIME, OLIVER had returned from Sheeran's house at Camlough Lake. He walked in to be met by the horrific sight of John Martin lying dead and the bright kitchen walls and floor splattered in thick blood. Oliver couldn't believe his eyes. The happy home he had left thirty minutes earlier was now a horrible bloodbath. He thought he was having a nightmare. He didn't know what to do as he took in the sight of the slaughter that lay before him.

Assuming John Martin was the only person dead from the attack and now in a desperate state of panic, Oliver rushed out of the house and ran up the road to O'Hanlons to discover that Anthony was there lying on the floor clinging on for dear life. Anthony, in awful pain, bleeding heavily, and weak told him about the horrific massacre and broke the news to him that Brian was also dead.

Oliver's shock now intensified, but realised he had to act quickly. Conscious that Anthony was hanging on to life, he rushed out of the house and ran to Fr Hughes, our parish priest whose residence was about 300 yards away, but he was not in. He then went in search of Fr Con Malone, a Rosminian missionary priest who happened to be home in Whitecross from Tanzania at the time. Fr Malone was not in either so he returned to the scene of the crime. Unknown to Oliver, Fr Malone had been alerted to the shootings by neighbours and was on his way to my house to break the bad news to me.

Meanwhile Jessie Murphy and her son Cyril, who were neighbours of the O'Hanlons, ran down to our house when they heard the news. As Jessie stepped inside the porch door at the front of the house, she almost tripped over the bullet shells scattered on the floor. Then nearly stumbled across John Martin's body and couldn't believe the bloody mess around her. She said a few prayers, unaware that Brian was dead as well. Once her prayers were complete, she couldn't wait to get out of the house and ran back home screaming.

By this time, Fr Hughes and Dr Joe Stewart from Newtownhamilton had arrived at our house. The last rites were given to John Martin and Brian by Fr Hughes and Dr Stewart formally confirmed that John Martin and Brian were officially dead. They then called to O'Hanlon's house and unsure of Anthony's survival, the last rites were given to him. The ambulance then came and Anthony was taken to Daisy Hill Hospital in Newry seven miles away.

Dr Stewart and Fr Hughes then went over towards Sheeran's House at Camlough Lake to break the horrific news to our parents. They were stunned and Dr Stewart gave both an injection of diazepam to prevent severe shock. Later in Daisy Hill, he dispensed a supply of Valium to our Seamus, in the hope that everyone would get a decent night's sleep.

Sometime afterwards, Fr Hughes told me that my traumatised Mother asked, 'Why was there no warning from the police? Why didn't they shoot me instead?' Our parents were absolutely devastated. As they struggled to take in and mentally comprehend the madness of what had happened, Fr Malone arrived at my door to break the bad news. He walked in and said in a very serious tone of voice, 'grab your coat, there's been an accident over at the cottage, we need to hurry'. I told Róisín to lock all doors and left the house immediately with Fr Malone and asked him what exactly happened. He told me there had been a shooting and he presumed there had been fatalities but he wasn't sure.

When we arrived at the house before 7 p.m., to my surprise, the road outside our gate was not sealed off. A police land rover and an ambulance were parked outside the gate. Two armed RUC men stood outside the door of the house. One of them was known to me as Constable George Cully from Mountnorris who was based at Bessbrook station. A small crowd of concerned neighbours had gathered outside the house and a few I spoke to, including Jessie Murphy, sympathised with me. I quickly realised that there was a definite fatality or more in the house.

I approached the door and Cully told me I was not allowed inside. I told him that I was Eugene Reavey and this was our family home, but he wouldn't let me in even though he knew that I was family. I was furious, and not accepting his stern authoritarian uncooperative diktat, I burst in past the two RUC men and was immediately followed by my cousin Kevin Reavey who was only fourteen at the time.

What I saw almost made me vomit. Amidst a room full of successful GAA trophies and 1975 Christmas cards wishing us peace and goodwill for the year ahead, John Martin was slumped face down on the floor in a dark pool of his own blood. There was blood everywhere. As I surveyed the chaos around me and took in the horrible sight I was witnessing, I almost overlooked the fact that an RUC policeman was busy in the kitchen rummaging through our china cabinet. Sensing he was up to no good, I asked him what he was doing?

He said, 'I believe there's ammunition stored here'.

'You won't find any ammunition in this house unless *you* are going to plant it,' I said.

The RUC man was Trevor Cartmill, a neighbour from nearby Kingsmills and I lost my temper completely. I grabbed him by the neck and then Kevin took hold of him as well. With strong force, we chucked Cartmill out the door. To my surprise, none of the RUC men said a word even though, technically speaking, we could have been arrested for manhandling a police officer. I went back in to the house and unaware that I was at the time, the RUC men gave Kevin a beating out in the yard. This was extraordinary behaviour for a so-called civilised police force at a time of inexplicable grief for us. They could not have been more insensitive if they had tried.

I surveyed the bloody mess around me in the kitchen and as I did, the trail of blood on the floor led me to the boy's bedroom. I looked all around at the mess and there on my left-hand side was Brian, slumped dead in his own blood in the fireplace. He was positioned as if he was like someone who had sat down and had fallen asleep. I was frozen with disbelief. Two of my brothers were dead. 'Jesus Christ,' I thought, 'what did we do to deserve this?' The ambulance men came in the door and asked if they could be left alone for five minutes.

Then my younger brother Paul, who was just fifteen at the time and had spent the evening with friends, arrived on his bicycle to a scene of utter chaos. Shortly afterwards, the ambulance took Brian and John Martin's bodies to the morgue in Daisy Hill Hospital, Newry. My brother Frank had arrived by now and he too was denied entry into the house. Our parents arrived shortly after 8 p.m. and sat outside in Dr Stewart's car. He persuaded them not to go inside.

Two plainclothes RUC detectives arrived from Newry and made themselves known to my brother Oliver. They asked him if he would accompany them to the home of our good Protestant farming neighbours and close friends, Bertie Hamilton and his wife Margaret, who lived 200 yards or so down the road from the massacre. Oliver and the two detectives travelled the short distance to the Hamilton house in an unmarked police car. They quizzed Oliver about the killings and wrote everything down. But no account of this mysterious written record has ever seen the light of day. To this day, we are baffled as to why Oliver was taken to the Hamilton home and I can only assume the detectives were on some sort of fishing expedition in search of intelligence.

During the evening while we were at our family house, I was constantly in and out the door as a result of anxiety trying to grasp the horror. On one occasion, I stepped outside and stood between the front door and the gate at the road. Two RUC officers stood at the door with an additional four at the gate. Every so often a voice in the distance could be heard on the police walkie-talkie radio sets. As I observed the scene around me, I overheard a significant nugget of information. The voice on the walkie-talkie revealed that a car had been found burned out. The voice gave a grid reference for the location. Curious to know where, I asked one of the RUC officers to identify the location and he said he didn't know.

Meanwhile my sister Kathleen, who was a nurse in London, had been out visiting friends. She was at home in Crouch End near Finsbury Park getting her children ready for bed when her husband Pat called her from downstairs. He had been watching the news on TV and the report said that three men from a large Catholic family in South Armagh had been shot. It showed a map in which Whitecross was highlighted on the screen. Kathleen assumed straight away that our family had been hit. She became hysterical and Pat tried everything he could to calm her down. Obviously when one is away from home, a crisis is even more dramatic than it is for those who have to deal with it face on. At that moment, Fr Con Malone phoned her and confirmed her worst fears. She ran out into the street crying and screaming at the top of her voice telling anybody who was prepared to listen what had happened. In London, of course, nobody was listening and that was a realistic metaphor for the entire duration of the Troubles.

Our cousins, the O'Shea's in Cheshire, also heard on the radio that two Catholic families in Co. Armagh were subjected to shootings. They rang Sheeran's at Camlough Lake to find out more. Meanwhile on the other side of the Atlantic Ocean, my auntie Winnie, who lived in Queens New York, caught something on the television and she too rang Sheeran's to be told the bad news. Sheeran's, I should point out, had a phone. We didn't.

In Belfast, Fr Malone's mother was a patient in the Ear, Nose and Throat Hospital. Con phoned the ward and spoke to the sister in charge. By coincidence, my other sister Eileen also worked in the ENT hospital but was based on a different floor. Fr Con told the sister not to tell Eileen of the killings but to let her know that there was an emergency at home and that she should go to Whitecross as soon as possible. Con's two sisters Bernie and Ann, as well as his brother-in-law Gerry McKeown, happened to be in the hospital on the lower floor visiting his mother and Eileen was told she could go home with them.

When Eileen was informed about 'the emergency' at home, she instantly assumed that our Dad had died but she was assured he was fine. Con's sister, Ann, helped Eileen to pack her bags and they made their way down to Newry. On the way home from Belfast, some diplomacy had to be applied in the packed car which consisted of Gerry and Ann McKeown, Eileen, Bernie Malone and her two children. As they travelled along in the car, Eileen wept in the back seat constantly talking about our Daddy and praying he would be ok. Every so often she would ask Ann 'is Daddy dead?' Ann would assure her that our Dad was fine. The last thing the Malones wanted was to reveal all and upset Eileen in front of the children for fear it would make an already bad situation worse. Shortly before they arrived at Daisy Hill Hospital around 9 p.m., Eileen was told by Gerry McKeown to be strong and that what awaited her was worse than she originally feared.

As Eileen dreaded what most of us knew, my brother Seamus was unaware of what had happened. Micky John Grant, a neighbour in Drumherriff, drove to Newry where Seamus and his wife Teresa were visiting their in-laws at Derrybeg Cottages. Micky John told him of the killings and then took Seamus and Teresa in to Daisy Hill where they met Eileen.

Alice Campbell from Cullaville South Armagh, who was engaged to our Brian, happened to be a trainee nurse in Daisy Hill Hospital. The two had planned to get married on Saturday 14 August 1976 and were spending every available moment together saving and planning for the biggest day so far of their respective lives. Brian was with Alice that Sunday afternoon and dropped her off at the nurses' living quarters in Newry around 5.30 p.m. He then drove to Whitecross and arrived home around 5.45 p.m.

Being the industrious woman, Alice always presented herself in the ward half an hour before she was due on duty to be briefed by her colleagues as to who was coming in, going out and to get an update on the status of various patients. Just as she was about to leave her room, shortly before 8.30 p.m., there was a knock on the door. Her ward sister, Agnes White, accompanied by a Dr Wahab, the casualty officer, wanted to talk to her. Sister White chose her words carefully and told Alice she couldn't go on duty that night as her boyfriend Brian had been admitted to A&E as a result of an earlier 'accident'. Alice was baffled and commented that it couldn't be true as she had been with him up until she arrived into the hospital earlier. Sister White made her sit down on the bed and repeated her line that she couldn't go on duty due to the 'accident'.

Alice was then told by Sister White that the Reavey family was in the building and she should join us. Alice met my brother Seamus first who told her what happened. She didn't see Brian laid out in the hospital that night and all these years later says her recollection of that evening is a complete blur. I can't remember how Alice reacted on hearing the news but we know that in the months after the killing, she was absolutely devastated and completely heartbroken at losing the love of her life.

As Alice took in the awful news on that Sunday night, all of us, except Kathleen, had made our way into Daisy Hill Hospital to grieve for John Martin and Brian while waiting desperately for positive developments on Anthony. Our states of mind were so confused, puzzled and disorientated at that time, anger hadn't entered our thoughts. We struggled with the tears, loud crying and horrendous sense of loss.

Meanwhile our Dad, who had been shaking like a leaf from distress since 6.50 p.m., was supposed to go into the morgue in Daisy Hill and identify the bodies. Dr Stewart wouldn't allow him to do it and must have felt that with Daddy's bad heart condition, such a task might adversely affect his health. Instead, my brother Seamus, accompanied by Gerry Crimmins, the mortuary attendant and Detective Constable William David Smyth, formally identified Brian and John Martin.

The rest of the family were waiting in an ante-room praying that Anthony would recover in the intensive care unit. As the evening wore on, Seamus and I called to Patsy McLogan who ran a pub and funeral undertaking business in Newry Town. Patsy advised us it was too late to get the death notices into *The Irish News* newspaper the next day. Of course the killings were going to be front page news everywhere so the word was out anyway. He suggested we come back next morning to select the coffins.

Throughout the evening, Anthony was being moved in and out of X-Ray and operating theatres where the bullets lodged in him were removed from his lower groin and upper legs by Dr Shankar-Naryan, the senior house officer at Daisy Hill. To our surprise, no vital organs were damaged despite the massive loss of blood but that didn't mean though he was in the clear.

At some stage during the course of the evening, someone in Daisy Hill Hospital told us that three Catholics belonging to the same family had been shot dead at Ballydougan near Gilford in Co. Down which was fifteen miles north of Whitecross. We were in such a state of shock that night, we didn't assume there was any connection between what occurred in Ballydougan and what had happened in our house.

Later Fr Malone said the rosary at which our Dad, being the good Christian that he was, prayed for the gunmen and pleaded with us not to take revenge. Fr Malone, an experienced public speaker, also told us not to talk to the media unless we had a properly prepared message in advance which he would supervise. None of us had dealt with the press and in light of the shock and emotional daze we were in, we gladly accepted Fr Malone's wise recommendation.

As we paced the corridors of Daisy Hill, the media had made their way to Whitecross. ITN, UTV, BBC, RTÉ and all the national papers and international news agencies who had people in Belfast, flocked to Whitecross for, what was for them, just another daily story on the Northern Ireland conveyor belt of horror. None of us spoke to the press on the Sunday night because we weren't there. We were about to become famous but for all the wrong reasons.

It must have been close to midnight when we left Daisy Hill and made our way back to Whitecross wondering as we travelled along the dark twisty bumpy drumlins of South Armagh how this happened and, more to the point, why *we* were targeted? We made our way home to Whitecross via Camlough village in a convoy of cars along the Tullyah Road which cuts across at The Mountain House pub between Newry and Newtownhamilton.

There wasn't a single soldier, Land Rover, RUC officer or security person on the route! That in itself was extraordinary as we lived in republican South Armagh, two of my brothers were dead while Anthony was clinging on for dear life. Fifteen miles away, three members of the O'Dowd family had been shot dead earlier that evening, so one would have thought the area would have been swarming with soldiers.

That night, our parents stayed in our house in Drumherriff. Róisín recalls them crying and sobbing constantly throughout the night and getting very little sleep. My sister Eileen and Alice Campbell, Brian's girlfriend, stayed in O'Hanlon's just up the road from our place. They sat up the whole night wailing and re-living all the great times they had while asking themselves repeatedly why the lads were targeted? Colleen stayed with my aunty Margaret and uncle Patsy Reavey who lived at St Killian's Park in Whitecross. In fact she stayed there for the subsequent six weeks.

One of my abiding memories of the night was the call I made to my brother-in-law Pat McHale who was married to our Kathleen in London. Pat, a lovely guy, worked for Gallagher's Tobacco and earlier in his life had done two years of compulsory national service in the Grenadier Guards, an infantry regiment within the British army, but had never seen active service. During our chat, he remarked, somewhat naively, 'don't worry, our boys are in the air and they'll look after you'. I'm sure he meant well but as we were about to learn, low level British soldiers might have been fine when engaging with the public on a one-to-one basis but the conduct of their superior officers and the instructions they issued, were a different matter altogether.

As we went to bed on Sunday night 4 January 1976 trying to get our heads around what happened, we assumed things couldn't get any worse. How wrong we were!

Hell on Earth

On Monday morning, 5 January 1976, every one of us struggled to get out of bed. None of us slept the night before as we tried to take in the enormity of what happened.

I got up and struggled to get my bearings. The story was all over the radio news. There was no rolling twenty-four-hour TV news in those days. As the morning wore on, I went to Loughran's shop in Whitecross to find that the O'Dowd and Reavey killings were splashed across the front pages of the regional and national newspapers. 'Five Catholics are killed in two raids', one paper read while another carried an inside headline 'Masked gang entered house and murdered Brothers'. Another publication ran with a splash headline that said 'Five Roman Catholics Murdered'.

Elsewhere it was 'Five die in raids on homes' while the London-based *Daily Express* seemed to be hinting at something when its front page read 'Five killed as Ulster Truce nears its end'. All the papers seemed to be pointing the finger of blame on the UVF. As the killings dominated the radio news and talk programmes, we were mindful that on the previous night, the RUC forensics team had visited the house to gather information as part of their investigation. But they didn't carry out any work and opted to return the next morning.

On Monday at 7.30 a.m., Seamus who lived in Whitecross village, a quarter of a mile from the killings, was the first one of us to visit the house. As he attempted to gain entry, Edward Boyle, a neighbour from nearby Kingsmills stopped for a chat. Edward Boyle was one of the local farmers who had been instructed to vacate his house the previous Tuesday but refused. Unable to gain access through the front door, Seamus climbed in the window of the boy's room, the very place where Brian and Anthony had been shot.

If the bloody sight that I saw the night before was shocking, what Seamus witnessed multiplied the hurt and anger we have felt ever since. The house had been completely ransacked. The British security forces clearly came in during the night and pulled the house apart. The place was wrecked and every stick of furniture was smashed beyond repair. It was bad enough that two of our brothers were dead, a third was hanging on for dear life and then the so-called protectors of the public came in and destroyed the place.

Seamus opted to return to my place and bring our Father down to the house to see the mess. They returned to the scene of the crime and weren't at the house five minutes when a van pulled up at the front gate. Three men from the Housing Executive office in Newry, at what was the early hour of 8 a.m., presented themselves and had 'work' to do. One of the men was Vincie Small from the nearby village of Meigh. My Father knew Vincie well through the football. He had been clearly sent by someone in authority to replace the doors and architraves. The presence of Housing Executive personnel at the house was unusual as normally most of these people could not be found on the same earth as the rest of us on a Monday morning! What's more, if you rang the Housing Executive people on a Monday to fix a problem with your house, only God knows what week they'd show up. I should add there is no evidence to suggest that Vincie Small acted any way other than in good faith.

Yet here they were first thing on a Monday parked outside our house ready to replace items which contained bullet marks and fingerprints, vital evidence in any murder trial. The Housing Executive offices normally open for business at 9 a.m. and after the Christmas break, the first day back at work would deal with a backlog of jobs from the previous year. Where would they get the materials from so soon?

Our Father, despite the state of mind he was in and to his credit, sensed straight away that all was not right. He attempted to persuade Vincie and his colleagues to go away and leave the house untouched. They refused. The timing of the Housing Executive people arriving at the house so early and what they were instructed to do had all the hallmarks of meticulous planning by somebody in an official capacity and all with one aim in mind, as I saw it, namely to conceal potential evidence. As well as that, such work could sanitise what the media might see when they showed up later in the day.

The forensics team returned later in the morning and, despite the mess they encountered, had their work completed by 11 a.m. As they left, our Protestant neighbour Margaret Hamilton, my sister in-law Teresa and Annie McClorey, our Mother's best friend who had been waiting patiently outside the house, walked in to the kitchen to see the chaos that lay before them.

To everyone's surprise, Margaret, Teresa and Annie found fourteen bullet shells in the house. This was extraordinary considering the forensic people had just left. One would have thought every single fragment of evidence would have been examined, logged, bagged and taken away, but no, these shells were left behind leaving us to believe the investigation into the killings was not being taken seriously, itself a suspicious development.

With almost everything in the house smashed and the floors by now a sea of hardened crimson blood, Margaret, Teresa and Annie cleaned up the place as best they could as we prepared for the wake. In the subsequent hours, locals came and went. They brought sandwiches, bread, eggs, cakes, biscuits, buns, meat, stew, knives, forks, spoons and all the food you could think of. Bobby Scott, our Father's close Protestant friend, brought cans of fresh milk as did Robbie McGuinness' family while Whitecross GFC provided plates, cups, chairs and tables. Both sides, Catholic and Protestant, rallied together in a wonderful act of community, something that rural Ireland is famous for.

Meanwhile Seamus and our Father were busy in Newry selecting coffins at P.J. McLogan Undertakers. Elsewhere Frank and Oliver had to go to Fr Hughes at Whitecross parochial house to get permission to open two graves in the family plot up the road in Ballymoyer cemetery. We also had to source grave diggers, a self-driven practice which was very much the norm at the time but is now the preserve of funeral undertakers. Black ties and white shirts also had to be purchased. It probably sounds like no big deal now but searching shops for shirts which fitted and their different sizes then was quite time consuming in the midst of all the chaos that was happening around us.

We also had to arrange a bedside vigil roster for Anthony who was wrapped in medical tubes, having taken seventeen bullets. While all this was going on, a growing group of media people were camped outside the house desperately requesting a quote or two from one of us.

After the forensic people departed, the British army stayed clear of our house but maintained a presence at both ends of the Kingsmills Road which ran past our front gate. Noisy military helicopters circled overhead all day. Such was the unbearable noise created by the activity in the sky, when our Father opted to speak to the broadcast media around 3 p.m., his voice was drowned out. It was as if there was a deliberate plan to silence or muffle the Reavey version of events.

At 4 p.m., something unusual happened – the overhead British army helicopters, all RUC and military soldiers in the locality returned to barracks in Bessbrook, four miles away. All UDR personnel returned to their local base at nearby Glenanne. This didn't appear to make sense in light of the killings that had happened in our house twenty-two hours previously.

As the day wore on, we became more aware of the O'Dowd killings which happened fifteen miles from Whitecross just outside the village of Gilford, midway between Portadown and Lurgan. At almost the same time as our Brian, Anthony and John Martin were struck down by UVF gunfire in the Whitecross massacre, the Catholic O'Dowd family had gathered for a post-Christmas get-together at their farm. The atmosphere in their house was a jolly one with members of the family enjoying a sing-song around the piano over a few drinks when suddenly at around 6.20 p.m., the door burst open, gunmen stormed in and sprayed the place with bullets. Oil rig worker

Barry O'Dowd (24) who was planning to return to work the next day in Scotland, his brother Declan (19) and their uncle Joe (61) were killed in the attack. Five Catholics were now dead and one seriously injured in two assaults that happened within twenty minutes of each other!

These attacks were planned so one would have thought that with such a blitz of bloody activity on the one day fifteen miles apart and republican reprisals an almost inevitability, security would have been stepped up, but no, that was not how it looked to us. All visible military personnel in South Armagh disappeared into thin air at 4 p.m. on Monday 5 January as darkness fell – or so it seemed.

With silence returned to the sky over our house, our Dad opted to give another interview to the broadcast media:

> I have lived in this house all my life and I've had good relations with my Protestant neighbours. I have worked all my life more for Protestant farmers than my Catholic neighbours.
>
> There is no reason at all for this attack on my family. My feeling is that if their deaths help to stop the killings, then they may not have died in vain.
>
> I appeal that there will be no retaliation for the murder of my sons. As we knelt down to say our prayers last night and prayed for my sons who died and the son who was injured, we prayed also for the men who shot them because they will have more to suffer as the years go on.

By now my sister Kathleen had arrived into Belfast Airport from London. She was picked up by Bill Harte, Seamus' brother-in-law. When Kathleen got to the house, she was in shock. She walked in to the kitchen and despite her arrival home, our Dad, who had been heavily sedated by injection, was sitting down with Dr Joe Stewart and Fathers Hughes and Malone. Despite Kathleen's return, Dad showed no emotion, such was the shock he was in.

While Kathleen surveyed the state of the house and observed the milling crowds outside the gate, we found ourselves with a decision to make. We were due to head in to Newry at 5.30 p.m. to bring Brian and John Martin's remains back to Whitecross for the wake. However, we all opted to delay our visit to Daisy Hill Hospital to see a UTV news update at 5.40 p.m. which would broadcast Dad's statement.

At 5.45 p.m. approximately, close on thirty cars departed in convoy from the Reavey household to make the seven-mile journey to the morgue along the Kingsmills Road past Bessbrook and on to Newry. I was driving the lead car accompanied by Róisín and her mum, Katie Quinn. We went through Kingsmills crossroads before we drove around what's known locally as the Manse corner.

As we turned this slight bend on the road, I became aware of some activity further up on the brow of the hill before us. I could see the headlights of a stalled vehicle about 300 yards further ahead. As I approached the brow of the hill, a man appeared from nowhere in the dark of night waving his hands frantically for me to stop.

He ran towards my car and I rolled down the window. I recognised local man Gerry Byrne who was the first person on the scene from the Newry side. Gerry was a Department of the Environment engineer who was based in Whitecross. He was clearly in a state of panic and shouted, 'Jump out quick Eugene. There's been a shocking massacre up the road'. You can't go any further. The road is blocked. There's been a slaughtering match up here.'

I pulled my car into the side of the road and all the vehicles behind me stopped. I got out of the car and ran twenty yards towards the stalled vehicle. Its lights were pointed away from me and as I got closer, I could see steam rising from the road as the rain fell. My immediate thoughts were that the red Ford minibus, Reg: EIJ 987, had maybe struck Henry Magee's cattle which had, perhaps, strayed from a nearby field. As I got closer, my assumption was completely wrong.

With each step, I could see dead bodies strewn across the road. The sight before me was just horrific. There were pools of blood and human bodies piled on top of each other. Ten men were dead. A heavy smell of death filled the air, something that has never left my mind after all these years. I didn't know who the dead people were or why they were there but following on from what happened in our house the day previous, I thought we were living at the end of the world. To my surprise, there were no RUC or British soldiers about the place. I tried to take in the awful horror but emotionally upset with our situation and unaware as to how many were dead, I said to Gerry Byrne, 'I can't handle this. We're on our way in to Daisy Hill Hospital to pick up my two brothers who were murdered last night and I just can't cope.'

Gerry fully understood and he went to Magee's farm to raise the alarm and to contact the RUC. With the road now blocked, I had to tell the people in the second car of the convoy to pass the word back down the line that everyone was to reverse to the nearby crossroads and take the Tullyah Road into Newry.

Shocked at what we just saw, we made our way to the morgue at Daisy Hill Hospital. A queue of over 100 people, one step at a time, filed past the two coffins containing Brian and John Martin's bodies. The two lay in their respective brown caskets like twin brothers who had gone to sleep. The mourners, all dressed in heavy overcoats and struggling to hold back their sniffling tears, edged past the coffins to pay their respects. There were very emotional scenes from close family relatives and friends. The silent atmosphere in the morgue was horrible and was only broken intermittently by the sound of crying. Fr Malone said the appropriate prayers for us as well as those who were shot dead at Kingsmills.

Eventually, the family was led in to a side room and as we waited, the lids were firmly placed on the two pine-coloured coffins. When the time came for the two hearse cars to leave and drive to Whitecross, they couldn't get out. While we and the many mourners were inside, the car parks outside had become a traffic jam as siren-blaring ambulances, brake-screeching RUC patrol cars and land rovers arrived at the hospital to deal with the bodies that were being ferried into A&E from the Kingsmills Road.

As our funeral cortege waited to depart, the families of those in the minibus massacre had arrived and were guided into a designated waiting room. Fully understanding their pain and grief, I walked in and identified myself, before offering the condolences of our family.

Eventually, the funeral procession, which by now had swollen to over 100 cars, could leave and we set off for home. The Kingsmills Road leading to our house was blocked off and we had to take a detour via Camlough and headed towards the Mountain House pub two miles away. As it edged closer to the pub, we were flagged down by very bright red lights. It was a British army checkpoint of eight or so soldiers and the positioning of their two land rovers meant we had to drive in a zig-zag manner to get through. The two hearses headed the procession and were gestured through the checkpoint. The drivers were told to wait for the remaining cars to be waved through.

Seamus was now in the first family car, a blue Peugeot 308 which was stopped, resulting in the entire procession coming to a halt. I was in the second car, a Ford Escort, with Róisín and my mother-in-law. Our two cars were jammed in between the two land rovers. The soldiers simultaneously approached both cars and we wound down our windows.

Far from being polite, the soldiers, in aggressive condescending tones, asked us who we were; what were we doing on this road; where were we going and then asked Seamus, our Mother and myself to step out of the cars. For some reason, they allowed our Dad to remain in Seamus' vehicle.

They knew who we were but it seemed they were instructed to make our lives as difficult as possible. Seamus and myself were put standing up against the two land rovers with our hands outstretched as if we had just committed a public order offence. As we stood facing the sides of the two jeeps, the soldiers began aggressively questioning our Mother. I shouted loudly to the soldier 'you leave that woman alone'. Then a soldier jammed a gun in my back and held it there. The gun was rattling like a jackhammer. The young soldier was clearly nervous. I thought to myself, that's it. I'm dead as well.

As I pondered what I thought were the last minutes of my life, the next thing was I heard a British soldier in a working-class English accent being abusive to our Mother and mocking her like as if she had been a captured criminal who was on the run.

In a completely condescending tone of voice, he said 'Mrs Reavey, isn't it great that you have no worries and here we are standing out in the rain trying to protect you while you are having such a good time'. To this day, I still can't work out what the hell he was on about.

Then, in a blatant act of provocation, he started to rub his fingers around our Mother's face.

'Mrs Reavey,' he said, 'I see you have only two ears. Where's your other ear? Mrs Reavey I see you only have one nose. Where's your other nose?' he mockingly asked. The arrogant, insensitive soldier then took a liberty in a depraved, disgusting and undignified way and I'll leave it at that.

At this stage, my temper was boiling. Our Mother was being tormented, degraded and humiliated. I was furious. I think she sensed I was about to do something that might put our lives in danger. Realising my frustration she said, 'Eugene, don't do anything rash! Don't'.

Sensing that we were about to be the victims of reprisal for what happened at Kingsmills and re-living the image in my head of the doors that were shot off their hinges in our house the night before, I could hear our Mother saying her prayers. She must have suspected as well that we were living our last minutes and it was all going to end on a dark wet Monday night in South Armagh.

No traffic was moving on the road which could divert attention from our plight. The cortege of cars following us was stalled and its occupants were unaware of the harassment we were going through. Meanwhile, as the rain poured down my face, I stood with my two outstretched hands placed on the side of the jeep, the rattling gun was still pressed hard up against my back. A wrong move or inappropriate word, I thought, and it would be all over for me. Fear and rage gripped me simultaneously.

Then Seamus was asked to open the boot of his car. The soldier who had been interrogating him, pulled out three transparent plastic bags through which, the spilled blood of my brothers was clearly visible. Without blinking an eye or even asking a question, the heartless soldier emptied the contents of the bags on to the wet road. The bags contained the blood-soaked clothes that Brian, Anthony and John Martin had been wearing when they were gunned down. John Martin, it should be remembered, was hit with forty-three bullets so one can only imagine the bloody sight.

The soldier, who removed the items from the bags, then began to dance on the blood-stained clothes much to the amusement and laughter of his colleagues. How could any soldier with the slightest ounce of humanity in him, be so ruthless, heartless and disgusting as to do such a thing?

It was as if the infamous ill-disciplined Black and Tans, who were sent to Ireland by Winston Churchill to put manners on the unruly Irish in 1920 during the War of Independence, had been sent all over again. These guys were the lowest of the low.

It quickly dawned on me as my blood boiled that but for the grace of God, the entire Reavey family would have been wiped away in seconds had our Mother not decided to go to Sheerans' house. Had we all been in the house that Sunday evening, as we usually were, the gunmen who burst through the door would have murdered all of us. It was becoming clear that there was some sort of a malicious agenda being perpetrated against us.

As I stood in the rain, thinking this torturous ordeal was never going to end, I sensed that evil in its fullest form had been visited upon us and it was all going to end badly. After about twenty minutes when the cortege of cars seemed to stretch all the way back in to Newry, our reluctance to buckle from the humiliation seemed to convince the British soldiers they had done as much as they could to provoke us without the desired result.

All of a sudden, 'our hell on earth' ended. The gun was removed from my back. The soldiers got back into their Land Rovers, headed off and as we breathed a massive sigh of relief, we gathered up the blood-soaked clothes from the road like wretched beggars picking up crumbs. It was hard to believe that these soldiers represented her majesty's government. It was close on 9 p.m. by the time we arrived back at Whitecross to wake Brian and John Martin. When the hearses got to the house, the place was heaving with people. Hundreds and hundreds of them showed up to pay their respects and sympathise.

When we eventually stepped in the door of where unthinkable horror had devastated our lives the previous night, Seamus, our Mother and myself, were emotionally distressed. Dealing with the killings was one thing but in the past half-hour our own lives had been on the line. Our energy levels couldn't go any lower but in times of such personal chaos, the human body seems to find strength from inexplicable sources.

As we tried to calm ourselves and deal with the massive crowd at the house, two noisy British helicopters hovered overhead and lit up the place with intimidating search lights. As the night wore on, the word from locals was that ten men had been shot dead at Kingsmills.

One notable visitor to the house was journalist Peter Taylor, then a reporter on the ITV programme *This Week* who later joined *Panorama* at the BBC. Peter, who became one of the great credible writers on The Troubles, stayed late that night and to his credit, kept in touch for many years afterwards. Other well-known visitors to the house were SDLP Assembly member and later to be an MP in the House of Commons, Seamus Mallon – a close family friend, Frank Feeley, Paddy O'Hanlon, and Jerome Mullen who were prominent members of the Social, Democratic and Labour Party

In response to questions from journalists, Seamus Mallon

said the murders were 'highly planned atrocities against innocent people. An all-out effort must be made by both the authorities and the community to bring the murderers to justice.'

On Tuesday morning, my aunties Winnie and Bridie in New York and Cleveland Ohio respectively, flew in to Dublin. The overnight flight in economy class from JFK is usually exhausting and the jetlag can knock one's sleep routine off course for a few days but when the murder of your nephews is on your mind, one can only imagine how miserable that journey must have been. When they came through security in Dublin Airport at 7.30 a.m. to meet Fr Con Malone, the first thing on their agenda was to get hold of the morning newspapers to read the details on what happened in their sister's house two days before. So imagine the shock they got when they picked up the *Daily Mirror* to see the headline that read '10 die in IRA Massacre'. Winnie and Bridie were so stunned and shocked at what they read, they were actually afraid to come to Whitecross. Fr Malone had a job on his hands convincing them over breakfast that as they had come this far, they had to complete the journey. After all, their two nephews were to be buried the next day. Eventually they agreed to travel to Whitecross.

At least a dozen people consisting of cousins and neighbours stayed up all night in the house with the corpses. Such was the fear in the Whitecross and surrounding areas over what had happened, some people, en route to work in Newry, called at 7.30 a.m. as they were terrified that if they called that night, their lives would be in danger while driving along the Kingsmills Road to get to the house.

As Winnie and Bridie were making their way to South Armagh, the names of the Kingsmill Road dead had emerged on BBC Radio Ulster throughout the morning. All were Protestant factory workers: Robert Walker (46) from Glenanne, Joseph Lemmon (46) from Bessbrook, Reggie Chapman (25) from Bessbrook, Walter Chapman (23) Bessbrook, Kenneth Wharton (24) Bessbrook, James McWhirter (58) Bessbrook, Robert Chambers (19) Bessbrook, John McConville (20) Bessbrook, John Bryans (46) Bessbrook and Robert Freeburn (50) Bessbrook. Alan Black (32), a fitter from Bessbrook was also shot but survived. Richard Hughes, a Catholic from nearby Bessbrook was spared by the gunmen in what was a blatant attack on members of the Protestant community.

As THE FAMILIES OF those who died on the Kingsmills Road grieved for their awful loss, we had our own situation to deal with. I was out for the count in bed having stayed up most of the night dealing with all the chaos around us. Róisín got up at 7 a.m. in our house at nearby Drumherriff and was making a bottle for Catriona when there was a very loud bang at the front door.

Assuming it was one of our family or a neighbour she opened the door to find a tall man from the British army who spoke in a posh educated English accent. At least eight other soldiers were at the front gate with two others in the garden. All were heavily armed.

'Yes, can I help you?' asked Róisín curiously wondering what he was there for.

'Can I speak to Eugene?' he asked.

Róisín told him I was in bed before asking what he wanted to speak to me about.

'I want to speak to him about the murder of the ten men at Kingsmills last night.'

Róisín slammed the door in his face. Unusually, the soldier walked away but as events and days passed by, that would not be the last visit from her majesty's armed forces.

We thought that the media presence was big on Monday but twenty-four hours on and with the atrocities on our road now global news, reporters, cameramen and photographers from all over the world, mainly London-based correspondents for far-off broadcasters and newspapers, had descended on to the Kingsmills Road in huge numbers. A journalist with a US newspaper remarked that the Kingsmills Road in South Armagh, on which our house was sited, was the most dangerous place in the world that week. While the media people were trying to piece together the madness of what had happened in the previous two days, we had to deal with growing crowds outside the gate while simultaneously attending to Anthony who was in intensive care and clinging on for life in Daisy Hill Hospital.

From 9 a.m. that morning, two of our family would go into the ward for a bedside vigil. Two hours later, another two would replace them and this went on all day. Not surprisingly, ourselves and the hospital authorities were fearful that someone might walk in and finish off Anthony. That may sound crude but remember, at this stage, Anthony was a live witness and could reveal information that the UVF and their pals didn't want known.

We learned that Alan Black, who was in the intensive care unit, had regained consciousness. Quoted in the *Irish News* next day, the consultant surgeon operating on Alan said, 'this man has multiple injuries. He is immobilised and there is always the danger of infection ... he is young and fit and I am hoping that he will recover but it will be at least a week before we can be happy about the situation.'

Although Anthony was hanging on for life, he was conscious enough to talk and gave interviews to BBC NI and UTV where he re-lived on film what happened.

Back in Whitecross, Rev. Robert Nixon, the Presbyterian minister in Bessbrook, called to the house and expressed his sympathies. Other local Protestant ministers to call during the day included Rev. Murphy, Topping, McLenaghan and Birney. Visits to Catholic homes from such prominent members of the Protestant faith were rare but their presence that day was greatly appreciated, treated with the utmost respect and never forgotten.

As WE TRIED TO cope with the swelling numbers outside the front gate and the emotional shock of our loss, seven miles away Newry and District Trades Union Council launched a campaign to end the bloody sectarianism that had now become 'the norm'. Over 2,000 people showed up at a meeting at Margaret Square on Hill Street. Tom Moore, chairman of the Trades Council, condemned recent murders and was backed by John McAleavey of the Irish Transport and General Workers Union as well as John O'Donnell of the Amalgamated Transport and General Workers Union. They called on the paramilitaries to get off the backs of working-class people and allow them to go about their work in peace. A minute's silence was observed but the large number in attendance, which was high, proportionate to the local population, was a reminder that the public had enough of the tit-for-tat killings that were now an everyday feature of life in Northern Ireland.

Unlike most civil rights and anti-sectarian gatherings, the one in Newry broke up peacefully and those in attendance from both sides dispersed and went about their business. Whether or not loyalist and republican paramilitaries would listen to the call had yet to be determined.

Back at Whitecross later that afternoon, our Father, Jimmy, who had recently retired from his job with Newry and Mourne Council owing to a bad heart, spoke to the assembled press:

> I hope in God's name they will see sense. I was shocked when I heard of last night's shooting and I know what the families of the ten men are going through, just the same as my family has been going through since Sunday night. I express sympathy to them.

Our Father made it clear that the Kingsmills atrocity was not in retaliation for the killings of Brian and John Martin but for recent killings and attacks in the area during the previous twelve months. He added:

> I was disappointed because I thought my appeal [last night] would have been listened to.
>
> One of them [Robert Freeburn] was reared in a house just a few fields away from our home and I worked along with another of them for a time.
>
> I wish the gunmen had shot me instead.

Our Father sent condolence telegrams to the families of all who died in the minibus massacre. We were grieving for those killed on Kingsmills Road just as much as others were grieving for us.

As Tuesday, 6 January, wore on, BBC Radio Ulster news was reporting that the mysterious group that carried out the Tullyvallen massacre the previous September calling itself The South Armagh Republican Action Force, had contacted the *Irish News* newspaper. It claimed responsibility for the Kingsmills massacre. According to the paper, 'the caller gave a pre-arranged code word. The caller said the murders at Kingsmills were in retaliation for the assassination, the previous night, of five Catholic men at Ballydougan and Whitecross.' He said '12 gunmen were involved and armalite and sub-machine guns were used. Immediately afterwards,' he added, 'the gang split up and dispersed into South Armagh.'

Asked if any further action would be taken by the group, the man replied, 'Not unless any loyalist paramilitary groups take retaliatory action.

'Meanwhile, there will be no further action on our part. We are a completely separate organisation and have no connection with the Provos.'

It was generally accepted in South Armagh that the Republican Action Force was a cover name for a bunch of rebels within the IRA. Remember, the IRA was 'officially' on ceasefire at the time and it was highly unlikely senior members of the Provisional movement would have approved the killings.

This was the second time the 'Force' had struck in the locality, having killed five Protestants the previous September at nearby Tullyvallen Orange Hall. The IRA told the *Irish Times* that it had nothing to do with those killings and warned that the 'Force' was likely to strike again in retaliation to atrocities carried out by British loyalists.

Throughout the Tuesday, thousands of people gathered at our home to pay their last respects. There were people there from Tyrone, Derry, Fermanagh and beyond. It seemed to me that every person I had met in my life called to the house. Rosminian priests came from Waterford to sympathise while GAA members from all over the island of Ireland turned out in huge numbers. We just could not believe the size of the crowds that showed up. It was probably the biggest wake ever seen in South Armagh up to that time.

Among the many hundreds to pass through our house were students from St Paul's secondary school on the Green Road in Bessbrook. As they made their way in to the house, our Mother, who sat between the two coffins, asked each one of them their names and how they knew John Martin and Brian.

One thing that was becoming clear as the day wore on was that some sympathisers were experiencing difficulty getting to our house. Visitors were telling us that their cars were stopped by the British army on approach roads to the house and checked thoroughly. We were told that young British soldiers, inexperienced and abusing their sense of military importance, were cheeky and intimidating when asking people to step out of their cars.

With Tuesday coming to an end, there was one positive development in the midst of all the madness – we were told that Anthony was making good progress in Daisy Hill Hospital.

The Village of Black Flags

On Wednesday morning, 7 January, we all got up early after another bad night's sleep and I decided to head to the local shop to pick up a newspaper. The sight before me, as I made my way into the village, was amazing. All of Whitecross was draped in black flags, a visible expression of sympathy and respect from the locals for John Martin and Brian who everybody in the area knew and loved. The flags were everywhere. I hadn't seen them the night before but now they were hanging from every window and telephone pole in the place. There were even flags hanging from the top of the goalposts in St Killian's football pitch. The *Daily Mirror* carried a headline the following day describing Whitecross as 'The Village of Black Flags'.

I made my way over to the family house at 8 a.m. and a sizeable number of local Protestants had gathered to kindly offer their sympathies. They too had obviously opted to call early in the morning because they felt that to do so the previous night would have been too dangerous. It was much appreciated that they went out of their way to sympathise with us at such an early hour.

As the crowd numbers continued to swell, local women who came to the house to feed and refresh our sympathisers, provided an extraordinary voluntary service for us. Shortly after 9 a.m., larger crowds began to assemble at the house to pay their last respects. The queue of people appeared to stretch forever in both directions. After the remainder of the wider Reavey clan arrived, we had to close the doors for a final family get-together in advance of the burials. As we gathered for what would be John Martin and Brian's last time in the house they were reared in, seven miles away in Daisy Hill Hospital, Anthony was being comforted by his girlfriend Lillian Savage who had arrived there just around 9.30 a.m. A plan had been put in place whereby Lillian would keep Anthony company until 12.30 p.m. while the funeral mass was taking place. Lillian would then be replaced in the hospital by our cousin Seán Reavey while she returned to Ballymoyer for the burial ceremony in her own car.

Shortly after 10 a.m., Fathers Hughes and Malone said prayers in the house and we prepared to bring Brian and John Martin to their final resting place at Ballymoyer cemetery, two miles or so up the road. The sight of our parents staring into the coffins that morning for the last time is an image I'll take to my grave. The endless hours, effort and love they gave in rearing Brian and John Martin were coming to an end as they prepared to bury their own flesh and blood who were gone too soon and gone too young.

When family prayers were completed, I remember walking outside the house and all I could see were thousands and thousands of sympathisers. Members of the Whitecross GAA Club, under the well-managed supervision of St Killian's chairman John Moley, lined up on both sides of the road outside the house to form a dignified guard of honour. The pine caskets were gently removed from the house by Patsy McLogan's undertaking staff and carried out to the road. They were then placed on two separate sets of coffin trestles. Seamus and myself stood at the front of the first coffin while Frank and Oliver stood at the second one. Positions at the rear of each coffin were taken up by our cousins Seán and Kevin Reavey followed by Seán Loughran and Gerard McDonnell.

From there, we lifted the coffins on to our shoulders and walked slowly for about 200 yards up the road towards O'Hanlon's farm before changing the carriers as others took over the task of carrying the caskets for a further short distance. We eventually made our way up the hill to the centre of Whitecross village where the funeral procession stopped outside the shop adjacent to St Killian's Gaelic Football ground for a minute's silence. Surrounded by the massive bunting of black flags, the stalled cortege was a poignant reminder to all of us of the place where Brian and John Martin spent every other minute of their youth playing GAA, developed their sporting skills and making friends. The cortege started off again and rotating the individuals carrying the coffins continued all the way to the front gates of St Malachy's Roman Catholic church at Ballymoyer where Seamus, myself, Frank and Oliver resumed the positions we took at the outset. Close on fifty children from the Whitecross Irish dancing group and youth club led by my niece Joanne and nephew Cathal Reavey, marched in front of the two hearses carrying wreaths and floral bouquets.

It was upsetting enough to be carrying your two murdered brothers with thousands of mourners and the world's press witnessing your suffering but to add insult to shocking loss, the slow walk from my parents' house to Ballymoyer church was made all the more difficult by the menacing, hostile and unwelcome presence of British army tanks, guns and personnel. Along the route, young British soldiers in dark green uniforms with camouflaged faces were pointing their guns at us as we moved along the road. In the midst of all this, a massive British army helicopter hovered overhead and the pounding noise of its swirling blades was so loud, we could barely hear our own footsteps. If that wasn't bad enough, mourners were photographed by certain soldiers at every opportunity.

At Ballymoyer chapel, Frank, Oliver, Seamus and myself, along with our cousins, carried the coffins up the avenue and into the church where we rested them on the waiting trestles. Half of the seats were reserved for the wider Reavey family. Thousands of mourners tried to fit into a church that only holds 300. The local parish priest, Fr Peter Hughes, said the funeral mass, assisted by Fr Con Malone. The eulogy was given by Bishop Francis Lenny, auxiliary to Cardinal William Conway who was the primate of all Ireland then. Bishop Lenny told the congregation that 'it was a time of great sadness and sorrow for the people of the parish as well as in Gilford where the O'Dowd family victims were being buried at a funeral mass presided over by Cardinal Conway'.

Bishop Lenny continued, 'Tomorrow the people of Bessbrook will be burying their dead. They understand how we feel at this time of great loss.

'It was practically a foregone conclusion that a reprisal attack would be made in South Armagh, the area, which in a matter of days, has become the graveyard of the new year dreams, hopes and prayers of so many thousands for peace … it is a day of great sadness and sorrow in the Parish with feelings too deep for words. Those who killed the ten Protestant workmen rejected the Christian plea of Jimmy Reavey that there should be no retaliation. We cannot understand the minds of those on both sides who can so brutally murder their fellow men and take upon themselves the awesome power that belongs to God alone as the Author of life,' he said.

At times, we struggled to hear Bishop Lenny's words as they were insultingly drowned out by the over-bearing humming sound of the British army helicopter that floated in the grey sky over the church.

During the service, my cousin Seán left after holy communion and made his way in to Daisy Hill Hospital to relieve Lillian, so she could attend the burial ceremony.

The church at Ballymoyer is about 300 yards away from the cemetery and when the coffins were taken outside, Brian's was draped with a jersey representing his beloved St Killian's Gaelic Football club in Whitecross. There, members of St Killian's GFC and workmates carried them up to the entrance of the cemetery. Once they arrived at the gate, Frank, Oliver, Seamus, myself and our cousins carried the coffins down the pathway to the family burial plot.

The graves were dug by neighbours under the supervision of Ted Finnegan who did a superb job to ensure John Martin and Brian received a solemn dignified burial. The inner sides of the deep brown earth in each grave were decked in cascading layers of moss while the bases were covered in palm leaves creating an entire green burial space. The highly impressive display was done by local man Hugh Kennon who lived in a farmhouse next to the graveyard. The two coffins were gently lowered in to the ground by the undertakers and gravediggers. Alice Campbell, Brian's fiancée, placed a single rose on his casket and those who remained on after the burial ceremony, took turns in filling the grave with the displaced earth.

The look on the faces of my sister Eileen, Alice Campbell and Teresa Reavey is something I will never forget. They stood linked to each other and had a look of despair on their faces as if they were lost in another world. As the damp dark clay was poured upon the coffins, shovel by shovel, the floral wreaths began to mount up – 225 bouquets and wreaths were left at the graves.

Looking back on the funeral after all these years, I cannot recall an occasion where so many people, young and old, dripped in tears. John Martin and Brian's workmates, football pals and those in the locality wept openly while the groans of loud crying filled the cemetery air on what was a wet and miserable January Wednesday.

Once the burial ceremony ended, people from far and near queued up in their hundreds to shake our hands, give us a hug and express their sympathies. It was at least ninety minutes before the last persons in the line made their way up to us and sympathised our loss. Some people had to be physically assisted from the cemetery while others, visibly shaken, were comforted by close friends. The scenes of misery were awful.

We left the cemetery in the chill of the January air only to be further sickened by the insensitive sight of uniformed British soldiers who had surrounded the graveyard with their guns and observed every person. The sense of intimidation they created was hard to take and to this day, we continually ask the perennial question, why?

As mourners quietly drifted away from Ballymoyer cemetery, those of us left by the gravesides, got into our cars and drove the three miles or so back to my house in Drumherriff where over 300 people called to the house for a comforting chat to reminisce about John Martin and Brian. People called, sympathised and chatted giving us much-needed and fully appreciated emotional support. As they did, a rotating team of neighbours kindly helped with what appeared to be the endless task of laying out cutlery and washing dishes. As one batch of volunteers prepared food, another was busy ensuring there was a steady supply of clean cups, plates, knives and forks. The house was packed even if it was somewhat claustrophobic.

Despite being together in our hours of grief, in the coming days, that close-knit bond would loosen again with my aunties heading home, while all of us would slowly return to getting our shattered lives together again not knowing what the coming weeks, months and years would bring as fear enveloped the Whitecross area of South Armagh.

Now that the funerals were over, our focus switched towards getting Anthony back on his feet as soon as possible. There was no shortage of people heading in to see him. The word from the hospital was that his condition was improving and with that good news, it was now felt that there was no need for twenty-four-hour vigils at his bedside.

Our parents were still staying at our house in Drumherriff and I recall that the house was packed with people who stayed overnight. One of the reasons for this was that some visitors who called to the house, stayed longer than planned and fearful of an attack while driving home along the dark rural roads of South Armagh where retaliation was expected, they opted to remain overnight on safety grounds. That's how scary and frightening it was around our area at the time.

EARLIER IN THE DAY as John Martin and Brian were being laid to rest in Ballymoyer, three miles away in Kingsmills, the funeral of Robert Freeburn aged fifty, a father of two children, was taking place. Close on 600 attended the funeral which was officiated by the Rev. Robert Topping who told the congregation that Mr Freeburn 'was a hardworking man with no enemies ... He believed in peace with his neighbours and would never have thought of any retaliation.' A number of Protestants who attended Robert Freeburn's funeral called in to my house at Drumherriff on their way home to express their sympathies on our loss.

Fr Hughes was a regular visitor to our house every Sunday night before the killings but now in light of the atrocities, he was calling three times a day. A visitor to other houses in the locality also, he updated us with scary stories of nearby farms that were unoccupied at night time. He told us that at least thirty farm houses, both Catholic and Protestant, were being vacated every day once darkness fell with the owners and their children spending the night at cousins or friends beyond the area only to return again next day to carry out work on their farms.

With revenge now very much the way of life in South Armagh, Catholic home owners were receiving threats to get out of the area from British loyalists while Protestant property owners were getting the same treatment from the IRA who, ironically, were on 'ceasefire'. Over a period of time, a significant number of Protestants along the Armagh-Monaghan border south of Newtownhamilton, sold their farms to local Catholics and moved further north.

ON MONDAY NIGHT/TUESDAY morning, 5–6 January, 600 members of the specialist Spearhead Regiment were deployed from Aldershot to South Armagh. They were joined by members of the SAS (Special Air Service) who engaged in covert surveillance and counter-terrorism activity. Within days of arrival, there was a notable increase of military personnel on the ground.

Col Philip Davies, commanding officer of the 1st Battalion Royal Scots Regiment, speaking to *Panorama* on BBC TV, a week after the killings, told reporter Michael Charlton that his members in the British army were up against twelve dedicated IRA gunmen operating mainly from south of the border and perhaps thirty in total across the area.

By Thursday, the media focus had, understandably, switched away from the Reaveys and the O'Dowds, to the funerals of the Protestant workmen who were shot dead on Kingsmills Road. Forty-four-year-old John Bryans, a widower and father of two was superintendent of the local Sunday School; twenty-five-year-old Kenneth Wharton, a married father of two and eighteen-year-old Robert Chambers, single, the youngest of the those killed, had their funeral service at the Church of Ireland church in Bessbrook.

In the nearby Presbyterian church, the service took place of Reggie Chapman, twenty-seven, father of two, a Sunday School teacher; his brother thirty-five-year-old Walter Chapman, single; forty-nine-year-old carpenter and married father of three Joe Lemmon, a grand master in the Royal Black Preceptory and an Orange Lodge chaplain; twenty-year-old single man John McConville and James McWhirter, fifty-eight, father of three and also a member of the Royal Black Preceptory.

The final victim to be buried was the driver of the red Ford minibus, forty-six-year-old Robert Walker from Glenanne whose Protestant cousin Davy Barbour was married to my Catholic cousin Nora Sheeran who was also in Doyle's pub the previous Saturday night with Brian and the Chapman brothers.

The funeral service was attended by Whitecross Roman Catholic parish priest Fr Peter Hughes and generated additional media coverage after, it appears, comments made by Rev. Robert Nixon did not go down well with some members of the congregation. It was reported in the papers that during the service, Rev. Nixon wept as he told the packed congregation that 'the murder of five Catholics, the Reaveys and the O'Dowds on Sunday night had led directly to the Kingsmills massacre.

'The five Catholics had been slain in the name of Protestantism but their killers were just as guilty of the murders of the ten sons of Bessbrook as if they had pulled the triggers themselves.'

It seems that it was interpreted to mean that the Protestants who killed the O'Dowds and the Reavey brothers might as well have killed the Kingsmills workers also.

Matters were further strained when Rev. Nixon's wife, Maud, was quoted in the Dublin-based *Sunday Press* newspaper as saying that she received threatening phone calls from angry loyalists. On occasions when she asked for the names of the callers, she was told she wouldn't get them as her husband would only 'pass them on to the IRA'.

The big fear now amongst locals was, would there be more fatalities in South Armagh?

From Hope to Heartbreak

THURSDAY, 8 JANUARY, WAS expected to be our first day of returning to 'normality' – if such a thing was possible – after the previous madness. We assumed it would mark the start of trying to get back to our regular daily routine. Even though John Martin and Brian had died, our main focus now was getting Anthony out of hospital as quickly as possible. As the days wore on and people continued to call to the house, I was told something of significance which, because of my dysfunctional dazed state at the time, didn't fully sink in but took on a whole new meaning as crucial information evolved in the subsequent years. Jim Malone and his brother Barry, who both lived in Whitecross village, called to the house and after the usual pleasantries were exchanged, the conversation eventually turned to the Kingsmills killings.

Jim told us that on Monday – the day of the massacre – he and his brother drove from Whitecross towards Bessbrook along the Kingsmills Road as part of our cortege. When our procession was stopped at the scene of the killings, we were eventually told to reverse our cars back to the Kingsmills crossroads and take an alternative road into Daisy Hill Hospital in Newry. Barry and Jim, like everyone else, reversed their cars and instead of following our procession into Newry, they returned home to Whitecross village to inform their family that a shooting had occurred less than two miles further down on the Kingsmills Road and to raise the alarm with their neighbours. They left their house in Whitecross at around 7 p.m. and headed back down towards where the massacre had occurred. With the Kingsmills Road blocked, close to where the killings took place, they turned right on to the Drumherriff Road where their sister Marie lived and immediately noticed something strange. A UDR Land Rover was parked at the side of the road next to the entrance to Eugene Malone's farm. The significance of this will become apparent later on in the story.

Malachy Murphy, who lived 150 yards up the road from our family home, also called to the house on Thursday. He too began to reveal some details about the events of the previous Monday. He and his son Cyril were part of the Reavey funeral cortege that was making its way from Whitecross to Newry when local man Gerry Byrne stopped it at the site where the Kingsmills massacre occurred. When it was decided that all cars should turn around and take the Drumherriff/Tullyah Road into Newry, curious Malachy opted to stay at the scene. As the vehicles eventually drove off to Newry, Malachy got out of his car and walked up towards the red Ford minibus where the killings took place.

Shocked and sickened with what he saw, he turned around, got in to his car, said nothing to Cyril and decided to return to his home at nearby Priest Bush Road. Fifty yards from his own house, he came across Charlie O'Neill, who also lived nearby at Priest Bush corner and was standing on the road looking for a lift into Newry. Malachy stopped the car, got out and discussed the killings with Charlie so as his young son Cyril wouldn't be aware of what happened. As they talked, a car came speeding down the road from Whitecross doing about seventy miles per hour. Charlie flagged down the approaching vehicle to inform the occupants about the massacre.

No sooner had he raised his hand when the car screeched to a halt. The doors burst open and three policemen jumped out carrying guns. One of them rushed to Malachy's car, opened the door and put a gun to Cyril's head, telling him 'switch those fucking lights out and don't move'. After the initial shock and fear at this horrible RUC behaviour, Malachy calmed the hostile environment down and eventually told the aggressive policemen what happened on the Kingsmills Road. The policemen took off again but instead of making their way to the spot where the massacre occurred, they drove further down the road and turned left at the next crossroads which seemed odd.

Thursday rolled on and people continued to call. Later that day, Michael O'Hare of Ballymoyer called with his parents, Mary and Jim. He too had a story of significance connected to the Kingsmills massacre – on the Monday, four days previous, he was driving along the Kingsmills Road between 6.55 and 7.05 p.m. to Newry. As he came towards The Manse Corner, close to the spot where the killings occurred, a policeman rolled out of the hedge and flagged him down, his uniform was covered with mud suggesting he must have there for some time. The policeman informed him of the killings and re-directed him to Camlough via a nearby road called 'The Backroads Loanen'. This all sounded like no big deal at the time but took on a significance later.

Fr Hughes called that day as well and told us that he feared living in the Whitecross parochial house as he felt isolated and had asked the RUC in Bessbrook if they could provide security for him. The RUC said 'no' as their resources were stretched at this horrible time. Fr Hughes told us that it was decided that in the interests of safety, all community activity should cease for a month, which meant no devotions in the church on Sunday evenings; youth club activities would have to be stopped; as would football meetings, band practice and bingo, etc. Each night, two members of Whitecross Gaelic Football Club (GFC) would drive around to the parochial house every half-hour to check on Fr Hughes' security. During that week, all of South Armagh was effectively closed down. Nothing moved, no work was done and business activity came to a halt. A curfew of sorts had kicked in and a number of local men provided security at each of the four Catholic churches in the parish for fear of loyalist gun attacks, firebombs or explosions during mass.

Normal daily life had almost come to a standstill in the area. People were afraid to leave their houses at night time; farmers were afraid to work in their fields during the day; suppliers were reluctant to do business with local shops and even children were scared to go to the local schools. Whitecross had effectively become a living 'ghost town' for fear of reprisal killings. The atmosphere of horror around the place was just awful. By the end of the week, the increased British military presence in South Armagh had become very visible.

On the Thursday evening, 8 January, my brother Seamus called to the cottage where the killings occurred and took our parents to Corlatt Drive in Whitecross village for their tea in his house. At around 7.10 p.m., they went to visit Anthony at Daisy Hill Hospital in Newry. A mile or so down the road, they were stopped by the British army at Kingsmills crossroads and asked who they were and where they were going? They answered the questions, were waved on and presumed they would have an unhindered drive in to Newry. However, three miles further down the road, as they approached the crossroads at the townland of Maytown, they were again flagged down at a British army checkpoint. Seamus stopped the car and wound down his window. The British soldier, like an excited child on Christmas morning, shouted, 'Ahhh … it's the Reaveys. Pull your fucking car in there Mr Reavey.'

It would appear that the previous British army checkpoint had sent on a radio message to the next one to let them know the Reaveys were en route. The cheeky British soldier asked Seamus his name and then requested his driving licence, which he handed over. The soldier took hold of the licence and walked to a nearby jeep to check that Seamus was who he said he was. A fellow soldier then radioed the details to an office, probably in Lisburn, to check that the paper work was in order.

There was an unexpected problem. The words on the licence didn't match the earlier verbal exchange. As everyone on the green side in Ireland knows, certain English words have a different meaning when used in an Irish context. For example, Liam is the Irish for William, Seán or Eoin can be the Irish version of John and in this case, Seamus is the Irish for James. Our Seamus was christened Patrick James and was known to us all as Seamie. Of course we knew that but the British soldier didn't make the connection.

Ten minutes later, the soldier returned to the car and asked for the names of the other passengers. Our parents didn't have a driving licence and therefore had no ID. The soldier asked all four occupants to get out of the car. Our Dad refused to do so as he had recently suffered a heart attack. The soldier then made a big issue about the fact that our Mother did not have ID and the intimidating questions went on and on for fifteen minutes. The soldier then undertook the same carry-on that occurred previously on the Newry to Newtownhamilton Road – rubbing his hands on her ears and saying things like, 'you only have two ears Mrs Reavey, where's your other ones? You only have one nose Mrs Reavey, where's your other nose?' She was subjected to mockery and degrading humiliation *again*. Our parents were mentally and physically in poor shape and the arrogant insensitive behaviour of the soldiers was nothing short of barbaric. By the time the British soldiers decided to wave Seamus, his wife Teresa and our parents on, it had passed the time slot allowed to visit Anthony in the hospital, 7.30–8.15 p.m.

Despite this, Seamus, Teresa, Mum and Dad headed in to Daisy Hill Hospital on the off-chance they might get in to see Anthony. Seamus had to take on the role of diplomat in explaining to the nurses what had happened with the British soldiers. The nurses understood their dilemma and allowed them to see Anthony. The nurses had gone through this familiar routine many times with other Catholic families in the area who found their journeys to the hospital frustrated by the behaviour of insensitive British soldiers

Around this time, I called to the home of Kinnear Elliott, a Protestant neighbour who lived in a large two-storey Georgian house at the Kingsmills crossroads, just to see how his family were keeping. I remember knocking on the door of his house to see if he and his family were there as most families in the area were not sleeping in their own homes. Eventually a voice in the distance asked, 'Who's there?'

When I said, 'it's Eugene Reavey', I could hear what sounded like scurrying going on behind the door. Eventually it opened and what caught my attention was that he had obviously wedged a massive tree trunk between the base of his stairs and the front door to prevent paramilitaries from bursting in. It was a stark reminder of the fear that locals on both sides were living in just to stay alive and keep their sanity intact. I had known Kinnear well over the years and found him to a be a quiet unassuming man and I know, in light of the sectarian tension at the time, he appreciated, my call.

Another unforeseen problem had emerged by now – our parents just didn't have the confidence to sleep in the cottage where their three sons had been shot the previous Sunday. What was once a loving Irish home full of happiness and laughter with a welcoming open door, had now become a place of horror – and they were now effectively homeless. Realising our parents didn't feel able to live in their home again, our sister-in-law Teresa discussed the matter with Seamus and decided the best way to handle this emerging 'accommodation crisis' was for them to vacate their own home at 9 Corlatt Drive Whitecross and invite our parents to live in their house. Seamus and Teresa, their children Cathal and Joanne moved out of No. 9 and moved in with my brother Frank and his wife Marie at 21 St Killian's Park Whitecross, a three-bedroom house.

BY THIS TIME, ALAN Black, who survived the Kingsmills massacre, had been released from intensive care and moved into the same ward as Anthony. Alan only stayed there for a day as the hospital board felt he and Anthony were serious security risks, in other words if a gunman burst in and killed them, two crucial witnesses with important knowledge, would be gone. Anthony and Alan were moved in to the maternity ward which was the next floor upstairs in the hospital and was a safer place. The two of them had a lot in common and quickly struck up a friendly relationship.

In the subsequent days, Fr Hughes visited Bessbrook Police Station and spoke to the sergeant on duty. It was not Fr Hughes' style to make a formal complaint but I know he told the sergeant of the physical, abusive and humiliating treatment our parents were subjected to. Fr Hughes' best intentions fell on deaf ears.

By this time, my sister Eileen had returned to her work as a trainee nurse at the Royal Victoria Hospital in Belfast, a place that probably dealt with more injured and dead bodies in the previous seven years than any other medical centre in the western world. She was working between the Royal in Belfast and Daisy Hill Hospital in Newry. Whenever Eileen was in Daisy Hill she felt very conscious about her name badge 'Nurse Reavey'. Well-meaning patients and visitors were constantly sympathising with her and referring to the murder of her brothers which she found very difficult to deal with. However she also felt that certain patients and visitors took a hostile tone with her whenever they noticed the name 'Reavey' on her identity badge!

This was hugely overwhelming for her to deal with so soon after the murder of her brothers and she was eventually given permission to stop wearing her badge whilst on duty. Eileen persevered with her training and I am glad to say she qualified and gave a lifetime of service to the NHS.

On Friday 9 January, Alec Robb, a Protestant publican from Markethill and a school pal of our Mother's, arrived at the door with a friend of his to sympathise. The chat was benign and shortly afterwards, Alec said he wanted a private word with our Father. The two men went in to the front room which was empty and they spent what felt like an eternity in there. When they emerged, they shook hands and Alec hugged our Mother before leaving with his friend. Five years later, the shocking contents of that conversation were revealed to me.

On the same night, my good friend and mentor Don Best from Poyntzpass outside Newry, grandfather to Simon and Rory who would later play rugby for Ireland, called to the house. He told us that he tried to call to see us the previous Monday with his son Craig but their drive from Camlough to Whitecross was blocked due to the Kingsmills massacre. Don was very apologetic saying that the murders of Brian and John Martin were definitely not in the name of Protestantism and he appeared to be embarrassed that the wider world thought it was. He praised our Dad for his call of no retaliation and said his words revealed his true Christian thinking.

As Don was leaving, I walked him out to the car and before he departed, he said, 'I didn't want to say this to you in the house but I have to let you know that there is a whispering campaign doing the rounds that your brothers were killed because they were in the IRA.' I was shocked but not surprised because all the intimidation from the British army and the RUC in the previous days led me to believe that we were being deliberately targeted in a hostile way.

I told him that 'none of the Reaveys have ever been in the IRA. It's complete nonsense.' Don knew this as he was a close friend of mine for many years. Ironically, in the five years I knew him up to that stage, having worked with him on a weekly basis, he mainly spoke business and rarely mentioned anything political at all. To me, he was one of nature's gentlemen.

From this time on, we all had to alter our travel routes from Whitecross in to Daisy Hill Hospital to avoid British army checkpoints. Anthony meanwhile was on the mend and his recovery was being described as 'rapid'. Such was his improvement, he was out of bed and attending physiotherapy. Alan Black had been making good progress as well but his recovery appeared to be slower as his injuries were more serious.

When Anthony was brought home to 9 Corlatt Drive from Daisy Hill, his return was like a whole new lease of life for our parents. When the ambulance arrived, a small crowd of neighbours had gathered to welcome him home. As his wheelchair was lifted from the rear door, he received a huge round of applause.

Our Mother was over-joyed on his return. For the first time in almost two weeks, she had something to take her mind off the atrocious killings. She had a new-found focus to occupy her long days and most importantly, one of her targeted sons had returned home alive, having been so close to death. There was definitely a spring in her step and her caring was directed Anthony's way again.

Anthony's welcome return created unexpected problems. Large numbers of people started calling to the house again to shake his hand, say hello and wish him well but the house could only accommodate so many at a time and managing the pedestrian numbers became a logistical problem. The importance of peace and space was crucial in this early stage of Anthony's recuperation and while the swelling numbers of people at the door meant well, their good intentions were creating the opposite effect.

Scores of media people began to show up again in the hope of securing an exclusive interview with him. We fully appreciated the valuable work the press had done in covering our difficulties in the previous weeks and were mindful that reporters and camera people were only doing their day job, but despite their desire to re-live the shootings all over again, we could not facilitate all of them this time around. Eventually, the press moved on and Anthony's mobility, bit by bit, was improving – he managed to stand on one foot and with the aid of crutches, could make his way out the door and hobble the short distance down the road to Malone's Shop.

Within two days of Anthony's return to Whitecross, our daily lives became frustrated again. The British army set up a checkpoint at the one and only phone box in the area which happened to be opposite No. 9 Corlatt Drive. This meant that every person who called to the house was checked and frisked.

ELSEWHERE IN NEWRY COURT of Appeal on 15 January, two RUC detectives were cleared of assaulting a man called Robin Jackson who was brought in for questioning around the Miami Showband Massacre. On 23 December 1975, Constables Norman Carlisle (26) and Raymond Buchanan (25) both stationed in Newry, were each fined £10 for assaulting Robin John Jackson, aged twenty-six of Lurgan, at Bessbrook RUC Station on 7 August. Judge Brown, to the surprise of all present, told the court, 'I am satisfied that, strange though the sequence of events was, the detectives neither attacked, struggled with or punched Robin Jackson. 'I cannot be 100 per cent sure how he [Jackson] got his injuries and lump at the side of his eye and a bump on his forehead,' the judge stated. If the RUC had been doing their job properly, this fellow Jackson would not have been released from custody. The reasons for this will become clear later on as his role with the notorious UVF Glenanne Gang becomes more apparent.

On Saturday afternoon, 24 January, Anthony decided to go and visit his girlfriend Lillian who lived in Belleeks, about two miles from Whitecross. Oliver opted to be his driver. Even though Belleeks is a short distance as the proverbial crow flies, they drove off and were hardly thirty seconds on the road when they were stopped at an army checkpoint. There was the usual British guff in 'who are you? where are you going?' and 'open up the boot of your car, Sir'. A half a mile up the road, they were stopped again at what's known as Priest Bush Junction and went through the same routine. Another half a mile on and they were stopped again at Kearney's corner and half a mile further on at Patton's Corner they were stopped and questioned again. When they finally got to Belleeks, the British army stopped the car and went through the same drill all over again. All this in the space of two miles.

Oliver dropped Anthony off at Lillian's house and was stopped at the same checkpoints on the return journey again only this time he had to say repeatedly where exactly he dropped off his passenger. Yet on the night of the Kingsmills massacre, there wasn't a soldier to be seen in the locality.

Throughout the day, Anthony was in great form in Lillian's house. People were popping in to say hello and wish him well. He was fed like a VIP and enjoyed the attention.

Either Oliver or Seamus were to collect Anthony that night from Lillian's house at around 11.30 p.m. after *Match of the Day* finished on BBC 1. However such was the increased intimidation shown by soldiers that day, our Mother crossed the road to the phone box and rang Lillian's house. She told Anthony that Oliver had been stopped five times earlier on the return journey and that it might be best if he stayed in Lillian's that night.

Mindful that the public phone in Whitecross was likely to be tapped and that the British army knew of his whereabouts, Anthony opted not to stay in Lillian's House. It was agreed he would stay in the home of Dolly McMahon, Lillian's aunt, whose house was 300 yards away at 2 Rockview Crescent in Belleeks. Lillian drove Anthony to Dolly's house, kissed him goodnight and he slept there.

The next morning, Anthony was given his breakfast in bed and according to Dolly, he was sitting up smoking a cigarette and was in a jovial mood. He had no plans to go to 11.30 a.m. mass as the approach driveway up to the church at Belleeks was rather steep and difficult for him to navigate. The McMahons left the house at 11.15 a.m. for mass and Anthony opted to stay in bed. Lillian left mass at communion time around 12 noon and made her way down to Tully's newsagent and grocery shop in Belleeks village where she worked part-time at the weekends. When Dolly and husband Pat arrived home after mass and entered the house expecting to see Anthony up and about the place, they found him fully dressed at the top of the stairs, flat out on the floor and unconscious. Dolly phoned the ambulance and the local medic, Dr Joe Stewart from Newtownhamilton. Somebody else ran up to the church and alerted Fr Hughes to come to the house as soon as possible.

Lillian was in the shop and became aware of the crisis when she looked out the window and saw the blue flashing lights of the ambulance outside Dolly's house. Instinctively, she dropped everything and ran across. By this time, Dr Stewart had arrived, followed by Fr Hughes who administered the last rites, before he was taken away to Daisy Hill Hospital. As Anthony was being rushed to Newry, Fr Hughes called to 9 Corlatt Drive and broke the news to our parents. He said that Dr Joe Stewart informed him that Anthony had been rushed to hospital suffering from delayed shock and that he would be fine in a few hours. He told them not to worry and to hold off on visiting him until later that day.

Our Mother, alerted the rest of the family and we all gathered at No. 9. She was uneasy but not unduly worried following the comforting words of Fr Hughes. At 4.00 p.m., she crossed the road and phoned Daisy Hill Hospital seeking an update. When she got through to reception, she asked the gentleman at the other end of the phone if there was any word on her son Anthony Reavey who had been admitted to the Accident & Emergency department earlier that day in an ambulance at approximately 1 p.m. The young man checked his sheets and told her that 'no one has been admitted today called Reavey'. He said he had been on duty since early morning and no person of that name had been admitted to A&E. He added, 'your son left Daisy Hill two weeks ago'.

'But he's been re-admitted again today.'

'No, that is not correct.'

He must have thought she was unwell. He told her to go home and stop worrying.

Sadie returned from the phone box sobbing. She told us that Anthony had not been admitted to the hospital and she feared that something suspicious was going on. We got in to our cars and rushed in to the A&E department at Daisy Hill. We asked the first nurse we came upon where Anthony was, but she didn't know. Seamus, Oliver and myself checked the wards in the hospital to see if Anthony was receiving treatment somewhere else in the building. As Oliver and Seamus went off in different directions, I headed down a corridor and checked every room on my way.

Within minutes, I found Anthony in a disused room on his own. Firstly, I was relieved but secondly, I found him lying on a trolley unconscious. He was not connected to any machines and it looked as if he was either ok, or else, nobody in the hospital was aware he was in the building. The scene before me was strange and highly suspicious.

I contacted the nurse we had spoken to earlier and asked her to get a doctor. Anthony was eventually brought to an intensive care ward upstairs where we were told to stay outside the door as we were now outside official visiting hours. We remained on the corridor for close on two hours and two of us were eventually allowed in. This time Anthony was wired up to numerous monitors and still unconscious. We subsequently learned that my sister Kathy, a nurse in the neurological ward at Whittington Hospital in London, rang Daisy Hill and enquired with the head sister, whom she knew, about Anthony's condition. The ward sister told Kathy that they were struggling in trying to determine a diagnosis. Kathy happened to say that Ian McColl, an eminent neurosurgeon, was on duty at Whittington Hospital that day. She rang and spoke to McColl. He told her, amongst other things, that if the pupils in the eyes were enlarged, the brain would be implicated. Anthony subsequently underwent an angiogram, a process whereby dye is injected in to the bloodstream to determine the possible cause of illness. Despite the sudden urgency by the hospital in treating him, we were told that they would know more, the next day, Monday.

Back home in Whitecross, the locals knew that Anthony was back in hospital. All we could tell anyone who called to the door was that Anthony was comfortable even though he was unconscious. What else could we say? We were not medical people and only relayed what we were told.

On Monday morning 26 January, none of us went to work. We all went to 9.00 a.m. mass where Fr Hughes prayed that Anthony would have a speedy recovery. Afterwards, we all popped in to 9 Corlatt Drive for a cup of tea and a chat with Mum and Dad. Mum rang Daisy Hill from the phone box near the house and was told Anthony had a comfortable night.

We then went into Daisy Hill where, only two at a time were allowed in to see Anthony in intensive care. The curtain around his bed remained closed all the time. When Mum and Dad emerged from the room after about twenty minutes, they told us that Anthony slept well without any further deterioration, even though he was still unconscious. An update would be provided once the specialist had checked his condition. We took turns in pairs to go in, sit by his bedside and say a prayer.

When the specialist arrived shortly before mid-day, Fr Hughes went into the curtained bed area with Mum and Dad. He checked the readings from the various machines, looked at our Mother's face and said, 'I'm afraid to tell you but your son is seriously ill. We don't have the facilities here at Daisy Hill Hospital to care for him. I will recommend to have him moved to Ward 39–40 which is the neurological department at the Royal Victoria Hospital in Belfast.' (Our Eileen was based on that ward as part of her nursing training.)

The rest of us were sitting outside at the end of the corridor when Fr Hughes, Mammy and Daddy came through the door. The empty look on their faces was something I will never forget. They said that Anthony would have to be transferred to Belfast and then it dawned on us that his condition was far more serious than we were led to believe up to that point. Mum, who sounded like somebody who had been hit by a sledge-hammer, was struggling desperately to find the appropriate words. She eventually said in her soft Armagh accent, 'Wee Anthony is fighting for his life. God help him. I can't believe this is happening'.

Having spent a huge amount of the time in the neurological ward of The Royal with our Catriona who was receiving on-going treatment for Crouzon's Syndrome, I knew that if Anthony was being transferred to this department, the chances of him leaving there alive were slim. I didn't let my thoughts be known as I, like the rest of the family, hoped for the best. We spent the rest of the afternoon sitting beside Anthony. I pressed the sister-in-charge repeatedly as to how soon would Anthony be transferred to Belfast and she couldn't tell me. That night, some of the family staged an overnight vigil in the hospital, praying to every saint that ever lived, for a good outcome.

On Tuesday morning at 11 a.m., Anthony was transferred to the Royal Victoria Hospital where he was immediately put on a life support machine. He lay lifeless in bed with burr holes in his skull to relieve pressure where there was a build-up of fluid on the brain. Dr Derek Gordon, one of the leading neurosurgeons in the world at that time, took charge of his treatment. He came in, took a look at Anthony and went away again without as much as saying 'hello' to us. Maybe he was naturally aloof, cold perhaps or else, he had nothing to tell us.

Next day we were none the wiser on Anthony's condition so I requested a meeting with Dr Gordon to seek an update. Róisín and myself went in to his office, fearing the worst and hoping for the best. He asked us to tell him how Anthony ended up in hospital. We explained as best we could and he told us that the prognosis on Anthony was not good. He said that if he had been able to treat Anthony the previous Sunday, he might have been able to successfully address his condition. Then, in a more serious tone, he delivered the bad news that we didn't want to hear. He was straight and to the point as no doubt this was the horrible type of situation he had to deal with, day in, day out. 'If there is no improvement by tomorrow [Thursday] and I can't be hopeful, we will have to consider switching off the life support machine.' He indicated that if the machine was left on, Anthony would spend the rest of his life brain dead and in a vegetative state. 'I'm sure your parents would not want that,' he said.

I sat frozen in the chair, speechless, and I might as well have been hit by a high-speed train. Róisín held my left hand and as the grim news was delivered. I was in a trance listening to his words. There were so many salient questions I wanted to ask but I just couldn't open my mouth to speak. Anthony was 'dead' even though he was still alive and now, I was faced with the task of breaking the dreaded news to Mum and Dad and the rest of the family.

We left his office in shock and barely able to stand. We didn't know what to say to each other or what to do so we headed to the staff canteen like zombies to join with the rest of the family. We sat at a table and I couldn't work out what I should do next, I just didn't know how to break news of this magnitude. I opted to say nothing for the time being and kept the information lodged in my mind, even though I convinced myself over and over that Anthony might pull through and go on to live a healthy life.

That night, Wednesday, Mammy and Daddy stayed in Terry Kelly's house, a family friend, on Broadway, just off the Falls Road in Belfast. Next day, we all gathered in the hospital and despite the secret I knew, I was still hoping that Anthony's condition might improve over night. As the rotation of pairs sitting with Anthony continued, my turn to sit with him came around 10 a.m. I was joined this time by Fr Con Malone as Róisín stayed at home for the morning. Shortly after Con and myself took our seats, Dr Gordon, accompanied by the sister-in-charge carrying Anthony's file under her arm, entered the room as part of their routine morning check-ups.

Having examined Anthony's pulse, Dr Gordon turned to me and asked if I had informed the rest of the family what he had told me the day before? I told him I didn't have the confidence to do it. He then said he would talk to us when he finished visiting the remaining patients on that ward. Twenty minutes or so later, Fr Malone and myself left Anthony and joined the rest of the family who were sitting in the lobby area of the hospital. Dr Gordon joined us shortly afterwards to deliver the bad news. He said that he regretted to inform us that Anthony was not responding to treatment and that he was brain dead, would remain in a vegetative state and recommended that the life support machine be switched off. His hard-hitting, no-nonsense, straight-to-the-point comments struck us right between the ears. There was silence as we all took in the enormity of his words.

None of us knew what to say or what to do. We all comforted each other and took the view, collectively, that switching off the machine was the appropriate thing to do. It would have broken our Mother's heart to spend the rest of her days feeding and caring for Anthony while he just existed, completely unresponsive, in another world.

Having absorbed the news we didn't want to hear, we all headed to the staff canteen. Oliver, who was in the hospital, rang St Paul's comprehensive school in Bessbrook and left word for his wife Marian to come to Belfast urgently. She brought our sister Una with her.

Fr Malone went to the ward around 6.30 p.m. and when he got to Anthony's bed, Oliver and Marian walked towards him. They were clearly distraught and fought hard to hold back the tears. As they struggled to compose themselves, they told him that Anthony, at the age of seventeen, had passed away. Three brothers were now gone in the space of four weeks, thirteen had died on our road. Those sixteen fatalities, including the O'Dowd family, were the latest statistics of a bloody murky conflict.

Fr Malone returned to the canteen and told us gently that Anthony had slipped away peacefully. Even though the news had been expected, it was remarkably difficult to take in. There was a horrible grim silence amongst us as men, women and children elsewhere in the canteen munched their way through food and chatted between themselves, unaware of the new-found darkness in our shattered lives.

We were asked to go to the ward by Fr Malone and as we made our way up to Anthony's room, my brother Seamus went to Terry Kelly's house on Broadway to break the news to Mammy and Daddy. Mum hadn't gone to bed as she stayed up, praying constantly. When she heard the news, she cried uncontrollably, so much so, that Dad, who was upstairs and alerted by her scream, attempted to come down as quick as he could. In a rapid dash however, he tripped, fell on the narrow stairs and damaged his ribs on the round wooden ball at the bottom of the banisters. He had a bad heart, his third son had just died, his wife was hysterical and now, here he was lying in severe pain on the floor at the bottom of the stairs. Mammy didn't know if he was having a heart attack or was dying before her very eyes.

As the Kelly family scurried to get to a neighbour's phone and call an ambulance, while simultaneously comforting and calming my distraught Mother, somebody else had to notify Eileen and Lillian in the Nurses' Quarters about Anthony's passing. The ambulance rushed Dad to the Royal Victoria Hospital and he had three fractured ribs. As he fought the severe pain in one bed downstairs, his son was lying dead upstairs. We feared that our

Father's weak heart and this fall, coming on the back of what happened in the previous four weeks, would see him die as well. With all this happening, our Mum and Dad did not get to see Anthony's body being wheeled out of his ward to the mortuary.

Fr Malone convened as many of the wider Reavey family that he could and said mass at the hospital chapel. I remember him saying that 'your faith will be tested in the coming days and you will be back in the public eye once again for all the wrong reasons'. The media had been notified that Anthony had died and his passing had become a prominent story on radio and TV news.

We returned to Whitecross in convoy to plan for his funeral, gather our thoughts and get some badly needed sleep. When we arrived home, a large crowd of locals had gathered at Corlatt Drive. The people who showed up at the house sympathised with us but their tone was different and was clearly one of anger as it was widely believed that Anthony would survive. After all, he had been seen out on his crutches only the previous week.

Next day, Sunday, with all the funeral arrangements organised, Anthony's body was returned to Corlatt Drive from Belfast. A staggering 250 cars travelled to Belfast and waited for the body to be released. Most nationalist families in South Armagh had rowed in with support. The funeral procession then moved from Belfast to the Camlough Road in Newry where we were joined by another 100 or so cars which continued the cortege to Whitecross stopping for a minute of reflection outside our family home at Greyhilla.

When we got to No. 9, the sight resembled what we saw for the funerals of John Martin and Brian. There were several thousand people for as far as the eye could see. The numbers were extraordinary and united all shades of political opinion in the region as they came to pay their respects. The number of people who showed up for Anthony's wake was much greater than those who attended for Brian and John Martin. I was particularly surprised at the number of young people who showed up.

Corlatt Drive isn't a big house and quickly we found ourselves with a massive traffic-management problem not helped by the fact that Anthony's body was laid out in an upstairs bedroom. This meant we had to devise a system whereby we could only let so many people into the house at a time; bring them up the stairs while squeezing them past those coming down. Then we would guide them through the back kitchen for a cup of tea and a sandwich. Visitors went out the back door and onto the main road via the pathway at the side of the house. The system worked although the flow of people was hindered every so often by Mum who tended to have a long conversation with some old friend she hadn't seen in years. The process was repeated all over again on the Monday. Our parents sat on each side of the coffin and stayed to the very end. On Tuesday, the burial of Anthony was almost a copy of the funerals of Brian and John Martin.

Dad, with his three broken ribs, insisted on walking from No. 9 to St Malachy's church, Ballymoyer, and further up the road to the cemetery, a journey of three miles. No one knows what sort of physical and emotional pain he was in that day as he buried his third son. Fathers Peter Hughes and Con Malone officiated at the church. Also present was Cardinal William Conway, the primate of All Ireland who told the mourners that 'the spirit of love and forgiveness which the Reavey family had shown after the brutal onslaught on their home was deeply Christian.

'The same profoundly Christian spirit had been shown by the Protestant families at Bessbrook after their equally horrible experience.' He asked 'why do those who speak of Catholics and Protestants hating each other not regard these people as typical rather than the tiny minority of ruthless men who are responsible for these crimes?

'I have spoken to many, many of these families who have been cruelly bereaved in this way and I have yet to hear a word of bitterness from any of them.' His words conveyed a message that any expression of bad feeling would only fuel what was an already awful situation.

With the church service over, we placed a Whitecross GFC green and white jersey on it and began the slow funeral march up to Ballymoyer cemetery.

Like before, the British army was out on full display with camouflaged soldiers positioned in ditches along the route – their guns pointed frighteningly in our direction. They were also busy taking photographs, while overhead, the humming sound of a massive military helicopter intimidated people. This conduct by the British was shocking.

Thousands of people from all over the country marched silently in procession and congregated around the burial site at the cemetery where, it was plain for all to see, the mounds of exposed brown clay hadn't yet settled on the graves of Brian and John Martin. Just like the previous two funerals, Anthony's light oak coffin, with the green and white jersey removed, was slowly lowered into the earth. As the shovel-fulls of soil were poured in, those close to the plot dropped red roses into the grave. Anthony's girlfriend, Lillian Savage, was devastated and her screams filled the air for all to hear. She was unable to stand and had to be held up to remain stable on her feet.

Amidst the loud crying and dripping tears, one by one, the thousands in attendance lined up to shake our hands, give us a hug and expressed their deep sense of sadness at our third loss within a month.

Unknown to me, our Father, Jimmy, who had become separated from us in the massive crowd, found himself fighting for his own life. Having lost his third son and having had his hopes built up about Anthony's improving health in the days after the shooting as well as the ongoing intimidation by the British army, the pressure from the stress became too much. Surrounded by a multitude of people, he collapsed. Such was the massive number of people in the cemetery at the time, we were unaware of his predicament.

Gerry McKeown, who lived in Corlatt Drive, spotted my Father patting his chest rapidly and realised in an instant that all was not well. He worked his way through the crowd, out the gate and made his way up to the phone box at Mary O'Hare's house from where he rang an ambulance. In the meantime, Dr Joe Stewart, our family GP, who had been shadowing my Father but lost him, eventually learned of the crisis and rushed to his car before returning to deliver a crucial injection. The ambulance arrived at the cemetery as thousands continued to queue to pay their respects and many of them must have thought the Reaveys were facing yet another funeral in the coming days.

The medical personnel escorted my Father to the ambulance, took his pulse and treated him there and then. He was clearly suffering from excess fatigue and stress. Fortunately, his life was not in danger. Dr Stewart was remarkably caring in the subsequent weeks and called several times every day to check on our parents.

Like before, family and close friends returned to my house at Drumherriff on the south side of Whitecross. Everyone who called got a hot dinner. To this day, I still don't know where all the food came from. Our neighbours were amazing all over again. We never got around to thanking them individually but after all these years I am belatedly humbled to express our sincere gratitude for their wonderful support. Their generosity was an extraordinary expression of kindness that seems to exist in great numbers amongst caring people of all persuasions in rural Ireland at times of personal loss and difficulty.

Back in the real world, the British army were showing no signs of relaxing their intimidation of the Reaveys.

Step Out of the Car Please

In the days after Anthony's funeral, we had a mountain of organised chaos to deal with. People were still calling to the door; cards from well-wishers all over the world were coming through the letter box; tables, chairs, knives and forks, etc., were being returned to their rightful owners. The media were still looking for interviews and all of us were desperately trying to get a decent night's sleep, fearful that more killings could happen in the locality any day at any time.

Lots of loose ends had to be tidied up; bills had to be paid and in the midst of all this, we had to keep a watchful eye on our parents whose mental state, like the rest of us, was far from ideal. We had a little more time to analyse all that had happened during the month of January 1976 and reluctantly began to accept the killings of Brian and John Martin. As we cried and held back our anger, there was nothing we could do about it except allow justice to take its course – or so we thought.

However, for some inexplicable reason, Anthony's death was harder to take in. He had survived the initial shootings; showed signs of improvement and then was taken from us in a way that left us wondering was all what it seemed to be? We went through all the 'what if' scenarios, a hypothetical area I'll return to later in the story.

Later that evening around 6.00 p.m., I called over to No. 9 to check on our parents. Shortly after I arrived, there was an unexpected knock at the door. A British soldier standing at the front door informed my Father that they were doing a census of all houses in Whitecross. [We subsequently discovered that ours was the only house they visited.] The soldier told my Father that they wanted to know who was in the house. He was asked why he was now living in a different place. Dad answered and was told that the response he gave didn't tally with the information they received during a previous visit.

Step Out of the Car Please

Where are Brian, John Martin and Anthony?
They were dead.
Who killed them?
They were murdered.
Who murdered them? Why would they be murdered? Were they in the IRA?

This line of questioning, designed to trip up our Father, went on for the best part of an hour. Anyone else would have over-reacted to the questions but our calm-mannered Dad knew what was going on.

The following morning, Monday, I needed to return to work so that I had something to focus my mind on and take my thoughts away from the depressing events of the past four weeks. I left my house at Drumherriff around 8.40 a.m. to be in Portadown for nine-ish or so I thought. I drove out the gate, turned left and down the hill. 150 yards away from the house, I encountered a British army checkpoint at Captain's Bridge over the Carrickananney River. All the soldiers had heavy camouflage paint on their faces. I was waved down, stopped the car and was greeted by an English accent that said, 'good morning, Mr Reavey. Can you step out of the car please?'

I got out, expecting the usual line of questioning. This morning however, the routine was different. A colleague of the soldier who 'greeted' me approached and said in a hostile tone: 'Mr Reavey I want to ask you who was involved in the shooting of the people at Kingsmills?'

'I wouldn't know. How would I know that?'

He turned around and said to his colleagues, 'Eugene says he knows fuck all about who shot the people at Kingsmills?'

At that moment, two soldiers approached me, grabbed me by the left shoulder and right arm and frog-marched me through an opening at the end of the bridge wall. They then told me to jump down off the bank and into the field, which I did. The two soldiers jumped after me and escorted me over to the river bank. They then told me to jump in to the freezing water. I refused.

The two soldiers then pushed me in to the water and made me get down on my knees. The fast-flowing water was up to my chin. Another inch deeper and I would have drowned. Here I was on my own and I am staring in to a deep dangerous river. One slip and I would be dead. Even if I didn't stumble on the stony bed underneath, I felt I was going to die. I kept asking myself repeatedly: 'what in the name of God did I do to deserve this?' Sensing the finality of my life, I prayed desperately to Brian, John Martin and Anthony to intercede and save me from certain death. Next thing, another soldier arrived and walked into the river. He was holding a pistol in his hand and put the gun to the temple on my forehead and asked aggressively, 'WHO shot the people at Kingsmills?'

'I don't know.'

He then pulled the trigger slowly and as I watched him do so, I thought straight away that I was dead. But the gun was empty.

Next thing, he put the gun above my left ear and repeated the question, 'Who shot the people at Kingsmills?'

'I don't know.'

He pulled the trigger. Nothing happened again. Not satisfied with my truthful answer, he then placed the gun at the rear of my head and asked, 'Who shot the people at Kingsmills?'

'I don't fucking know.'

He pulled the trigger. Nothing happened.

He put the gun at my right ear and asked, 'Who shot the people at Kingsmills?'

'I don't know.'

He pulled the trigger again. Nothing happened.

With each attempt, he was getting more aggressive and I was beginning to think he was playing Russian roulette with only one bullet in the gun. That meant I was running out of options while at the same time my heart was beating so fast from nervousness and fear, I felt I was either going to have a heart attack or simply collapse and drown.

This time he put the gun on top of my head pointing downwards before saying, 'Who killed the people at Kingsmills?'

'I don't know', and presumed that was the end of the road for me.

He pulled the trigger again and nothing happened. In the middle of this drama, I was trying to work out how many shots he had left before the fatal bullet would finish me off. He then pushed the pistol in to my skin at the top of my nose between my two eyes and asked, 'Who killed the people at Kingsmills?'

'I don't know' and assumed the next trigger would end it for me.

An English accent somewhere behind me shouted, 'Blow his fucking brains out Sarge'.

He pulled the trigger and … nothing happened.

The soldier holding the pistol, turned around, lifted himself on to the grass and walked away. I stayed on my knees in the fast-flowing water, numb with the cold, fearing that if I turned around, a British army marksman would finish me off.

Fifteen minutes later, I eventually plucked up the courage to turn around and see if the soldiers were still there. There was now another problem The water in the river was so cold, I had lost all feeling in my legs. I had to reach out with my arms to the edge of the muddy river bank and drag myself out of the water before trying to get my blood-flow back to normal. Eventually I got feeling back in to my legs and soaked to the skin, I walked out of the field and into the car, conscious that at any second, a fatal shot could ring out and end it all for me.

I returned home, shaking like a leaf and covered in mud. Róisín wasn't at home as she had left earlier to teach at St Malachy's in Camlough. Our housekeeper Lily Finnegan was in the kitchen when I arrived back and I told her what occurred. I told her not to tell Róisín as she was upset as it was. The killings of Brian, John Martin and Anthony was bad enough but Catriona, our daughter, was in an out of hospital. The last thing Róisín needed at this vulnerable time was to hear my horrible story.

I rang Ross Poultry and told the receptionist to pass on the message that I was working from home that day and I'd be making local calls. I changed my suit and took it into McParland's dry cleaners in Monaghan Street, Newry. It was bad enough having had so many sleepless nights during the month of January but now I sensed I was being targeted by the British army and what happened that morning, could soon happen again.

I was harassed and threatened again in the freezing cold waters in the same way on Tuesday, Thursday and Friday. Each time, a gun was put to my head, trigger pulled multiple times and nothing happened. I have asked myself every so often in subsequent years, how many innocent people in Northern Ireland had a gun put to their head by the British army and facing possible death, said the first thing that came in to their head to avoid a bullet and in the process, their words landed them in jail? There are so many people who 'admitted' to things they didn't do just to avoid an early death but ended up with a court conviction that will scar their respective families for generations to come.

The actions perpetrated by the British on the Ballymurphy 11, The Maguire Seven, The Birmingham Six, Guildford Four, Judith Ward and Bloody Sunday killings, etc., took on a whole new significance for me in later years and highlighted how brutal, immoral and dishonest British conduct can be.

Fr Hughes called to the house on the Friday. He had met the officer in charge at Bessbrook barracks and relayed the abuse I had been subjected to that week. Over tea and biscuits, the well-spoken officer made it quite clear to Fr Hughes that he was 'shocked' that his soldiers would engage in such unacceptable conduct. After much 'yes it happened' and 'no it couldn't have', the officer, who had a posh English accent, said he would go away and check the army logs. He returned half an hour later and told Fr Hughes that there were 'no records whatsoever of his soldiers stopping and questioning Mr Reavey'. Fr Hughes was annoyed at what he heard but in light of all the skulduggery that had gone on in South Armagh during the previous six weeks, nothing surprised him.

The meeting convinced Fr Hughes that the British couldn't

be trusted when it came to fairness and justice. I subsequently told Fr Hughes what had happened to me that morning following which, he confided in me that the British army had undermined his word. He went on to say that he was so afraid as a local Catholic leader, he sensed he would be shot by a British army death squad in time. Such was his level of fear and anxiety, he told me he was thinking of requesting a transfer out of the local Loughgilly parish to ensure that he would not succumb to British dirty tricks.

Apart from Róisín, Catriona, Aisling and the rest of the Reavey family, Fr Hughes and Fr Malone were the most important people in my life in early 1976. They were two men I could trust. Their advice was always spot on and I could confide in them on issues that I just couldn't tell my parents at the time.

Fathers Hughes and Malone were like bonded brothers. They got on great, their outlook on life, politics and the evolving sectarian madness was exactly the same and each fully valued their respective close friendship. At times, I became the person each one of them confided in. Often Fr Hughes would tell me things that he didn't want Fr Malone to know and vice versa. We were like a trio of pals who lived for each other.

Despite the increase in security operations around South Armagh in early February, one sensed that things were beginning to settle. Of course, nothing ever settled as terror attacks continued in waves elsewhere around Northern Ireland as the weeks, months and years moved on.

The tension that had engulfed the Whitecross/Bessbrook area in the previous six weeks had relaxed somewhat and I thought the worst of this dark period in my life was over. I was clearly wrong.

Welcome to South Armagh

In the weeks following Anthony's death, the killings in South Armagh ceased for a short while. The atmosphere around Whitecross was still scary. We were all aware of what the British military could do at any moment, legal or otherwise.

I was back at work and my daily routine had all but returned to normal, even though I continued to travel in and out of work using a different route every day.

As all the Reaveys continued to grieve for Brian, John Martin and Anthony, unfortunate families elsewhere in the six counties, Catholics and Protestants, were going through the daily horror of losing a loved one as The Troubles showed no signs of ending. Just when we thought South Armagh had enough of sectarian murder, the next local killing hit the headlines on 26 February 1976. Joe McCullough, aged fifty-seven, was a Protestant farmer from Altnamackin just outside Newtownhamilton, which is about six miles from Whitecross. A member of Tullyvallen Orange Order, he lived with neighbours to avoid being attacked by the IRA

On the day in question, he returned to his farm to feed his dog when he was set upon by an IRA gang who stabbed Joe five times and cut his throat twice. It was yet another slaying in the growing catalogue of death in dysfunctional South Armagh. There was absolute revulsion over Joe McCullough's death and the bad news meant that for every person killed on one side, a retaliation on the other, would follow.

Around this time, Michael Stroud, who was a sales manager, suggested accompanying me on my rounds in South Armagh to meet and engage with the various egg producers in the area. It was a sort of PR exercise, one where he could put a face to the producer and assess any feedback or issues they might have from their dealings with Ross Poultry Limited. We travelled from Portadown to Whitecross and called in to my house for a cup of tea and a chat. As we left, Michael remarked how scenic the countryside was and asked, 'where are all these British soldiers you keep going on about who keep abusing you?'

No sooner had he asked the question, we were stopped at a British army checkpoint outside the Mountain House pub on the Newry to Newtownhamilton Road as we made our way to Hughie Largey's farm in Crossmaglen. A soldier ordered me out of the car and asked me to open the boot and bonnet. The boot was full of veterinary medicines and supplies for the poultry industry. It also contained scissors and a butcher's boning knife which, no doubt, aroused suspicion. The supplies were removed and scattered on the side of the road. The car, like myself, was searched inside out and upside down.

Michael, who was a well-spoken tall man from Wales and an atheist, sat in the front seat of the car and observed the way the soldiers behaved. He then, unexpectedly, got out of the car and said to the bemused soldiers, 'I'm going for a leak' and proceeded to walk across the road into the pub. His accent, which was completely foreign compared to the local dialect, stood out like the proverbial sore thumb. Suspecting something suspicious was afoot, the soldiers followed him into the men's room and proceeded to semi-strip him. The soldiers forcibly removed his jacket, shirt, his socks and shoes. They emptied his pockets and thoroughly checked the contents.

There was one consolation in the middle of this unwelcome humiliation namely, they protected his dignity by leaving his pants on which, knowing the hostile manner in which they operated, was unexpected. He was asked repeatedly who he was, where he lived, what he was doing in South Armagh and more to the point, what he was doing associating with me? Michael was eventually released and returned to the car.

'This is the most undignified experience I have ever endured in my entire life,' he said in a posh disgusted tone.

'Michael, welcome to South Armagh!'

'Turn this car around and bring me back to Portadown. I have never been so humiliated in my life.'

'Michael, we haven't even got near Crossmaglen yet and we have to visit these farms.'

Michael demanded I head for Portadown but I wouldn't budge. When I eventually got my licence returned to me, we headed for Crossmaglen and I reminded him that the experience he just endured was everyday life in South Armagh.

We eventually made it to Hughie Largey's farm at Creggan- duff where Michael, unknowingly, was somewhat insensitive to local feelings towards the British army. During the course of a jovial conversation, Hughie, who with his wife were the salt of the earth, happened to ask Michael what his son was working at these days.

Michael replied, without thinking, that he was 'in Sandhurst' [the Royal Military Academy] training to be an officer in her majesty's military. Fortunately, he made his remarks in front of Hughie Largey. Others in the locality might have taken a different view.

Hughie joked, 'You didn't have to send him that far to be a soldier. If you sent him to Crossmaglen, he'd learn all he needs to know in six weeks.' Michael made it clear in subsequent days that he would not be returning to South Armagh any time soon in the foreseeable future.

About a week later, I returned to some farms to collect outstanding monies due to the Ross company. The amount totalled £2,400, a sizeable amount of money in 1976. Having collected the cash, I placed it in an envelope and noted the amounts paid by each farmer. Next morning before I left the house, I placed the envelope inside my shirt just to ensure I wouldn't be robbed by the IRA or the British army and thought nothing of it. As I made my way towards Whitecross village, I was stopped by an army checkpoint at Priest Bush Corner and ordered to get out of the car for the routine check. A soldier asked me for my licence and then proceeded to frisk me. Not surprisingly, he felt this bulge under my shirt and when he asked what it was, I replied 'that's money I collected on farms yesterday'.

In an instant he swung me around, tore open my shirt ripping off all the buttons and grabbed the envelope. He took it to his superior where a long chat ensued. An RUC officer approached me and asked me what I was doing with the money? I told him I had collected it from some farms as outstanding payments for private egg sales for Ross Poultry in Portadown. The RUC officer walked away and spoke to the soldier. The soldier in turn came back to me and in an aggressive tone accused me of robbing the post office in nearby Mullaghbawn the previous day. Totally unaware of the robbery I replied, 'you must be joking. I robbed no post office'.

The soldier went back to his superior and together with the RUC officer, they had a long discussion and radioed back to Bessbrook army station where details on my work were queried and clarified. Eventually, the money was returned. I threw the envelope on the driver's seat and sat on it. I was waved on but I was furious. As I drove to Portadown, I questioned myself and hoped nobody in Ross Poultry would question my loyalty. I also asked myself about whether or not I had a future with the company as the constant harassment and intimidation was becoming too much to handle.

I eventually got to Ross Poultry and furious with rage, I walked straight in to Bob McCammond's office without asking his secretary to check if he was free to meet me. I stormed in, flung the envelope on the desk and said to Bob in an unwarranted raised voice as I pointed at my ripped shirt, 'This is the price I have to pay to get you your bloody money in Cullyhanna'. To his credit, Bob immediately sensed something was wrong, raised his hands and said 'settle down Eugene, we'll sort this out'. He knew straight away that something serious had happened and fully understood my anger. He rang his secretary, and asked her to bring in tea and biscuits. He began the process of counting the money before asking me to explain what happened. He wanted me to go to the police in Portadown and make a formal complaint. I knew that this was pointless. He suggested a break would do Róisín and me good and that hopefully by the time I returned, the chaos in South Armagh would have stopped.

I told him that the unbearable stress of all that was happening was getting to me. It was also having an effect on Róisín and that maybe it would be best if I left the company. Bob wouldn't hear tell of it and said I was only feeling that way because of what happened earlier that morning. He added that he was very happy with my work and that he had recognised my contribution to the company.

I returned home that day and asked myself if Ross Poultry was where my future lay? Bob McCammond was a gentleman to work for and he had been most understanding about my recent difficulties but I kept asking if it was time to work for myself or was there any business or profession that I and the rest of the family could tap in to that would be more lucrative or would give us more independence not to mention peace of mind?

BY THIS TIME, FR Con Malone had returned to Tanzania. He got a commitment from me before his departure that I would definitely go and visit him soon. We booked a holiday and looked forward to our adventure in east Africa.

On Wednesday 31 March and shortly after 9.30 p.m. Róisín's mother, rang to say she had a blistering headache and enquired if we had any aspirin in the place? Róisín told her there was a packet in the cupboard and she would send me up to the house. I got in the car to drive the mile or so towards Belleeks and as I turned right into Carrickgollogly lane, there in front of me was a big boulder in the middle of the road in the centre of the bridge. I stopped the car, got out and forcibly moved the huge rock to the side of the road. I headed on up to Mrs Quinn's house, delivered the aspirin, had a brief chat and got back in to the car.

When I came to the bridge on the return journey, the boulder was back in the middle of the road again. I sensed that something strange was going on. I got out of the car and gently pushed the boulder to the side of the road before heading on home driving as carefully as I could. Just as I put the key in the front door of the house, this massive explosion went off one mile up the road that shook every house in the vicinity.

Welcome to South Armagh

I guessed in an instant what had happened although I didn't know how big the blast was. Next morning, the news on Radio Ulster revealed that an explosion occurred at a bridge in South Armagh. Later in the day it emerged that three British soldiers from the Royal Scots Regiment were killed when their land rover was thrown twenty yards downstream after two creamery kegs packed with 300 pounds of explosives were detonated by remote control. One soldier survived the blast.

The following Sunday, after a football match, we visited my parents. At around 5.15 we decided to head home and as we approached Kingsmills crossroads noticed a large number of soldiers on the road. We got to the checkpoint and I was waved over to the right-hand side.

As I opened the boot, a small portly reserve RUC police officer edged up to my left and told me in a very gruff tone to take all the football jerseys, boots, water bottles, poultry accessories, etc., out of the boot. I didn't like his tone and told him, 'take it out yourself. I'm not getting paid to do your dirty work'.

There were heated exchanges between the wee RUC man and myself for at least fifteen minutes. Róisín opened the door and told me in no uncertain terms to take all the items out of the boot as she wanted to go home. I got the message loud and clear and started to remove all the items from the boot, when the RUC reserve officer said, 'You know Eugene, your boys weren't shot for nothing. They must have been in the IRA'. Then he hit me in the ribs with the butt of his rifle. I collapsed into the boot of the car and held myself upwards with my elbows while my knees were jammed in to the rear number plate. I was in serious pain but eventually recovered my breath.

I turned around, looked up and there he was staring down at me. In a fit of rage, I hit him on the side of his left jaw with a right hook that even Mike Tyson would have been proud of. He fell into the ditch collapsing like a bag of spuds. I was grabbed by five soldiers, dragged across the road and subjected to a severe kicking and beating. To complicate matters, Róisín was furious with me. She could see the RUC were antagonistic towards me and felt it would be better if I kept my mouth shut instead of answering them back. She decided to drive off and leave me stranded to fend for myself.

With Róisín out of sight, I was dragged into the back of a land rover and kicked all the way as we drove in to Bessbrook RUC barracks. From there, I was dragged out and thrown on to the floor of a cold cell with no seats, no window and no water.

Around 8 p.m. that evening, I heard a familiar voice outside my cell. I knew it was Fr Hughes. I didn't know it then but he had a far better relationship with the RUC than he had with the British army. If he vouched for your character, that was good enough and so after much chit-chat outside my cell with a senior RUC official, next thing, the door opened. The RUC man popped his head in and said, 'you're free to go'. No questions were asked and no details were sought. As I was walking out the door, he said, 'if you wish to make a complaint, call back tomorrow'. I never called back as I felt that my complaint would amount to nothing.

AROUND THIS TIME, RÓISÍN'S mother Katie Quinn, who lived at Carrickgollogly Belleeks, had her hands full trying to raise six of her eight children and run a small farm of thirty acres on modest land. After the bomb explosion at the bridge which claimed three British soldiers in March, a number of houses in the locality had received menacing visits from the British army. One day while I was moving cattle from one field to another with young Killian Finnegan along the old Carrickgollogly Road, Killian walked in front of the cattle and as he approached Deighan's Lane, a platoon of soldiers confronted him. After the cattle were guided in to the nearby field, the soldiers challenged Killian about his movements in recent days. He was intimidated and quizzed at length.

I closed the gate into the field and walked towards the soldiers who had formed a circle around Killian. When I got to them, I asked what was going on.

'We're asking this young man some questions.'

'It's not a wise idea to be interfering and intimidating the boy.'

My words were the verbal equivalent of stepping on a landmine. The soldiers were furious and started shouting at me. How dare I, an Irish Catholic, tell soldiers in her majesty's army what to do. I was grabbed and pushed against the stone wall with a gun put to my head and asked the usual plethora of bullying questions.

After the soldiers eventually moved on, the reasons for their presence became clear. Across the road, the entrance into Deighan's farm, which comprised two dry-stone walls on either side, had been blocked. The British soldiers had pulled the stone walls apart which meant that the Deighan family could neither get in or out of their house. The Deighan's were hard-working people who stayed as far away from politics as one could get. But, British soldiers, with plenty of time on their hands, came in to the area, caused chaos and upset the daily routine of innocent people in the locality.

Shortly afterwards, when I was home from work in midafternoon I went up to check my cattle on land I had leased from my mother-in law. I always popped in to see her on the way home for a chat and as I approached her house, I could see the place was overrun with heavily camouflaged soldiers. I presumed they were doing a census to see who lived there, i.e., who was home and who was not but I quickly learned it was something far more sinister. I made my way to the front door and could hear Mrs Quinn screaming and remonstrating with a senior member of the platoon.

Soldiers had burst in and wrecked the modest one-storey building, itself an old-style stone-built farmhouse. They pulled the place apart and despite their determined efforts, they couldn't find what they were looking for. One of the soldiers climbed up into the roof space and once he searched that section, he attempted to break through in to the next room only to find his way blocked by the original gable wall. He used his sledge hammer to knock out large stones which fell through the ceiling and down on to the floor. The house was wrecked.

The one-time home of the Quinn family had been destroyed by the British army and Róisín's mother and six siblings were left with nowhere to live.

As the heavy stones were falling from on high, I had to leave the house for my own safety. When the soldiers felt they had done enough damage to make the house completely uninhabitable, they left. I walked back in to the house and was shocked at what I saw.

I was even more alarmed when I discovered Mrs Quinn lying unconscious on the dusty kitchen floor. 'Jesus Christ,' I thought. 'What the hell happened here?' I wasn't too sure what to do so I shook her and quickly saw that she was alive. I got her a glass of water, she sat up and eventually came around. Katie was shaken and very upset. The actions of the ruthless British army were so severe, she was left with no option but to find somewhere else for her and her family to live.

If Mrs Quinn's life wasn't tough enough to contend with up to now, her family were now like local refugees. Katie and her six children moved in temporarily with her eldest daughter Mary Murphy in her small council house in Camlough while the home place was left to fall in to dereliction. As one can imagine, all members of the wider Quinn family and those in the locality were outraged over what happened. Eventually Mrs Quinn was offered a council house in St Oliver Plunkett Park in Camlough.

On 5 April 1976, thirty-two-year-old Robert McConnell, an unmarried Protestant farmer and a member of the UDR, was walking along a laneway leading to his home at Tullyvallen in Newtownhamilton to put his disabled sister to bed. According to the book *Lost Lives*, his mother had died three weeks earlier and his seventy-six-year-old father was in the house waiting for him. The IRA set up an ambush and shot him several times in the head and face. He died on arrival at Daisy Hill Hospital in Newry. I didn't know him but I knew that he and his sister spent a lot of time at the home of their Catholic neighbours, the O'Neill family. Kevin O'Neill was a gentleman and looked after Robert and his disabled sister like they were members of his own family.

Ten days later, on 15 April 1976, the first known killing by the British SAS (Special Air Service) in Northern Ireland occurred in the South Armagh/North Louth area. Peter Cleary, twenty-five, who lived three miles on the Newtownhamilton side of Belleeks, was due to get married in the coming month and went to a social gathering at the home of his fiancée, Shirley Hulme, who lived in North County Louth just south of Forkhill. There was loud music in the house and the beer was plentiful.

According to writer Mike Ryan, the SAS, had, it seems, Peter under surveillance following recent IRA activity in the area.[1] He was a wanted man and had moved some time earlier south of the border to take up residence in Dundalk. On the night in question, an SAS unit lay in wait outside the Hulme residence and using specialist listening devices, eavesdropped on what was being said in the house.

Somebody at the party walked out in to the back garden to urinate and accidentally stumbled upon the unit lying in wait. The four-man SAS team, realising their cover had been blown, sprung in to action, entered the house and singled out Peter. When asked to identify himself, he gave a false name. The SAS stripped his clothes off and gave him a severe beating. It is reported that his neck was broken with a karate chop before being shot in the chest at close range 'trying to escape'.

The book *Lost Lives* quotes an editorial from *The Cork Examiner* newspaper at the time as saying that the standard British response of saying 'shot while trying to escape' is one of the oldest and least credible excuses put forward by armies across the world to try and justify a killing. 'It has usually been greeted with cynicism and deservedly so'. *Lost Lives* says an SAS operative who entered the house to single out Peter Cleary for killing was later identified as being Robert Nairac.

Peter Cleary was buried in Belleeks and given full IRA military honours however his death sparked widespread controversy not so much because he was shot dead by the SAS but because this unit of the British military establishment had killed in the Irish Republic.

The media had a field day with this story. It had escalated to what is regularly termed a 'diplomatic incident'. It amounted to being a 'military invasion', a blatant breach of international law. From my recollection of the time, Taoiseach Liam Cosgrave, did nothing about it apart from issuing a few wishy-washy statements to the press.

If the SAS could go into the Republic and get away with a serious violation, it would happen again. Not surprisingly, republicans were given another excuse to hit back and if the IRA got a 'spectacular' revenge, the British would intensify their activities in South Armagh.

AROUND THIS TIME, A customer told me that he had been speaking to a Raymond Bell of 'Bell's Eggs' at Crossgar in Co. Down who was keen to speak to me. My customer told me that Mr Bell was looking for a technical poultry adviser to manage a new egg-supply network. I met him and he offered me a very attractive proposition. I would have a much-improved salary, expenses, a company car and I could spend more time working from home. The dangerous daily commute to Portadown would be replaced by travelling to Crossgar instead, a daily difference of forty miles extra in the car. Crossgar incidentally, is where Ian Paisley founded the Free Presbyterian Church on that most 'Irish' of days, 17 March in 1951. As part of the plan, Bell's had a new arrangement with Thompson Feed Supplies in Belfast whereby a new egg-supply group would be established. I liked what I heard from Mr Bell and the additional managerial responsibility with the role gave me a new sense of importance.

I had to tell Bob McCammond the news that I had been offered an improved role elsewhere. I informed him as gently as I could and there was a lengthy silence. I wasn't sure if he was going to wish me well or call me all the names under the sun in light of his previous flexibility. Bob said, 'I am very disappointed at this news. Ross Poultry did all it could to accommodate you.

I am personally disappointed that you are leaving. I will not stand in your way. I wish you well and I would ask that you keep in touch. You have shown great resilience and you're the type of man I would like to keep in Ross Poultry.'

He told me to take the company car and hold on to it until I returned from our holiday in Tanzania. He showed remarkable consideration and understanding. I was paid for the following month and Bob gave me two pre-paid open airline tickets from Belfast to London Heathrow.

Five days after terminating my own employment with Ross Poultry, Róisín and myself got on a plane in Belfast courtesy of Bob McCammond and flew off to London and onwards to Tanzania.

British Brutality in Ballymoyer

When our enjoyable month in Tanzania was over, it was back to the cooler climes of Ireland where I was about to begin a new phase in my life. On Monday, 31 May 1976, I started work with Bell's Eggs, Crossgar, Co. Down. My first role was to pick up my new car, a yellow Renault 12 from Bell's Motors in Crossgar. I met Raymond Bell in the office where we discussed my duties and the territory I would cover in the coming months. My main focus was to familiarise myself with how Bell's ran their operation and to grow their customer numbers. Raymond allowed me to leave the office at noon and gave me a half-day. Tomorrow I would 'officially' start work full time.

I got into my brand-new car delighted with myself. I adjusted the seat, altered the mirror and headed south via the scenic picturesque countryside of Co. Down through Downpatrick, Clough, Castlewellan, Kilcoo, Hilltown, Mayobridge, Newry, on towards home, enjoying the drive and the lovely smell of fresh new upholstery along the way. I made my way up towards Whitecross preparing to turn left at Kingsmills crossroads and on to home at Drumherriff. About 100 yards short of what's known locally as Finnegan's Corner, I was waved down by the British Parachute Regiment. 'Oh no,' I thought, 'here we go again'. I stopped the car, rolled down the window and a large blunt soldier with green and black camouflage paint on his face said, 'Good afternoon, Mr Reavey'.

I said, 'Hello.'

'We haven't seen you around Mr Reavey in a long time.'

'That's right.'

'You were away on holiday Mr Reavey'.

'That's right.'

'Where were you Mr Reavey?'

'I was on holiday.'

Then his tone changed.

'You were on holiday in fucking South Africa, Eugene.'

'No you're wrong. It was fucking *east* Africa.'

'Buying fucking guns for the IRA, Eugene?'

'Yeah, whatever you say.'

At this point I noticed two other soldiers were placed in the hedge with their rifles pointed in my direction.

The soldier in charge, pointed his rifle to the side of my head and said, 'Get out of my fucking sight before I shoot you'.

I took off slowly and drove the 200 yards or so to my house. I changed my clothes and put on casual wear. Twenty minutes later, after a cup of tea and a biscuit, I decided to head over to Camlough village to buy worm drench for the cattle.

I drove out the gate and turned right to take what is known as the back road to Camlough. I hadn't travelled 200 yards when I was stopped by the Parachute Regiment again. I rolled down the window and there before my eyes was the same large British soldier. It seems, he was in bad form.

'Get out of the car you little fuck,' he said angrily.

I got out of the car and he directed me to the opposite side of the road where he issued a stark instruction to a soldier of lesser rank.

'Don't move you little fuck, and [looking at the other soldier] if he does, shoot him.'

While I was standing looking ahead of me, next thing I saw the back seat of the car flying over the hedge and in to the field in front of me. I didn't move. Five minutes later, I heard a thud sound. Something had been thrown in to the field behind me. The next thing was the front seat of my brand-new Renault 12 went flying past in mid-air and into the field before me. Before I knew it, another wheel went hurtling past me. This was followed by another thud sound from the field across the road before the next wheel came flying past me followed by another thud and wheel.

All of a sudden, the commotion stopped. The big soldier came over to me and in a loud and aggressive voice said, 'kneel down'. I knelt down on the road fearing my luck at these hostile checkpoints had finally run out. The soldier pushed his rifle in to the back of my neck and said, 'the next time I ask you where you were on your holidays you little Irish cunt, answer me'.

He threw the keys of the car as far as he could into the field before me. Next thing, the dozen or so soldiers at the checkpoint turned around and walked into the field in front of me where a noisy chinook helicopter descended from the sky and picked them up.

I turned around rattled after what had happened and there was the shell of the brand-new yellow Renault 12 sitting on the road on its axles without its four wheels and seats. I couldn't believe the lengths these people went to in order to intimidate me. It just seemed to be getting worse with each passing day and I wasn't the only one in the area receiving this type of treatment.

I walked back to the house and rang Bessbrook RUC barracks to report what happened. The officer I spoke to was as intimidating and abrupt as the soldier who put the gun to the back of my neck. He laughed at me and said, 'if you weren't shooting at your neighbours, this wouldn't be happening to you'.

I was furious with his comments. Where this line of 'shooting your neighbours' came from, was a mystery, however a picture was slowly becoming clear – somebody was briefing against us, wrongly implying we were in the IRA.

On 5 June, fifty-four-year-old bachelor Mick McGrath called down to The Rock Bar at Granemore, a rural townland between Whitecross and Keady at around 10.30 p.m. to buy six bottles of Guinness and bring them home to his brother. As he walked out the door, he stopped at the railings for a chat with barman Francis Powell. As Francis headed back in to the bar, a car quickly approached and three masked men got out and fired on Mick. He was hit in the tummy and hip before falling to the ground. The men were carrying a bomb which failed to go off but as Mick lay in pain on the ground, he noticed something. The boots worn by one of the gunmen looked remarkably similar to the type that would be worn by a police officer. The boiler suits worn by the gunmen however did not reach down all the way and revealed that the trousers underneath were dark green, standard RUC issue. One of the RUC officers was back at the local station in time to take part in the 'investigation' of the attack.

The British army bomb disposal team arrived and defused the device before taking it away to Belfast for further examination. Strangely enough, all of the bomb's components were conveniently destroyed in what was termed a 'malicious fire' at the Forensic Science Laboratory four months later.

Friday 25 June was a beautiful summer day. I came home from Crossgar around 5.30 p.m. and later, Róisín opted to serve a salad meal in the back garden. I had cattle to attend to when the meal finished and Róisín asked me if I would take Catriona, by now, two and half years old, to Whitecross where her grandparents looked forward to seeing her before she went to bed. I got into the car and headed over to Corlatt Drive and as always, my parents were delighted to see Catriona.

Shortly after my arrival sometime around 9.30 p.m., I answered the new telephone that had been installed in the house as Mammy and Daddy were too busy giving their undivided attention to their grandchild. Róisín was on the line and she was struggling to get the words out. She had just received a call from her brother Paddy Quinn who was trapped in a house owned by Paddy O'Neill at Sturgan, close to the Mountain House pub on the Newry to Newtownhamilton Road. The house was under siege by British army soldiers and their shots were targeting the house.

Paddy asked Róisín if I could bring Fr Hughes up to the house to negotiate his safe release with the British. I didn't realise the extent of the situation Paddy was in and put Catriona in to the car before heading off to find Fr Hughes to head up to Sturgan. When we got to Paddy O'Neill's house, there were British soldiers everywhere. We pulled in to the side of the road and when we got out of the car, the seriousness of the situation became apparent. There were tracer bullets flying in all directions lighting up the air as darkness began to fall.

A platoon of British soldiers placed on a Mass Rock in Lislea overlooking Paddy O'Neill's house, were firing shots at the rear of the building and many were heading in our direction. The soldiers lying on the road we had just travelled, shouted at us 'get out of the fucking way'. No words can express how frightening the situation was.

I was trying to avoid deadly bullets whizzing past me while all I could think of was protecting Catriona at all costs. Realising our lives were in danger, I had to get Catriona out from the back seat and place her under the car and even then, there was no guarantee we were safe from gunfire.

Fr Hughes, in a scene similar to the famous walk of Fr Edward Daly in Derry on Bloody Sunday, waved a white handkerchief and courageously shouted back at the soldiers 'cease fire and I will speak to whoever is in the house'. The soldiers stopped firing and waited. Fr Hughes, stood up waving the white cloth shouting 'hold your fire, hold your fire' and approached the front of Paddy O'Neill's house. When he got to the front window of the building he shouted 'put your guns down and I will talk to the commanding officer. Put your guns down and I will get you out safely, no more firing.'

Fr Hughes then spoke to the commanding officer and told him that he would speak to the gunmen and get them out. The commanding officer agreed to the proposal. Meanwhile I was lying down on the ground under the car with Catriona. I knew Paddy was inside but obviously, he wasn't alone.

With firing stopped, Fr Hughes bravely put his head in the window and spoke to the men inside. He persuaded them to put down their guns and walk outside with their hands in the air. They did this and were instructed to lie down on the ground. I could hear a lot of aggressive shouting in the distance from bolshy British soldiers in the infamous 3rd Parachute Regiment. The men were cautiously frisked for fear of hidden explosives. Catriona and myself weren't allowed to move an inch. We continued to lie under the car in a way that made us look as if we were dead.

Eventually the two men who were in the house were taken away to Bessbrook station in green army land rovers. I didn't see everything that was happening at the house as I was on the ground under the car.

Fr Hughes returned to the car and got in to the passenger seat. With a huge sigh of relief, he said, 'that's another job done'. I brought him back to the parochial house in Whitecross and as soon as we got there, he got into his car and drove to Bessbrook station where he met senior officers to discuss what happened at Paddy O'Neill's house. Several hours later, he returned to our house, walked in to the kitchen and said, as if nothing at all had happened earlier, 'get that kettle on for a quick cup of tea'. In the meantime, Mrs Quinn had called to our house and was anxiously awaiting his return for an update on the shootout. Fr Hughes revealed that two of the four-man IRA unit apprehended by the British army were local IRA volunteers Paddy Quinn (25) from Belleeks and Raymond McCreesh (19) from Camlough.

Fr Hughes said that Paddy and Raymond would, in all likelihood, be charged with IRA membership as well as possession with intent. Mrs Quinn cried loudly. He added that the RUC could hold Paddy and Raymond for up to seventy-two hours before deciding to either charge, extend their period of detention or release them. The raid and horrible destruction of Mrs Quinn's house by the British army raised questions. Did the British know something about Paddy that the rest of us didn't or did Paddy join the Provos because of the damage done to the house? Either way, Mrs Quinn was a severely distressed woman.

The news was a huge shock for us. I thought at the time that the unexpected revelation that my brother-in law Paddy Quinn was in the IRA would now give the British army even more justification to harass me and the Quinn family as well. On the instruction of my mother-in-law, I contacted my solicitor Rory McShane in Newry. I told him what happened, the family connection and asked him to enquire on Paddy's condition. I also asked him to act for Paddy.

The next morning, it emerged that a third man in the unit, Danny McGuinness (19) had been arrested in possession of a rifle by the security forces in a nearby quarry. There was talk that a fourth man had escaped the siege but nobody knew who he was at this stage. The following Tuesday, 30 June, the three men, looking somewhat dishevelled, were charged at a special sitting of Newry Court and remanded in custody until 8 July. Mrs Quinn, who was in court, looked sad, gaunt and lost during the hearing. Paddy Quinn, Danny McGuinness and Raymond McCreesh were subsequently given lengthy sentences and sent to the Maze Prison.

It was around this time I contacted my solicitor Rory McShane again. We had a long chat and following his advice, I decided to set up a construction company not so much to make a few quid but to honour the loss of Brian, John Martin and Anthony. All the elements were in place as my brothers Seamus and Frank were plasterers, Oliver was a joiner, while Paul and my Dad were painters.

We called the company 'Reavey Brothers (Contractors) Ltd' and would focus, at the outset, on renovations and maintenance of 1940s and 1950s property stock for the Northern Ireland Housing Executive (NIHE). All we needed now was sufficient funds to pay wages for the first month and a couple of contracts to get us up and running. We had to get employers and public liability insurance and above all else, we had to learn the system, i.e., how to fill in tender forms; meet the criteria and most importantly to get on the list of approved contractors particularly when you had no track record of maintaining and renovating houses.

AT THIS TIME, REPORTS were circulating that more and more people were being threatened, intimidated and harassed by the 3rd Parachute Regiment in the South Armagh area. The behaviour of the paras ranged from soldiers exposing themselves to young girls; to hay barns being burned down; to young men and women being threatened that they would be shot unless they became informers.

We thought the savage behaviour of the British army in South Armagh couldn't go any lower. Well, it did on 14 August 1976 when one of the worst and sadly, most overlooked killings to happen on the island of Ireland, took place. Twelve-year old Majella O'Hare lived in the townland of Ballymoyer just two miles up the road from Whitecross. She was the youngest of five children and her parents Jim and Mary were lifelong friends of our parents. That day, Róisín and I were in Navan, Co. Meath with Robbie McGuinness and his wife Erin. He was looking at a farm he was interested in buying. Robbie, who lived on the Kingsmills Road, also had enough of the daily intimidation from the British. The stress of living where we are and fearing for the plight of their six children persuaded him that it was time to pack up and move on.

We looked at the 150-acre farm and Robbie and his wife weighed up their options. On the way home we detoured via Dundalk and got to a British army checkpoint at Carrickasticken close to Forkhill. The soldiers were clearly agitated when we arrived. They were aggressive and told us 'get the fuck out of this car'. At that point, shots rang out from everywhere and we quickly had to lie down on the road on the passenger's side of the car. A ferocious gun battle between the IRA and the army broke out and lasted for at least half an hour. Robbie McGuinness, cool as you like, took out a cigarette and lit up as shots whizzed past us in all directions.

Eventually it ended and a British soldier asked us for our names and ID. We told him we were from Whitecross. He told us that a shooting had taken place there earlier in the day and sent us on our way. Our curiosity was in overdrive as we headed home, wondering who might have been involved. When we finally made it to Robbie's house, Phelim McGuinness told us that Majella O'Hare had been shot. Horrific and all as it sounded, we assumed it was a non-fatal shooting. We then left McGuinness' house and headed up to my parents' house. When we arrived there, the story we were told was even more chilling.

14 August is one of many dates I will take with me to the grave. It was the day that our brother Brian was to marry Alice Campbell. A day that was expected to be a happy and memorable one became unforgettable for all the wrong reasons.

My brother Seamus had arranged to collect Alice at Daisy Hill Hospital at 9 a.m. after her shift ended. They then went down the town and bought flowers in a local florist to put on Brian's grave. En route to Whitecross, they stopped at our family home where Brian, Anthony and John Martin were killed. While there, Seamus cut roses from a floral arch in the garden and put them in to the boot of his car.

They popped into No. 9 for some breakfast and a chat. About 11 a.m., Seamus, our Father, our youngest sister Colleen and Alice headed up by car to Ballymoyer graveyard where the three boys are buried. When they got out of the car, Seamus noticed soldiers entering the graveyard from an adjoining field on the Whitecross side. Alice and our Father took the flowers out of the car while Seamus brought a knife and a bucket which he filled with water inside the graveyard wall. As they made their way down the hill towards the grave, they met six soldiers coming towards them. Five of the soldiers were marines and one was a member of the parachute regiment.

The member of the parachute regiment called out in a menacing tone, 'Seamus Reavey? I want a word with you when you're finished'. Seamus cut the roses, put them in to the vase and tidied up the grave. Seamus, Alice, Colleen and our Dad, having said a few prayers, deliberately waited at the headstone in the hope the army platoon would go away and they would not be subjected to harassment. To add to the atmosphere, Alice was in floods of tears. She was still in the depths of misery after Brian's killing in January. The bouquet of flowers she had hoped to display at her wedding was instead being placed on Brian's grave. Eventually they made their way back to the entrance gate when a voice from somebody in a position of authority within the platoon rang out, 'Seamus Reavey come up here or

I'll knock the fucking block off you'.

Seamus walked the twenty yards or so towards the paratrooper who was standing at a roadblock. He told the para in a civilised tone of voice, 'I wasn't going to run away. You have no call to be shouting at me'.

Whilst the soldier was berating Seamus, a car pulled up and local man Hugh Kennon told the soldier, 'that's nice language to be using in front of a graveyard'.

The soldier quickly replied, 'fuck off you'.

Hugh drove on and as he did, a group of eight local schoolgirls came along walking nonchalantly towards Ballymoyer church where they were heading for confessions. The girls were giggling and skipping along the road as youngsters of that age do. The soldier continued to be abusive towards Seamus telling him that the IRA murdered his brothers because 'they refused to shoot UDR men'.

It was seven minutes before mid-day and as the soldier continued to verbally abuse Seamus, from nowhere, a loud shot rang out. There was screaming and pandemonium. The schoolgirls, in a state of distress, huddled around each other and clearly knew something was seriously wrong – twelve-year-old Majella O'Hare had been hit. Majella's father, Jim, was digging up weeds outside Ballymoyer church 150 yards away, heard the shot and subsequent commotion. He dropped his shovel and ran to the scene only to discover that the young girl struggling for her life and in deep agony on the ground, was his daughter. Amidst the chaos, he lifted Majella in to his arms. She was bleeding heavily from a wound on the left side of her tummy. Jim was in a state of shock and cuddled Majella, not knowing what to do next. Just then, a completely insensitive arrogant British soldier approached Jim and asked, 'what the fucking hell are you doing here?'[1]

Jim couldn't believe his ears and somewhat startled by the hostile nature of the question said, 'I'm the girl's father.'

'Well close your fucking mouth,' responded the soldier.

Sixteen-year-old Una Murphy recalled that the soldier told

Jim in an aggressive tone of voice to 'take his fucking hands off her [Majella]'.²

Jim O'Hare replied, 'this is the only wee girl I have left'.

The soldier said, 'I don't give a fuck'.

Jim was forced to put Majella down on the road and let her continue to wriggle in screaming pain and ooze blood before she was carried away by another soldier. Jim was offered a sip of water and a couple of puffs from a cigarette.

Seamus and Alice who were watching the commotion from a distance were shocked at what they heard, asked the soldier that was beside them, if they could go down to where the schoolgirls were screaming and crying.

The soldier said 'no'. Seamus explained to the soldier that Alice was a qualified nurse and asked again if he could take her to the cluster of screaming girls?

'No,' was the loud heartless blunt answer once again.

Then, the soldier's conscience must have caught up with him as he unexpectedly grabbed Alice by the hand and took her down to the scene of the shooting. Alice, already upset because of the day that was in it, found Majella lying on her back. The exit wound in her abdomen was clearly exposed. A soldier shouted to a colleague to bring some bandages.

With seeping red blood all over the place, Alice tilted Majella's chin to ensure a proper air flow in to her lungs and as she did, the soldier nearby said, 'this is your fucking Provos for you'.

Fr Hughes arrived shortly afterwards expecting to hear confessions. As he did, the soldier remarked, 'there he is [Fr Hughes] again, He's always stuck in it'.

Shortly afterwards, my friend Barry Malone arrived in his car. A paratrooper made him stop and as Barry rolled down the window, the soldier shouted, 'that's what your fucking Provos do, there it is for you, look'. The soldier thumped the top of Barry's car and said, 'drive on to fucking hell'.

The Brits were clearly up to their usual dirty tricks of trying to create the impression that they were innocent in all this. As far as they were concerned, this shooting was carried out by the IRA and that they, the British, wouldn't do such a thing. The thinking being that if you convinced enough people that the IRA were responsible, they might, in turn, lose all local support.

All subsequent statements made to the RUC by local witnesses had a common thread running through them – that when questioned by the British army, soldiers continually referred to six and nine shots being fired. Of course, everybody else present when Majella fell, only heard one shot. Just like Bloody Sunday in Derry and the Ballymurphy Massacre in Belfast, this was once again trigger-happy immature British soldiers playing with guns and it didn't matter who the casualties were. The Kitson practice of killing innocent people without justification was still going strong.

At this stage, a British army helicopter hovered in and landed on the sun-drenched road stirring up a cloud of choking dust in the process. The soldiers threw Jim O'Hare in to the helicopter – then they also *threw* Majella on board, head first, in the most undignified way imaginable. According to Alice, Majella's legs were left dangling out of the helicopter as were her blood-dripping exposed intestines. Alice climbed on board and she too was afforded so little space, her red-trousered legs were left dangling over the edge of the helicopter doorway while she held on to a strap with her right hand as the noisy helicopter rose into the sky. As it did, she used her other hand to push Majella's intestines back in to her young tender body.

According to Alice, Majella lay on her back struggling to breathe. A British solider put his arm on Majella's throat in what appeared to be a deliberate attempt to obstruct her breathing. Alice couldn't believe her eyes. She had to thump the soldier, tell him to 'stop' and pull Majella's legs in, which he did. She added that a fellow soldier, who appeared to have some sort of a conscience replied, 'this will only take five minutes. We have a doctor standing by'.

Alice had witnessed the injured in the aftermath of the Miami Showband massacre and nursed musician Stephen Travers back to good health. She lived through the torment of seeing Brian and John Martin's bodies coming in to Daisy Hill; she comforted Alan Black and Anthony as well and to add to all this heartbreak; the wedding she so longed-for, was taken away from her, and now this.

To make matters worse, she was verbally abused on the helicopter as she fought desperately to resuscitate Majella. The heartless British soldiers piled on the abuse without any sense of remorse.

'Go on you fuckin' Provo nurse. You're stuck in this again', they said repeatedly.

Brave Alice worked on the noisy intimidating British army helicopter, giving Majella the 'kiss of life' and saying the Act of Contrition into her ear just before it landed in Newry. She carried Majella into the casualty department at Daisy Hill Hospital where three doctors attended immediately.

Two of them applied stethoscopes and the third attached an oxygen line but, unfortunately, it was too late. Within seconds, one of the doctors removed his stethoscope and said, 'she's gone'.

Twelve-year-old innocent schoolgirl Majella O'Hare was dead and those responsible were the infamous Parachute Regiment of the British army.

As Alice walked out of the emergency department, she met Mary O'Hare, Majella's mother, on the way in. Mary O'Hare said to Alice, 'Tell me please, honestly, is she dead?' Alice, already in shock, didn't know what to say and left the difficult job of relaying the bad news to Fr Hughes. Once again, the Whitecross area of South Armagh was global news.

What made this killing even more difficult to accept was the way the British army issued one press statement and then changed it as the day went on in a blatant attempt to divert blame. The news bulletin on Downtown Radio at 1 p.m. that day said 'a gunman had opened fire on an army patrol in Whitecross near the border in Co. Armagh and a twelve-year-old girl has been hit'.

By 2 p.m., the British army statement read 'that a gunman

had opened fire on the army patrol and it was "believed" that the army may have returned fire'. By 3.30 p.m., the Ministry of Defence press office said, 'it was then certain that the army had returned fire but had failed to hit the gunman and added that Majella O'Hare had died in the crossfire'.[3]

Majella's killing created tension between the RUC and the British army. The RUC arrived at Ballymoyer and asked the army to hand over the weapon that was central to the shooting. The army refused to co-operate, but with their credibility declining by the hour, they eventually capitulated. With the army rapidly losing the PR battle on news coverage, the next day the Royal Ulster Constabulary issued a statement saying that 'the fatal bullets probably came from an army weapon. A Report that the army came under fire is still under investigation'.[4] This brutal killing was a major embarrassment for the British Ministry of Defence and government in London.

The post-mortem revealed that Majella had been hit by two bullets, both of them believed to have been fired by an army general-purpose automatic machine gun. The IRA issued a statement shortly afterwards insisting that none of their units or members were responsible for Majella's death. The British army insisted for some time afterwards that there was a 'phantom gunman' in the area but nobody in the area believed them.[5]

Majella's dreadful killing shocked even the hardest of hard men and women around the world. Loving parents of schoolchildren in Britain, Ireland and beyond were disgusted. Close on 3,000 people attended Majella's funeral at Ballymoyer church.

Just like the burials of Brian, John Martin and Anthony, mourners came from all over the country. Majella's coffin was carried by members of her family and friends in relays. They included pupils from St Paul's School in Bessbrook where she attended, Whitecross Youth Club and St Killian's GAA Club where her brother Michael had been a prominent player and member in the 1960s and 1970s.

The pain on the faces of Jim and Mary O'Hare and their

children Marie, Michael, Anne and Margarita at the funeral was plain for all to see. The British army was conspicuous by its absence that day. They were obviously aware that if they put the O'Hare family through the same intimidation as we experienced, locals, already fuming with rage, would have moved hell and high water to drive them out of the place.

There was outrage in the locality towards 'The Brits' after Majella's killing. As far as everyone in South Armagh was concerned, it was blatant murder. The question now was, would anybody be held accountable? Parents were afraid to send their children to school. If the British army could shoot dead an innocent young schoolgirl, who was going to be next? The atmosphere and sense of fear around the place was as toxic and dangerous as it could get.

In 1977, Pte Michael Williams was acquitted for the manslaughter of Majella O'Hare by the clearly biased Justice Maurice Gibson who, ten years later, was murdered by the IRA. In 2011, the British government apologised for the killing of Majella effectively admitting their army and Justice Gibson got it wrong.

Two days after the horrific slaying of Majella, a car bomb exploded in Keady, Co. Armagh. If ever there was an example of collusion between the British security services and the UVF, this incident captured it all.

Building an Empire

WE HOPED AND PRAYED that Majella O'Hare's killing was the last of the atrocities in the area, however, we were wrong again. Two days later on 16 August, the day Majella was buried, a bomb blast took place that night in Keady which is about ten miles from Whitecross. Thirty-two-year-old mother of three Betty McDonald, who, with her husband Malachi, ran the 'Step Inn' Bar, was killed when a no-warning car bomb exploded outside the premises. The explosion also claimed the life of twenty-two-year-old plumber Gerard McGleenan who lived across from the bar in St Patrick Street when he caught the full force of the blast as he stood outside his home. Twenty-two people were injured in the explosion after a Ford Consul vehicle had been hi-jacked on the loyalist Shankill Road in Belfast a week earlier.

After atrocities like Dublin-Monaghan, Kay's Tavern in Dundalk, the Silverbridge murders, the Miami Showband massacre and the Reavey-O'Dowd killings, there was growing talk locally that something strange was going on as the UVF was able to carry out these horrific attacks with remarkable ease, accuracy and efficiency yet nobody was being arrested, prosecuted or convicted. Surely, they could not have the protection of the RUC or the security services? After all, we were living in that part of Ireland that is in the United Kingdom, a self-promoted beacon of democracy, so quick to condemn human rights violations in other parts of the world, it wouldn't engage in deliberate murder of its own citizens?

AROUND THIS TIME, I purchased a second-hand Commer van for our new enterprise at a local auction. Seamie Quinn, a fitter from Tyrone who lived locally in Whitecross, made the van roadworthy and we were on our way. Oliver, my brother, fitted out the rear of the van to hold tools and implements and by the opening week of September, we started our first maintenance contract at Newtowncloghoge on the southern side of Newry. Even though I was in charge of the new company, I was still putting in a 9–5 day with Bell's Eggs in Crossgar. This meant that when I arrived home in the evening, I would attend to my cattle and if that wasn't enough for one day, I would then have to lock myself away in my newly designated 'office' and study the detailed process of cumbersome tender applications and the crucial importance of every comma, dot and sentence in a complex contract.

We put a sign on the side of the van with the words, 'Reavey Brothers (Contractors) Ltd.' It seemed logical at the time but it turned out to be a foolish move. The very display of our family name on a van was like a magnet for abuse from the British security services. Every time we pulled up at a British army checkpoint whether in Co. Armagh or elsewhere, they could see us coming in advance and as usual, we were subjected to the habitual threats, abuse, intimidation and guns pointed in our faces.

ON 28 OCTOBER, THE Ulster Defence Association of which the ruthless Ulster Freedom Fighters were also members of, struck again when one of their senior officers took sectarian killings to a new level. Mrs Máire Drumm, aged fifty-seven, was a mother of five children. A native of Killeen on the Louth-Armagh border, she was a former vice-president of Sinn Féin before stepping down due to ill health and had served four terms in prison for republican activity on both sides of the border. Máire caused quite a lot of controversy earlier in the year when commenting on the death of IRA hunger striker Frank Stagg at Wakefield Prison Yorkshire in February 1976, she said:

> If they send Frank Stagg home in a coffin, I would suggest the fighting men of Crossmaglen would send the SAS home in boxes.

Needless to say, her comments were pounced upon by unionists, loyalists, British MPs and the Tory press in London. She had set herself up to be a target.

Máire Drumm was a patient in the Mater Hospital on the Crumlin Road in Belfast. On 28 October, she was awaiting a cataract operation when a number of men wearing white coats and pretending to be hospital staff, walked into her ward and shot her dead. Among those charged with the killing was Jimmy Craig, a senior and notorious member of the Ulster Defence Association. Jimmy told me some time later that the charges against him were dropped. Sam Mathers, who was a security officer at the hospital was the only person convicted for the killing.[1] Jimmy Craig was to become a big thorn in my side later.

Cover-up Starts to Emerge

The long-awaited inquest in to the deaths of our Brian, John Martin and Anthony were scheduled to open on Friday 28 January 1977 in Armagh Court. Inquests are an official record as to the actual cause of a sudden death.

Where a murder or manslaughter is believed to be the cause, then that is a matter of criminal investigation by the police. As we headed to the court, we actually didn't know what an inquest was. We had never attended one before and assumed, wrongly, that we were heading to a lesser form of court case.

Our family solicitor at the time was Brendan McNamee who was based at Lower Catherine Street, Newry. Brendan, who passed away in the mid-1980s, took on the services of barrister Éilis McDermott, Northern Ireland's first female QC and now a leading King's Counsel on the NI legal circuit. Brendan had spotted her obvious talent at a younger age.

When we arrived at the courthouse in Armagh City, all twenty of us were surprised at what we perceived to be an over-the-top and intimidating security presence. We assumed it was for the expected arrival of someone more high profile than us. We were wrong. The RUC and British army were there in full regalia to give us a 'VIP welcome'. As we walked up the steps, members of the security forces engaged in provocative and hostile behaviour. One RUC officer made an attempt to strike me with the butt of his rifle and muttered, 'Go on yiz murdering bastards'.

There we were on our way in to the court thinking we were going to get some answers and a RUC policeman was doing all he could to provoke a fight.

The inquest got underway at 3.45 p.m. which we thought was a rather late commencement time for a triple murder. It should be pointed out that then there was no internet, reporters didn't have mobile phones, some didn't have cars and relied on buses to get out of Belfast at a time when public transport timetables were disrupted on a daily basis. Because this hearing was taking place so late on a Friday afternoon, we later took the view that this was a deliberate tactic to minimise press coverage and ensure it got as little publicity as possible.

As it commenced, all I could hear was mumbling voices in the distance. Our parents couldn't hear a word, in fact the acoustics in the place were so bad, they might as well have stayed at home.

I moved up to the front, sat in beside our solicitor and re-lived the horror of what happened on 4 January the previous year as various RUC officers recalled how they were notified of the killings and what they witnessed when they visited the scene of the shootings. The inquest was suspicious for the non-attendance of the surgeon who operated on Anthony in Daisy Hill Hospital, namely, James Blundell.

Surgeon Blundell also treated Anthony during his return visit on Sunday 26 January 1976. Our solicitor had written to Coroner Noel R. Anderson on several occasions requesting Blundell to attend the inquest. From correspondence I have in my possession, on 10 January 1977, Surgeon Blundell wrote to the coroner saying the 3.45 p.m. commencement time was inconvenient. He asked if the start time could be brought forward to either 2 p.m. or 2.30 as he had an appointment later that day in the Royal Victoria Hospital, Belfast.

We don't know what the coroner wrote in response but we later learned from legal correspondence that on 24 January, Blundell wrote to Anderson again and told him he could *not* attend the inquest as he was going to the Middle East. The letter, which I have in my files, was received by the coroner on the morning of 28 January, the day of the inquest.

The reply was strange as Blundell had indicated in earlier correspondence that he was willing to attend on Friday 28 January if the commencement time was brought forward to 2 p.m. By cancelling at the last minute, it was too late for the coroner to terminate the hearing as legal teams on both sides had committed to attending.

The state pathologist, Thomas K. Marshall, professor of forensic medicine at Queens University in Belfast told the court in his autopsy that the injuries to Brian and John Martin 'were caused by bullets of low or medium velocity'.

In my opinion, this was a blatant lie.

He added, 'there was nothing to indicate that any of them had been fired at close range'.

When we heard that particular line, we couldn't believe our ears. Remember, the shootings occurred at close proximity in the house not in some big open field. We all quickly concluded that something was amiss here.

There was worse to come. The pathologist told the court that when it came to the 'Cause of death' for Anthony Reavey aged seventeen years:

> 'Death was from natural causes. It was due to a massive haemorrhage into the left side of the brain arising from a small leash [bundle] of abnormal blood vessels called a haemangioma.
> 'This was a congenital abnormality and the bursting of one of the blood vessels which precipitated the haemorrhage was a spontaneous event.
> 'No other disease was found.
> 'He bore scars on the lower limbs as a result of the bullet wounds he had sustained about three weeks before his fatal illness.
> 'This episode of wounding played no part in his death.'

When this unconvincing cause of death was read into the court record, we smelled the proverbial rat straight away.

Éilis McDermott, QC, knew that what she heard was suspicious and took to her feet immediately. She told the Coroner Noel R. Anderson in no uncertain terms that she did not agree with the pathologist's findings. She made it quite clear in a very forceful and firm manner that she wanted the causes of death in all *three* killings to be recorded as 'open verdict'. 'Open verdict' would mean affirming the occurrence of a suspicious death but not specifying the actual cause.

A confirmation of 'natural causes' would also mean we could not make a compensation claim against the British state. Com-

Cover-up Starts to Emerge

pensation of course, no matter how much, could not replace the loss of our three brothers.

However, as a point of principle, denying us an 'open verdict' in Anthony's case, was simply closing down another avenue for us to seek justice as we had suspicions all along about the circumstances surrounding his death. It would also mean the controversial and mysterious circumstances of the killings would not have to be re-lived in some other legal forum!

As far as we were concerned, the Brits were trying to cover up something about the death of Anthony. It shouldn't be overlooked that Anthony was the only survivor of the atrocity. Maybe in their eyes, he saw things and could later reveal names and faces – if he survived. Éilis verbally lashed Coroner Anderson and made her objections and concerns known in clear and robust language. Coroner Noel Anderson, in response, insisted that based on the Pathologist's Report, the injuries Anthony received on 4 January 1976 when he was shot at close range had no bearing on his death. There was an audible gasp of disbelief in the court.

We went into the Coroner's Court expecting fairness, honesty and independence from the British legal system. We left feeling as if the British had kicked us again. They were up to their dirty tricks and their sinister sleazy way of conducting affairs made us all the more determined to question what was going on.

That wasn't the end of the matter. The official inquest documents handed to our solicitor Brendan McNamee contained details on Brian and John Martin that didn't make sense. According to the section on the page marked 'Date, time and place of death', the official record shows that Brian and John Martin died on 4 January 1976 at approximately 7.30 p.m. in Daisy Hill Hospital [Newry]. Of course this is incorrect as Brian and John Martin died at 6.10 p.m. on the same date in their home at Greyhilla, Whitecross, Co. Armagh.

When we eventually got back to Whitecross, it was like a funeral wake all over again. The word had leaked out about the inquest. The neighbours were as shocked as we were and began calling to the house to sympathise. We had no answers for them and our parents eventually found the influx of people too much to deal with.

Roll on forty-four years and as conscientious twitter users remembered the anniversary of the Reavey killings on 4 January 2020, a reply to a tweet from Suzanne Breen of the *Belfast Telegraph* who recalled the anniversary, caught me by surprise but strengthened my suspicions.

The tweet came from a Dr Allister Taggart, now in South Africa, who worked as a medic at the Royal Victoria Hospital in Belfast in the 1970s. In his reply to Suzanne, he left the reader in no doubt that he was not convinced with the findings of the inquest.

He said, 'Anthony Reavey came under my care in the neuro-surgical unit in the RVH with a brain haemorrhage just a month after the attack ... Tragically, he never recovered. No one will ever know if the two [the shooting and the brain haemorrhage] were connected. RIP.'

Dr Taggart would have seen hundreds of victims caught up in The Troubles come through the doors of the RVH in his time but, Anthony's death stood out and remained in his memory after forty-four long years. The fact that he still had doubts about the exact nature of his death confirmed to us that the finding of death by so-called 'Natural causes' on Anthony's inquest report endorsed our belief that the British engaged in a blatant cover-up.

Shortly after the time of the inquest, Catholic Sergeant Joe Campbell of the RUC was maintaining law, order and peace in the picturesque nationalist village of Cushendall, a mainly Catholic community where Irish culture was alive and well on the Co. Antrim coast. When he discovered that some of his colleagues were assisting the UVF to import weapons at nearby Red Bay Pier and brought it to the attention of his RUC superiors, his fate was sealed. Joe was shot dead at the gates of Cushendall RUC station on the night of 25 February 1977 and his killing shocked everyone in the locality who viewed him as being a friendly and flexible policeman. His death put

Cover-up Starts to Emerge

a focus on the dangerous relationship between certain senior members of the RUC and loyalist paramilitaries, even though such affiliations were always strenuously denied.

Elsewhere in the month of April 1977, what appeared to be 'just' another killing took place in a small Co. Antrim village. An horrific event for the suffering family, it disappeared off the news radar within hours as it was overtaken by events of higher profile. This particular murder later proved to be a pivotal moment for those that suffered in the Dublin-Monaghan bombings, Miami Showband massacre, Reavey-O'Dowd killings and a significant number of other mysterious murders in the mid-Ulster area during the 1970s.

On the night of 19 April, William Strathearn (39) a married Catholic with seven children who lived over a chemist shop in the small village of Ahoghill in Co. Antrim, answered a call to his house. A former GAA inter-county footballer with Derry, he opened the upstairs window to see two men down below at the front door. One of them shouted up that his daughter was ill and needed medication indicating that this was some sort of emergency. William Strathearn went down to the door to let the two men in and was gunned down before he could say hello. He was shot twice. His killing was reported on the news and was treated as yet another regrettable sectarian murder. Nobody claimed responsibility and no arrests were made at that time. As later events would reveal, his death proved highly significant and revealing.

Elsewhere, with each passing day, I began to notice that a certain British army officer was spending more and more time in the locality. I subsequently learned his name was Captain Robert Nairac. A number of times when I was stopped at British army checkpoints, it was he who dealt with me. He stood out head and shoulders from the rest of his regiment and clearly knew the local lie of the land and all who lived in the area. His uniform was different, he spoke with a contrived Northern Ireland accent and occasionally let his English twang slip. To my own surprise, he seemed to know more about the

Reaveys than I knew myself. He knew all about my cousins and wider family with remarkable detail.

I'd roll down the car window and he'd say things like, 'Ahh Eugene, good man, how are things? How is Róisín and the family doing? I see you're busy with the construction business. Whitecross football team had a good win at the weekend! How is 'Johnny' [so and so] doing these days?'

Immediately, my back was up. I couldn't figure this guy out. His behaviour was inconsistent with that of his colleagues at other checkpoints. I didn't know his name at the time and was somewhat surprised at his exceptional local knowledge but as time moved on, he became something of a household name for all the wrong reasons.

His nature of engagement was such that he applied what's known in interrogation as reverse psychology. He would attempt to persuade you he was 100 per cent Irish, a republican from west Belfast, Catholic, spoke the Irish language, knew the history of Ireland and was sympathetic to the IRA. He would ask you questions like 'how soon do you think it will be before there's a united Ireland?' Ensuring his colleagues didn't hear his words, he would almost whisper to you words like 'the quicker the British leave Ireland the better, I hate the way they treat the Irish'.

On one occasion, he tried what can only be described as an old British army trick. He was chatting away in an over-familiar tone. In the middle of this 'friendly' conversation, he pretended to search his pockets looking for a folded map when he said, in a most uncharacteristic manner for a British soldier, 'Here, will you hold this rifle for me?'

I twigged straight away what he was up to and I promptly said 'no'. He wanted me to hold his gun so that I could leave my fingerprints firmly lodged on its metal casing. If I held the gun, the British could shoot me there and then and claim afterwards that they shot me because I made a grab for the rifle.

This, of course, was symptomatic of the dirty tricks the British got up to every other day. They did it all the time with scores of unfortunate innocent men and women ending up in jail. All this for simply identifying themselves as being Irish. It was a classic divide and conquer tactic by the British.

I can reveal here that Nairac stayed in the homes of certain South Armagh republicans. Of course this wasn't known at the time but it does say something of his daring persuasive charm in that he convinced a small number of hardline republicans to believe that he wanted the British out of Northern Ireland when in fact he had successfully infiltrated the RUC, UDR, loyalist organisations, IRA and the INLA, an impressive achievement.

It should be pointed out that Nairac was fulfilling the very brief that he had been trained to do namely, to recruit informers, gather as much information as possible from the enemy while simultaneously creating as much hostility as possible between the Catholic and Protestant communities. He also applied the same tactics with groupings on the loyalist side.

We learned many years later that Nairac was implicated in several high-profile killings. His many additional roles included planned attacks, ensuring that RUC personnel were not present in the locality when these attacks occurred and setting up military hits in such a way as to convince the public that the atrocities were the work of paramilitaries only. By giving the impression that the UVF had taken ownership of these attacks, it would send out a message that that IRA had serious opposition and that the British security forces were 'innocent' bystanders stuck in the middle who, as far as the wider public were concerned, were only trying to 'keep the peace'.

These operations were structured to deliberately provoke one side against the other but all were designed to ensure that British military personnel were viewed as having no involvement whatsoever.

We now know that this strategy was applied in the Reavey-O'Dowd killings and the Dublin-Monaghan bombings, etc., but it all went horribly wrong for them at the Miami Showband massacre in July 1975 when the nature of their evil operations was exposed. The British were prepared to break every law in the rule book to achieve victory over nationalists and republicans.

Robert Nairac who, by now, was a well-established treble agent, continued to be a menace in South Armagh. However despite Nairac's strong belief that he was invincible and could talk his way out of any dangerous situation in South Armagh, it all came to an end on the night of Saturday 14 May 1977.

Nairac had left Bessbrook army base around 9.30 p.m. in his red Triumph – not your typical Irish republican car – and headed for the Three Steps pub, about nine miles away, a rural hostelry at Drumintee not far from the villages of Jonesborough and Forkhill in South Armagh. His car contained radio transmission equipment to allow him communicate with Bessbrook barracks.

As it was Saturday night, there was a good lively crowd, circa 100, in the pub and the John Murphy Céili Band, which had members from nearby Silverbridge, Crossmaglen and Forkhill catchment area, drew a large gathering as they played a mix of popular Irish ballads and traditional céili tunes.

While in the pub, Nairac, who was conspicuous as he wasn't a local, did his usual trick of attempting to circulate with the pub's regular customers and eventually went up on stage to join the house band by singing two popular republican ballads about the early 1920s IRA called *The Boys of the old Brigade* and *The Broad Black Brimmer*. His methods were clearly designed to try to convince the locals that he was one of them. It seems his audacious attempt to 'fit in' and entertain the locals turned out to be a step too far. As he took the microphone into his hand to commemorate the Old IRA in song, Nairac, with long hair, wearing a donkey jacket and denim jeans, launched into the opening words:

> Oh father why, are you so sad
> On this bright Easter morn'?
> When Irish men are proud and glad
> Of the land where they were born.
> Oh, son, I see in mem'ries few
> Of far off distant days
> When being just a lad like you
> I joined the IRA ...

Cover-up Starts to Emerge

Nairac's movements in the pub that night and his frequent visits to the toilet are believed to have aroused suspicion. When he eventually left the pub to make his way to the car, it's understood he spoke to a local man who had been in the pub that night. It's believed a verbal dispute and scuffle developed. The heated exchanges were not helped by the earlier consumption of alcohol.

A number of local republican sympathisers, not believed to be in the IRA, came on the scene. Quickly realising that Nairac was engaging in a heated dispute with local man Terry McCormick – who happened to be a former champion boxer – they apprehended him before asking who he was and where he was from, etc.

Despite Nairac responding saying he was 'Danny McErlean', a 'mechanic' from west Belfast, a subsequent beating and rough search of his body resulted in a British army browning pistol falling out of his shoulder holster and on to the ground. His fate was sealed.

Nairac was bundled into the boot of a car and taken to a field at nearby Flurrybridge Ravensdale, Co. Louth. He was questioned further about his identity, origins, etc., and despite refusing to blow his cover, he was shot dead by a member of the IRA who was called to the scene.

The subsequent trial for his killing made legal history as it was the first time suspects were tried in Northern Ireland for a crime that happened in the Republic of Ireland. The trial was all the more remarkable, as legal process goes, because no body was found and therefore proof as to the actual cause of death could not be proven beyond reasonable doubt.

Why is all the above relevant? Nairac was central to the execution and planning of the Dublin-Monaghan bombings, the Miami Showband massacre, the deaths of John Francis Green, Peter Cleary as well as the Reavey-O'Dowd killings. His role in these murders and the skulduggery he got up to in framing people for crimes they did not commit was nothing short of inhuman and vicious.

Robert Nairac was honoured by the British state with a

posthumous George Cross medal, the second highest award that can be bestowed on UK citizens. It is given for 'acts of the greatest heroism or of the most conspicuous courage in circumstances of extreme danger'. One man who worked closely with Robert Nairac and knew all about his doubled-edged activities in South Armagh was Julian 'Tony' Ball of the SAS. He died in suspicious and mysterious circumstances in a car crash in the middle east state of Oman in 1981. There were no other vehicles involved or witnesses. The SAS took full and suspicious control of his funeral. It seems Tony Ball knew too much and had passed his sell-by date.

The Slaughter Continues

By January 1978, we were two years on from the deaths of Brian, John Martin and Anthony. No suspects had been charged, prosecuted or convicted. There wasn't one single shred of information coming our way on who might have been involved in the Reavey and O'Dowd murders.

There wasn't even the occasional courtesy call from the RUC just to say 'How are things? 'We're still on the case and we haven't forgotten you.' Quite clearly, they had. We found this very disrespectful but by this stage we were well and truly suspicious of the sinister forces around us.

Surely, we thought, the slick professional nature of the murders suggested that those responsible must have been local? These killers were able to get into the area, carry out their attacks and get away using 'safe' local roads like invisible ghosts in the night.

Tragedy struck again in the locality on 24 June when sixty-four-year-old Joe Porter, a UDR private and farmer who lived locally on Creggan Road, Mountnorris, was gunned down by the IRA. Joe's death caused some concern locally as fears grew that revenge would not be far away. Despite our fears, no local revenge was enacted at this time.

As 1979 moved on, tragedy struck just up the road from Camlough village. Martin Rowland (26) a single man and Catholic, was found dead at the local dump, 400 yards from his own home on 5 October. With no involvement in paramilitary or political activity, he was shot twice in the head and once in the shoulder. The UVF said they did it and the motive was driven by the fact that Martin was a Catholic. Once again like so many occasions in the past, the UVF were able to get in and get out as if there was no British army presence in the area. Nobody was ever arrested, charged, prosecuted or convicted.

On 2 January 1980, our locality was hit again. This time, sixty-

The Killing of the Reavey Brothers

two-year-old Samuel 'Cliffy' Lundy, married with one child and a former member of the UDR, was shot dead by the IRA at Drumnahuncheon Road just down the road in Kingsmills. The Lundy family were good friends of my Mother and would pop in for a cup of tea and a chat 2–3 times per week as they would head up on foot to nearby Ballymoyer to visit relatives. We were all very upset at Cliffy's killing. The Lundys were good, decent people and daughter Jennifer and her mother eventually moved away from the locality.

BETTER TO LET SLEEPING DOGS LIE

IN LATE 1980, REPUBLICAN prisoners commenced a hunger strike at the Maze in a dispute over concessions. The strike was called off when the British agreed to a deal but then reneged on its word by indicating that they were on the verge of crushing the IRA. However, determined IRA prisoners in the Maze prison had other things in mind and were determined to go all the way to embarrass the British.

As the prisoners decided on their next move, tensions moved up a notch when the Provos killed former unionist MP Sir Norman Stronge and his son James on 21 January 1981 and burned their mansion to the ground. Aged eighty-six, Stronge represented 'Big House' unionism and lived in Tynan Abbey with its 800 acres near Caledon, Co. Tyrone close to the Armagh-Monaghan border. At one stage, the land at Tynan Abbey was up to 8,000 acres. A former speaker in the old Stormont parliament, Sir Norman Stronge had been an MP from 1938 to 1969; was a member of the Derryshaw Boyne Defenders Orange Lodge and area president of the British Royal Legion. He was seen as being an ally of Basil Brooke, the former prime minister of Northern Ireland from 1943 to 1963, the pompous man most observers say sowed the seeds of the Troubles. He maintained and even encouraged the centuries-old bitter divisive culture of discrimination against all Catholics in Northern Ireland.

According to the book *The Life of Sir Basil Brooke* he said in an infamous Orange Order speech at Newtownbutler, Co. Fermanagh in 1933 that while many of his Protestant and Orange counterparts employed Roman Catholics, he himself 'would not have one about the place'.[1] Brooke went on to say, 'I would appeal to Loyalists, therefore, wherever possible, to employ good Protestant lads and lassies ... I recommend those people who are Loyalists not to employ Catholics, ninety per cent of whom are disloyal.'

The following day the prime minister of Northern Ireland, James Craig, referring to Basil Brooke's comments, told the Stormont parliament, 'there is not one of my colleagues who does not entirely disagree with him and I would not ask him to withdraw one word.'

I have always taken the view that Stronge, Brooke and the large land-owning unionist elite not only trampled all over Catholics, but also treated working-class Protestants in an appalling manner. Had they been fair to all sides, the Troubles might not have erupted at all.

According to *Lost Lives*, the IRA said the Stronges had been chosen as 'symbols of hated unionism', meaning they represented all that was unjust about British rule in Ireland in so much as their ancestors came here, stole all the land from the Catholics, enforced the penal laws, put the locals out in the ditches to fend for themselves and lived like oppressive kings at the expense of the poor Irish. The ease at which the IRA were able to get access to Sir Norman Stronge and his son James to end their lives, frightened a lot of land-owning unionists who all felt they could be next.

As of February 1981, the feeling amongst the IRA prisoners was that those planning to go on hunger strike would have to do so on a phased basis so that the pressure on the British would be applied increasingly and consistently over a lengthy period of time rather than reaching a short intensive peak. The most important thing, as they saw it, was that anybody who volunteered and didn't have a medical condition, would starve to the death unless that is, the British compromised in the meantime. It was 'do or die' in every sense of the phrase.

Nobody was forced to go on hunger strike – volunteers formed an orderly queue and a carefully constructed plan was put in place. The first to refuse food was Bobby Sands. Aged just twenty-seven, he commenced his hunger strike on 1 March 1981. Twenty-two more volunteers followed, averaging three per month. Among those who volunteered to go on hunger strike was Róisín's brother, Paddy Quinn, from the nearby village of Belleeks South Armagh, so the outcome of the hunger strikes was as critical to us as it was to the families of all those involved. For the first time in four years, Paddy was allowed to accept visits from his mother. Such requests during the blanket protest were rejected as prisoners couldn't leave their cells without wearing prison uniforms.

Raymond McCreesh was the third volunteer to join the strike on 22 March after Bobby Sands and Francis Hughes. Aged twenty-four, Raymond was a friendly young man and I knew the McCreesh clan well. A fourth volunteer joined on the same day when Patsy O'Hara of the Irish National Liberation Army (INLA) took his place in the hunger strike. As the weeks passed, the hunger strikes gained more publicity as hundreds took to the streets to voice their protest against the prison conditions. The tension in South Armagh began to grow as the nationalist community expressed opinions that left nobody in any doubt that the lives of two of their own locals were on the line.

Even families who had no interest in the republican cause felt that the British were playing with the lives of two South Armagh men over issues that were key points of principle to republican prisoners. From the IRA perspective, the volunteers were in prison as a result of political oppression. As far as the British were concerned, the IRA were just thugs involved in everyday crime and murder. In Republican areas, this difference of opinion was highly significant. For the McCreesh family, Raymond was a freedom fighter trying to end British rule – he was not a criminal. Victims of brutal IRA actions of course, took the opposite view.

The weeks rolled on and more people, including female prisoners in Armagh Gaol, joined the strike. As Róisín's brother was a prisoner, a series of meetings between the families of prisoners and the Republican leadership outside took place at a number of centres in west Belfast. On occasions, Gerry Adams and/or Martin McGuinness would attend and update us on the condition of the strikers. They also updated us on what the

British officials were saying in terms of meeting the demands for political status.

Motherly emotions don't always tally with political objectives. Paddy Quinn's mother, Katie, could live with the fact that her eldest son was in jail fighting for a united Ireland, but was not prepared to let him die. It seemed to me from our conversations at the time that Mrs Quinn didn't appear to be won over by what Adams and McGuinness were saying. On one occasion, Róisín had strong words with Gerry Adams: 'Why don't you go into Long Kesh and tell these prisoners to call off the hunger strikes and save us all a lot of grief?' Adams replied with words to the effect, 'It has nothing to do with me. The prisoners decided to go on strike and it's up to them to call it off.' This suggested that Gerry Adams and the republican leadership either had total or no influence on the prisoners' decision.

The plan was quite clear. The hunger strikes would generate worldwide publicity for the Provos and would see concerned governments elsewhere put pressure on the British. Increased support would also translate into more financial donations for the republican cause. It would also create a scenario whereby the British government would be seen to have let these men die unnecessarily. As well as that, hundreds of volunteers would sign up for the cause, a bunch of new martyrs would emerge and the extra pressure on London might force officials in Whitehall to compromise and all of the above would be a strategic victory for the IRA – that was the perception. On the other hand, if the hunger strikes were called off, the republicans would be seen to have caved in twice in six months leading to a major PR victory for the British, a falling off in IRA recruitment and the slow death of the provisional movement.

Enter Fr Denis Faul. Originally from mid Co. Louth, he was a teacher at St Patrick's school in Dungannon, Co. Tyrone. By 1981, he had emerged as a vocal critic of violence on all sides but had a profile high enough to be listened to seriously by opponents in the green and orange communities. A regular visitor to the prison where he frequently said mass, he had built up a relationship with a number of republican prisoners. He regularly appeared on radio and television critical of the inhumane way the British treated prisoners. Having seen so much discrimination in Northern Ireland during the 1950s and 1960s, he never stopped calling on the British and unionist authorities to treat Catholics fairly in areas like housing, education, employment and human rights.

Fr Faul was highly critical of the hunger strikes. For him, any loss of life whether through 'terrorism', murder, self-infliction or by accident, had to be avoided at all costs. When Paddy Quinn was incarcerated in 1976, Fr Faul became a regular visitor to Katie's house. IRA prisoners who were on the blanket protest had been refused family visits unless they wore prison uniforms, which meant Katie hadn't seen Paddy in over four years. As Fr Faul was a regular visitor to the prison, he could update her on the state of play inside the Maze.

An unforeseen development on 5 March led to an unanticipated domino effect that ultimately changed the profile of the hunger strikes, altered the course of Irish history and sowed the seeds to ending the conflict. Frank Maguire, a native of Gort, Co. Galway, had been an independent republican MP for the constituency of Fermanagh/South Tyrone since 1974. At the age of fifty-one, he died unexpectedly of a heart attack. Realising the massive publicity and political opening the subsequent by-election presented, republicans, to the complete surprise of the political establishment in London, Dublin and Belfast, decided to put the name of hunger-striker prisoner Bobby Sands on the ballot paper in the hope of winning Frank Maguire's seat.

This was seen as a daring development at the time as the republican movement was then, and is to this day, totally opposed to sitting in the British parliament in London and therefore one might ask, what was the point? With potential PR embarrassment coming for the British, Prime Minister Margaret Thatcher and her officials were faced with a delicate dilemma. They could go against their principles, cut a deal on special category status for prisoners and the problem would be solved, a move that would see her face a massive potential backlash from unionists, Conservatives and right-wing newspapers in London.

Should Sands get elected and die, Mrs Thatcher would be seen to let an elected parliamentary 'colleague' die and that would create negative PR. It would enrage republicans, with potentially horrific consequences. On the other hand, if Sands was elected as an anti-H-Block MP, he would also deny the seat to the hotly tipped Official Unionist candidate and former leader of the party, Harry West. (The Official Unionist Party had been a sister party of the Conservatives since 1909.)

As things stood, the ruling Tories had a serious image problem looming. With public sympathy for Sands and the hunger strikers growing in republican areas, the intransigence by the British only helped to swell support for the anti-H-Block candidate. British failure to bring IRA paramilitary activity to an end was further stretching the already strained relationship between the Conservative government, official unionists and Ian Paisley's Democratic Unionist Party. The British secretary of state for Northern Ireland, Humphrey Atkins and Mrs Thatcher were getting it in the neck from all sides.

My memory of the time is that republicans and nationalists from all over Ireland flocked to Fermanagh/South Tyrone in the weeks leading up to the by-election to canvass people who could vote. This was the first democratic test of significance for the republican movement since the British formally partitioned Ireland on 3 May 1921. If Bobby Sands could beat Harry West in his own back garden, it could set a template for the future.

As the weeks rolled on, more and more of the London-based media outlets, including worldwide TV networks, were visiting Fermanagh/South Tyrone and asking what happens if Bobby Sands wins the seat? Would the British prime minister let an election candidate die in a dispute over prison status? The British dug their heels in and wouldn't budge. Margaret Thatcher refused to accept that the republican cause was political, saying on television that 'crime is crime, is crime'.

The more belligerent she became, the more determined the republicans were to win a moral and PR victory over her. Republicans and nationalists on the ground in Fermanagh/South Tyrone worked morning, noon and night canvassing every house in the constituency – the contest was clearly one of green versus orange. The election was just as important as the hunger strike itself as there were huge symbolic principles and risks at stake.

Danny Morrison, the former director of publicity with Sinn Féin, summed up the dilemma that determined republicans faced. He told the Trevor Birney-produced *66 Days* TV documentary made in 2016 that if Bobby Sands lost the election by just one single vote, Margaret Thatcher and the Tory media could gleefully tell the world that republicans were not capable of winning the seat for their man. That would be the cast-iron proof that there was no public support for the hunger strikes, the prisoners' demands and the existence of the IRA. This by-election had become a political version of Russian roulette. Whoever lost would be severely damaged. The pressure continued to mount on Margaret Thatcher but to quote her own words, 'The Lady was not for turning', at that stage anyway.

When the votes were cast on 9 April, Bobby Sands election caused a political earthquake. The anti-H-Block candidate won the seat and was elected to her majesty's parliament He secured 30,493 votes. Close behind was hotly tipped Harry West of the Official Unionist Party on 29,046 votes. The story was global news. Unionists and members of the Conservative Party in Britain were furious as the IRA had done the unthinkable and won this hugely symbolic battle. Global media interest was again firmly fixed on Northern Ireland. The big fear that emerged in the hours following the election of Bobby Sands was that if he died in prison due to a lack of flexibility from the British, a civil war could break out in the six counties. The atmosphere across Ireland was toxic.

In South Armagh, particularly around Camlough where Raymond McCreesh grew up, the number of British army and RUC checkpoints seemed to increase with each passing day.

At nearby Bessbrook heliport, helicopters were landing every 2–3 minutes. The noise alone created by these machines added to the tension around the place. Everybody was afraid of what might happen next. Even at night when I went to lock the gate, I was nervous that a bullet might hit me from somewhere.

The clock was ticking. Bobby Sands moved closer to death and with his sight failing and his body unable to take water, it was only a matter of time before the newly elected member of parliament for Fermanagh/South Tyrone died. Religious leaders including then papal envoy Monsignor John Magee, a native of Jerretspass outside Newry, visited the prison and spoke to Sands in his final days. He did all he could to get him to call off the strike. Despite presenting Sands with a crucifix sent from Pope John Paul II, his calls fell on deaf ears.

As THE WORLD WATCHED on and the hunger strikers drifted towards their demise, we had a crisis of our own to handle. On Easter Sunday 19 April, our Father, Jimmy, died at 5 a.m. in Daisy Hill Hospital Newry. At the relatively young age of fifty-seven, he had suffered fourteen heart-related attacks since 1976. The fact that he lived as long as he did was thanks to the superb medical assistance and nursing care he received in Daisy Hill. It's very hard to explain to people outside South Armagh but the constant harassment, intimidation and threats from the British army day in, day out while the wider security forces were allowed to kill and abuse, almost unchallenged, caused our Father endless sleepless nights, high blood pressure and ultimately, his death. To lose a young father was horrible.

Some days before he passed away, we visited him in hospital to keep him company and after a long chat, the time came for us to leave. As family members left the ward close to midnight to head home, our Father called me back for a private word. Laying on the bed and very weak, he asked me in a low tone of voice, 'Eugene, do you know who shot our boys?'

'No, not really. I've heard a few rumours but I don't know.'

'I want you to keep this a secret. I'm going to tell you who they were ... Alec Robb, a publican from Markethill, called to our house in the days after the killings. He told me that he overheard a conversation in his bar on the day after the shootings. During the chat amongst the lads, he learned who carried out the killings and heard them say that a large number of people were involved and that five UVF men did the murders. He gave me their names.' My Father told me who the murderers were and then said, 'I don't want you to pass on these names to the IRA. The last thing I want is retaliation.'

I was stunned that our Father knew who was responsible and told nobody. Now that I look back, it says something of his calm and mature character that he kept the names to himself because he could see the bigger picture – if he revealed the names, the IRA, perhaps, might seek revenge. It was a shocking burden he put on me but I fully understood where he was coming from. I'm glad now that I didn't know for the previous five years because we were all in such a state of shock and with the continuing intimidation by the security forces, I might have said something to somebody I would later regret.

Based on past experience, we felt going to the RUC to report the names would have been a dangerous exercise as sectarian officers would have informed the suspects. I was in mental agony wondering repeatedly what I should do with this crucial information. After much emotional torture, I believed it was 'better to let sleeping dogs lie'.

Our Father's funeral on Wednesday 22 April in Ballymoyer church and cemetery was massive. All the local councillors, my Father's old GAA pals and officials as well as the SDLP deputy leader Seamus Mallon, amongst others, attended. Our Mother had lost her life-time partner – her rock.

WHILE WE GRIEVED FOR our Dad in South Armagh, frantic talks were going on in the prison with many important people of note in and out of the place trying desperately to bring the hunger strikes to a halt. Across the Atlantic Ocean, the ongoing coverage was producing a momentum that was creating serious PR damage for the British. On 29 April, the highly influential *New York Times* put the metaphorical boot into Margaret Thatcher. A story titled 'Britain's Gift to Bobby Sands' on page 26 read:

> On the question of principle, Britain's prime minister Thatcher is right in refusing to yield political status to Bobby Sands, the Irish Republican Army hunger striker. But this dying young man has made it appear that her stubbornness, rather than his own, is the source of a fearful conflict already ravaging Northern Ireland.
>
> For that, Mrs Thatcher is partly to blame. By appearing unfeeling and unresponsive, she and her Government are providing Bobby Sands with a death-bed gift, the crown of martyrdom.

At 1.17 a.m. on 5 May 1981 after sixty-six days of starvation, Bobby Sands died. His death was the lead story on news bulletins all over the world. The *Nightline* programme on the *ABC* TV network fronted by Ted Koppel from its HQ in New York, broke into its evening programme to announce his death, a reflection on how big this story was.

Not surprisingly, angry residents in nationalist areas came out in large numbers. They lit fires, overturned cars, banged dustbin lids, set up barricades, rioted, threw petrol bombs at the RUC and vented their fury at British soldiers. Clusters of women gathered on street corners and recited what seemed like endless decades of the rosary. The Brits couldn't work out if the huge turnout on the streets was actual support for Bobby Sands or an expression of revulsion for the way the prisoners had been treated by Mrs Thatcher's administration in the prison.

The Sands funeral on 7 May was the largest ever seen in Belfast up to that time, with close on 100,000 attending. Bobby Sands was given the customary send-off with IRA men in combat uniform wearing balaclava helmets firing a volley of shots over the coffin. The identity of the gunmen was partially shielded by the use of black umbrellas which were held in place by the female wing of the IRA as British helicopters hovered overhead with close-up cameras. The scenes, which the London *Daily Mail* described as being a 'macabre propaganda circus' were viewed on television screens all across the world – the IRA got sympathetic publicity it couldn't buy.

Up to that week, politicians on all sides kept banging the drum that the republican movement had no support and therefore no mandate to pursue their campaign. As events later showed, the amazing outpouring of support and sympathy for the Sands family and the other hunger strikers, switched on a highly significant light within Sinn Féin thinking. Their senior personnel realised that if they could convert that support in to votes, then that would move them from being seen as isolated evil pariahs on the margins of society to sitting in the best seats at the negotiating table. Such a move would be slow, long and difficult but as things evolved, it became clear that the origins of what became known as the peace process were born in Belfast that week.

As the days rolled by, the media coverage was endless and reached a new crescendo when twenty-five-year-old Francis Hughes from Bellaghy in Co. Derry became hunger striker number two to die when he was pronounced dead on 12 May after fifty-nine days on hunger strike. The global coverage for Francis Hughes' death was as plentiful as for Bobby Sands. Each passing hour saw greater focus in South Armagh on the plight of Raymond McCreesh from nearby Camlough. He, by now, had passed the point of no return. With media and political attention on Belfast and Bellaghy in the previous seven days, the IRA turned up the heat in South Armagh. On 19 May, five British soldiers were killed when their Saracen tank was blown up on Chancellor's Road just off the Newry route to Camlough. The 1,000 pounds bomb was so powerful, it destroyed the tank which weighed a hefty ten tonnes. It was clearly planned to send a message to London.

With so much media around the place, TV crews dashed to Camlough to cover the atrocity. This meant the IRA campaign ate up most of the time on television news bulletins across the world that night. The print and broadcast media were just about to pack up their bags in Camlough when two days later, local man Raymond McCreesh, twenty-four, died after sixty-one days on hunger strike.

The fact that the media were in the locality ensured maximum coverage again. On the same day 21 May, Patsy O'Hara of the INLA became number four to die and that meant media attention also took in the Bogside in Derry City. With five British soldiers dead and Raymond McCreesh being number three to die in prison, the atmosphere in South Armagh was frightening. Emotions were high on both sides. Raymond McCreesh's coffin was taken from the prison and transported to the morgue at Daisy Hill Hospital in Newry by the authorities. The RUC informed the McCreesh family that they could take Raymond's remains back to their home in Camlough where he would lie in repose.

The Reavey clan made our way to Newry. There were thousands of people there. The plan was for all of us to march the three miles or so from Daisy Hill all the way to Camlough. It was quite a sight. Thousands marched to the sound of a local piper as the hearse with coffin draped in an Irish tricolour, made its way along the road to Camlough village. As the march moved along, hundreds more joined in along the way. Eventually the hearse arrived at the McCreesh home and the coffin was carried inside. The wake seemed to last for ever. Thousands filed into the house one by one. It took us over an hour to make our way in to the front room and the queue from where we stood, seemed to stretch all the way back in to Newry. I never saw anything like it before or since.

With tension gripping South Armagh and Northern Ireland, the IRA showed no sign of taking a break. On 28 May, Mervyn Robinson, a forty-seven-year-old RUC policeman and married father of three children, went into Robb's Pub on the nearby Tullyah Road. Mervyn was well liked locally and lived 400 yards away from our house and any time he met me on the road, he would always stop and ask how Paddy Quinn was getting on. As he left the pub, the IRA shot him less than 200 yards from his house. There was widespread shock as he was a popular community policeman and had no known enemies in the locality. It would appear his sin, as far as the IRA was concerned, was that he wore the wrong uniform. His funeral at Belleeks' Church of Ireland was attended by large numbers from the Catholic community, a reflection of the esteem he was held in.

By mid-June 1981, nine Republican prisoners were on hunger strike and four had died. The evolving story was still head line news around the world but one began to sense that with the belligerent British failing to budge on the political status issue, the impact of the ongoing deaths was going to lessen in the weeks ahead. Not deterred though, there was still a lengthy list of prisoners lining up to join the hunger strike.

One of those was my brother-in law, Paddy Quinn. On 15 June, Paddy refused food and became the twelfth prisoner to do so. Róisín, her mother and the other six members of the Quinn family were devastated with Paddy's decision. As they saw it, Paddy was on the slow agonising road to death. There were no signals from the British that things were going to change any time soon, if at all, and Mrs Quinn's interpretation of the various meetings with senior republicans in the previous months took on a new relevance.

When somebody else is dying, the sympathy is with that person's family. When it's on your own doorstep, the value of life becomes more precious and focused. As the days and weeks rolled on, we hoped and prayed that commonsense would prevail on all sides and that this nightmare would soon stop.

The political and religious leaders were still in and out of the prison and talking to the British government trying to end the hunger strikes. Before the hunger strike, Róisín and I had booked a holiday to New York earlier in the year and despite our concerns about going to the Big Apple, Róisín's mother told us to go ahead as at that stage, Paddy's underlying condition wasn't an issue.

In early July we arrived in New York and headed for Sunnyside in the borough of Queens, where we stayed with my Aunt Winnie and her husband Tom, a native of Co. Laois. They had two sons, Thomas & latterly Joseph who, as a volunteer ambulance driver, later died from complications arising from the 9/11 attacks on the World Trade Centre. One would think that being so far away from home, the hunger strikes wouldn't be of interest to your average native New Yorker. But we discovered the number of people of Irish stock protesting in the city, targeting British companies and institutions, was much bigger than we expected.

The Irish in New York had clubbed together to generate publicity in the hope of putting pressure on the newly installed Ronald Reagan administration in the White House as he had Tipperary roots. Margaret Thatcher persuaded President Reagan not to get involved as it would amount to 'political interference in foreign domestic affairs'. This has become one of the most abused phrases in the world of diplomacy.

WHEN WE BOOKED OUR holiday to New York, we had assumed we could put our feet up, take it easy and stroll around the city. That was the plan but it didn't exactly work out that way. No sooner had we unpacked our bags and sat down at the kitchen table for a cup of tea and a biscuit when word seeped out within the Irish community that a sister of an IRA hunger striker was in town. As the New York anti-H-Block organisers saw it, Róisín would make a good story for the local media. Before we knew it, calls were coming in from TV, radio stations and newspapers all across the city. Within days, she spoke on radio which targeted the Irish community in the city and to a number of newspapers, TV stations as well and gave a detailed description of what was happening to Paddy at the time.

She articulated how the Quinn family had a tough upbringing following the death of their father in 1962 in his early forties when Paddy was just ten. With eight children to feed in the house on what was a small farm of rough ground and little income, Paddy took on a lot of family responsibilities at a young age. She also highlighted her house being destroyed, the numerous severe beatings Paddy received from the British army which ultimately drove him and others in the locality to join the IRA. She explained how the persistent savage conduct of the British army, the belligerence of the government in London and the hunger strikes were impacting the Quinn family.

To get away from the constant demands we were receiving in Sunnyside New York, we opted to move out to Long Island to the small tranquil town of Riverhead where a brother-in law of Seamus, Seán Harte and his wife Mary, lived in a very classy upmarket area. No sooner had we emptied our suitcases there when the word got out again that a sister of a hunger striker was in the area and the phone started ringing again. This time, a hunger strike rally was planned in the local community hall and everybody of Irish heritage in the area would be there that night. We went along and the place was packed with about 400 or so in attendance. The locals couldn't believe that a sister of an IRA hunger striker was in their midst to talk about the situation in the prisons.

Róisín told the gathering about the history of protest by republican prisoners and how they had tried to get political status. She explained that despite numerous calls for concessions, the British wouldn't budge and that after four years of refusing family visits, there was only one thing the prisoners felt they could do to achieve their modest demands – fast to death. Those in attendance couldn't believe there was so much commotion over prisoners wanting to wear their own clothes. She revealed to the gathering that her mother hadn't seen Paddy in person for four years and that the option to volunteer for the hunger strike was a personal decision for each prisoner. The prisoners were putting their lives on the line, but having been so abused by the British, they felt that this was the only way to achieve what were basic concessions. As Róisín spoke, a growing number of mothers in the audience wiped tears from their eyes.

With the Riverhead event over, we felt it was time to enjoy our last few days in New York. We didn't take any more calls and decided it was time to take it easy. We knew that once we left the bright lights of New York City and headed home, we were back to our real world which was an awful one.

The Hunger Strikes hit Home

In the meantime, Paddy Quinn was four weeks into his hunger strike. His condition wasn't helped by the fact that he had a serious underlying kidney problem. That made him vulnerable to die earlier than expected due to his hunger strike. Unlike the other hunger strikers who were lasting for around two months or so, Paddy was fading at a quicker rate. The pressure was great on the Quinn family.

After we arrived back in Ireland, one of the first things we did was call to Róisín's mother, Katie Quinn, to see how she was and to get an update on Paddy's condition. When we walked in the door of her house, we were shocked at what we saw. Katie was frail, the skin on her face was dotted with red blotches, a sign of her enormous stress. She was having difficulty sleeping and had lost weight. The ongoing situation and lack of information from the prison; the hostile media coverage from the London press; the increased British army presence in the area; the sense of anger in South Armagh after the death of Raymond McCreesh and the prospect of losing her first boy, was taking a worrying toll.

Katie travelled to the retreat in Lough Derg, Co. Donegal, three weekends in a row and prayed to every saint known to try to bring the hunger strikes to an end. Unknown to us, three visitors from Sinn Féin had called to see Katie in her newly renovated home in Belleeks. They were clearly preparing for Paddy's eventual death. One of the three was Jimmy Drumm, whose wife Máire was shot dead in 1976 at the Mater Hospital Belfast by Jimmy Craig and his pals in the UDA.

Their presence made Katie realise that the focus would soon be switching to the Quinn family. Paddy's condition was worsening and her unwelcomed moment in the spotlight was quickly coming. She had seen all the media coverage surrounding Bobby Sands' death and the difficulties it posed for his family. The onslaught of global attention that was about to come crashing down on her was something she felt she would not be able to handle. Katie was frightened, nervous and clearly didn't know what to do. Matters weren't helped by the fact that she was a widow and lived with her daughter Philomena in the middle of the countryside. She was all alone every day during working hours. The sense of loneliness and fear over what was expected to happen, left her feeling isolated both physically and emotionally.

With the British army setting up intimidating checkpoints down the road from her gate on a frequent basis, the thoughts that they might raid the newly renovated house, wreck it for a second time and leave her homeless yet again, was constantly on her mind. Prayer and devotion to her Catholic faith kept her going.

At a time when we hadn't a clue about how bad Paddy was because nobody told us, access was difficult and media reports were not always prisoner-specific. The days were ticking along and the word coming to us was that Paddy was deteriorating fast. He had developed ulcers in his mouth and throat and was finding it difficult to swallow water. Even though he was offered treatment, he refused it.

Fr Denis Faul was still in and out of the prison trying to find a successful solution to the hunger strikes, but his pleas, and those of Cardinal Tomás Ó Fiaich, to the British were ignored. Fr Faul was pushing the point that if a hunger striker went in to a coma, it should be left to the discretion of his family to end the fast. With Kevin Lynch close to death and surpassing Bobby Sands' number of days on hunger strike, Mrs Quinn knew that Paddy was drifting closer and closer to his end.

On the morning of Friday 31 July 1981, I was leaving my home in Drumherriff at around 9 a.m. to head to my office when the phone rang. A well-spoken RUC inspector in Newry station introduced himself and asked me if I would pass a message on to Mrs Quinn? I asked him why he was ringing me and he said 'you're the contact number we have for the Quinn family'.

I told him that Mrs Quinn was now living in Belleeks and

that he should call to her house and deliver the message himself. He replied by saying that 'it was too sensitive an issue for him or the RUC to visit the house'. I took that as code for saying the RUC were actually afraid to go near the Camlough and Belleeks area so soon after the death of Raymond McCreesh.

He informed me he had received a phone call from the prison governor who told him that Paddy Quinn only had hours to live. He stressed the word 'hours' not days. He said that Paddy had deteriorated rapidly overnight and that Mrs Quinn needed to know the protocols in place for the removal of a dead body from the prison in the event of Paddy's death. He went on to say that the RUC would transport Paddy's remains to the morgue in Daisy Hill Hospital and that the funeral undertaker would then take ownership of the body.

He wanted an assurance from me that there would be no interference in the transfer of the body to Daisy Hill. Of course I couldn't give that guarantee but I promised to pass the message on. He added that if the Quinn family respected the wishes of the RUC on the first leg of the journey the RUC would not have a presence at Daisy Hill Hospital morgue and en route to Belleeks.

I asked myself 'why is this inspector ringing me' considering all my previous dealings with the RUC were hostile? Now, *they* were asking *me* to do *them* a favour When I put down the phone, I thought that maybe the RUC was playing some sort of a game. Maybe Paddy was not close to death but they were saying he was to persuade Mrs Quinn to try to get him to end his fast and thus manipulate a deceptive end to the hunger strikes.

After all, Paddy was forty-seven days in to his fast and going by the trend of the previous hunger strikers, he had at least another fifteen days or so left to live. If Paddy was the first hunger striker to be taken off his fast, the likelihood was that the British would boast to the world that they had broken the determination of the IRA and that would be a major symbolic victory for London which had not made one single concession to the prisoners. I went to Mrs Quinn's house in Belleeks and relayed the message. As sceptical as I was to what we presumed was a British trick, she didn't believe the message from the RUC either. Mrs Quinn, like myself, took the view that Paddy was too early into his hunger strike to be so close to death.

I went back home and was no sooner in the door when the phone rang again. This time it was the governor's office at the prison. He said if we wanted to see Paddy alive, we would need to visit the prison hospital within the next hour. His body was closing down and the end was near. I wondered if the parents of the other six dead hunger strikers at that stage had received similar calls?

This call was more convincing than the previous one. The governor's office asked for the registration number of my car, the make and colour, etc., and enquired as to who would accompany us? I was told that once we arrived at the gates of the prison, we would be waved straight through without delay. Suddenly, my inner alarm bell went off and I sensed we really did have a life-or-death crisis on our hands and I had to act quickly

I rang my office and told secretary Briege Carroll that I would not be in for the rest of the day. I drove to Camlough as quickly as I could and picked up Paddy's sister Mary. I explained to her the dilemma we were in as she was hearing the news for the first time. Very agitated, Mary was upset at what she expected to see when she got to the prison. I told her to prepare for the worst although my words did little to calm her down.

I called to Mrs Quinn and delivered the news. She hurriedly fixed her hair, changed her clothes and before we knew it, we were heading for the prison outside Lisburn. I repeatedly discussed with Katie the two options available to her. She could leave Paddy on hunger strike, respect his wish to die for political status and he would be dead before the day was out. On the other hand, she could try and end his fast but in doing so, he would be the first prisoner of this group to be formally taken off the hunger strike. If that was to happen, the Quinn family ran the risk of getting a tough time from the wider republican community and the possibility of being isolated and unpopular in South Armagh. As well as that, the Tory press in London would ridicule Paddy and the Quinn family for not going all the way, and all this before hostile Conservative and unionist MPs had their say in the House of Commons.

The options I put to her had been turning over in her mind repeatedly in the previous few weeks. She knew exactly what the potential implications and consequences were if Paddy was taken off his fast but was determined to keep him alive. Whatever the cost, she had her mind firmly made up. She would do all she could to prevent him dying.

The trip from Belleeks to the prison is about thirty miles but it felt like the longest journey I had ever made in my life. My opinion didn't really matter as the final decision rested with Mrs Quinn. We got to the main gate and as promised, it swung open automatically as did the second and third inner ones. When we got to the door of the prison hospital, an official was there to meet us. We were escorted to the ward and stopped at the door of Paddy's room. He lay lifeless on his bed, itself the only item of furniture in the room. It had an over-bed table firmly placed on it containing an untouched breakfast. A prison officer arrived and replaced the breakfast tray with a hot steaming lunch which was put directly under Paddy's nose, a consistent tactic that had been a deliberate ploy by the British to break his fast. We were then allowed to enter the room. Mrs Quinn, who hadn't seen her son in five days, was shocked at how much his condition had deteriorated since her last visit.

Paddy's hair was untidy, greasy and long. It hadn't been washed and cut for almost three years apart from the occasional burst from a power hose which was used to cleanse the cell walls during the dirty protest. Every so often, he would endure a cleaning session from a scrubbing brush, forcibly applied by a couple of prison officers holding him down against his will.

His skeletal bones protruded through his delicate white skin and his shrunken face was drained of all its blood. His eyes had sunk deep in to his skull and his heartbeat was dangerously low – he was pure 'skin and bone' with no fat in his body. Riddled with bed sores, such was the lack of muscle and strength in his body, he was naked from the head down to his waist as his weak body couldn't take the weight of the bed sheet. You could count every rib in his emaciated body. Even though he was barely alive, she cried and struggled to take in the horrible sight that lay before her.

Some of the words from *The Mother* by Pádraig Pearse sprang to mind as I looked at Mrs Quinn and the desperate situation she was in:

Lord, thou art hard on Mothers,
We suffer in their coming and their going;
And tho' I grudge them not, I weary, weary
Of the long sorrow – And yet I have my joy:
My sons were faithful, and they fought.

Paddy had by now drifted into a deep coma. He couldn't see or talk and he didn't know his mother, sister Mary and brother-in-law were in the room beside him. He had almost passed the point of no return. Once Paddy had fallen into a coma and reached a point where he couldn't think for himself, the onus for his fate switched to his mother, Katie.

Dedicated Irish republicans all over the world were supportive of Paddy and the other hunger strikers but *they* were not in Katie's shoes. For Mrs Quinn, the time she feared most over the previous weeks and months had finally arrived. The atmosphere in the room was surreal.

As we looked at Paddy waste away before our eyes, Mrs Quinn asked to see the medic in charge. The doctor, a tall pleasant man, happened to be coming along the corridor and came in to the room. He asked the prison officers to leave in order to have a private chat with us.

Mrs Quinn asked the doctor, 'how bad is Paddy?'

'Paddy is in a very critical condition. The only way I can put this is, his body is in the process of closing down. His kidneys are in a very bad state due to an underlying condition.'

She then asked, 'how long has Paddy to live?'

'I can't be precise but he has hours rather than days.'

Katie then put it to the doctor: 'If I took him off hunger strike now, what are the chances of him living?'

'I'd say 60/40 against.'

I recall there was a short but grim silence in the room. It reminded me of 1976 when we had to make the awful decision with Professor Gordon to switch off the life-support machine that kept our Anthony alive.

Mrs Quinn had made her mind up. She looked at the floor and then lifted her head. Katie was adamant that saving her son from death was far more important for her, than the principle of whether or not prisoners should wear their own clothes. She made eye contact with me and Mary before saying to the doctor, 'I want to take him off. Is there a form I have to sign?'

'Yes,' he said.

An assistant had the consent form in a folder and presented it to Mrs Quinn before the doctor said, 'you will need a second family member to sign as a witness'.

She asked, 'if I sign now, will you get him to a proper hospital?'

'I will. Thank you very much Mrs Quinn. You're a very brave woman,' said the doctor.

Mrs Quinn signed the consent form, followed shortly afterwards by Mary.

Katie's request and decision turned out to be a defining moment in the history of the hunger strikes and as later events unfolded, the future direction of Ireland and its divided people. A Catholic priest appeared on the scene and blessed Paddy before giving him his last rites. He said a prayer holding hands with Mrs Quinn and Mary.

As we prayed for Paddy's life, we could hear constant loud crying further down the corridor. I learned minutes later that the noise was from the room occupied by twenty-year old INLA hunger striker Kevin Lynch from Dungiven, Co. Derry. The news that Paddy was taken off hunger strike spread quickly around the prison.

The Hunger Strikes hit Home

What should have been a private moment between Mrs Quinn and her son was anything but. Prison staff, who wrongly thought that the IRA had capitulated, spread the word as quickly as possible to other prisoners and the media. Katie Quinn's personal decision was global news within seconds. The revelation that a republican hunger striker had come off hunger strike dominated the headlines around the world and was manipulated by the Tory Press in London who presented the story as victory for Mrs Thatcher and defeat for the IRA.

Shortly afterwards as we stood waiting for Paddy to be carried out to the waiting ambulance, a woman came rushing down the corridor and hugged Katie. It was Kevin Lynch's mother. Both of them were in floods of tears and hugged each other for a number of minutes. Mrs Lynch wept uncontrollably and said to Katie through her tears, 'you did the right thing Mrs Quinn'.

She appeared to speak as if she would have liked to have taken her own son off the strike. But Kevin Lynch had drawn up a will which, it appears, included an instruction that he be allowed to die.[1]

Nobody knows what sort of pressure families, who found themselves in the same situation as we, were going through. Kevin Lynch died within twenty-four hours, on 1 August 1981, having refused food for seventy-one days.

Paddy was put on a drip and wheeled out to an ambulance before being rushed off to the Royal Victoria Hospital in Belfast. Despite his mother and sister wanting to travel in the ambulance with Paddy, they were not allowed which led to some very heated words with prison staff.

We got into my car and drove out on to the main road. As we exited the gate, we spotted Paddy's two brothers, Laurence and John, who had been unable to gain admittance to the prison. We explained what happened inside, before heading off to Belfast while Laurence and John returned home to Belleeks after we informed them they would not be allowed into the the Royal Victoria Hospital.

We drove to the RVH in Belfast and made our way up to

one of the top floors before eventually finding out what room Paddy was in. The British army and RUC had taken over the floor that Paddy was on and put us through their customary security checks. When we stepped out of the lift, there were the usual ridiculous questions; 'Who are you? Where do you live? Why are you here? What was Paddy Quinn doing in the prison?' and that was just for starters. They even asked his mother: 'what relation are you to Paddy Quinn?'

I had to take off my shoes and socks, empty my pockets and answer a range of mindless and humiliating questions. Of course, they knew exactly who we were. They also knew why we were in the hospital but applied their usual silly tactics of making life as difficult as possible.

Then we were asked to produce ID. I had my driving licence and while Mrs Quinn and Mary had welfare documentation, they didn't have photo-identification. There were ructions, Katie Quinn couldn't believe her eyes and ears that the British army and RUC were trying every trick in the book to stop us from getting in to see Paddy in his hospital bed. I pleaded with the RUC over and over but, predictably, they wouldn't budge. I asked them what a fifty-five-year-old woman in 1981 would need photo-ID for? They wouldn't give an answer. Katie had no ID because she couldn't drive, never had a car and had no need for a driving licence, nor did she have a passport. I explained that Paddy was her son and all she wanted to do was sit by his side.

Having pleaded our case over and over, eventually we got in and the sight before us was horrific. Paddy lay life-less on the bed in a coma, encased in what appeared to be a spaghetti-like arrangement of tubes pumping fluids into his life-less body. Mrs Quinn sat down at the side of the bed and, with black beads in her feeble wobbling hands, started to recite the rosary. At intervals, she would dip a white cotton handkerchief in to a small silver dish of water and moisten Paddy's lips and forehead.

Meanwhile, teams of medical people in long white coats were in and out of the room undertaking tests; monitoring the many screens that were hooked up to his body; opening and closing vials of medicine and assessing voluminous notes on his condition. A doctor told us that because Paddy's body was totally drained of vital vitamins and nutrition, his eyesight would probably be impaired and his kidney function was likely to cause endless problems. The ethical Hippocratic Oath, which medical practitioners must honour in accordance with their profession, was clearly working effectively again in the RVH. Doctors, specialists, consultants and nurses never once expressed a derogatory comment about why Paddy had ended up where he was.

Five hours on, Paddy was still in a coma. The nurses told us not to expect anything positive, if at all, for a number of days. There was nothing more we could do. Exhausted and worried, we eventually opted to go home.

Next morning, 1 August, there was a steady stream of Irish, British, US TV crews and newspaper people calling to the house. Mrs Quinn, who was staying with us, was in demand and in all interviews she gave, Katie kept her message simple – Paddy was her son and she was entitled to take him off hunger strike once he drifted in to a state of unconsciousness. She had her mind made up and didn't owe anybody an apology.

As the media reported and analysed the political implications of Katie Quinn's decision, twenty-five-year-old IRA volunteer Kieran Doherty, TD, single, from Andersonstown, Belfast, died on 2 August. Francis Hughes' cousin and IRA volunteer Thomas McElwee (23) single from Tamlaghduff, Bellaghy, Co. Derry died on 8 August. Twelve days later, Micky Devine (27) a father of two from Derry and a member of the INLA, was the final hunger striker to die in the Maze prison. With Joe McDonnell (29) and Martin Hurson (24) already dead, the hunger strikes had claimed ten lives.

Paddy Quinn and others who were on hunger strike were not aware in their final days that serious pressure had come on the IRA leadership from the relative families and wider republican movement to bring the whole process to an end.

Brendan Duddy, who died in 2017, emerged as a crucial behind-the-scenes player in a process that ultimately led to the

1994 IRA ceasefire. So many people have so much to be grateful to him arising from his contribution and efforts for peace.

OVER MANY MONTHS, BIT by bit, Paddy clawed his way from the verge of death back to a point where he could function independent of hospital equipment. His eyesight and kidneys were damaged and other body organs strained. He was alive, but just about, and began the very long road back to what might be classed as 'normality'.

Danny Morrison and convicted IRA prisoner Richard O'Rawe have subsequently told me that there was no bad feeling within the republican movement over the decision to take Paddy off the strike. As they saw it, the decision to end Paddy's fast was not of his doing as he was in a coma, but was one taken by his mother on medical grounds and respected by Republican prisoners. Mrs Quinn has stated many times that her decision to take Paddy off his fast was one she never regretted.

It paved the way for other worried families who found themselves in a similar position. Prisoners such as Pat McGeown, Matt Devlin and Laurence McKeown were taken off their hunger strikes by their families in the subsequent weeks. The remaining eight volunteers ceased fasting when the hunger strikes formally ended on 3 October 1981.

There was a massive sense of relief on the island of Ireland when it ended. The expected civil war that so many know-all commentators in the media predicted, never materialised. Within a week of Jim Prior issuing the Tory version of 'no surrender' to the IRA, the British government shocked the political world by granting the prisoners four and ultimately their five demands. Margaret Thatcher, who had said repeatedly 'I shall never give them political status' and 'crime is crime is crime', finally caved in. The phrase *Perfidious Albion* to describe public deception by the English in Ireland, was clearly still alive and well. The British government conceded to all demands, except one. IRA prisoners could now wear their own clothes, were allowed to associate freely and could receive a certain number of visitors and mail.

Jimmy and Sadie Reavey pictured shortly after their wedding in 1942.

Below: *The Reavey family pictured in 1965,* back row, *Seamus, John Martin, Eugene, Brian, Frank, Oliver, Kathleen.* Front row, *Una, Jimmy, Colleen, Eileen, Anthony, Sadie, Paul.*

Communion days, Anthony, Brian and John Martin.

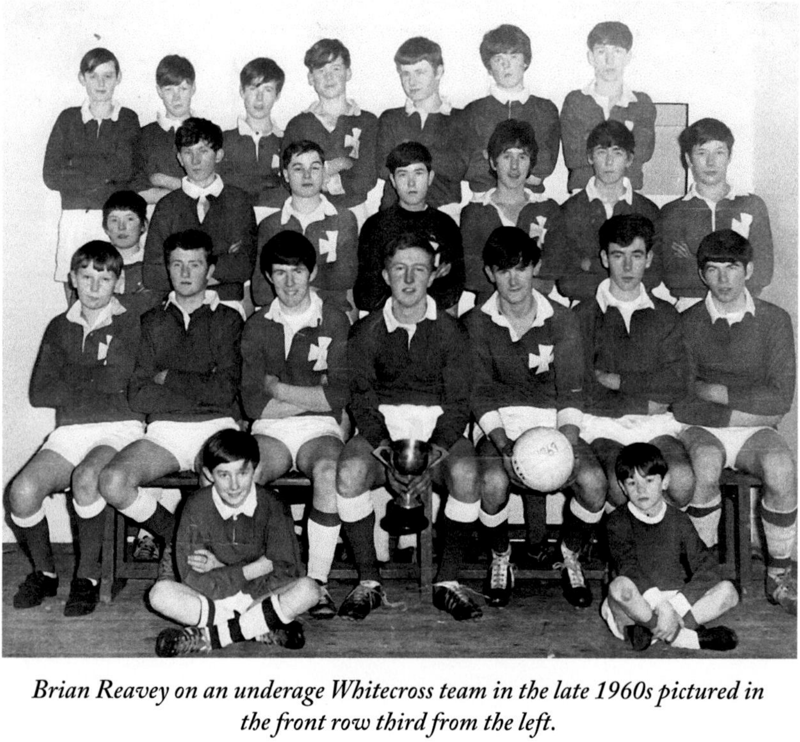

Brian Reavey on an underage Whitecross team in the late 1960s pictured in the front row third from the left.

Eugene and Róisín's wedding, April 1972.

John Martin

Brian

Anthony

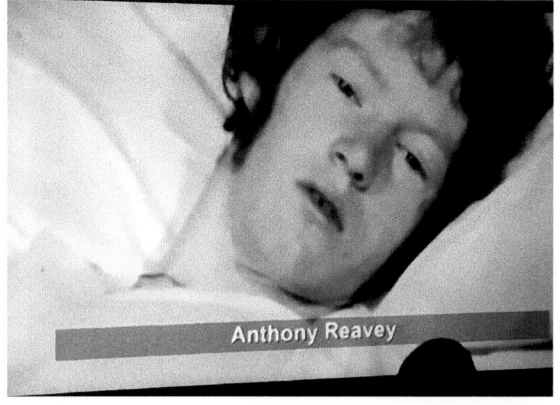

The scene in the living room of the Reavey cottage in Greyhilla immediatly after the boys were shot on 4 January 1976.

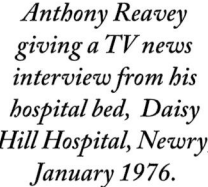

Anthony Reavey giving a TV news interview from his hospital bed, Daisy Hill Hospital, Newry, January 1976.

Eugene pictured with Barney O'Dowd. Barney's two sons and his brother were murdered by the Glenanne gang on the same night as the Reavey brothers, 4 January 1976.

Mary O'Hare pictured with her son Michael, holding an image of her daughter Majella who was murdered by a British soldier in Ballymoyer, Co. Armagh in August 1976.

Eugene's brother Oliver and sisters Kathy McHale, Colleen McKenna and Eileen Reavey at the unveiling of the Reavey brothers monument, January 2016.

Amnesty International projected the image of the Reavey brothers onto the Houses of Parliament in London in protest at the British government's Legacy Act.

Alan McBride, Stephen Travers, Trevor Ringland, Eugene Reavey, Rory McShane and Joe Campbell at a Truth & Reconciliation Platform (TARP) event in Newry, Co. Down.

Eugene surrounded by his grandsons and grand nephews at a football match in Whitecross between Armagh & Donegal which was held to commemorate the Reavey Brothers fortieth anniversary in 2016.

Eugene and Róisín celebrating 50 years of marriage.

The Hunger Strikes hit Home

Educational facilities were provided and eventually they were allowed to refuse to work within the prison.

The hunger strikes turned out to be a significant watershed in the history of the Troubles and as events slowly evolved, they marked the embryonic beginnings of a long and hard-earned closure to the most horrific period of conflict seen in Ireland during the twentieth century.

Meanwhile Mrs Quinn received a visit from award-winning writer, the highly respected Christopher Whipple and photographer Harry Benson of the New York-based *LIFE* magazine. Her difficult dilemma and the implications of the hunger strikes were given a two-page splash in the October edition and read all over the world.

Questioned if it was Paddy's wish to be taken off the hunger strike, Katie told *LIFE*, 'he never pledged [me] to let him die but even if he had, I think I would have done the same thing'. As her dramatic story was absorbed, discussed and analysed by political observers in Washington DC and around the world, I had some very distressing news of my own to deal with.

A NUMBER OF HIGHLY dangerous paramilitaries in the Ulster Defence Association, based in Belfast, wanted to see me for an urgent 'chat'.

Pay up or Pay the Price

With all the turmoil going on in the H-Blocks and the Quinn household, it was easy to forget that everyday life went on. Babies were born, children went to school, the sun shone, the rain fell, the grass grew, bills had to be paid and Reavey Brothers Contractors Limited had construction projects to chase.

The Grove Housing Association in North Belfast was seeking tender applications from suitably approved contractors to carry out remedial works on existing deteriorated housing stock on the nearby Shore Road. The advertisement was conspicuously small and I asked myself if a contractor had already been earmarked? Eager to secure the contract, I got in to my car next day, drove up to Belfast and did a drive-by reconnaissance inspection of the buildings which were ones we were totally familiar with namely, the *Coronation Street*-type, two-up two-down red-brick structures built after the First World War. The Shore Road is in the Tiger's Bay area of Belfast and while I had heard it mentioned several times on TV news, I was unaware that this was, and is, a staunch loyalist area.

However, that didn't bother us at all. As I saw it, business was business and all we were interested in was getting the work done, building up our reputation as a credible construction company, making a few pounds and moving on to the next job. The following Monday morning our company secretary, Briege Carroll, rang the Grove Housing Association and asked if Reavey Brothers Contractors Limited could be added to the tender list. This was necessary as to be considered eligible, the company would have to demonstrate a proven track record of successfully completed projects of a similar size and budget. To get on the list, a resumé or CV of previous jobs; their completion dates; who the hiring local authority was; the consultants; quantity surveyors and architects involved and the relative budgets for each particular project, had to be included.

Pay up or Pay the Price

In the following weeks, the tender documents were issued, priced up and delivered by hand. This was necessary in applying for such projects in Northern Ireland as certain papers were known to mysteriously 'go missing' or arrive 'late' by post. Sabotage and sectarianism, it should be stated, were always daily features of everyday life in Northern Ireland. Shortly after we submitted our application, I was somewhat surprised when I received notification that Reavey Brothers Contractors had actually won the tender. We attended a Grove Housing Association meeting on the Shore Road.

With our papers signed and Reavey Brothers Contractors Limited ready to go, I placed an advertisement in the local South Armagh/South Down newspapers seeking labourers, joiners, electricians, block-layers, etc., for the Shore Road project.

The Ad insisted that all applicants must have a current tax exemption certificate better known as a 715 Form. In other words, I hired these people as self-employed contractors, paid them the agreed rate for their services and they in turn paid their own taxes and social security contributions to Revenue. This was very much the norm in the construction sector. Within a week of meeting the Grove Housing Association, we commenced remedial works on phase one of the project. This involved renovations on thirty-five houses along the Shore Road. Rooftops had to come off and the affected residents had to be accommodated in caravans which we had to supply. The local tenants were very receptive, welcoming and were delighted that their houses were finally getting the long-awaited cosmetic make-over that they had long been lobbying for. All they wanted was for us to get the job done so that they could live in their homes happily ever after.

Most of the houses were in poor to mediocre condition inside but a sizeable number needed extra special work. The conditions in some of the houses were so bad, it quickly dawned on me that Catholics were not the only ones in Northern Ireland who were being treated as second-class citizens. Large numbers of working-class Protestants were living in appalling slums as well and had been completely discriminated against and forgotten by the rich ruling unionist elite down through the decades.

The Basil Brooke rhetoric of encouraging people to look down their noses and ignore poor Catholics had also applied, but in a less obvious way, to low-income Protestants. What I saw on the Shore Road was an eye-opener I will never forget and made me develop a sympathetic approach to their plight.

Our lads were less than a week on the job when one day out of the blue, a black BMW car drove on to our site. I was at home in my Whitecross office at the time and was unaware of this mysterious visit until my brother Frank arrived in that evening, having completed the day's work.

Frank said, 'Two suspicious-looking men arrived at the site today. One was 6'3' and the other was 5'7' in height ... They said that if we wanted to continue working in the area, we would need to pay protection money.

'You're talking to the wrong man,' said Frank. 'You will need to talk to Eugene.'

I had heard stories about protection money being paid to paramilitaries. I had been sort of expecting one of these visits from the minute we were granted the tender but hoped it would never happen

A veil of nervousness came over me. The question now was, who exactly was I dealing with, what sort of money would they be seeking and would the sums demanded make it financially worth my while continuing with the job? Frank handed me a piece of paper containing a phone number that I was requested to ring next morning. I was conscious that if I didn't engage with these people, the consequences were likely to be dangerous not only for me but for the fifty or so employees working on that particular job, the majority of whom were Catholic.

I was caught in a classic 'Catch 22' situation. If I paid too much protection money, I would complete the job at a financial loss. If I didn't pay, the likelihood was that someone would die and if I walked away from the project, not only would I have breached the contract, I might never get Housing Association work ever again.

All that before the discommoded Protestant families on the Shore Road would express their anger at being let down by a bunch of Catholic builders from South Armagh who had abandoned them. I was in a scary dilemma. I could face potential bankruptcy or pay out to a bunch of loyalist bullies. The bottom line for me was the safety of my employees.

Next morning, having built up courage, I phoned the number Frank gave me and to my surprise, the voice at the other end was none other than prominent mobster and senior member of the Ulster Defence Association – the notorious Jimmy Craig.

To complicate matters and it shows up the sinister way the British government ran Northern Ireland, the UDA, whose paramilitary group the Ulster Freedom Fighters (UFF) worked closely with the UVF, was a *legal* organisation at this time. Jimmy was the UDA's chief 'fundraiser' and their number one extortionist. Practically nothing commercial happened in most loyalist areas without Jimmy getting a financial cut.

His ruthless reputation was so bad, he was reported to have colluded with IRA and INLA extortionists he knew to ensure that certain loyalist rivals such as the 'Shankill Butcher' Lenny Murphy and UDA Commander John McMichael, who threatened to expose his lucrative rackets, were actually killed by republicans as a 'favour' to ensure they conveniently disappeared off the scene. Jimmy Craig was such a menace, he was even dismissed by the West Belfast UDA unit after he was allegedly involved in the murder of two Catholic and Protestant men in 1977. He clearly had angry enemies on both sides.

I was nervous before I made the call but when I did, I was pleasantly surprised at how polite he was on the phone. The call didn't last very long. Jimmy wanted to meet me in Belfast next day for what he said was 'a more detailed chat'. That is code in loyalist circles for saying 'do as we say or else expect consequences'. Jimmy was insistent that I should bring some cash, plenty of it. The thought crossed my mind as I drove to

Belfast that Jimmy wanted to do a deal with me as quick as possible just in case somebody else muscled in ahead of him.

The meeting was scheduled for the Shore Road in the Tiger's Bay area. At 2 p.m., Jimmy showed up in the company of his driver and minder, one David 'Artie' Fee, himself an intimidating and prominent loyalist in his day who also had a 'hard man' reputation.

There was only one item on the agenda, namely the amount of cash that would have to be handed over every week. Jimmy kept saying 'Eugene, if you can't pay up, I can't stop the locals from breaking your equipment however, if you're prepared to pay the right price, I'll do my best to guarantee protection.'

He was leaving me with no options. We didn't argue in a heated way but debated at length on the sums which he insisted would be on a per-house basis. I pleaded the 'poor mouth' and told him it was a tough competitive tender. Protection money, I reminded him repeatedly, was not built in to our original costings and would totally absorb all my projected profits. I told him that paying such protection money had the potential to put me out of business. As far as he was concerned, it was pay up or pay the price.

Jimmy was not sympathetic at all as I'm sure my pleas were ones he heard over and over from every contractor and business owner he had dealt with down through the years. He went on to add that he could provide 715 tax exemption certificates belonging to people who were in prison.

In other words, as far as Her Majesty's Revenue was concerned, payments would be issued to certain names who were supposed to be block-layers, electricians and plumbers, etc., but as it happens, some of these individuals were actually convicted criminals behind bars and the authorities never cross-checked. All we had to do was pay the cash, itself a difficult resource to get hold of on a weekly basis as most contract payments were made by cheque.

Alternatively, we could give Jimmy a cheque written out to the 'hard working tradesman' whose name was on the 715 form. Jimmy had an arrangement with a pub close to the Sandy Row area of the city where he would then cash it in for his own benefit. As this stage, I didn't know enough about 715 forms and unaware of how the system he proposed, worked, I didn't take him up on his offer. Jimmy told me what the rate of payment was and added that he was receiving protection payments from chemists, hairdressers, pubs, taxis, bookies, fast food shops, furniture outlets, you name it and they paid him.

He went on to say that the IRA had been doing it for years and the UVF simply copied the practice. To my surprise, he even revealed that UVF people in prison had formed close friendships with IRA prisoners who passed on details of various republican scams that loyalists ultimately benefitted from!

The wider public would be most surprised to read that many of those friendships from hitherto sworn enemies have lasted to this day!

After much haggling with Jimmy, I paid him £1,000 in cash and we agreed a weekly fee. The agreed arrangement severely ate into my projected profits and a way would have to be found to recoup our losses. With the deal now agreed, we could get on with the job of refurbishing the houses on the Shore Road without any hassle, or so we thought.

In the meantime, I engaged in negotiations with a certain senior official in the Grove Housing Association (who we cannot name for legal reasons) to try to secure additional 'contingency fees'. This is generally known as 'rainy day' money for unforeseen circumstances that may arise during the contract period. I told the him about the outrageous menacing demand for protection money I had received. He listened but as far as he was concerned, it had nothing to do with him. It was prudent for him to turn a blind eye and a deaf ear on the subject of protection money. That way, he kept his job and most importantly of all, he lived a longer life.

Part of the contract for re-furbishing the houses on the Shore Road was to hold monthly meetings with the Grove Housing Association to update their people on how the project was progressing. The meeting would be nothing more than a construction update and a discussion on any difficulties we were experiencing. Despite repeated efforts by me to get the issue of protection money on to the agenda and accordingly, into the minutes or record, Frankie Millar, who headed up the Grove Housing Association, wouldn't hear of it.

Unionist hardliner Frankie was an interesting character. He said in 1988 that 'Irish travellers should be incinerated' and that Nelson Mandela was a 'black Provo'.

Frankie would ask who the money was being to paid to and I would respond 'Jimmy Craig'. In response, Frankie would say, 'give him nothin' and if Jimmy asks again, tell me and 'I'll give him a box in the face'. Of course, Frankie was just acting the hard man and never did anything about it.

Despite Frankie's expressed bravado, our relationship with the association was strengthening with each passing week. Every morning our lads would show up for work and nothing would be touched. The 'security service' we were paying for seemed to be working.

Such was our growing friendship, Frankie Millar one day told our Frank he had a problem in his house. Our Frank, on understanding what the issue was, said 'leave it with me and I'll call up to fix it'. Frankie Millar could not believe his ears that a Catholic, from South Armagh, was offering to do a small house-job in a staunchly loyalist area of Belfast. When our Frank got to his house, it turned out to be a watershed moment in Frankie's life. Frankie met him and said, 'do you realise you are the first Catholic to cross the door in this house?' Our Frank did the required job and as an act of goodwill, refused to take payment.

Phase Two of the Shore Road programme was coming up for tender and involved another forty houses. Phase One was coming to an end and at a monthly meeting with the association, Frankie Millar suggested that it would be logical to retain Reavey Brothers Contractors and the same team of architects and QS people to maintain continuity of delivery. For this to happen, there would have to be an upgrade on the rates of payment across the board despite the fact that we were already on site in a compound with the necessary equipment. The contract and fees for the work were signed and we continued on.

We commenced phase two and were hardly a week on the job when Jimmy Craig and Artie Fee arrived on site again. The lads presumed it was a 'courtesy call' as Jimmy, in the best interests of good working relations, popped in every so often just to see how we were getting on. His occasional visits were more so for the good of his bulging bank account and less so for ours. This time, Jimmy was up to his old tricks.

It seems, he was not in a good mood. He said to Frank, 'give this message to Eugene. Tell him to have the compound cleared and all the workforce, diggers and equipment off site by Friday.'

Frank suggested that Jimmy give me a call. Jimmy said, 'I won't be giving him a call. We made an agreement and he [Eugene] hasn't stuck to it.'

I rang Jimmy first thing next morning and asked, 'Jimmy, what's going on?'

Jimmy didn't respond so I said, 'I'll be in Belfast later. I'll meet you at the site at 2.00.'

On the way up to Belfast, I couldn't work out why he could be so irate when he spoke to Frank. After all, I was honouring our 'contract' and he was getting paid every Friday. What more could he be looking for?

Jimmy and Artie Fee showed up at 2.00 as agreed. Jimmy jumped out of the car and contrary to his earlier behaviour, was his usual bubbly, smiley self. Glum Artie however, looked like someone who had lost his life savings. Jimmy came in to the site hut while Artie stayed outside.

'So Jimmy, what's going on?' I asked.

Jimmy said he had been on another building site the day before and the builder told him that I had got a contract for 200 extra houses on the Shore Road. I started laughing and told him that there was no way I could get an extra 200 houses as a project of that size would have to go out to tender. I told him that I got an extension on my existing contract to refurbish an additional forty houses.

Jimmy said, 'I have to get more money if you are working on extra houses'.

I said, 'Jimmy, I'm only starting on this new phase of forty houses and we agreed I would pay you on a per-house basis. The payments are the same because I am on the same rate as the houses are the same size.'

Jimmy insisted and the exchanges went on for an hour as he repeatedly said that I should pay him more money. I refused to pay extra. He asked if we had received any further contracts from the Grove Housing Association? I told him 'No'. Eventually, agreement was reached that I would continue to pay Jimmy the same rate per house as agreed for the original Phase One.

The next day, Thursday, we were working on a new build of eight houses at Orby Place in South Belfast for private developers Frank Boyd and Kevin McKay which our lads had started three weeks previous. I had to go to the site with our assistant QS Paul Meehan to assess work done in order to prepare payment for the brick-layers next day. We did what we had to do and just as we were leaving the site, our exit was suddenly blocked by an incoming car. The occupants just happened to be Artie Fee and Jimmy Craig. The minute the car stopped, Jimmy jumped out and asked, 'so Eugene, what the fuck is going on here?'

In response, I said, 'this has nothing to do with you so please move your car.'

'You pay me for these houses or else the deal is off,' he said in an angry voice.

I explained to him that this particular job had been priced long before I applied for the Shore Road project. I had even asked Frank Boyd if any paramilitaries were operating in the area. Frank assured me there were none. I told Jimmy that as the number of houses here were only eight, the margins were tight and there was no room to pay protection money.

Jimmy asked for £500 per house. I told him what to go and do with himself. He wasn't impressed. I offered him £50 per house and he laughed at me. I insisted that the profits were too tight for protection money. He said that this was his area and if I didn't pay up, he threatened to wreck all the houses we were working on along the Shore Road. Artie then intervened and said if we didn't pay up, he would knock down all the block work on the site where we were. I now knew the calibre of individuals I was dealing with. While I was scared that this might go one step further and 6'3' Artie might draw a gun on me, I told Jimmy to tell his mate to get off the site as this was an issue between me and him.

After a long series of heated exchanges, I agreed to pay Jimmy a round figure of £2,000 or £250 per house. Then there was another snag. He wanted the money there and then.

The next day was a Friday and I headed to Belfast early in the morning with a lot of cash to pay various trades people working on our sites. When I got to the Shore Road compound, I rang our secretary Briege in Whitecross and she told me that a man had been on the phone looking for me and wanted to meet as soon as possible.

His name was Jackie and he wanted to meet me at the South Belfast site. I presumed he was somebody local looking for a job perhaps or a difficult neighbour who thought our noisy cement mixers were way too loud.

So I headed over to the South Belfast site and when I got there, the man in question was waiting for me. He said to me, 'I'm Jackie McDonald. I'm from the South Belfast UDA and you owe me money for operating this site'.

I thought this was some sort of a bad joke and said, 'are you for real? I paid protection money yesterday. You're getting nothing off me.'

He asked who I had paid the money to and when I told him it was Jimmy Craig, the complexion on his face changed.

'Jimmy Craig doesn't operate this area. I do. You owe me money. This is my patch.'

'Good Jesus,' I thought. In a growing rage, I quickly realised Jimmy Craig had tricked me, but what could I do?

There were angry words with Jackie. I told him that his gripe was with Jimmy Craig and not with me. I repeatedly reminded him that this was a small building site where we were only constructing eight houses.

As he saw it, we dealt with the weekly payment of wages and were an easy touch for extortion.

As I argued over and back with Jackie and began to wear myself down in the process, we eventually agreed that I would pay him £1,000. For that, Jackie would walk away and not bother me again. I never set eyes on Jackie McDonald in person from that day to this.

Jackie McDonald effectively disappeared off my radar but Jimmy and Artie did not. As we edged towards the completion of Phase Two of houses on the Shore Road, other scary problems emerged. I was sitting in my office in Whitecross one day around lunchtime when Briege knocked on the door and entered. She had some worrying news: 'there's a 'Captain Black' of the UFF on the phone and he wants to speak to you.'

'The Ulster Freedom Fighters?' I said to myself. Maybe they wanted to tell me something about the killings of Brian, John Martin and Anthony? It wasn't unusual for loyalist gunmen to be in the UFF this week and the UVF next week. I had heard of 'Captain Black' as he was the spokesperson for the UFF, a group of ruthless killers who were part and parcel of the legal UDA.

I lifted the phone and said 'hello'.

In reply, he said, 'this is Captain Black. We have just murdered your brother [Frank] on the Shore Road'. He didn't say anything more and put the phone down.

I sat in my chair frozen. My mouth went dry. We were reliving the killings of Brian, John Martin and Anthony all over again and I didn't know what to do. I thought about ringing the Grove Housing Association to enquire if somebody had been shot but then decided not to.

Briege, all flustered and in something of a panic, came in with a cup of much-needed tea. She said, 'get that in to you before you go anywhere'. After some conversation with Briege, she told me that 'Captain Black' told her that he was from the

UFF. She asked if I should bring one of our guys in the yard, who was busy priming timber, to accompany me to Belfast as she could see I was visibly shaken?

I said 'no', got in to my car and drove straight to the Shore Road site in Belfast. I tuned in to Radio Ulster news at the top of the hour but they had nothing on the 'killing' which I thought was a bit strange but I assumed the BBC wouldn't run with something unless the RUC confirmed it first.

Something of a nervous wreck, I prayed to my dead brothers and Father that what 'Captain Black' told me was not true or if it was, that Frank would still be alive. I was in such a daze at the time, I promised myself that if Frank survived, I would quit construction work and pursue some other business for a living. The extraordinary stress of dealing with these monsters in the loyalist community was driving me over the edge. Life had got to the point where it was one crisis after another with the UDA.

I couldn't live with the scenario that my decision to tender for projects in Protestant communities was putting the lives of my own family and employees in constant danger. I was in a tricky dilemma. I couldn't down tools and walk away from a project as that would be a breach of contract that would leave me open to being sued in court. The other problem was if I walked away from an incomplete project, I would not be able to recover monies owed to me by the NIHE.

I got to the site on the Shore Road and to my surprise, there was no commotion, no RUC Land Rovers, no army, no scene-of-crime tape and no indication that anybody had been shot. As I turned in to the compound, I spotted Frank up a ladder. I thought I'll say nothing about the call from the mysterious 'Captain Black'. I got out of the car and shouted up at Frank, 'come down here and we'll walk around the houses'.

Frank came down off the ladder and there wasn't a bother on him. I asked him how he was getting on? Had he any hassle? 'No,' said he. He added, 'there was talk around here of a child getting knocked down out on the main street but we didn't see anything.'

The site was busy, everybody was working away and I left it at that. I decided to call to the Grove Housing Association for a courtesy chat and test the water, so to speak. I didn't ask any questions and they were clearly unaware of anything sinister that day. I took it upon myself to go looking for Jimmy Craig but he was out of reach. I had three phone numbers for Jimmy but still couldn't track him down.

Later that night Jimmy rang me at our new house in Ashgrove, Newry. I asked him to meet me the next day in Belfast and he agreed. I'm sure Jimmy being Jimmy must have assumed we were meeting to discuss money. We arranged to meet at a fish and chips shop not far from the Shore Road.

Craig and Artie showed up and I made it clear to Jimmy that I needed to speak to him on his own. I suggested that Artie head off and I would give Jimmy a lift home. The two agreed. Jimmy had 'rent' to collect from the chipper and having done so, got in to my car before suggesting I bring him to his house at Northland Street off the Shankill Road.

I stopped the car outside his new-built NIHE red-brick house on Northland Street and he invited me in. I walked through the front door and was impressed at what I saw. The interior was luxurious and somewhat spacious. We made our way in to the kitchen and I sat down at the table.

As I glanced around my surroundings, I was shocked to see on the wall a picture of The Blessed Sacred Heart with a red-lit crucifix flickering at its base. Most Catholic houses across the world would have had one of these on display at this time.

I laughed my head off and said to Jimmy, 'what the hell's going on here, is this for me?'

'No' said Jimmy. 'Mary my wife is a Roman Catholic, goes to mass every day and is a daily communicant.'

I couldn't believe that a staunch hard-man Protestant and loyalist paramilitary from the Shankill Road area who approved the murder of Catholics and opposed everything that Irish nationalists stood for would marry someone from the opposite side of the divide in Northern Ireland.

Mary made us a cup of tea and a sandwich and left the house to go shopping. I got down to business and said, 'so Jimmy, can you tell me, who is Captain Black?'

'How do you know Captain Black? You wouldn't have any business with him.'

'Do you know who he is?'

'I do know but I can't understand why he would want to ring you.'

I told him that I had received a phone call the previous day from someone saying he was 'Captain Black' and for all I knew, that could have been anybody.

The so-called 'Captain Black' whoever he was, told me that my brother Frank had been shot dead.

'"Captain Black" didn't ask for money. He just said Frank had been shot dead but Frank is actually alive. I mean Jimmy there is no point in me paying you for security when I'm not getting what you promised.'

Jimmy was clearly agitated, went to the phone, dialled a number and asked the person at the other end his name. What followed next was heated and hostile.

Jimmy said to 'Captain Black', 'what the fuck were you ringing Eugene Reavey in Whitecross for yesterday? The Reavey Brothers are my clients. I've been dealing with them on this site all along, now you go and fuck off.'

Obviously, I don't know what 'Captain Black' said in return but one thing was obvious, there was tension amongst at least two senior members of the UDA in an ongoing battle over turf and money. The Reaveys were now in the middle of it

'Captain Black' was a name usually associated with UFF spokesperson John White. The same John 'Coco' White, left the Shankill area of Belfast in something of a hurry in 2003 following a loyalist feud with Jackie McDonald and his pals.

White was convicted for the 1973 murder of Catholic SDLP Senator Paddy Wilson who he stabbed a staggering thirty-two times and sliced his throat. In the same frenzied attack, he killed Protestant woman Irene Andrews for which he was sentenced to life in jail.

The only problem in trying to link John White to the call was, it seemed he was in prison serving his sentence. Unless he was running operations from the inside, it left me thinking that 'Captain Black' had to be some other person or else Jimmy was making a fake 'call' and nobody else was on the other end of the line.

I should add that 'P. O'Neill' was the pseudonym used by the IRA for all official announcements but no such living person was known to exist so this 'Captain Black' may have been somebody else or simply didn't exist at all.

Jimmy continued his rant and threats on the phone, 'If you don't leave my customers alone, I'll send Artie over to you and he'll kick the living daylights out of you, ye specky-eyed fucker.' Jimmy wasn't very nice when he was angry.

He slammed down the phone and was clearly upset. He knew that if I was put out of business, a chunk of his lucrative income would dry up. He said, 'drive me down to the Shore Road site'.

We left the house and headed for the compound. Along the way, Jimmy was determined to reassure me that I had nothing to worry about. He was going to sort this out by hook or by crook and both if necessary.

We got to the site and Jimmy proceeded to talk to Frank even though I had asked him in the car en route not to discuss the matter. Jimmy spoke to Frank and sounded him out by asking him in a civilised way if anybody had called the previous day? Frank told him that nobody had called and that it was a rather quiet one on the site.

I presumed that once Jimmy Craig spoke to 'Captain Black', that would be the end of the matter. It wasn't. It later transpired that following the theft of weapons at a UDR Station in Coleraine, Co. Derry, a prominent loyalist was stopped at a check-point and called in for questioning by the RUC. In the course of his interrogation, the same 'hard man' found the questioning too difficult to handle and began crying over his paramilitary past. As pent-up guilt came over him, he wept into his hands and revealed some of his past sins. He told the RUC that he was part of a death squad that was en route to kill Frank Reavey at the Shore Road in the Tiger's Bay area of North Belfast. The mission didn't exactly go to plan.

As 'Captain Black' was on the phone to me breaking the 'bad news', the death squad was approaching the site when a young child walked out on to the roadway and was knocked down. The RUC was told that the mission had to be aborted as the hit-and-run incident pushed their plan off course. In the process of building a case against the same loyalists, the RUC wrote to Frank and asked him if he would talk to them about his planned 'execution'?

Frank passed the letter on to me. I rang the investigating officer and asked him why it was necessary for Frank to co-operate seeing as he had no hand, act or part to play in his planned death?

I explained that we knew nothing about the planned UFF hit and anyway, if we participated in the prosecution of certain suspected loyalists, we would be signing our own death warrant. We didn't participate any further in the RUC investigation but at least we suspected where the whole 'Captain Black' story came from.

By now, we more or less knew how to play the scary extortion game in Belfast but as events evolved, the greedy boys in the UDA kept moving the goalposts and changing the rules. The bottom line though was, if you wanted to do business at street level, you had to pay money for protection.

It was purely a case of, play ball or deal with the consequences. You couldn't go to the RUC to make a complaint because if you did, you would have to face your 'protectors' in court and that in itself would, in all likelihood, mark the end of your time as a building contractor followed by an unwanted funeral with all the grief and bitterness that would bring.

Protection rackets were so rife, the RUC made little or no attempt to end this way of doing business as many of its members were sympathetic to the UDA cause which, from what we could see, was more about making money than maintaining loyalty to the crown.

We learned some time afterwards that as far as the NIHE was concerned, Reavey Brothers Contractors were the 'only' ones in Belfast they were aware of who were paying so-called 'protection' money. Of course what the NIHE didn't tell us was that other construction companies were paying phantom 'security companies' to look after their sites.

These so-called 'security companies' never existed even though they had the exact same 'shareholders' who benefitted from our work. They were UDA fake companies that only existed on paper. So when a construction company issued a payment, the invoice came from a company that had no office, no staff, no assets but, surprise, surprise, the payment always ended up in the pocket of a loyalist paramilitary.

As far as the NIHE and various housing associations across the six counties were concerned, these were 'legitimate payments' simply because the invoice and receipts could account for the money spent. Just like the 715 certs, it was then up to Revenue to engage with these mysterious 'companies' to ensure they paid their taxes to the British exchequer – which of course did not happen. This anomaly was going on all across the UK but was a dedicated way of life for certain people in Northern Ireland.

The frustration and endless fear of working in Belfast was a continuous battle every single day. One morning we would show up at one of our sites and 100 brand new doors ready for fixing on to frames would be missing. No sooner would that number be replaced when the next day all our ironmongery such as door handles, nails, hinges, etc., would be stolen and sold to a competing contractor.

It emerged sometime later that anybody who supplied us with goods would have to pay protection or delivery money. Jimmy Craig was making money on the double, treble and even quadruple in some cases from each site where his grip was firmly in place. Nothing moved unless he got a financial slice.

Jimmy Craig, 'An Innocent Man', so to speak

By 1984, we successfully applied for a contract at Greenisland outside Belfast. The result of our application at Greenisland had a familiar menacing pattern to it. In other words, we knew in advance our application was the successful one thanks to our old 'friend' Jimmy Craig. Within forty hours of our application being submitted to the NIHE, Jimmy could always tell us with remarkable accuracy if we were successful or not. This of course raised a number of questions. How did Jimmy know before us? How did he have access to such sensitive confidential information and more to the point, who in the NIHE informed him of who had applied? Jimmy also knew how much the project was worth. One can only speculate how Jimmy had access to such sensitive information.

One thing was clear though, Jimmy had access to inside information which made it difficult for us to budget for such jobs knowing that he would ask for his cut while simultaneously being aware of how much we would get. As time moved on, it became clear that Jimmy was keeping this confidential information to himself and did not share it with his superiors in the UDA.

Jimmy did not extort money from us for the Greenisland job but we still had to pay up to a local UDA extortionist called Charlie McCann. We wondered at times if Charlie in turn was paying a sub-contractors fee to Jimmy for the privilege of 'minding' us.

As our work at Greenisland got underway, this project became something of a poisoned chalice. In the first week of setting up camp, local youngsters stole hammers and tools from our inventory. These thefts always occurred during the various tea breaks throughout the day. The local thieves were so brazen that on one occasion we took a tea break only to discover that when we resumed work, a generator worth about £750 had gone missing. With our work on the project set to expand in the subsequent weeks, I had to buy three generators and as many heavy-duty chains. We tied the generators with the chains to the on-site lamp posts.

Our lads laughed at the time saying the use of chains would stop the local thieves from running off with the generators. How wrong they were. No sooner had the generators been brought on-site, our guys finished a tea break to discover that one of the machines had been hacked off its pole with a heavy-duty chain cutter.

My brother Seamus rang me to tell me about the costly ongoing theft from the site. I decided to give Jimmy Craig a call and tell him in clear terms that our tools and machinery were disappearing on site and that Charlie McCann was unwilling to retrieve the items for us. Jimmy got the message and said 'leave this with me'. True to his word, Jimmy showed up at the site the next day with every single tool and generator that had disappeared but he wanted £150 for being a 'good Samaritan'.

Despite the sense of relief that we had recovered all that we lost, it didn't make any difference in the long term. The tools and the generators continued to go missing. I would call Jimmy. He would retrieve them and Jimmy would get £150 for his efforts each time. The cycle of disappearance, complaint, return of goods and payment went on and on like an overworked boomerang.

Another costly stunt was one whereby some local young bucko would climb up on our scaffolding and jump on to a pile of sand. Next thing out of the blue, we would get a solicitor's letter with a claim that one of 'our employees' had broken his leg in a fall.

Of course, the so-called 'employee' never worked for us at all and when the matter was processed, for some bizarre reason, our insurance company would pay out £7,500. When we questioned this outrageous payment, we were told that it was cheaper to settle rather than contest it in the courts as legal fees would see the overall cost mount. Of course most of the £7,500,

I was informed, went to the UDA with the 'stunt man' getting a tiny fraction for supposedly 'breaking his leg'. In the meantime, payments of this kind increased our annual insurance premium.

The scams and the extortion were getting worse and more creative by the month. Paying for so-called 'protection' seemed like an endless stressful experience. The Italian mafia would have been easier to deal with.

On a separate matter, we were working on a project in Poyntzpass in South Armagh. The job was a series of new-builds, renovations and refurbishments, which we did every other day. It was around this time, a man called to my office in Whitecross. His name was Gerry Quinn and he was from the Department of Health and Social Security, commonly referred to us as the Dole office. I knew Gerry from old as he was an active GAA man with Clonduff GFC in Hilltown, Co. Down.

Gerry wanted to know the status of some people who were working on our site in Poyntzpass i.e. how many were direct employees of Reavey Brothers and how many were hired in by sub-contractors? He also sought to know the hours they worked and if they were paid by cash or cheque? The problem here was that if I required a joiner to work on six houses, I would agree a fee per house with him. The joiner would in turn hire in the appropriate number of people to complete the job. The people hired in worked for the joiner and *not* for us. I would pay the joiner who in turn paid his own team but it was up to them to pay their own individual taxes, etc. The joiner, as a sub-contractor, submitted the Cert to our office to get paid for work done. The Cert and an accompanying identity card, similar to a driving licence, were issued by her Majesty's Revenue Commissioners subject to companies like mine that met the required criteria, i.e. we were a legitimate operation turning over X amount of pounds per year and honouring our commitments to the Revenue by paying our taxes, etc. This was a practice we complied with at all times.

When the Cert was handed into a company, the picture on it would have to match the physical appearance of the person who owned it so that the individual seeking the payment was who he said he was. The company would then check with Revenue that the card was valid and hadn't expired before making the respective payment. The ultimate objective of the 715 cert was that companies like ours could issue a payment without having to charge tax at source. The theory of it all sounded fine. However major flaws were emerging.

Republicans initially and laterally loyalists, took full advantage of the 715 Certs. According to Jimmy Craig, they set up dummy companies and applied for 715 certs for individuals who were actually locked up in the H-Blocks and who, as it happens, were sometimes unaware that the certs were being applied for in their name. That may sound slightly complicated but, in a nutshell, paramilitaries were obtaining 715 Certs from her Majesty's Revenue, each worth on average £100,000 and sold them on usually for ten per cent of their value.

It was win-win for all involved except HMRC which was taking a huge financial hit. However, red flags were starting to be raised with the Revenue people in Whitehall as large numbers of workers hired in this way were not paying tax. The initial concern was the amount of people drawing the dole and working at the same time. The small amount of tax being paid relative to the high number of 715 Certs in circulation eventually, after many years, became a cause of concern for the authorities in London.

IN THE MEANTIME, HARASSMENT from the security forces showed no signs of ending. Every other morning as our vans, drove in to Belfast, we were stopped at Loughbrickland and Sprucefield. As always, we were asked the same usual questions – who are you? where are you from? where are you going, etc? Lunch boxes would be opened and emptied. Tool boxes thrown on the ground and contents in the van tossed in to the grass margins.

It never seemed to stop. We noticed that lots of other vans like ours drove the same road every morning and were not stopped at all. One can only imagine the amount of precious working hours, translated into money, that we lost at RUC, British army and UDR checkpoints day in, day out.

There was no point in complaining. How do you complain to the RUC about the RUC at a time when Catholics are being treated as second-class citizens and with deep suspicion?

One night in early 1986, at 5 a.m. in the morning, police personnel arrived at my door in Ashgrove Newry, where we lived at the time. The RUC did everything to kick the door in. As I heard the commotion, I jumped out of bed and peeped through the curtains where I could see at least ten officers and a number of cars outside the gate. My initial thoughts were, 'Great, at least it's the RUC and not the UVF'. I thought at the outset that maybe there was something wrong at one of the properties we were working at, like a fire perhaps or maybe a major theft. Maybe, a family member had been injured in a car crash? I put on my clothes and went to the door. There were at least four officers at the door and as many again out on the road.

The RUC officer asked me, 'Are you Mr Eugene Reavey?'

'Yes,' I replied.

'Are you the Managing Director of Reavey Brothers Contractors Limited?'

'Yes,' I replied again.

'I'm arresting you under the 1973 Northern Ireland Special Provisions Act.'

'What have I done wrong?' I asked in disbelief.

'You're coming with us. We have a warrant for your arrest.'

Before I knew it, the RUC officers pushed their way in to the hall and one of them made a grab for the phone book that was on the telephone table. He opened the book and the first name and number he looked for was that of Jimmy Craig to which he said, 'well, we have the right man here'.

I knew exactly in an instant why the RUC were there. I told them that they didn't have to search the house as my children and Róisín were in bed and all my documents were in my office in Whitecross. The senior RUC officer took my word and said, 'put your jacket on and we'll head there'.

I said to Róisín, 'I'm off to Whitecross with these boys. Don't be worrying. I'll be back.'

I was handcuffed to an RUC officer and bundled in to the back of a police car. We drove to the British army compound at Bessbrook and I was escorted to a helicopter which was full of soldiers and police. The noisy chopper made the short journey to Whitecross and landed in the GAA field. As we touched down, I noticed soldiers on the roof of Loughran's shop and a further armed batch crouched on the ground behind the wall inside my office grounds. The security presence was way over the top but I presume the RUC were sending out a message to the locals aimed at humiliating me and conveying a notion that I was involved in crime. (From the time Brian, John Martin and Anthony were killed, I never had a kind or courteous word sent my way by the RUC even though before January 1976, they were polite.)

The RUC removed every single sheet of paper and filing cabinet in the place, including the bins to the thirteen vans outside the office. All the material seized and myself were taken to Castlereagh interrogation centre in east Belfast. The questioning at times was ridiculous. They went through every contract I ever signed and wanted to know the names of persons who worked on the respective sites. They wanted to know was I paying money to the UDA?

'Yes I am'.

'Who are you paying the money to?'

'You know better than me who I am paying. Your people are very negligent in your duty. You know damn well because you have photographs. You should be ashamed of yourself. You have never given me protection, in fact I should have taken a case against you for failing to carry out your duties.'

Despite constantly asking for my solicitor to be present, a request repeatedly denied, I was quizzed over and over by three senior RUC detectives and I was shocked at the way they attempted to set me up for a possible charge. In the room was a flipchart with a number of names, each with lines heading off in different directions, attempting to link me with other individuals, companies we did business with and possible crimes. Intimidating as it was, the map of companies and individuals, failed to have the desired effect in getting me to say something that might incriminate me.

Of course I refused to name who I was paying protection money to, fearing what could happen as a result. Craig had previously warned me that if I implicated him or others in any way to the police, he would shoot me and members of the Reavey family.

I continued to remind them about the hassle Reavey Brothers Contractors had been receiving from the RUC, the delays at checkpoints, the removal of equipment from our trucks, the time and money lost because of their conduct, etc. I even asked them, 'what have you done to find out who killed my brothers? You've probably done F-all. You know who shot them and you won't do anything about it.'

Not surprisingly, I got no response. I must have touched a raw nerve. The RUC interrogators then started a line of questioning that focused on my parents. One of them said, 'your mother was a decent woman, I saw her on TV and you're going to be a big embarrassment to her if you don't own up and reveal who you're paying money to.' It was quite clear that all they wanted was for someone to go on the record to say something that would implicate Jimmy Craig. After numerous rounds of questioning, on one occasion my response to a silly query was to sing a verse of *The Boys from the County Armagh*. The RUC eventually released me. They mustn't have rated me as a singer!

A day after my release, I got a call from Jimmy Craig. He asked me how I got on with the RUC? He said jokingly, 'if they're asking about me, then they're leaving somebody else alone.' I told him that the RUC knew every site I was working on and that they had photographs of me talking to him but they had no pics of money being handed over. I also told him that the RUC had knowledge of individuals who had 715 certs that I had been using and I felt that some of the people who possessed these certs may have been talking to the police. As I saw it, the RUC had information that could only have come from somebody with a 715 cert.

'That's interesting,' said Jimmy.

Four days later, Jimmy rang me again. He had important news and wanted to meet me in a hurry. We met in the car park at The Halfway House pub near Dromore in Co. Down. Jimmy sat in to my car and left Artie Fee on his own in the other vehicle. He proceeded to tell me that he had an inside contact who managed to photocopy my statement to the RUC. He had the photocopy in a package in his hand. I was gobsmacked. Jimmy, who was able to know who had tendered for building projects, had access to RUC statements as well within hours of them being written up!

Certain people in the RUC were clearly looking after Jimmy, itself enough to ask how could Catholics have faith in the police service when some of its members were blatantly working hand in hand with British loyalist paramilitaries? Jimmy showed me the statement and I looked at it over and over before saying 'yes that's my statement all right'. I wondered if the RUC had made recommendations on what actions they might take against me? Jimmy didn't know. He was satisfied that my statement had not implicated him and so I got to live on for the foreseeable future.

The following Monday, the big news story of the day was that 'Leading Loyalist Jimmy Craig has been arrested in connection with alleged extortion'. Surprise, surprise, Jimmy was not charged and walked out of Castlereagh RUC Station an 'innocent man', so to speak. He told me later that the RUC said I had implicated him during my interrogation but as he had seen my statement he knew that was not the case. If Jimmy hadn't seen the statement, only God knows what would have happened to me and my wider family.

The episode was a sharp reminder about the way malicious individuals within the RUC could deliberately set people up for a fall. One can only imagine how many people were jailed in the wrong or shot dead during the Troubles because of conniving policemen with their own sectarian agenda.

Reavey Brothers Contractors had to continue business following the raid on my office without important files such as diaries, cheque books, maps and contracts, etc. I waited and waited thinking I'd be arrested again but the RUC couldn't find anything to link me to a crime.

Making a payment isn't illegal but harassing someone for such money is. It was quite clear they were on a mission to frame me. Two months later, the RUC gave up and the files were returned to Whitecross.

Every other day, local loyalists looking for money would come on site wanting to talk to me.

The foremen of the day would make excuses but they kept coming back. The cheeky and arrogant ones would come on-site making menacing threats that if we didn't pay up, we'd be found dead in a ditch. It was a scary experience and the threats could be executed any day at any time.

On one occasion, a local bolshy man came looking for me. Thinking we were a soft touch for money, he made the usual threats of 'I'm in charge around here, pay up for your own safety'. Our lads would always deal with such unwelcome individuals by saying, 'We have nothing to do with money. You'll have to talk to Eugene. He'll be here on Friday around 10 a.m.' Friday, as it happened, was always Jimmy's pay day. I rang Jimmy and asked him who this thug was? He replied, 'I don't know. I'll meet you at the site and we'll deal with him'.

At 11 a.m., Jimmy and Artie Fee arrived at the site and asked where this individual lived. Oliver pointed to a blue door across the way and Jimmy decided to confront this man. When we arrived at the house a short distance away, Jimmy burst in to the hallway and severely assaulted the man. Artie Fee lifted this man up from the floor and gave him a brutal beating in the kitchen before smashing up presses, cutlery, tables, chairs and everything he could get his hands on. The place was like a bomb site. I was horrified at the scale of the brutality I witnessed.

In the midst of the noisy commotion, Jimmy Craig then went into the kitchen and told his host in clear terms, 'don't you ever say anything to these people ever again. You're no UDA fundraiser. If I have to come back again, it will be a different story. This is only a warning.' The man, who was dripping in blood, clearly got the message. All I was thinking was, there will be revenge for this and the Reaveys will suffer.

As we drove away through unionist Woodvale, I said to Jimmy, 'don't involve me ever again in something like this'.

The UDA continued to give me 'special treatment' and to this day I still can't work out why, although with hindsight, I presumed that as long as I continued to pay up every Friday, I felt safe despite being a walking bag of nerves.

Jimmy remained in his role as the top extortionist in the UDA and as his riches multiplied, others, who made a comfortable living by extracting money from businesses, were doing all they could to move in on his growing empire. One such man was thirty-three-year-old John Bingham. A prominent member of the UVF and the Orange Order, he spent two and a half years in jail for conspiring to import weapons. He was convicted arising from evidence given by UVF 'super grass' Joe Bennett, a development that caused a lot of loyalist internal tension. A shop owner, Bingham was a married man with two children.

In the early hours of 14 September 1986, the IRA broke into his house in the Ballysillan area of north Belfast and shot him dead. According to the book *Lost Lives*, an IRA statement said: 'Relying on accurate intelligence reports, we were able to pinpoint the whereabouts of UVF murder-gang leader John Bingham, who after a period of intensive activities which resulted in the deaths of at least five innocent Catholics, had just, in the last number of weeks, felt safe to return home … The fact that his whereabouts were so closely monitored, led to speculation that the IRA had the assistance of loyalist paramilitaries … Reliable Shankill sources said they believed the killing was related to a territorial dispute over protection

Jimmy Craig, 'An Innocent Man', so to speak

money collection involving UDA leader Jim Craig.'

Jimmy, it seems, was working hand in hand with the IRA and was prepared to go to any length to protect his bulging bank account even it meant killing his colleagues in the UVF.

Speaking in the Northern Ireland Assembly shortly afterwards about Bingham's killing, DUP leader Ian Paisley decided to have a go at BBC Northern Ireland over its coverage of the murder. He said, 'A man is innocent until proved guilty. The BBC has no right to destroy a man's character. The IRA had no right to claim that Mr Bingham was a murderer.'

The Collusion Intensifies

Jimmy Craig was getting greedier by the day and had developed a new tactic to grow his already lucrative income. Every site we worked on by now had two young loyalists sitting in our work hut or on-site office. They monitored every batch of timber, cement, tiles, blocks, bricks, slates, window frames, the vehicles and their registration plates, you name it, that entered the site. They would report the comings and goings to Craig who, with Artie Fee, would contact the suppliers and 'persuade' them to 'donate' money to 'the UDA' otherwise they would be barred from selling their products to construction companies with potentially dangerous consequences.

It was around this time I met Tommy 'Tucker' Lyttle, the second-in-command to UDA leader Andy Tyrie. Our unplanned meeting came about when I agreed to see Jimmy Craig in the Europa Hotel in Belfast for a chat about 'business'. Jimmy and Tucker were in the hotel to give veteran journalist Jim Campbell of *The Sunday World* newspaper a proper earful following a revealing piece he had recently written. Jim, who had been shot at his own home three years previously by UVF paramilitaries, had an office in the hotel at the time for safety reasons.

Tucker Lyttle was the opposite in personality to Jimmy Craig. While Jimmy was Mr Alpha Male with muscles and dripping of gold, Tucker was very unassuming. Even though he was number two in the UDA, he was modest and was on record at that time as being opposed to killing Catholics for the sake of it. He believed the time had come for Northern Ireland to be a separate independent state. In 1978, he co-founded The Ulster Political Research Group which showed he had a different intellect to Jimmy who just wanted to beat up anybody who wouldn't give him money. After a lengthy conversation, Tucker told me that he knew my brother Seamus and lived close to where he was working. Tucker also said that he had something of importance in his house that he wanted me to see. All I could think of was, 'am I about to be lured to my death if I take up this offer?' But as I had become a generous and fiercely reluctant 'donor' to the UDA, they needed me more than I needed them.

Later that day I called to Tucker's house off the Shankill Road. His modest residence was heavily fortified with a thick steel door and when I walked in, I felt once again that I was entering a place where Catholics just didn't go. After a short chat, Tucker disappeared for a few minutes, returned and presented to me a collection of close on twenty-five sheets of paper, each containing twenty-four photographs. 'Here, have a look and see if you know any one of them?' he said.

As I stared with some bewilderment at the pictures before me, Tucker said, 'these photographs of republicans were given to me by the RUC Special Branch'. The more I browsed through the photographs, the more faces, complete with their respective names and dates of birth, I recognised. Fifty of the pictures, approximately, were of persons who worked for us and the batch included photographs of me, my brothers Seamus, Frank and Oliver. I also recognised a young man called Loughlin Maginn. We and others were targets and the RUC had handed this list to the UDA, proof, if ever proof was needed, that collusion between the security services and loyalist paramilitaries, was widespread.

I took the pics home asking myself in the car, 'why would Tucker Lyttle show these to me and more to the point, what did it say about the murky relationship between the RUC police force and the UDA? I came to the conclusion, rightly or wrongly, that Tucker Lyttle wasn't particularly interested in killing Catholics, republicans maybe and that these pics were of no benefit to him. What I would do subsequently with the photographs didn't seem to bother him either. There was always speculation about collusion between loyalist paramilitaries and the security forces but now for the first time, I could see the proof with my own eyes.

The Killing of the Reavey Brothers

I went home and said nothing to Róisín, Frank, Seamus or Oliver. I didn't sleep too well that night asking myself repeatedly, 'what should I do with this shocking information?' I decided to have a chat with my solicitor Rory McShane in Newry. When I showed the photographs to him, he asked where they might have been taken? I told him we were being stopped repeatedly at RUC checkpoints and in all likelihood, those were the places we were snapped. Rory advised me to inform all of the employees I had who were in the photographs. Once that was done, they would all be more vigilant in their

The Collusion Intensifies

movements and if anything happened, I could not be accused of withholding crucial information that put their lives in danger. He also suggested talking to the newspapers so I contacted Fabian Boyle, the local correspondent for *The Irish News* and a reporter I knew in the *Belfast Telegraph*.

Both papers, and latterly BBC NI as well as UTV and Downtown Radio, gave it prominent coverage. My name was not mentioned in print or broadcast so as far as the UDA was concerned, the source was unknown. The revelations made uncomfortable reading for some people in the security services and the British government. This confirmation of collusion meant that a long hitherto suspected genie had finally escaped from the political bottle. Despite my initial fears, Jimmy Craig and Tucker Lyttle never uttered a word to me about the revelations in the papers. For all they knew, it was somebody else and that led me to believe that these photographs or similar batches were circulated to many persons other than Tucker Lyttle.

Later Tucker phoned me as he had work for Reavey Brothers Construction. He wanted *us* to upgrade *his* security which did not make sense. Frankie Millar must have recommended us! The very thought of us carrying out a job on the Shankill Road area was scary enough at the time but to be working for one of the senior bosses in the Ulster Defence Association within which the ruthless anti-Catholic UFF operated, was frightening. As we upgraded Tucker's modest house, the UFF and UVF continued their respective strategies of killing Catholics. One can only imagine how the unionist community would have reacted if they knew that Tucker hired us from South Armagh instead of a loyalist-owned construction company!

In the summer of 1987, Jimmy Craig's fearless wingman and dreaded minder, Artie Fee, got married. Among the observers that showed up to see the happy couple take their vows was a crew from *The Cook Report*, an investigative current affairs programme which was produced by Central Television in Birmingham for ITV. Dedicated reporter Roger Cook was in town to make a documentary about how Jimmy Craig and his pals were extorting money from building developers, running rackets to fund terrorism and exploring the ultimate cost to the unsuspecting British taxpayer! I recognised Mr Cook from his TV programme. His producer contacted me and asked for a meeting over dinner. We agreed. One thing caught my attention when we met up though. He did not introduce me to all of his team which left me a bit uneasy and somewhat guarded as my initial instinct was that the other people at the table might have been police pretending to be part of the TV crew.

I sat down at the table with Mr Cook and at his insistence, ordered a dinner. He told me he was making a programme about the extortion game in Belfast which left me wondering how he became aware that I was paying money to Jimmy Craig?

After much too-ing and fro-ing about 715 forms, threats, intimidation, thefts, payments and the entire racketeering game, etc., in Belfast, Cook asked if he could do an interview with me about the extortion money I was handing over to the UDA? He promised that my identity would be protected, my voice replaced by an actor and my face would be obscured on screen. He also said that what he really wanted was for me to go on camera and reveal that Jimmy Craig was extorting me.

I told him he must be joking. If I went on camera, obscured or not and said something that left Jimmy Craig in no doubt it was me, I'd be dead in no time. The safety of my family and work force was always paramount for me. I thought Cook was very presumptuous. I felt that he thought that all he had to do was show up, ask me to go on camera and I would just say 'yes'.

The more I listened to his rhetoric on extortion, the more I felt that he must have received inside information from a source within the RUC and that worried me. I suggested we discuss this in the morning, after I gave this some thought.

Cook said he had to go to Portadown next day where he was going to do an undercover interview with a Mr Eddie Sayers, a prominent member of the UDA in mid-Ulster, who was also extorting money from local building projects. I said to him, 'I will go home and think about it. I'll see you here for breakfast in the morning and I'll let you know my decision.'

I discussed the matter with Róisín who reached the same conclusion that was uppermost in my mind namely, to give this interview a miss. I met Cook the next morning and told him of my decision not to go ahead with the interview. He said he was disappointed and added he would make it worth my while financially if I spoke. I also told him that no appearance money whatsoever would justify an interview. As usual, somebody flying in from England for a few days and leaving just as quickly clearly didn't know the local consequences when it came to speaking to the media on such sensitive issues.

WE GOT CONFIRMATION FROM the NIHE that we had submitted the best tender application for a new-build project on the Whiterock Road, a Catholic area just off the Falls area in west Belfast. One day in Jimmy Craig's company, I remarked that I had to pop in to the Housing Executive office in Adelaide Street to sign the contracts.

Jimmy asked if I knew who I would be dealing with on the Whiterock Road. In other words, who would I be paying extortion money to? I told him I hadn't a clue to which he said, 'I'll introduce you to the man you have to deal with on the Republican side'. I thought I was hearing things again. Here was a prominent member of the UDA offering to introduce me to a member of the Republican movement who he worked closely with. The 'sectarian war' in Northern Ireland, was, in my opinion, a deceptive farce at times. One thing was emerging and it was, the senior people on both sides were a 'protected species' while the foot soldiers on opposite sides were killing each other every week.

Jimmy arranged the meeting. Paddy Lynch, my foreman, and I went to the site on the Whiterock Road where we met our republican contact. Paddy recognised the contact having worked with him in the past. 'You leave this man with me and give me a few quid,' Paddy said to me. He had his own particular way of doing business over a pint in the pub. It turns out that Paddy did an extortion deal with the IRA which amounted to a bargain!

THE ITV *COOK REPORT* titled 'Worse than the Mafia' was broadcast on 19 August 1987. It described Jimmy Craig as being a 'UDA extortion specialist'. It reported how Craig and other loyalist extortionists worked hand in hand with the IRA in carving up Belfast City for so-called 'security' jobs. It told the viewer that Jimmy Craig and his counterparts in the IRA would meet regularly to discuss rackets. The programme stated that for some people in the UDA and IRA, accumulating money came first and the constitutional position of Northern Ireland within the UK came a distant second but as long as the war continued, both groups had a reason to extort money as it supposedly financed their respective causes.

As expected, the TV programme also focused on the abuse of 715 certs and how the British taxpayer was being fleeced under the system. To the wider public, the revelations were shocking but this was Northern Ireland and nobody in London cared.

The episode also featured an undercover interview with Eddie Sayers, the main UDA extortionist in mid-Ulster. In the interview, Roger Cook pretended to be an English property developer who was investing over £3 million in a project and wanted to know how much he would have to pay for 'security' but more so, why he should pay?

After all, this was not the way business was done elsewhere in the UK where loyalists supposedly got their law-and-order inspiration from. Eddie told Cook that he would be seeking £9,000 per million invested for 'security'. A demand of £27,000 for a fifteen-minute chat in a Craigavon car park wasn't a bad day's work even if the so-called 'security' was never delivered.

However most worrying on the *Cook Report* was an undercover interview with a man wearing an anorak standing beside the edge of Dundrum Lake with a fishing rod. The man whose identity was not revealed and whose voice was replaced by that of an actor, told the programme that he paid extortion money for 'protection' on a construction project carried out in the Shankill Road area. He told Cook that such was the level of intimidation he suffered, he couldn't get anyone to work for him and as a result went out of business with significant debts.

The interview and the programme didn't ruffle a single feather in London but caused quite a stir locally. In the days after the broadcast, my phone was hopping off the table with calls from other builders and the media wanting to confirm if the contents of Cook's report were accurate and if I could identify the man with the fishing rod at Dundrum Lake?

I told reporters that I spoke to Mr Cook and refused to take part in the programme. I said that I had no knowledge of who the man at the side of the lake was. The follow-up media coverage created greater awareness amongst the weary public, other building contractors and their respective families. It also set off a number of alarm bells within the UDA. The heat on Jimmy Craig was about to turn up a notch. As Jimmy's activities were subject to increasing scrutiny from a number of sources, Reavey Brothers Contractors were flat out with work. Our monthly turnover had reached a peak of almost £600,000 per month. Our cash flow was healthy and with sub-contractors taken in to consideration, we were paying close on 300 people every week. That was a lot of pay cheques at any time whether in Belfast or elsewhere.

ON 9 NOVEMBER, THE day after the Enniskillen poppy day bombing, the madness and stupidity of sectarian warfare reached another new low when an incident at one of our sites had fatal consequences. We were doing a job for the NIHE at Highfield Estate close to Woodvale in North Belfast. Jimmy Craig had insisted putting two UDA subordinates on to our site to monitor our staff and all the firms coming and going with building materials.

The two young UDA buckos turned out to be a menace, always in the way and trying to assert authority that they didn't have. John Rush, a very talented joiner by trade, was our foreman on the site. Something of a mathematical genius, John was a dedicated employee with a high standard of professionalism in his everyday work. It was customary for John to walk around his site every morning where he would speak to team leaders one by one and to tell them what was expected in the coming days.

He would also enquire what products were required in their respective areas and if materials needed to be delivered to the site. John Rush, a native of Crossmaglen, was highly respected by the tradesmen on site. He would always return to the site office at around 10 a.m., have a quick cup of tea and sandwich before making calls to our HQ office in Whitecross where he would tell our secretary, Briege, to place orders for cement, bricks, blocks, timber, etc.

On this particular Monday morning, he returned to the site office, poured tea from his flask into a cup and reached into his lunchbox for a sandwich only to discover it was empty. The two young UDA hoodlums sitting in the corner who had treated themselves to the contents of the lunchbox, laughed their heads off when they saw the expression of bewilderment on John's face over the missing sandwiches. They thought this was funny but John Rush did not.

Furious with rage, John grabbed each one of the boys by the hair and banged their faces together. He kicked them out of the office before telling them to go home and never come back. The boys, wincing in pain, made their way to the nearby Highfield branch of the Glasgow Rangers supporters club where they told their story to loyalists who were present. A few hours later, the two boys and a lookout person, returned to the site. A number of men, unknown to us, were undertaking an environmental project on a roundabout which was part of the site but not included in our contract.

One of the workers was nineteen-year-old Adam Lambert, a student from Ballygawley in Co. Tyrone. Thinking he was a Catholic, the two young UDA upstarts looking for 'a taig', shot Adam Lambert dead, having wrongly assumed he worked for Reavey Brothers. It turned out that Adam Lambert was a Protestant student. Later that day it was reported on radio that the killing was in retaliation for the Enniskillen bomb which happened the day previous. To me, this excuse for the killing was nonsense. Adam Lambert was shot dead as his three loyalist killers wrongly presumed, that because of where he was working, he was a Catholic. There was revulsion over the killing as Adam Lambert was working his way through college and had no political affiliations whatsoever.

To make matters worse for us, Reavey Brothers Contractors, were drawn in to the blame game as the killing happened on a site we were working on. Once again as in the past, we had difficulty getting people to work for us. None of our team wanted to work in the heart of loyalism where innocent people were shot in revenge for atrocities happening elsewhere.

WITH NOVEMBER COMING TO an end, one of the most vocal critics of Irish nationalism went to an early grave. George Seawright (36), a unionist councillor who was born in Scotland, was a member of the UVF and the Ballysillan Orange Order Lodge. His thinking was so extreme, his abhorrence of Catholics made him sound like something from the stone age. He once said, 'Taxpayers money would be better spent on an incinerator and burning the lot of them. Their priests should be thrown in and burned as well.'

Seawright's loathing of Catholics was so intense, the Irish People's Liberation Organisation, decided he had to go. He was shot in the head on 19 November 1987 as he sat in his parked taxi in Dundee Street, Belfast, and died fourteen days later. According to author Martin Dillon, Jimmy Craig was later implicated in his murder.[1]

With Christmas fast approaching, a killing of major significance took place that I believe radically altered the trajectory of the Ulster Defence Association and probably prolonged the

Troubles. It seems there was serious fallout from the broadcasting of the *Cook Report* on UTV/ITV. Jimmy Craig emerged from the programme as the leading extortionist in Belfast, taking money on a weekly basis from close on 100 businesses. One can only guess as to how much money was ending up in Jimmy's bank account. The problem for Jimmy was, senior people in the UDA had seen the TV programme and serious questions were being asked behind the scenes as to how much of this extorted money was going to the Ulster Defence Association, where it was supposed to go and how much was Jimmy Craig keeping for himself?

Stories had been circulating in loyalist circles about Jimmy's lavish expenditure. Pressure was coming on him from within the UDA. He was making lots of money, treating his friends to foreign trips and parties and the UDA wanted answers to certain questions.

A later report by journalist Ed Moloney published in Dublin-based *Village* magazine on 25 September 2021 revealed that Jimmy Craig had formed a cosy friendship with members of the Official and Provisional IRA that seemed to go beyond just business. According to Moloney's piece, Craig negotiated what was secretly known as 'The Top Man's Deal' whereby senior Republicans and Loyalists didn't kill each other. Both sides would meet regularly in places like The Lagan Social Club in the predominantly Catholic Markets area and The Royal Bar on the Shankill Road.

Ed Moloney reported that Jimmy Craig even went on holidays with his pals in the Official IRA, the non-violent wing of the Republican movement who, like Craig, were driven more so by making money through rackets than fighting for, or resisting, London rule in the six counties. A story on the *Village* website says that on one occasion the UDA and IRA men with their wives lapped it up in Italy where their holiday even took in a visit to the Vatican in Rome. Imagine if George Seawright knew that!

John McMichael, a commander in the South Belfast Ulster

Defence Association brigade, decided to investigate. He had been on an evolving mission to drive the UDA down the political route and away from violence, a plan that was not well received in the lower ranks of loyalism. From what Jimmy Craig told me, McMichael had the authority to either bring the rackets to a stop, divert more of the extorted money to the UDA or dismiss Jimmy from its ranks altogether. Whichever way one looked at it, the excesses of the party were coming to an end for Jimmy.

On 22 December 1987, thirty-nine-year-old John McMichael, a married father of two children who ran a local pub, opened the door of his car at Hilden Court in Lisburn to deliver turkeys to the families of loyalist prisoners. As he did, a bomb exploded and he died shortly afterwards. The IRA said they carried out the killing but the word was soon out that Jimmy Craig set it up as he believed John McMichael's investigation was going to bring his money-making rackets to an end. The RUC chief constable at the time, Sir John Hermon, issued a statement implicating Craig saying the killing 'was designed to cause grievous dissention and disruption and to eliminate a threat to whosoever that threat may have existed. I would not wish to take it further than that. But think of my words very carefully.'

John McMichael's killing caused outrage within the senior ranks of the UDA. Jimmy Craig was now seen to be out of control. Something would have to be done to put manners on him and prevent further solo runs that were being carried out without the approval of senior members in the organisation. An exception had been made for the 'Top Man's Deal' that Jimmy had put in place with the IRA, but as time passed on, there would be repercussions for John McMichael's death.

He calls himself 'Doctor Death'

Every year since 1976, the first week of January is a time that all of our family find themselves in a state of renewed trauma and emotional upset. Each festive season, the days between Christmas Eve and 4 January are like re-living the same period all over again.

In the first week of January, the annual memorial mass for Brian, John Martin and Anthony takes place on a Saturday evening in nearby Carrickananney church. For us, it's an occasion to formally remember the boys, re-kindle old family friendships and catch up with people who knew them well at the time but have since moved away from the area.

In the first week of January 1988 as we went through the annual trauma, I got a surprising phone call from my solicitor's office in Newry. Paul O'Kane had bad news for me, the more he spoke to me, my mouth became dryer as I absorbed the news. He asked me to accompany him to Bessbrook RUC barracks where charges would formally be made against me in relation to the operation of Reavey Brothers Contractors. I sensed straight away that these related to the 715 certs but I wasn't sure at this stage. I met Paul in Newry and we drove to Bessbrook. Having eventually negotiated our way in to the heavily fortified RUC barracks, we were brought into a room. An RUC inspector came in and read out the charges. The RUC were taking me to court for alleged false accounting.

A few days later on Friday 8 January, I was in Belfast. Friday, as always, was payday for the UDA mafia. We had eighteen new-build houses to develop on a site that up to then, had been completely hassle free. I was in a makeshift office upstairs in a completed house. There was a knock on the door downstairs and when I opened up, Jimmy Craig and Artie Fee were there. Jimmy walked in and Artie remained outside the door on watch. There was the usual bit of chat between us and I handed over the envelope which contained several thousand pounds which Jimmy quickly buried in his inside pocket and quipped, 'See you next week Eugene'. I walked them out to the main street and watched as they crossed the road and enter a nearby pub.

Tommy Lynch was the foreman and at around 2 p.m., he came up to me and said, 'there's a strange man down here and he wants to talk to you.'

'What's his name?'

'He calls himself "Doctor Death".'

'Really? send him up.'

When he walked into the office, I asked him, 'Who are you?'

'I'm Davy Payne. I'm in the UDA and I'm looking for protection money.'

He had a vindictive look on his face. I didn't realise it then but I was dealing with one of the most vicious and feared killers to grow up in Northern Ireland and I also later learned that his nickname was 'Psychopath!' To put Davy Payne in context, Jack Holland, the Belfast-born journalist, in the New York-based *Irish Echo* on 26 March 2003 described him as, 'the UDA's most violent and feared killer'. That was quite a title to have considering the long list of ruthless loyalists who lined out for the UVF, UFF and LVF down through the decades.

These included Lenny Murphy, fellow Shankill butcher Robert 'Basher' Bates – who was given ten life sentences, John Gregg, Stephen 'Top Gun' McKeag and our old 'friend' 'Captain Black' namely John White. Other notables included Billy Wright, Kenny McClinton – the religious pastor who wanted to chop off the heads of Catholics and place them on railings in Woodvale Park – Michael Stone, Frankie Curry – who boasted of killing nineteen Catholics, Jimmy Craig, savage killer Robin 'The Jackal' Jackson and terrorism director Johnny 'Mad Dog' Adair.

Davy Payne also had a volatile temper and when operating so-called 'romper rooms', was known to use electric drills to kneecap victims when torturing them. Unknowingly at the time, I was clearly 'rubbing shoulders' with the man at the top of 'the depraved' club.

As I stared Davy Payne in the eye, I jokingly said to him, 'You're too late mate. Jimmy Craig was here before you'. He said, 'This is my area and Craig has no business taking money from you.' His mood quickly turned and all of a sudden, he produced a gun from under his coat. 'I'll blow your fucking head off if you don't pay me.' He pressed the gun towards my mouth and I pushed it away before I said to him, 'I don't have any more money with me and I can't pay you.' I told him to contact Jimmy Craig and get the money from him. Davy pressed the gun in to the back of my head as I stared out the window.

He told me to turn around, face him and open my mouth. He pushed the gun in to my mouth again and I stood shaking like a leaf on a windy day.

'Don't give any more fucking money to Craig. I'll be back next week and I want that money.'

He took the gun out of my mouth, put it in his pocket and left. Rattled by this frightening experience, I followed him at a distance and watched his movements. He crossed the Lisburn Road and to my surprise, he walked in to the same pub that Jimmy Craig and Artie Fee had entered half an hour before.

'Something strange is going on here. Are these boys trying to extort me twice over?' I wondered.

I had three numbers for Jimmy Craig and I usually connected with him on one of them. There was a café close by which had a pay phone and I popped in there. I rang the first number on my list and to my surprise, Jimmy answered the phone.

'Jimmy what the fuck is going on here? I've just had Davy Payne here looking for money and he put a gun in my mouth and to the back of my head.' I vented my anger and told Jimmy I was not going to tolerate anybody coming on to the site to intimidate me or any of my workers. I reminded him that I was paying for 'security' and I wasn't getting it.

Jimmy calmly said in response, 'You're very lucky he didn't shoot you'.

I told Jimmy, 'You better get over here to the site'.

Shortly afterwards Jimmy and Artie returned to the site and

I told him I was thinking of pulling out of this and other sites in Belfast. I made it clear to him that if he couldn't guarantee our safety, I wasn't going to put my team in danger and I'd stop applying for projects in the city. This was news that Jimmy did not want to hear.

I was very shaken by this incident as it was the first time in a long time that I really feared for my life. Jimmy replied by saying that Davy Payne was a very violent person whose attitude to extortion was usually one of, 'shoot first, ask questions later'. He tried to calm me down by saying that Payne would not be back on this site, a comment which, at the time, made me feel the two were, perhaps, partners in crime.

Jimmy asked Artie to go down to the café and bring back two coffees and pastries. As Artie headed off, I went downstairs and told Tommy Lynch to instruct all the on-site crew to go home. My fear was that Davy Payne might return and if he did, this time he would pull the trigger and that would be the end of me. About half an hour later, Craig arrived and confirmed that the man who came on-site actually was Davy Payne. I wasn't sure if he was trying to calm me down but he went on to say, 'I want you to watch the late-night news on BBC tonight. Make sure you do. He then left.

I locked up the office and site entrance gates. My car was parked around the corner close to the café. I was so afraid over what happened, I went in to the café for refuge and got a coffee. Like hundreds of times before, I repeatedly asked myself, 'why am I putting myself through all this hassle? Is it worth it and more to the point, is it justified to put the lives of my brothers and my workers on the line because loyalist thugs want all our hard-earned earnings?'

When I eventually arrived home that Friday, I must have looked bad. Róisín kept asking me, 'Are you all right?' She knew something was wrong. I told her that it was just another Friday and I had to deal with the usual Belfast hassle.

After I had my tea, I walked up in to the back field at Ash Grove, where we were building houses, to check how the lads on that particular project were getting on. When I returned to home, I couldn't sit down after the fright I got earlier that day such was the fear, tension and adrenaline-flow in my body.

Róisín was watching *The Late Late Show* on RTÉ TV with Gay Byrne. It was one of those 'specials' that one didn't interrupt. I walked up and down repeatedly in the kitchen clocking up time trembling with nervousness and waiting for the BBC NI TV news to come on air.

I did tell Róisín there was an item of interest coming on I needed to see, even though I didn't know what it was going to be. I hadn't a clue what was coming next. As the story was introduced, it quickly became clear what Jimmy Craig meant when he said I 'wouldn't have any more trouble from Davy Payne again'. The news reader said the RUC had stopped three cars outside Mahon Road police station in Portadown. The drivers had been detained. The reporter said, 'A large consignment of rifles, hand guns and ammunition were found in the cars'. The report said 'a third man has also been detained. It is believed the man is a senior loyalist from Belfast'. It was reported that Davy Payne had the telephone number of a leading loyalist written on the back of his hand. It was subsequently reported that the leading loyalist was Noel Little from Markethill, whose daughter Emma Little-Pengelly is now the deputy First Minister of Northern Ireland.[1] It was clear to me that Jimmy Craig knew that a consignment of weapons was destined for the UVF and Ian Paisley's newly created Ulster Resistance Movement which was set up with the intention of collapsing the 1985 Anglo-Irish Agreement.

The weapons were being transferred from a 'farm' in South Armagh to personnel in the greater Belfast area. Determined to isolate Davy Payne from his money-making patch, Jimmy tipped off his pals in the RUC that the deadly consignment was en route. The cache consisted of 90 Browning pistols, 161 AK-47s, 250 grenades, 6 RPG 7'S, 184 magazines and 11,000 rounds of ammunition, along with 200 lbs of deadly Semtex. Davy Payne was sentenced to nineteen years in jail for his trip to Portadown that day thanks to Jimmy Craig. This was proof once again of how ruthless Craig was to prevent rivals from moving in on his lucrative rackets.

The episode was also a massive blow to the UVF who invested huge money, resources and time in securing the weapons. The senior personnel in the UVF were furious and put two and two together that somebody within their ranks had tipped off the law-abiding wing of the RUC.

The Davy Payne episode left me scared. I was one of the last people to see him before his arrest and I feared that people within the UVF ranks might think that it was me who had reported him to the RUC for harassment. I lived nervously during the subsequent weeks.

Meanwhile the fallout from *The Cook Report* which was broadcast on UTV/ITV the previous autumn continued. Pressure was coming on Jimmy Craig and he decided to take legal action against the makers of the programme. By early 1988, Central TV had persuaded 'the man in the anorak' who was seen with his fishing rod on the edge of Dundrum Lake, to be a key witness in their defence. The 'man in the anorak' whose face was covered and voice altered on-screen, happened to be an old friend, forty-five-year-old Jack Kielty from Dundrum village in Co. Down, an active member of the GAA. One of his three sons, Patrick, went on to have huge success in Britain as a comedian/presenter and now fronts *The Late Late Show* on RTÉ TV.

Jack was a popular man and at one time early in his life, he forged out a successful career as a band promoter bringing big names like Roy Orbison and Tom Jones to Northern Ireland. I also knew Jack well through the music business. At one time, I managed a country music band called *The Clipper Tones* which did gigs in the South Armagh/South Down area. I would regularly ring Jack and ask him if he could get us gigs and from that, a close friendship developed. Added to this, we both had plenty to talk about through our involvement in the GAA.

Jimmy Craig had intimidated Jack Kielty to pay protection money on a building project in Belfast. Jack was paying protection money until he couldn't pay any more and went out of business. When Jack spoke in disguise on *The Cook Report*, the average TV viewer hadn't a clue who he was but Jimmy Craig watching in Northland Street, off the Shankill Road in Belfast, identified him straight away. With Jack lining up to condemn Jimmy in the dock, events took a sinister turn. On 25 January, three members of the UDA's UFF burst in to Jack's office and shot him dead. A grieving widow was left to raise three sons. To the rest of Northern Ireland, it was just another sectarian death but everybody in the building trade knew what lay behind Jack's killing.

I was sick and somewhat nervous for a week, not just because I knew Jack but also because I could see that Jimmy Craig was turning into an uncontrollable monster and all it took was for one cross word between me and him, and I could be next.

The Cook Report had, unintentionally, contributed to Jack Kielty's death. I told Cook of the consequences for persons that went on camera and said critical things. Because Britain has a population of just under sixty million, one can do that in England and disappear into a different community. Northern Ireland, which can be somewhat parochial at times, is a more difficult place to hide in and the makers of that TV programme failed to understand this particular nuance of life here.

Porridge

In August 1988, my solicitor Rory McShane informed me that my trial would take place on 8 October at Craigavon crown court. I asked him for the best legal representation I could get. He contacted James McSparran, QC, who previously represented Reavey Brothers Contractors in our action against the NIHE after they removed us from the tender list. James was committed to a murder trial and wasn't available. Rory had another barrister in mind. He called Michael Lavery and when he picked up the phone he said, 'Mr McShane I haven't heard from you in ages'. Rory replied amusingly, 'Mr Lavery, it's not every day one of my clients can afford your services'. I went to Michael Lavery's house on the upmarket Malone Road in Belfast and explained my predicament to him.

To cut a long story short, I appeared in court and to the surprise of my legal team and myself, I was found guilty for my illegal use of 715 Certs. Before I knew it, I was on my way to prison.

An hour later I was taken in handcuffs out of the cell, down a corridor and escorted into what is called 'the horsebox'. My handcuffs were attached to the side rail on the inside and I was driven the bumpy road to Crumlin Road Gaol. As far as I was concerned, I had been deliberately set up to satisfy an RUC agenda which was to put Jimmy Craig behind bars. Trying to get someone to testify against Jimmy was another day's challenge altogether.

When I was escorted into the Dickensian jail on 12 October 1988, a prison officer remarked, 'Oh Mr Reavey, we've been waiting on you all week'. It all smacked to me as if a pre-determined decision had been made that I was going to jail whether I was innocent or not. Why would a prison officer say what he said unless somebody notified him in advance that I was expected here even though the outcome of the trial only occurred several hours previously?

After official registration in the prison, I had to hand over all my worldly goods such as my wedding ring, watch, wallet, etc. My Pioneer Total Abstinence pin which lets the world know that I don't drink alcohol and is distinctly unique to Irish Catholics, was a major cause of curiosity. One of the prison officers remarked to a colleague when he saw the pin, 'we have a right one here'.

One of the first things I had to do, was strip off and enter the human equivalent of an ancient wooden cattle crush. I was then doused with lice powder. It was humiliating. As the powder rained down on me and I was conscious that some of the most dangerous men that stood in shoe leather had passed through this process, I was somewhat taken aback when I noticed a name carved into the nearby wood. 'Bobo Price was here'. I laughed to myself as I went to secondary school in Newry with Bobo.

As I emerged from the shower of lice powder, one of the prison officers bundled my suit in to a basket and I said to him, 'hi boy, go easy with that suit of mine,' to which he replied bluntly, 'when you're in here, you're a nobody. You own nothing.'

As I had not expected to be convicted that day, I had no spare clothes with me. I had to wear out-of-shape prison garb with the only positive thing being that it had been recently washed. I was led to C Wing where my cell was no bigger than twelve feet by seven feet in size. If that wasn't bad enough, I had to share it with two loyalists. I didn't get any welcome from my two cell mates. All they knew was I was from down the country.

The two loyalists slept in the bottom beds while I had the upper bunk. My two cell mates were thin on conversation. I couldn't work out initially if they were just shy or whether they despised sharing a cell with someone like myself who was from the opposite side of the divide.

When teatime arrived, I went to the canteen where I noticed very quickly that the republican prisoners ate on one side and the loyalists on the other with respective tattoos determining where one was seated. I sat on my own and observed their manoeuvres.

When the man with the library trolley came my way the

next day and I gazed at his selection, I was shocked at what I saw. Practically all the books were of primary school standard. *The Famous Five: Five on a Treasure Island* by Enid Blyton was about as intellectually challenging as it got!

Next day, Róisín visited the prison. She brought clothes, food and copies of the *Irish Farmers Journal*, the British *Farmers Weekly* and a good thick GAA book. I had plenty to keep me occupied.

That evening sometime after 5 p.m., I went down to the canteen for my tea. Everything seemed normal when I walked in. I got in the queue like everyone else and selected my food before sitting down at an isolated table. As I tucked in to my food, I could see that a number of loyalists were huddled in a corner having, what appeared to be, a dramatic discussion.

'Something must be wrong,' I thought.

As I ate and read one of my farming magazines, I finished my meal and headed towards one of the in-house bins in the canteen to dispose of waste food. As I did, I drifted into the loyalist side of the line that divided the orange side from the green one. As I was leaving, two loyalists blocked me.

'Come on over here, we want to talk to you for a few minutes,' one of them said. I thought I was in trouble and that my loyalist cell mate had finally told his colleagues that I gave him a slap in the cell over an earlier dispute about keeping the light on in the cell and sensed I was about to be punished for my actions.

As I moved into a corner, I noticed that the twenty or so loyalists who had earlier on been in a huddle, were now moving in my direction. Before I knew it, there was an angry crowd around me. There were far more of them than there was of me. I sensed, with great nervousness, I was about to get a serious kicking.

Next thing, I was told something that totally shocked me One of the men asked me, 'Did you hear the news?'

'What news?' said I.

'Your friend Jimmy Craig has been murdered and your crowd did it. He was murdered by the Fenians.'

I didn't know whether to believe it or not.

'How could Jimmy Craig be murdered? After all, he was "untouchable" and had connections high up in the IRA.'

Next thing was, I got a whack in my lower ribs followed by a thump in the stomach. I fell to the floor and before I knew it, I was being kicked from all angles. I screamed in pain with every kick fired into me. Even though it lasted for ten seconds or so, it felt like an eternity. The kicking came to an unexpected stop when a tall man appeared from nowhere and said, 'lads, knock it off'. I don't know if he was a leading loyalist or a senior member of staff in the prison but the gang dispersed almost immediately. Having rolled around the place in agony, I eventually lifted my battered body up off the cold floor and dusted myself down. Despite the severe pain I was in, I hobbled back to my cell and turned over repeatedly in my bed howling in pain.

The news was out – Jimmy Craig really was dead. The man who had been the recent bane of my life was finally gone. His treachery, bullying, intimidation, murder of fellow loyalists, rackets, extortion and insatiable hoarding of UDA money in his own bank accounts, finally caught up with him.

He had been lured to, what he believed was, a UDA meeting at The Castle Inn pub on Beersbridge Road in east Belfast. It emerged that prominent loyalist Charlie McCann from Greenisland in north Belfast had attended an earlier meeting of UDA brigadiers in which the decision was reached to take out Craig. For some unknown reason, Artie Fee did not accompany Craig to the pub. The man who brought him there was Charlie McCann. Within minutes of arrival, McCann got a whisper in his ear and was told to go to the men's room.

Just as Craig commenced a game of pool, two masked gunmen walked in and shot him dead firing eleven rounds. As Craig lay dying, dripping in his own blood, McCann emerged from the men's toilets and ripped an expensive thick gold chain from Jimmy's bloody neck.

A bystander called Victor Rainey, a pensioner, was also killed while four others were injured. The UDA said they killed Jimmy

Craig for 'treason' following the death of John McMichael. According to the book *Lost Lives*, no UDA leaders attended Craig's funeral.

The next day Sunday, newspaper reports revealed to the public that Jimmy Craig had been shot by men instructed by the UDA leadership, a development that took the focus off me in Crumlin Road Gaol.

The officer in charge of republicans at the prison, whose name I didn't know, came to see me. He had heard about the beating I received and wanted to know if I wished to make a formal complaint to him?

I said 'no' because I understood why they thought it was a republican that killed Craig. In the interests of long-term safety and getting out of prison with full remission, it was best to say nothing.

On Monday morning, I went to the prison doctor. He too asked me if I wanted to make a formal complaint. Likewise, I said 'no'.

As I nursed my painful injuries, republican prisoners took the view that loyalists in the jail would have to pay for the wrongful kicking I received. Several days later as loyalists had their turn in the TV room, a group of angry republicans gathered up all the balls and cue-sticks from the billiards rooms and decided to take action. The group stormed in to the TV room and fired the balls at the television set smashing it instantly. They then beat the twenty or so loyalists with the billiard cues. The room was wrecked. The unexpected nature of the attack caught the loyalist prisoners by surprise.

The officers in charge on both sides met afterwards to discuss what happened and on the basis that the republican side deemed it justified, there was no further retaliation. The very loyalists who were hammered by the republicans in the TV room, filed in to the canteen next day and sat on their side of the dividing line as if nothing had happened at all.

Within days, I had some good news – I was transferred from C to D Wing where, to my surprise, I had a cell and a bed to myself. I felt like a VIP prisoner. I didn't have to worry about lights being switched off against my will. D Wing had a more civilised bunch of prisoners which probably sounds like a contradiction. None of the prisoners I met in the wing were there for paramilitary activity. They were all short-term inmates. While in D Wing, I undertook a fitness campaign.

I also met up with leading loyalist Eddie Sayers who was in prison arising from his appearance on the *Cook Report*. Eddie was civilised compared to the now departed Jimmy Craig. I got talking to him one day out in the yard and in the course of the conversation, he had some revealing news for me.

'Come here, do you see that fellow over there? Do you know him?' he asked.

'No'.

'His name is John Weir and he used to be an RUC policeman up your way in Newtownhamilton and Newry. He would have information about the killing of your brothers and he would like to talk to you'.

At that stage, I didn't know who to trust and what he suggested, at face value, didn't sound right. When you're in jail, you don't trust anybody.

One day I was walking around the yard and as I did, I heard two prisoners right behind me in conversation. They happened to mention 'The Reavey Brothers' which caught my attention immediately. When I turned around, I recognised the two faces. They were the young loyalists who were convicted for the murder of nineteen-year-old Adam Lambert. He was shot dead close to the Glasgow Rangers social club in Highfield Belfast the previous November, the day after the Enniskillen bomb in the mistaken belief he was a Catholic.

On recognising me, one of them said in an aggressive tone, 'We want to talk to you. Our wives have no money. We are in prison and can't earn any money so we want you to tell your wife to bring us up £500 every Saturday OR ...'

'Listen lads, any money you got in the past, that day is over'.

'We'll see about that. We'll get the number of your wife's

car.' I dismissed their implied threats and viewed them as little brats who weren't very bright.

Before Christmas I was transferred to Magilligan Prison in Limavady, Co. Derry, which caused some inconvenience as it meant Róisín now had to drive from South Armagh to the north coast, a round trip of 170 miles – and took up the best part of a full day.

Magilligan was a more modern prison and compared to the stone-age confines of Crumlin Road, it was like a luxury hotel, although the library trolley was still full of primary school books. Although I was listed for parole at Christmas 1988 which was posted on the notice board, it didn't happen.

Then one day, I discovered that my two young loyalist 'friends' from Belfast had also been transferred to Magilligan. Not surprisingly, they approached me again looking for money. I wasn't in the mood for any more hassle so I made a complaint to the OC on the republican side. Let's just say, I was never approached again and one of them was last seen requiring serious dental treatment having received prison 'punishment' as a result of my intimidation.

The refusal to release me on parole at Christmas left me worried. I sensed that either the RUC or British military intelligence were still plotting against me. Of course I couldn't prove that but these are the things that go through your mind when the state is making your life a misery. I wouldn't be spending Christmas Day with Róisín, Catriona, Aisling, Anthony, Fergal, Laura and Sarah. God knows how they felt.

As January 1989 approached its second week, I was surprised when one day I saw my name on the prison notice board. It said I was due for release on the tenth of the month. I was excited but another part of me felt this could be yet another false dawn. On 9 January, a welfare officer in the prison called to my cell. She confirmed that I was going to be allowed home the next day.

I walked out the gate next day, inhaled the fresh Derry air and was back in the real world again. My cousin Seán Loughran was waiting for me outside. En route home, we stopped off in

Dungiven and I got my first decent breakfast in three months. We then went to north Belfast.

My first port of call was to see UDA boss Tucker Lyttle. I wanted to clear any possible misunderstanding he might have had about me arising from the trial, if he had any at all. Seán, who had never been on the Shankill Road before, was a bundle of nerves as he sat in the car waiting for me.

I knocked at the door and one of Tucker's daughters answered.

'Is Tucker in? Tell him Eugene Reavey is at the door.'

Tucker came to the door and invited me in. The initial chat was all along the lines of 'when did you get out?' and 'how did you get on in prison?'

After some pleasantries, I got straight to the point. 'Well Tucker, I am just out of jail and this is my first stop. I wanted to speak to you personally and let you know that I had absolutely nothing to do with the murder of Jimmy Craig.

'I never gave any evidence at my own trial implicating anybody from the UDA. I said if word came out about anybody paying money to the UDA, it came from the revenue people. I paid my dues to the UDA to the tune of £1.35 million approximately.'

A surprised Tucker replied by saying, 'Really? We had you down for £350,000. I didn't think he was into you for that much money. It was a pity you didn't have a word with me about Craig any time I met you.'

'Most times I met you, Craig was always with me. I just wanted you to know all this so that you would be the first to know the truth.'

Tucker Lyttle was grateful for my visit. I brought some clarity to a situation where there might have been doubt about the evidence presented at my trial. Tucker assured me, despite my concerns, they knew that I had no part to play in the execution of Jimmy Craig.

He went on to say that a UDA meeting of its brigadiers took place where the internal investigation into the killing of John McMichael and other contentious issues were discussed. It was decided that Craig's working relationships with republicans, in particular those who killed prominent loyalists and his ongoing embezzlement of funds that were supposed to be destined for the UDA, meant he had to be taken out. His comments were what I suspected, but a huge relief for me. I could sleep a little easier when I got home that night.

I returned home to a good roast beef dinner. Róisín and the family were delighted to see me.

Many months after my release from jail, I experienced more terrible news. A leading member of the IRA has received some information about me and got his details completely back to front. A localised newsletter appeared in an edition of *An Phoblacht* which stated that I was a financial donor to the UDA. This was the equivalent of treason in South Armagh where in the eyes of some, it was seen that I was financing the UDA war against the IRA. I was an angry man. Somebody in the republican movement it seems, didn't know the difference between intimidating extortion and donation. As I drove around South Armagh in the subsequent weeks, I sensed that the IRA had it in for me as well as the Brits. I just wondered at times, where and how these people got their information? Despite our protestations, no apology was ever published.

MEANWHILE AFTER ALL THESE years, we were still anxiously waiting for word from the RUC about their so-called 'investigation into the killing of the Reavey brothers'. Every time I was stopped by the RUC at a checkpoint, I would ask them if there was any update? They would always reply 'no'. As we waited anxiously for a development, the UVF and British security services were planning more sinister deeds against innocent Catholics.

Brits Signal Desire to Leave

With Craig dead and Davy Payne doing time behind bars at her majesty's pleasure, I feared that other extortionists would move in to take their place. With the way things were going with Inland Revenue, I was also beginning to have serious doubts as to whether or not Reavey Brothers Contractors should work in Belfast again. If I took the decision to abandon Belfast, a whole new approach to generating income would have to be looked at and in all likelihood that would be via farming.

My time in prison allowed me to have a long think about life. I weighed up where I was at, the chaos caused by the killings of Brian, John Martin and Anthony, the hassle with Jimmy Craig and the ongoing intimidation from the RUC and British army.

Then I received a letter from the taxman. He was looking for £850,000 from my farming income. I was no sooner out of prison for the 715 Certs conviction – which brought no benefits to me at all – and here I was now facing a bill of over £800,000. The British state was leaning on me again.

I happened to know a tax consultant in one of the biggest accountancy firms in Belfast. I rang him up and he invited me to his house for a chat. We had a long discussion and he said something that proved crucial to my dilemma. He said, 'If you were a Protestant man and you lived in Bangor, I could take you to the taxman and we could do a deal but you would still have to take a hefty financial hit. On the other hand, the fact that you live so close to the border, there is no reason why you couldn't sell your properties in Northern Ireland and move five miles down the road to the Republic where the tax laws are different. All you have to do is live there for seven years, you can still cross the border every day as long as you are resident in the south. The choice is yours.'

I asked him repeatedly if his proposal was above board and how much it would save me? He assured me it was and the

Brits Signal Desire to Leave

amount I would save, would make it worth my while.

The next job on my hands was I had to run this proposal past the boss – Róisín. Naturally she had concerns. Such a move would be a major upheaval and create, at the outset, immense inconvenience. The one thing she insisted on was that any new home would be sited between Dundalk and the border. With Róisín's shopping list of demands and concerns firmly lodged in my head, I gave myself seven days to make my mind up. The best part of 400 cattle would have to be sold as would close on 160 acres of land and our house at Ashgrove in Newry. I spoke to a couple of estate agents and they put the word out.

While all this was going on, I had to look for a suitable property. I spoke to a number of estate agents in Dundalk and they in turn recommended several houses. We eventually settled on a property in Ravensdale about two miles from the border on the Co. Louth side which we purchased at public auction. With deposit paid and house purchased, I now had to get some cash to pay for the property. I quickly had to dispose of my assets and to my surprise, I offloaded the bulk of my land and cattle within a month. The house in Newry took a little bit longer to sell.

I gave more thought to the future of Reavey Brothers Contractors Ltd. In the spring of 1989, I called a meeting of the company's directors. The four of us had a long chat and in light of the ongoing hassle from the RUC and efforts to put us out of business, I felt that the time had come to take a change in direction. After much soul-searching and heavy hearts, we decided to liquidate the company. Approximately 300 or so tradesmen who had depended on us in the past, would now have to seek work elsewhere. As well as that, the local economy in South Armagh would be taking a notable hit. It was a massive decision to take. We were no longer working for others. I promised myself that no matter what future venture I entered in to, I would never pay extortion money again. A special era in my life had come to an end.

In the weeks/months that followed, most of our tradesmen and women managed to re-locate to different companies. One or two even started their own business ventures. I undertook to make arrangements to pay off small operators and individuals that were owed fees for work done as sub-entities on behalf of Reavey Brothers Contractors. While Reavey Brothers Contractors Ltd was no more, we formed a new construction company with the aim of doing local jobs. We were never going back to Belfast to work and would instead operate in the South Armagh, South Down area. To our surprise, we were inundated with offers of work. The jobs were not as big as the ones in Belfast and the financial rewards were not as lucrative. However, on the flip side, no paramilitary extortionists came looking for money.

ELSEWHERE, THE COLLAGE OF photographs shown to me some time back by Tucker Lyttle featuring targeted republicans, took on a new significance in the summer of 1989. One of the faces was a twenty-eight-year-old called Loughlin Maginn of Rathfriland, Co. Down. Known to his pals as 'Locky', he was a married father of four and worked in the poultry business. The UDA/UFF said he was a member of the IRA, a claim strenuously denied by his family.

On the morning of 25 August at 12.45 a.m., UDA/UFF gunmen smashed the front window of his house and burst in before shooting him dead. 'Locky' had been targeted intensely by the RUC and the British army in the months before his killing in ways that were similar to what the Reaveys had experienced since 1976. The 2012 Desmond De Silva Report into collusion found that Mr Maginn featured in the files that were taken from a UDR barracks in December 1988.[1]

The British had used the UFF again to carry out their dirty work. Andrew David Smith, Geoffrey McCullagh and former British soldier Andrew Neville Browne, who happened to be full-time members of the UDR and a fourth man, Gary Martin Quinn, were subsequently convicted for his killing. Gary Martin Quinn from Lisburn, was sentenced to five life-terms for other Catholic killings and only expressed remorse for Loughlin Maginn's murder because he was married to a Protestant.[2]

In the months that followed, Locky's wife Maureen was subjected to relentless harassment from the RUC and the British army. As she had raised her children Catholic, she quickly found herself isolated from her own Protestant community.

To add further insult to the dead, members of the British Parachute Regiment – the ruthless division that killed fourteen innocent people during Bloody Sunday in Derry – took it upon themselves to open up Loughlin Maginn's grave some weeks after his burial.[3] In an act of sickening disrespect, they rammed a spade into the lid of the coffin. Loughlin's wife told me in 2022 that the soldiers then removed Loughlin Maginn's gold-coloured name-plate which they subsequently put on display in their accommodation quarters as a form of victory trophy.

It took thirty-three years for the Maginn family to get what might be classed as 'justice' – British style. They accepted an out-of-court settlement on 16 September 2022 which meant the devious details of what the British security forces and the RUC/PSNI/UDR got up to with the UDA were never exposed to the wider public. At time of writing, the Maginn family are still seeking an inquest.

MEANWHILE ON THE POLITICAL front, relations between Dublin and London over the future of Northern Ireland were changing. The British Association of Canned Food Importers and Distributors is not exactly a name that instantly springs to mind when one thinks of the big corporate names that drive UK industry. The association's profile is so low, most members of the public would be unaware that it is an umbrella body that oversees its members' activities and issues in the retail and recycling sector.

On 9 November 1990, the secretary of state for Northern Ireland, Peter Brooke was invited to address the association's annual Christmas lunch at the Whitbread Restaurant in London. A secretary of state addressing an institution of this nature didn't make much sense but we now know his attendance was all part of a choreographed plan to get a delicate message out in a low-key way so as not to cause uproar.[4] He showed up with a prepared speech in hand. No members of the media were invited to attend except for a lone cameraman from BBC TV News who set up his equipment at the rear of the restaurant and attached his microphone to the podium.

Whatever Brooke was going to say needed to be recorded for history but not reported in a sensational way with splash-flash headlines all over the front pages of the next-day's newspapers. Not surprisingly, he spoke at length about the futility of violence before moving on to explain where the British government stood on moving things forward in a way that might eventually bring the never-ending killing spree to a much-needed end. Then, in a totally unexpected and remarkable development, he uttered the following words: 'The British Government has no selfish, strategic or economic interest in Northern Ireland.'

When the words got out, there was a silent earthquake in the six counties. We couldn't exactly work out what was going on but we sensed something was up. Such significant words would not have been said in isolation and would have been cleared by Prime Minister Margaret Thatcher who, two weeks later, would be gone from 10 Downing Street.

He was effectively saying London no longer wanted to hold on to Northern Ireland and that it would leave as soon as possible, if there was a guarantee that no mess would be left behind.

Even though the public was in the dark, developments were happening behind the scenes. While the killings continued and Sinn Féin was becoming more involved in democratic politics, the question was, would Peter Brooke's speech motivate a positive reaction from the republican movement or was it a gesture in vain from London?

With over 3,000 now dead from the Troubles and Peter Brooke sending out signals that some sort of change was in the air, we prayed that the years ahead would bring it all to an end and in the event of a possible ceasefire, we might get long-awaited answers on the massacre in our house.

Talks about Talks

As politicians talked, the IRA wasn't holding back. On the night of 31 May 1991, it attacked the British army base at Glenanne, just up the road from Whitecross. A red Mercedes tipper lorry had been stolen in Kingscourt, Co. Cavan, the day before and kitted out with 2,500 pounds of home-made explosives. At around 11.30 p.m., the lorry was driven down a steep hill close to the barracks and let freewheel through the perimeter fence before the bomb was detonated by remote control. Three UDR soldiers were killed and over forty people injured. Such was the power of the blast, it was heard fifty miles away in north Co. Dublin. A massive crater was left in its wake.

Windows were reportedly smashed in Dundalk while sixty houses were wrecked in the locality. Numerous cattle were also killed in nearby fields. The British army base was destroyed and never re-built. A local farmer called to see me and remarked that some of his cattle were killed and that the British army had removed security bollards three days before the blast which begs the question, why? The explosion raised a lot of local suspicion.

There had been talk in the years previous that the British army base at Glenanne had been a terrible blight on the locality and an indefensible embarrassment to the Ministry of Defence. It would suit certain establishment people if it was closed down. Much of the sinister activity that had happened in the South Armagh area, implicating the British security forces, originated from the Glenanne area. The attack all smacked as if somebody in the British army, a contemporary version of Robert Nairac perhaps, had worked hand in hand with the IRA to destroy the barracks. Something was peculiar about it.

Meanwhile our newly created construction company was busy and had increased its operations in Dublin. We managed to land a job at Trinity College which marked a noteworthy change from the intimidation we had endured in Belfast. Our team couldn't believe that we could drive to Dublin every morning without being harassed by police at checkpoints or that we could do a day's work and not have to look over our shoulder to see if a ruthless extortionist had come through the gate. What was normal and peaceful in the south was a welcome world for us and we loved it. We even felt that the weather was milder in Dublin compared to north of the border. As Van Morrison sang in 'Coney Island', 'Wouldn't it be great if it was like this all the time?'

Throughout the summer of 1994, senior republicans continued behind-the-scenes talks with the British and their own volunteers. Lots of coaxing had to be applied and each movement had to be slow and diplomatic to ensure the entire republican community was moving as one entity. Not all republicans were won over by Gerry Adams and Martin McGuinness who, they felt, had sold their souls to the British without delivering a united Ireland. Many hardline republicans asked, 'what was the war campaign for if there was nothing to show for it after twenty-five years'?

The long-awaited IRA ceasefire was formally announced on 31 August 1994, bringing their twenty-five-year armed conflict to an end. The sense of pleasure on the day was difficult to describe. For us, and so many other families, it meant hopefully, that the days of harassment from paramilitaries, the British and RUC were over. Our children and grandchildren could now grow up in a society where they didn't have to worry about being shot in the head, blown to pieces and hopefully could get through the rest of their lives without being discriminated against for being nationalist or Catholic.

Northern Ireland could now return to being a 'normal society' if such a thing was possible in the sectarian-divided six counties. Unfortunately this did not mean an end to all 'terrorism'.

With the IRA now on ceasefire, the UVF, UFF and other loyalist groups began to look isolated. They were still active yet who were they 'defending' their people from? Pressure was coming on them from the British government and on 13 October, they

Talks about Talks

called their own ceasefire. Gusty Spence representing several loyalist groups, addressed the media. There are many people who say Gusty Spence single-handedly started the killing culture during the Troubles when seventy-four-year-old Protestant woman Matilda Gould was burned to death on 7 May 1966 having been mistaken for a Catholic.[1] Three weeks later, Spence and his cronies in the UVF killed twenty-eight-year-old Catholic John Scullion on 27 May 1966.[2] Sectarian killing was underway. The killing of Matilda Gould and John Scullion show that the UVF fired the first shots of the conflict in Belfast but unionist politicians and leaders never acknowledge that fact when bashing republicans and nationalists. The irony is that the actions of the UVF at the time, kick-started an almost redundant IRA and brought them back with catastrophic consequences. If Civil Rights had been granted and the 1966 killings never took place, would 3,500 or so people have lost their lives in the subsequent years?

Gusty Spence read out a prepared statement from the Combined Loyalist Military Command. He said that the UVF offered 'abject and true remorse' to the loved ones of all the innocent victims of the Troubles and thirty years after his colleagues carried out the first murders, called a ceasefire.

KING RAT

1994 MAY HAVE BEEN a momentous year in the history of Ireland but it was also one the Reavey family will not forget. Our younger sister Una, who was born in 1963, took ill. She had emigrated to London in 1981 and graduated as an SRN Nurse eight years later. While in London, she met Armagh man Paul McKenna and married shortly afterwards before bringing baby girl Kirsty in to the world. The family returned home to Armagh but health-wise, all was not well. On 4 December, her breast cancer proved too much and she died at the young age of thirty-one in Daisy Hill Hospital. Our Mother had lost a fourth child and it devastated her.

Around this time, a figure emerged in mid-Ulster by the name of Billy Wright. Known as 'King Rat', he was a ruthless loyalist killer. Wright grew up in a foster home in Mountnorris, not far from Whitecross, after the break-up of his parent's marriage. It is said that the Kingsmills massacre in 1976, led the young Wright to get involved in loyalist activity. It is believed that he was responsible for at least twelve murders in mid-Ulster and when the UVF declared its ceasefire in 1994, he felt they had sold out to let the IRA in.

On one occasion in 1994 when we were working at a Housing Executive site at Laurelvale between Tandragee and Portadown, we learned that Billy and his gang had planned to pay us a visit. Fortunately, a neighbouring man overheard a revealing conversation at the Shamrock Park clubhouse of Portadown Football Club on the previous Saturday. The man who was doing most of the talking was Richard Jameson, a prominent member of the mid-Ulster UVF who died six years later in a shooting following a feud with members of the LVF. The conversation was all about a bunch of guys from 'Crossmaglen' who were working at Laurelvale and would have to be dealt with as issues had arisen over the failure to pay protection money. The neighbour tipped off our Seamus that a hit was planned for the Laurelvale site the following Wednesday morning at 9.50 a.m.

The RUC, who subsequently became aware of the planned hit, visited the site early on the Wednesday morning and warned our crew of an impending attack. The police instructed all present to vacate the site and escorted them to Markethill and away from danger.

Our lads returned to the site on the Thursday and Friday thanks to an RUC escort. However we were informed by the RUC on the Friday evening that security could not be provided on a daily basis and that any future work undertaken would be at our own risk. We were not prepared to put the lives of our men in danger any more. Between Jimmy Craig, Artie Fee, Jackie McDonald, Davy Payne, Billy Wright and all their loyalist pals, we had enough. We walked away from Laurelvale, even though we were owed a six-figure sum for work completed. The days of Reavey Brothers building and renovating houses in loyalist areas were over.

In the weeks before our exit from Laurelvale, loyalist paramilitaries had been making regular visits to the site seeking so-called 'security' money. Our solicitor Rory McShane was informed about these intimidating loyalist visits and got in touch with the anti-racketeering squad of the RUC in Belfast. He suggested to the RUC that a meeting involving Seamus Reavey and himself should take place at Tandragee Station to discuss the matter. The anti-racketeering squad told Rory that they didn't want to meet at Tandragee RUC station as they tended to operate independently of other units.

When one wing of the police didn't trust another, what chance did the public have? An alternative meeting venue was found, the complaint was made and to this day, we are still waiting on a response from the police. Even though the RUC knew in advance who was planning to carry out the expected hit, nobody was arrested or charged.

Billy Wright was jailed for eight years for threatening to kill a woman and having spent time at Maghaberry, was transferred

The Killing of the Reavey Brothers

to the Maze prison. He was housed in a punishment wing in H-Block 6 with members of the INLA. On 27 December 1997, he was shot dead by the INLA. The killing raised all sorts of questions as to whether or not certain people in the British security services, facilitated the hit to ensure Wright left the stage for political purposes.

PAISLEY PUTS OUR LIVES IN DANGER

ON FRIDAY 22 JANUARY 1999, my son Anthony phoned me. He had spotted a disturbing story in The *Belfast News Letter* paper under the headline, '25-year trail of terrorism – "Super-terrorists" responsible for Kingsmills and Omagh killings.'

The story included the text:

> The *News Letter* has learned that the ringleaders of the team which committed Ulster's single worst atrocity [Omagh bomb] in August also carried out the Kingsmills and the Tullyvallen massacres in the mid 1970s.
> ... and we have police documents to prove it – details of which lift the lid on the identities of a gang of so-called 'super terrorists' who embarked upon their careers as terrorists with the provisional IRA, later operating under the phoney tag of the South Armagh Republican Action Group during the ceasefires of the 1970s.
> ... one theory for why the massacre happened put forward at the time was that it was an act of retaliation for two IRA men murdered the day before.

When I read this, I was furious. The story stated that the Kingsmills massacre occurred because two members of the IRA were shot [locally] the day previous, implying our Brian and John Martin were killed for being members of the IRA – *our brothers were never ever in the IRA*. I was now afraid of possible retaliation on our family as a result of the false story. I had to act quickly.

The *News Letter* also carried another article under the headline 'Dossier shows RUC know the killers'. The 'papers' are also reported as containing very detailed information about the identities of those involved and that 'raids were carried out on the homes of the individuals in question'.

Even though the newspaper itself disputed that the Kingsmills massacre was an act of retaliation, *no* RUC or army raids were ever carried out at our house in relation to the Kingsmills massacre – proof that the contents in the dossier were wrong. That didn't address the issue at hand, namely that the Reaveys had been wrongly implicated in one of the most horrific attacks of the conflict.

I needed to get clarity on this emerging crisis from *The Belfast News Letter*. On Monday 25 January, I made a call to the journalist at the paper who wrote the offending story. Her name was Jeanette Oldham. What she said stunned and astounded me. She said sensitive British military documents had come in to her possession and I was named in them.

I gave her a proper earful down the phone and told her repeatedly that my brothers were never ever in the IRA. I requested a written apology, otherwise I would be heading to the courts. According to her, she could not write an apology unless her editor approved it. There were plenty of heated words exchanged between us before we ended the conversation.

The next day, no apology appeared in the paper. I called her again and she said that the paper's lawyers stated that she could write what she wanted to about dead people [Brian and John Martin]. Of course the issue here was, she was saying our brothers were in the IRA, when they were not and this had dangerous implications for our family.

She went on to accuse me of being a leader in the IRA and she had documentary evidence to prove it. She said she was quoting from an official police document. I hadn't a clue about these documents or where they had come from. Despite pleading with her on the phone to write a correction, my determined attempts fell on deaf ears.

Although the Reaveys were not named in *The Belfast News Letter* story and only we appeared to be paranoid about being implicated in the Kingsmills Massacre, we took the view that the story would fade from public consciousness and that would be the end of the matter. Two days later on 27 January, I was driving home to Whitecross in South Armagh around 5.30 p.m. and was listening to BBC Radio Ulster. A news reader came on and said words to the effect that DUP leader Ian Paisley would be naming names in relation to the Kingsmills massacre later that evening in the House of Commons.

Paisley puts our Lives in Danger

I thought no more of it and when I arrived home, I sat down to watch the TV news as usual. Róisín then called me in to the kitchen for dinner and I missed the promised broadcast. While I was working my way through Róisín's cooking, a speech was being given in London that would have a chaotic effect on my life and the Reavey family.

Shortly after 6 p.m., Ian Paisley MP, leader of the DUP and founder of the Free Presbyterian Church, took to his feet in the House of Commons in London. What started off as yet another speech on the evils of 'terrorism', turned out to be a shocking life-changing moment for me. The blatant lies that came next about me and others, caused me severe shock.

What he said made me a hated target. To this day I still can't believe what he said and more to the point, why he said it. The following is an extract from Paisley's speech by *Hansard*, the service which records every spoken word in the House of Commons. Paisley being the bombastic man that he was, didn't just say the following, he yelled it out as loud as he could:

Rev. Ian Paisley (North Antrim):

> Some of us will remember that, 23 years ago, there was a massacre in Kingsmills. It sparked off one of the greatest revulsions against terrorism that I have seen in the Province.
>
> Ten Protestants were gunned down in cold blood when the bus in which they were travelling was stopped by an armed gang. An 11th Protestant, Alan Black, survived, but was maimed for life. The only Roman Catholic on board escaped with his life after the killers told him to flee.
>
> At that time, we were told that steps would be taken to bring those responsible for the atrocity to trial. If the Government of that day had done their duty and gone after those men ruthlessly, we would not be reaping other atrocities, and perhaps we would not even have had the sorrow of Omagh.
>
> There are hard men in the republican movement who can fly flags of convenience whenever they like. I believe that the IRA leadership condones their actions, and allows them to return to the ranks after a time. There are all sorts of flags of convenience.
>
> It is interesting to note that a police dossier carefully prepared on

the Kingsmills massacre has recently come to light. It shows that the police did thorough work, had definite evidence and could, if they had been encouraged, have got men into the courts; but that did not happen. Now we are told by the police officer investigating the Omagh atrocity that he knows the identity of the bombers but he cannot secure a conviction.

The Tullyvallen massacre, another terrible atrocity, was thought to be the work of some group calling itself the South Armagh Republican Action Group; but that, too, was undoubtedly a cover name for a gang of cross-border PIRA terrorists. The fact must be faced that, under the surface, there are those who are ready to act, whose actions will be condoned and who will probably be re-incorporated into the republican movement after they have acted.

There is something seriously wrong with any country – and any Government – that permits known killers to walk the streets with impunity while their victims lie in cold graves. The fact that the killers could operate both inside and outside the IRA name, according to political circumstance, is no comfort to the community. It is an indictment of the Government's and the legal system's failure to address the problem.

The documents that I have mentioned reveal that top PIRA players are free to operate as PIRA, or under any other name during times of ceasefire, in the knowledge that they will be accepted back into the PIRA fold when they are required. The futility of those who believe that the IRA ceasefire is foundation enough on which to build the peace process stands exposed.

According to the dossier, Eugene Reavey, a well-known republican, 'set up the Kingsmills massacre …'

Paisley went on to name over twenty local men in his speech. He had put blatant lies into the House of Commons record.

Within an hour, the phone in my house was bouncing off the wall with calls. All the callers were friends and they all knew that Ian Paisley was stirring up trouble. The big fear for me was, what did my local Protestant friends think and how would they react?

Before we knew it, friends were calling to the door. Philip McCabe, our Protestant quantity surveyor, called to the house from Poyntzpass as did Dr Seamus Cassidy from Dungannon and Seamus McManus from Mayobridge to name some of many. The yard outside the house was full of people in no time.

They all gave their support to me and knew well that Paisley had told a big defamatory lie and completely misled the House of Commons. The problem for us was that whatever is said in the House of Commons is protected by parliamentary privilege. That means we could not take a legal action over what was now on the House record.

We were in an awful state. Róisín was fearful that we might get some unwanted visitors from the UVF calling. We couldn't believe that twenty-three years after our boys and those at Kingsmills were killed, this was happening again.

To make matters worse, BBC Northern Ireland broadcast a clip of Paisley in full flow featuring the names of those he had read into the record including my own. But we couldn't take an action against the BBC as the words uttered in the House were covered by parliamentary privilege.

Realising the family name was taking a hammering, Dr Seamus Cassidy and myself wrote a press release in which I totally rejected the comments made by Ian Paisley. I also called on him to make the same remarks outside the confines of the House of Commons and upon doing so, I would issue legal proceedings for defamation. The press release also stated with emphasis that at no time was I ever interviewed by the RUC in relation to the Kingsmills massacre and that I would be seeking an urgent meeting with then Chief Constable Sir Ronnie Flanagan. It also asked if this mysterious dossier actually existed and if so, from what security source or agency?

The next morning after Paisley's speech, I called to a house fifty yards down the road to chat to builders. The house had one time been owned by the Scott family who were Protestants. The Reaveys had been friends with them going back to the 1940s and always milked cows for the Scotts on 12 and 13 July as an act of good neighbourliness to help them mark Orange Day. The Scotts might as well have been part of our family, we were that close. In recent times they had sold their house to Catholic man Mickey Murphy, a sale that saw them subjected to abuse from certain local Protestants.

As I entered the gate of Murphy's house, two neighbours saw me coming and ran out past me as quick as they could. They didn't want to be seen next or near me. I couldn't believe it. I was now being shunned by certain long-time neighbours. The harm done by Paisley and his big mouth was causing untold damage.

What was particularly hurtful for Róisín and myself was that Eugene junior, then aged eight, came running in from school that day asking all sorts of questions. He asked, 'did you shoot those men?' While we explained it was all lies, the worrying thing was he was being quizzed at school by other children over what Paisley said. These children were obviously hearing the chatter at home.

While we as adults could defend ourselves, our children didn't know where to turn. Our Sarah, then eleven, was at Our Lady's Grammar School in Newry. A teacher in her school, Sister Yvonne, realising the turmoil that was going on, took her aside and reassured her that everything would be ok and not to be worried.

That evening, there were sixteen people packed in to our kitchen. Half were Catholic and the other half were Protestants. They all gave us their full support. The big worry for me now was, every time I got in to my car and drove down the road, I feared being ambushed and shot dead. If I crossed the road from our house to our local shop and there were Protestants I knew inside, I was anxious they would ignore me.

Over the following days, Róisín constantly locked the doors, fearing that anybody who called, would have a gun in their pocket. As the word got out that Paisley had named me and others, people in the nationalist, republican and GAA communities were shocked. *The Irish News* newspaper published a special editorial on Friday 29 January condemning Paisley's word and accused him of being very selective on what he said. The editor wrote:

The deaths of those innocent Protestants and Catholics in less than 48 hours were all equally shameful but Mr Paisley, tellingly, could only bring himself to mention the victims from one side of the sectarian divide.

It quoted SDLP MP Seamus Mallon who said, '... the DUP Leader had been guilty of an act of the "grossest irresponsibility" which had placed lives at risk.' Seamus Mallon was also critical of BBC NI for broadcasting the names as stated by Paisley in the House. However, the BBC said the privilege rule meant they were free to broadcast same and the fact that what is published on the *Hansard* website, is available around the world for all to see.

In the following days, serious pressure was mounting on Ian Paisley to withdraw the remarks and apologise. Journalist Greg Harkin writing in *The Sunday People* newspaper reported on 31 January what we all knew, but certain people in the DUP wouldn't acknowledge namely, that the dossier containing the names was fake and was compiled by renegade loyalists.

Harkin wrote that the sources of the dossier – the Red Hand Defenders and Orange Volunteers – whoever they were – had fooled Paisley. He went on to write that 'Senior RUC officers have now confirmed that the 'security files' containing the names raised by Paisley are in fact crude copies of original documents, doctored by those who made them. *The Sunday People* understands that the documents may be old UDR files.'

I learned many years later from journalist Tom Kelly of the *Irish News*, that SDLP MP Seamus Mallon was so furious with what he had heard in the House of Commons, he ran up a side corridor after Paisley following the speech and grabbed him by the scruff of the neck. Apparently what Mallon said to Paisley is unprintable.

The matter then came up for special mention at the next meeting of Newry and Mourne District Council in early February where all unionist councillors withdrew from the Chamber when the matter came up for discussion.

Sinn Féin councillor Brendan Lewis from Camlough told the meeting that 'the people named are now living in fear for their lives and those of their families'.[1] He added that the decision of the BBC to broadcast the names was 'totally irresponsible' and that the whole exercise was 'an attack on the entire nationalist community of South Armagh'. SDLP Councillor Pat Toner from Forkhill was also in full voice. He condemned unionist councillors for failing to voice their disapproval of what the DUP leader had said in the House.

The Irish World newspaper in London weighed in and in a lengthy editorial piece: '*The Irish World* challenges Ian Paisley to repeat his allegations [outside the House of Commons] against the men. In naming them, without foundation, or substantiation, in the House of Commons, he has sidestepped and ducked all sense of moral, civil and public responsibility.'

With the controversy raging on and no sign of an apology or clarification from Mr Paisley, Rory McShane and SDLP Assembly member John Fee from Crossmaglen arranged an urgent meeting with RUC Chief Constable Ronnie Flanagan. The delegation which also included myself, Brendan Ferris, a joiner from down the road near Glenanne – who was also wrongly named by Paisley – and his solicitor Ciaran Rafferty, met Ronnie Flanagan at RUC HQ in Knock, east Belfast.

Fully aware of the controversy that had unfolded, Ronnie confirmed to us that Brendan and myself were NOT suspects in the Kingsmills massacre. While this came as a welcome relief, the problem for us was, the people of Northern Ireland, in particular active loyalist paramilitaries, needed to be informed in order to clear our names, I had to persuade Ronnie that I didn't need to be convinced of my innocence but that he had to address the media which were gathered in large numbers outside the gate. This was, after all, the big news story of the day.

At first, he was reluctant to do this at that particular time. His approach was to talk to his officials and make a statement later in the day. I pushed the point with him on the urgency to talk to the assembled press as soon as possible. They were outside the front gate and they needed a story. If he spoke now, it would be win-win for them, him and us. Ronnie gave my plea some thought and agreed to face the cameras. He told the awaiting journalists, 'we have absolutely no evidence whatsoever on which to connect these two men with the Kingsmills massacre and there are no matters which are outstanding on which we wish to interview Mr Reavey and Mr Ferris.

'The dossier in question was not a police file. I am satisfied at this stage of the investigation that it is not part of a detailed police dossier as has been alleged.'

Standing beside Ronnie as he made his remarks, I was asked how I felt about the chief constable's comments to which I replied, 'I was happy that the chief constable has cleared my name. I am calling on Paisley to come out and do the same thing.'

I thought that upon being given the all-clear by the RUC, Paisley senior would have put his hands up and admitted he had made a major error. Well as it turns out, the man who headed up the Free Presbyterian Church, had a memory lapse from his weekly sermons where he would regularly preach lines like 'Repent for your sins and heaven awaits you'.

That night, Ian Paisley junior made himself look out of kilter with public opinion when he accused Sir Ronnie Flanagan of prejudicing the outcome of the RUC's internal investigation. In reaction to newspaper enquiries, he said that 'the Chief Constable's comments made it clear that the investigation was not concluded'. He added that his father, Ian senior, had no intention of apologising for the remarks made in the House of Commons.

These were worrying comments as Ian Paisley junior suggested that even though Brendan Ferris and I were innocent, a possible conclusion of the RUC investigation might produce a different result. This cast doubt on our innocence. His comments were scurrilous, unfounded and were clearly designed to make me look like a pariah within the local community. The Paisleys had got themselves on to an embarrassing hook and to back down and apologise to nationalists for such a humiliating error would be seen as an act of weakness within the loyalist community where a sizeable chunk of the DUP vote comes from.

Such an apology would also raise questions about Ian Paisley senior's credibility. If he was prepared to tell lies in the House of Commons and resist repeated calls to clarify his remarks, how could he taken seriously on anything else he would say subsequently.

The man who preached the word of God every Sunday at his church in Ravenhill, Belfast and told his followers they would burn in hell if they didn't repent for their sins, was not prepared to engage in the principle of forgiveness, one of the fundamental messages in the bible. His hypocritical sense of morality and decency didn't correlate with his bullish political drive to paint Catholics as bad people.

Paisley embarrassed true Christians around the world when he had to be forcibly removed from the European Parliament in Strasbourg in October 1988 for shouting insulting abuse at Pope John Paul II. In his full booming voice and carrying a placard which read 'Pope John Paul II, the Anti-Christ', he shouted, 'I refuse you as Christ's enemy and anti-Christ with all your false doctrine'.

The Paisleys were not prepared to budge and I was not going to let them away with it. Sometimes when mud is fired, it tends to stick regardless of whether it's real mud or not. Despite Sir Ronnie Flanagan stating publicly on TV, radio and in the newspapers that I was not a suspect in the Kingsmills massacre investigation, unfortunately some locals took the view that there was no smoke without fire!

I continued to be shunned by certain people in the Protestant community in South Armagh. Some of the families of those that died in the Kingsmills massacre that I had known since I was a child, disowned me. As far as some of them were concerned, what Paisley said in the House was true, even though there was not one single shred of evidence to back it up.

Nobody has ever been convicted for the Kingsmills massacre. Why?

While the fight with Paisley was only just beginning, the lid was about to be lifted on a shady group of brutal UVF gunmen,

RUC officers, colluding members of the British security forces and people, who I thought were friends, that lived just up the road from us.

THE COLLUSION CAT ESCAPES FROM THE BAG

WITH THE FALLOUT FROM the Paisley comments continuing to make our lives a misery and no sign in sight of an apology or correction, events were about to make a major turn for the entire Reavey family and others in South Armagh.

On the morning of Sunday 7 March 1999, I got up out of bed shortly after 7.30 a.m. I opened the presses in the kitchen anticipating a good breakfast but realising I was short on bread, I nipped across the road to our local shop. I scanned the collection of Sunday newspapers on the stand next to the window and what looked like a typical run-of the mill story about the IRA caught my attention.

I purchased *The Sunday Times*, paid for my groceries and tucked the paper under my arm before heading back across the road to put the toaster and kettle on. As the kettle began to whistle in the corner, I was drawn to a headline that was about to open a can of worms.

The paper carried a lengthy confession with John Weir, a former member of the RUC who was serving time in jail for murder. The piece was written by journalist Liam Clarke, a one-time member of Official Sinn Féin, the political wing of the Official IRA.[1] Clarke's piece carried the headline, 'RUC men's secret war with the IRA'. This was, to use an inappropriate pun, explosive stuff that all but confirmed everything we and others had suspected since January 1976 but couldn't prove.

John Weir, then forty-nine-years of age, was the man who UDA leader Eddie Sayers told me in Crumlin Road Prison, wanted to have a chat with me. At the time, I didn't trust anybody after the kicking I got in the jail and let the moment pass. Weir had now decided to go elsewhere with what he knew about a long list of killings and contacted Liam Clarke. The disgruntled former policeman who had done his bit to keep

The Collusion Cat Escapes from the Bag

Northern Ireland in the UK and got a fourteen-year conviction for his efforts, was about to sing like a canary.

John Weir was found guilty for his part in the murder of William Strathearn, the thirty-nine-year-old married father of seven children and chemist who was gunned down at his home in Ahoghill, Co. Antrim in April 1977.

His revelations were shocking, scandalous and beyond belief. Weir's interview with Clarke was about to help clear the fog on some of the many controversial killings mentioned in this book.

Liam Clarke wrote:

> ... like many Protestants, Weir had been deeply affected by the Kingsmills massacre ...

The suspects were still at large. Weir and others in the RUC feared they [the killers] would strike again. The [RUC] unit [he was in] would not stand idly by.

Thus began a killing spree in which Weir and certain rogue members of the Royal Ulster Constabulary, the Northern Ireland police force of Her Majesty's Government, began a deliberate campaign of killing Catholics, nationalists and republicans.

To make matters more sinister, these rogue RUC members worked side by side with terrorists in the Ulster Volunteer Force, the British army, the UDR and numerous shadowy figures from various UK security agencies.

Their mission was clear, namely to take the war to Catholic communities with the intention of wiping out the IRA even if it meant killing innocent people like the Reaveys, the O'Dowds and others.

Weir was one of the rare breed of Protestants who was actually born in the republic but joined the RUC to keep 'law and order' at a difficult time but through the influence of a horrible culture in the police, became the very type of evil person that he initially set out to prevent from gaining a foothold in society.

Raised in Castleblayney Co. Monaghan and educated at a Protestant boarding school in Dublin, he originally had ambitions to join the Gardai but opted for the RUC instead due to his family background.

Having joined the RUC, his first posting in 1971 was to Strandtown Station in loyalist east Belfast. At a time when the IRA was upping its bombing campaign and the auxiliary police force of

B-Specials had been disbanded, morale amongst police officers was low.

According to Clarke's piece, 'by late 1973, Weir said a consensus had formed among his peers that they should break the rules to curb the terrorists'.

Three years later at an RUC Sports Day on 23 June 1976, a number of officers from the Special Patrol Group (SPG) approached him for a chat. They told him that the IRA was winning the war, the RUC was seen to be soft and was applying policing with one hand tied behind its back, so to speak. Tactics had to change or else the days of British rule were coming to an end.

Weir went on to tell Clarke that Billy McCaughey, an RUC constable in Lurgan, had a dedicated hatred of Catholics and had close links with senior people in the Ulster Volunteer Force:

> McCaughey had been a member of the Ulster Protestant Volunteers [a loyalist paramilitary group set up by Ian Paisley in 1966], before he joined the RUC.

The Sunday Times piece went on to say that 'Weir, McCaughey and Gary Armstrong, a constable, became friends and drinking companions. Senior officers were suspicious of the trio. They were right to be. All three were destined to link up with the wild men of the loyalist paramilitaries.'

Clarke's story went on to reveal that Weir was introduced to the most notorious UVF killer of all time in Mid-Ulster if not in Northern Ireland by his RUC colleague Gary Armstrong. His name was Robin Jackson. Known as 'The Jackal', Jackson is believed to have taken part in the killing of at least fifty Catholics and maybe many more.

Worst of all though, Jackson operated under the protection of certain senior officers in the RUC. Imagine the global outcry if a paramilitary went around London killing critics of the British state but was found to be protected by senior members of the London Metropolitan Police? We were now learning what we suspected for so long, namely that there was a deliberate shoot-to-kill policy targeting innocent Catholics in order to spread fear into the nationalist community with the aim of defeating the IRA.

Clarke went on to reveal that Weir had told him that one senior RUC officer approved of [Weir] working undercover with the UVF. Weir had been asked to plant guns on Donal Walsh, an innocent farmer from Belleeks and that he should round up a group of top-notch UVF gunmen to kill Thomas 'Slab' Murphy and his family. As the RUC saw it, 'Slab' Murphy was, allegedly, the top IRA man in South Armagh. If 'Slab' was eliminated, the IRA would be a weakened force in South Armagh, so went the RUC thinking.

However, despite the fact that Weir and at least sixteen RUC officer pals were working and assisting UVF killers to target republicans and Catholics, senior law-abiding members of the RUC were hearing rumours. Fearing that their own careers were on the line, they decided to move on Weir and McCaughey for the killing of William Strathearn. According to *The Sunday Times*, 'after they were arrested for the Strathearn murder, both McCaughey and Weir started to talk under interrogation. Weir offered to turn queen's evidence against Jackson in return for immunity –

> 'He was offered a deal whereby he would have his sentence reviewed after five years but would still be prosecuted and have no guarantee of early release.'

I must have read Liam Clarke's story about twenty times to fully absorb the enormity of what I was reading. Was it any wonder Catholics didn't trust the police service?

Every mysterious thing we questioned about the Reavey killings since 1976 and beyond suddenly began to make sense. While we were slightly the wiser, the revelations by Liam Clarke only intensified our curiosity even though the Reavey-O'Dowd killings only got a brief mention in the piece.

The proverbial 'collusion cat' was out the bag. Certain elements within the RUC were up to their neck in colluding with paramilitaries, a charge which of course the authorities would deny repeatedly for many years to come. As the enormity of

Liam Clarke's story began to sink in, we wondered what we should do in response. Lots of people were ringing the house asking me if I'd seen the piece? They had all read the story and fully understood its implications.

Journalist Sean McPhelimy, who wrote a controversial book around this time called *The Committee*, found himself in a legal action against *The Sunday Times* newspaper. While compiling his defence, Sean secured an affidavit or sworn statement from John Weir which went into detail about the skulduggery that went on and his knowledge of various murders across mid-Ulster.[2]

A summary of its contents revealed here, gives a greater insight in to how certain members of the RUC colluded with some of the most malicious people ever to have lived on this island.

Given on 3 January 1999, Weir stated:

4. 'In 1972, I was transferred to Armagh RUC Station and I served in a specialist anti-terrorist unit, the Special Patrol Group (SPG) ... I quickly discovered that many members of my SPG unit had loyalist connections and supported the activities of loyalist paramilitaries.

'I recall that, during the Ulster Worker's strike in 1974, all member of the SPG unit fully supported the loyalist efforts to bring down the power-sharing Executive and we toured the barricades and encouraged the strikers to persevere.

'When my colleagues and I learned that we were going to be sent to Portadown to contain loyalist protests, we sabotaged our police vehicles by putting sugar in petrol tanks and disabling our vehicles.

'As a result, we were not sent to Portadown. My SPG had about 30 members of whom 29 were Protestant and the only one Catholic, Maurice Coyle, who resigned and went to Canada.'

5. 'It is important to make it clear that my SPG unit, following (Maurice) Coyle's departure, was entirely Protestant and committed to the Loyalist cause ...'

6. '... I recall one incident near Glenanne in South Armagh when I was on patrol with Constable [Tom] Moorcroft. We were called to a shooting incident which had occurred at Glenanne Lake and Mowhan village, the incident involved other members of our SPG unit and had led to the accidental death of two British soldiers, shot in error by my colleagues.

The Collusion Cat Escapes from the Bag

'I recall that, on the way to the scene of the incident, Constable Tom Moorcroft told me that he was concerned in case the dead men would turn out to be loyalist paramilitaries operating in the area. He mentioned the name of one such paramilitary, James Mitchell, who was also a member of the RUC Reserve in Markethill at that time.

'The incident confirmed my growing realisation that the security forces were involved in loyalist terrorism.'

7. I recall a visit to my SPG unit by RUC Assistant Chief Constable Charlie Rodgers, who asked us our views on how best to combat the rise in IRA activity in South Armagh. South Armagh was, at that time, an area which was experiencing much terrorist activity from both sides, Loyalist and Republican.

'We used the opportunity presented by Rodgers' visit to express some extreme solutions to the problem, such as that we use commercial lorries with armoured plating which would enable us to remove illegal IRA roadblocks by shooting everyone dead or that we should perform road stops wearing civilian clothes and carrying illegal weapons, pretending to be either UVF or IRA units, thereby learning the true allegiance of those who had stopped.'

'ACC Rodgers expressed his support for these proposals and other extreme measures with the result that some of us later implemented them. One of my colleagues, who later murdered an innocent Catholic, tried to justify his action by saying that Charlie Rodgers, on one of his visits to Armagh SPG, had authorised an RUC shoot-to-kill policy.

9. 'Two murders in 1974 and 1975 led to my transfer from Armagh SPG to another SPG unit in Castlereagh, Belfast. The IRA had murdered an Ulster Defence Regiment officer called Elliott.

'After his death, I received information that he had been held and murdered at the home of X [name provided] at [place Y, name provided] Castleblayney across the border in Monaghan. I passed this information on to Sergeant John Poland in RUC Special Branch Armagh.

'A short time later John Francis Green, a known IRA man who was on the run from Lurgan Co. Armagh was shot dead at [the home of person X] ... I later became aware that the Green murder had been committed by an Ulster Defence Regiment soldier Robert McConnell and by one of the men I met in "Norman's Bar", the loyalist paramilitary Robin Jackson.'

10. 'Some time after my transfer to Belfast, I received a visit from

two of my former colleagues in the Armagh SPG, Gary Armstrong and Ian Mitchell ...

'They told me that they had decided for themselves ... that the time had come to take direct action against not merely known Republicans or IRA activists but against the Catholic community itself so that it would put pressure on the IRA to call off its campaign.

'... They had [already] started their campaign by carrying out a bomb and gun attack near Keady village, in June 1976, at the Rock Bar which is located within yards of the border of the Irish Republic.'

12. 'I agreed ... in Castlereagh RUC station that I would attend a further meeting in Gary Armstrong's house in Rosemount Park, Armagh on a date which was also set.

'When I first arrived at the meeting a few days later, the following RUC officers were present: Gary Armstrong, Laurence McClure, Ian Mitchell, David Wilson and William Scott.

'We decided at the meeting that we would press on with a second attack but we did not settle on a particular target.'

13. 'I recall that McClure told me, at that meeting in McClure's house, that there was a farmhouse at Glenanne from which they had already carried out several operations. He did not tell at that stage who owned the farmhouse but he said it was owned by an RUC officer ... The farmhouse had been used in connection with the Dublin and Monaghan bombings in 1974.

'McClure informed me about this attack and others which he and others had carried out from this location.

'These included: (1) The Dublin and Monaghan bombings. I believe that 33 people were killed and scores seriously injured in these two bombings which occurred on the same day. The explosives for both attacks had been provided by Captain A [name provided], an intelligence Officer in the UDR.

'The bombs had been assembled at the farmhouse in Glenanne which was owned by the RUC officer James Mitchell. The main organiser of both attacks had been a loyalist paramilitary and UDR Captain Billy Hanna from Lurgan, Co. Armagh.

'The bombs had been transported in cars with Robin Jackson, Billy Hanna and David Payne taking part in the Dublin attack and person B [name supplied] taking responsibility for the one in Monaghan.

'... those responsible for them were never even questioned by the RUC even though both the RUC and Army intelligence knew within days of the bombings, the identities of the culprits.'

(ii) 'a bomb attack and gun attack on two pubs in Crossmaglen, carried out by McClure and Robert McConnell in November 1974 with the getaway car provided by James Mitchell and his housekeeper Lily Shields. A local man, Thomas McNamee, was seriously injured and died from his injuries a year later. No one has been prosecuted for this crime.'

(iii) 'The murder of two Gaelic football supporters at Tullyvallen, near Newtownhamilton in August 1975 by McClure, McConnell and other loyalists belonging to the UVF. These men were wearing military uniforms when they stopped the two football supporters and after identifying them as Catholics, shot them dead.'

(iv) 'A gun attack and bomb attack on Donnelly's bar in Silverbridge, South Armagh in December 1975. This was carried out in retaliation for the murder of an RUC Reserve Constable William Meaklim who, the group believed, had been held at the bar after being kidnapped by the IRA.

'I understand that three people were killed in this attack and that several more were injured. Mr Donnelly's 14-year-old son was one of those shot dead in the attack.

'Those responsible for the attack are Stuart Young, Sammy McCoo [Phillip], 'Shilly' Silcock, [Robert] McConnell with the get-away car provided by Laurence McClure and Lily Shields. After the attack, the group reassembled at Mitchell's farmhouse.

'I believe that no one has ever been prosecuted for these murders but that the RUC has known the truth for many years. On the same night, Robin Jackson led a gang which placed a bomb in Dundalk south of the border. One person was killed in that attack. Both attacks were co-ordinated.'

(v) 'The murder of three Catholic brothers, the Reaveys at Whitecross, South Armagh in January 1976. This attack was carried out by McConnell, Laurence McClure, RUC Reserve Constable Johnny Mitchell and one [of] McClure's brothers, who, alone, was not a member of the security forces. On the same night, Robin Jackson shot the three O'Dowd brothers dead. Both attacks were co-ordinated.'

So there it was in startling black and white. A UVF gang

working out of Mitchell's farm up the road from our house with the assistance and encouragement of certain people in the British security forces, had been killing Catholics.

Weir's statement was shocking but the more we absorbed it, the less uncomfortable we became because everything we presumed had happened, now made perfect sense. The only difference to our original expectations and Weir's statement was, we now had names.

Weir went on to reveal details about a number of other controversial killings in his statement but the word was out. The Glenanne gang, as they had become known, were central to most mid-Ulster murders. So murky was the relationship between the gang, the UVF and other British operatives, Weir went on to add in his statement that a Republican informant told him that the name of Robert McConnell, who was central to the Reavey Brothers killings, 'had been passed on by army intelligence to the IRA'.

Weir added that his Republican informant told him that our old 'friend' Robert Nairac knew that Robert McConnell was involved in the attack at Donnelly's Bar in Silverbridge. According to the informant, Nairac knew that the IRA was aware of who was involved in the Silverbridge attack.

This development highlighted the sinister activity that treble-agent Robert Nairac played in the middle of all this as he worked with the Provos one day and the UVF the next. The fact that he was playing one side off against the other but pretending to be loyal to both, made Weir realise he would sooner or later be an IRA target or an official RUC suspect.

When Nairac had made it known that the Provos knew who was in the Glenanne gang, Weir became a worried man. It came as little surprise to those in the RUC/UVF/UDR/UDA/ British army vicious circle that Robert McConnell was shot dead by the IRA three months after the Reavey-O'Dowd killings on 5 April at Tullyvallen, Newtownhamilton.

Weir, in a later affidavit statement to the Barron Inquiry in Dublin said the Brits, in their various under-hand forms, passed his name on to the IRA as they felt he had reached his sell-by date as an operative for their cause, itself a reflection on how dirty the war in Northern Ireland had become.

It was also a development that should have made loyalists realise how much they were being manipulated by their invisible political masters in London but they never ever saw it that way as they presumed that the British security services were always on their side. The Brits, of course, *were* on their side – but only when it suited their agenda.

Arising from John Weir's statement, it was now official that Mitchell's farm up the road from Whitecross in Glenanne, had been playing a key role in UVF activity in mid-Ulster. I knew James Mitchell as I called to his farm approximately once a month when I was with Ross Poultry. Every time I called to his house I was struck by how conservative he was. He was friendly and all he seemed to talk about was cattle, pigs, hens and farming. He never ever discussed the political situation of the time regardless of how severe the latest atrocity was. However, he was a reserve member of the RUC and he was a policeman one day and aiding the UVF the next with the support of the British security services.

The government in Dublin eventually set up a Commission of Inquiry under Justice Liam Hamilton to investigate these killings and upon his death, he was replaced by Justice Henry Barron.

Un-Fair, Fair

As the summer of 2001 rolled on, the Paisley saga took on a new, unwelcome twist. An organisation called FAIR (Families Acting on behalf of Innocent Relatives) began to add more misery to my life. FAIR was set up by Willie Frazer and posted a link on the www.victims.org.uk/ internet site to Paisley's speech. This amounted to a repeated publication of what was said in the House of Commons even though the *Hansard* record was online anyway. What bothered me though was the intent behind it.

Willie Frazer's father Robert, known locally as Bertie, was in the UDR. He was killed on 30 August 1975 by the IRA. His killing was supposedly in retaliation for the murder of two GAA supporters six days previously at Altnamackin by the UVF with the assistance of the UDR. Bertie was allegedly seen at Altnamackin when the killings occurred.

Willie, it seemed, had an axe to grind over his father's death and his anger was pointed in my direction. I had been hearing from locals that Willie had been telling people that I was present when the Kingsmills massacre occurred. Willie, from what I could gather, had got his wires crossed. Willie had assumed, wrongly, that I had a part to play in his father's killing in 1975. As I was later to learn, it was Willie Frazer who persuaded Paisley to make the erroneous parliamentary speech in the House of Commons.

In the meantime, I'm angry because Willie is trying to inform as many people as possible that what he thinks is the truth, is in fact completely wrong. Wondering where I should go next to deal with this re-emerging crisis, I raised the matter with The Pat Finucane Centre which then had an office in Newry. The conduct of FAIR was nothing short of appalling. Here was an organisation being subsidised by the tax payer while putting the lives of certain individuals in danger. If anything, it should have called itself 'UN-FAIR'.

There's a New Sheriff in Town

Hugh Orde, OBE, had a very impressive CV as a policeman. He joined the London Metropolitan Police Force and had worked his way up to the position of deputy commissioner. He was assigned to assist The [John] Stevens Inquiry into allegations of collusion between loyalists and British security personnel in Northern Ireland. The Stevens Inquiry was not published in full which, as usual, indicates that it contained details the British don't want the public to know.

On the retirement of Ronnie Flanagan in 2002 as chief constable of the newly created PSNI, Colin Crampton became the acting head until formally replaced by Orde in May of that year. When well-spoken, highly educated men arrive in Northern Ireland, having done everything by the rule book in England, they seem to think that they can do their work with the same effectiveness, efficiency and transparency. However, they quickly learn that Northern Ireland is different to the rest of the United Kingdom. In Britain, transparency is usually the norm though not always, as the Birmingham Six, Guildford Four, the Maguire Family, Judith Ward and many others found out to their cost.

In Northern Ireland, the common denominator is that too many people in senior positions have too much to lose if they are found out for their sinister activity. Northern Ireland, as some of the imported police chiefs learn fast, is the 'wild west' of honest policing.

When Hugh Orde took over as the top cop in the PSNI, one of the first things he set about doing to get his period in charge off to a good start was to revisit some controversial killings, where families were looking for answers from the uncooperative British security services. Orde decided to put dedicated teams in place to meet with as many families as possible to record their respective stories.

His intentions seemed honourable. There was only one

problem. What he had in mind didn't tally with the suspicious attitude-culture of other people in the PSNI, many of whom still had a bigoted RUC mindset. The PSNI set about contacting families like ours and also contacted the Pat Finucane Centre (PFC) in Armagh who gave them a list of Glenanne gang-related murders, including our brothers. A meeting was arranged with my brother Seamus and myself and the PSNI at The Banville Hotel in Banbridge. Also present would be Paul O'Connor, Alan Brecknell and Johanna Keenan of the PFC. The PSNI were represented by Detective Constable Inspector Derek Williamson and Detective Sergeant Lorraine Dobson. The meeting was supposed to be a 'sharing' exercise. In other words, we told the PSNI what we knew and wanted to know while they were supposed to tell us what they knew. It didn't exactly work out that way.

We began by asking DCI Williamson, 'if there was any record of any person offering vital evidence in relation to our case?'

He said, 'nothing had been added to the Reavey File following the 1978 investigation'.

Apparently, the Reavey killings were re-investigated in 1978 after RUC conspirator and bad-boy William McCaughey revealed to his pals that a colleague was involved in the Reavey killings. McCaughey subsequently said to one of his pals that he had been involved in the killings of Brian, John Martin and Anthony.[1] Nobody in the RUC contacted the Reaveys either to let us know or just to ask what we remembered of the night. It was, as I saw it, as if one wing of the RUC was investigating the other with the outcome known in advance.

According to Williamson and Dobson, the suspects in the killings had been hauled in for questioning in 1978 and, their names and their statements were not added to the file.

Derek Williamson was obviously a dedicated member of the RUC and was asked if ballistic tests were carried out on any weapons in the context of the Reavey investigation?

'No weapons were recovered at the scene'. We found Williamson's response unconvincing.

I was subsequently told by an ex-member of the Glenanne gang that the weapons used in the Reavey killings were spirited away on the night in an RUC Land Rover.

From shell casings of bullets found at the scene, the results showed that the following weapons were used namely, a 9mm Luger pistol, a 9mm Parabellum sub-machine gun (SMG), a 9mm Sterling SMG and a .455 Webley revolver.

Subsequent revelations in a HET Report showed that the 9mm Parabellum SMG was used in the killing of Denis Mullen on 1 September 1975 in Moy, Co. Tyrone. UVF operative Garfield Beattie was sentenced in 1977 to life in jail. His close pal William John Parr was sentenced to life in 1979 for the same killing. The same weapon was used in the killing of Peter and Jane McKearney in October 1975 at Moy, Co. Tyrone. UVF gunman Garnet Busby was convicted to life in jail on 23 October 1981 for these killings.[2] It was also used in the killings of Trevor Brecknell, Michael Donnelly and Patrick Donnelly on 19 September 1975 at Donnelly's Bar in Silverbridge, Co. Armagh.

A HET Report as well as a map of killings and weapons used by the Glenanne Gang presented in the Belfast High Court in February 2015 on behalf of Edward Barnard connected the guns to Laurence McClure, Ian Mitchell, Lily Shields, Robert McConnell, Davy Wilson and William McCaughey. Nobody was charged in relation to the murders at Donnelly's Bar!

The same weapon was again utilised in the non-fatal shooting at Tully's Bar in Belleeks, Co. Armagh on 7 May 1976. A week later, it was used again in the killing of Frederick McLoughlin at The Eagle Bar, Charlemont, Co. Armagh. Garfield Beattie, David Henry and Dalzell Kane were sentenced to life in prison on 12 September 1977. Joseph Norman Lutton, an RUC reservist and UDR member, was convicted in February 1979 to life in jail for the McLoughlin murder.[3]

The Parabellum sub-machine gun was also used in the murder of Patrick McNeice at Loughgall, Co. Armagh on 25 July 1976. The weapon was found following this killing and its horrendous ballistic history later emerged. Garfield Beattie and Henry Garfield Liggett were each sentenced to life in jail, while Edith Dorothy Mullen was given ten years behind bars.[4]

It emerged some years later that the gun was stolen from Glenanne UDR barracks in May 1971. Interestingly, the gun was not reported as 'stolen' or 'missing' in the Glenanne UDR logs.

The revolver was used in the killing of GAA fans Seán Farmer and Colm McCartney on 24 August 1975 at Altnamackin as the two men returned from the All-Ireland semi-final in Croke Park. While the identity of the killers is now common knowledge in South Armagh, nobody was prosecuted or convicted at the time. The Webley revolver was sent to the RUC weapons control department for destruction in 1980 in accordance with police policy at the time.

RUC constable, UVF gunman, Orange Order, Royal Black Preceptory and Presbyterian Church member William McCaughey, was convicted for the wounding of Mick McGrath and received seven years imprisonment. For causing an explosion, he received two years, possession of explosives he got four years, possession of firearms and ammunition, he received three years. He was given a total of sixteen years. These concurrent sentences came on top of his ongoing life sentence for the murder of William Strathearn in Ahoghill, Co. Antrim in 1977. McCaughey was also a former bodyguard to one-time minister in the Northern Ireland Assembly, former MP and MEP John Taylor of the Ulster Unionist Party.

Also convicted for the attempted murder of Mick McGrath were RUC constables Laurence McClure, Ian Mitchell and David Wilson. Constable Laurence McClure kept some interesting company in his time. According to John Weir, McClure was a member of the Co. Down Orange Welfare Volunteers, a vigilante loyalist group that operated in rural areas during the 1970s.[5]

John Weir also revealed that UVF co-conspirators included RUC reservist Constable James Mitchell, he of the infamous

Mitchell's Farm in Glenanne, Jackie Whitten of the UVF, RUC Constable Billy McBride, Constable Gary Armstrong, and RUC Inspector Harry Breen. The RUC denied the involvement of their respective officers in the Down Orange Welfare Volunteers.[6]

As for the home-made Sterling sub-machine gun (SMG), it was used in the shooting of Michael McGrath. Asked if any of the above weapons were standard British army/ RUC/UDR issue, Williamson replied, 'there is no suggestion that any of these weapons were from an RUC, UDR or British army armoury.' We found his response was unconvincing.

We also questioned Williamson about statements taken from our neighbours in Whitecross. His answers on this aspect were not convincing also in light of what we aleady knew. At 5.50 p.m. on the evening of 4 January 1976, a vehicle checkpoint or VCP, took place near Wesley Robb's pub on the Tullyah Road, just down the road from Whitecross. Yet when questioned as to why such a VCP existed, Williamson said there was no official record of a checkpoint in the area that evening. Maybe there was no official record, but as far as we were concerned, the answer didn't corrolate with the knowledge we had.

When asked about a statement that Anthony Reavey apparently gave in Daisy Hill Hospital before his death, Williamson said that, 'Anthony was the only witness who provided vital evidence in terms of its usefulness'. This comment was strange and unconvincing to us. If Anthony gave a statement that was useful, surely by now there would have been convictions and our ongoing search for answers would be over but that was and is not the case. Towards the end of the meeting, I questioned him about our family's concern over the lack of a full investigation in to the triple killings. His response said that 'things were different in 1976. The manpower wasn't there and the technology wasn't as advanced as it is now.'

He added, 'of all the case files I have reviewed recently, this is the most complete file from this period in terms of things being logged. This is one of the most complete investigations, there is nothing more that can be followed up in terms of leads, etc.' When I heard this, I thought to myself that this RUC man is not on the same wavelenght as ourselves. We found Derek Williamson to be a most unhelpful participant at the meeting.

There was another sinister dimension to this prolonged investigation. RUC officer Gerry McCann who led the Inquiry into the killing of the Reavey brothers, appeared to be making progress. However, after he hauled in a number of suspects for questioning, he was, surprisingly, removed from the case and it was handed over to another senior RUC officer whose leads 'dried up'. We could see certain elements within the RUC were rotten to the core when it came to assisting Catholics who were seeking justice, though there were genuine police officers too who upheld the law in a fair and balanced way. However, families like ours who were seeking information leading to justice were interested in exposing the prejudiced collusion. Hugh Orde may have meant well but his plan just wasn't working.

Garda File goes Missing

As 2003 drew to a close, the first of several reports from the Barron Inquiry was published. Its three-year investigation into the 1974 Dublin-Monaghan bombings was somewhat vague and certainly didn't provide Margaret Urwin and her team at Justice for the Forgotten, and other groups representing relatives of the deceased, with all the answers they were seeking. While the finger of blame was pointed directly at the Glenanne gang, the report used a lot of unconvincing language that could be interpreted different ways.

According to a summary of the report in the *Irish Times*, 'the loyalist groups who carried out the bombings in Dublin were capable of doing so without help from any section of the security forces in Northern Ireland, though this does not rule out the involvement of individual RUC, UDR or British army members'.[1] In my opinion, the Barron Report was vague in places although one has to be fair by saying that he received little co-operation from the Northern Ireland office and the events he was investigating had happened twenty-nine years previously!

This meant that a lot of the players caught up in the Dublin-Monaghan bombings were now dead and those who were alive had hazy memories. This situation limited Barron's ability to get to the core circumstances behind the bombings. Why did it take so many years before a decision was reached to hold a state inquiry?

Matters weren't helped for Judge Barron by the stream of misinformation he was fed from those who were reluctant to give him the answers he needed. What caught my attention in particular about the Barron Report was a reference to Lily Shields who worked as a housekeeper for James Mitchell in Glenanne. Judge Barron told me that his office sent a query to the RUC/PSNI about Lily Shields. The police replied to Judge

Barron and said that Lily Shields was dead. But she was very much alive and didn't die until 2011 at the age of fifty-nine, seven years or so after the Report was published. The PSNI seemed to be doing all they could to frustrate his Inquiry which ultimately left him dealing with a lot of information that could not always be verified.

Lily Shields, who was central to a lot of the sinister activity that the Glenanne Gang got up to, gave an interview to journalist Hugh Jordan of *The Sunday World* shortly before she died. In her interview, Hugh asked her a number of key questions about Glenanne Gang activity and Lily played dumb. However, in her own words she said, 'I will take all my secrets to the grave'. It seems Lily was being very loyal to her close friend James Mitchell and she revealed to Hugh that Mitchell had left her a substantial sum of money in his will shortly before he died in 2008.

A subsequent report by Senior Counsel Patrick McEntee published in 2007, made appalling reading for An Garda Síochána. It stated that garda intelligence failed 'to meet an adequate and proper standard' and 'The commission considers that it is probable that this serious organisational deficit provided an inadequate standard of support to those Gardaí involved in the criminal investigations.'

'Photograph albums of suspects were missing, including records of the contents. Garda notebooks were 'presumed lost, abandoned or destroyed ... A finger print was found on a registration plate of the Monaghan bomb car ... this registration plate is no longer in the possession of the Garda Síochána.' The Report further stated that 'it had been hampered by inadequate information provided by the British authorities and by loss of an unknown amount of information in the possession of the Gardaí.'

McEntee considered that his investigation, like the Barron Inquiry, was limited 'by not having access to original security and intelligence documents in the possession of the British Government.' The report said its terms of reference were not wide-ranging enough to allow it to comment further.

No definitive finding was possible on why the garda investigations ended in July (Monaghan) and August (Dublin) 1974, due to loss of material, deaths of witnesses, and a practice of 'not committing decisions to writing'.

The fact that garda files went missing was shocking for a police force in a democratic society. One would have thought that the investigation into the worst day of terrorism in the history of the Irish Republic since An Garda Síochána was founded in 1922, might have led one to believe that the files would have been given the VIP treatment and handled with special care. Alas, this was not the case.

The Report also revealed an incident in which files, which potentially included some on the Dublin and Monaghan bombings, were burned in a bonfire at the Garda Technical Bureau in December 1974 on the instructions of a senior garda.[2] The damaging findings by Patrick McEntee, SC, left one to consider if British intelligence had infiltrated senior members of the gardaí with inducements to ensure certain files of information went missing and that standard policing procedures were not adhered to?

Not surprisingly, Justice for the Forgotten were unhappy with the contents of the McEntee Report. One of their main concerns was that they – Justice for the Forgotten – had not been allowed access to the evidence gathered.

The Cover-up Continues

After persistent lobbying, the British government gave Sir Hugh Orde the go-ahead to establish the Historical Enquiries Team or HET in 2005 to re-visit the 3,269 unsolved killings between 1969 and 1998. The HET would have a budget of £30 million and it would function under the watchful eye of the PSNI, itself suspicious considering that many serving members were sectarian policemen and women during their time in the bad old days of the RUC. Despite the hope offered by the creation of the HET, there was one other major problem, the Enquiries' Team would only review but not re-investigate the respective killings.[1]

Dave Cox, would head the HET, formerly of the London Metropolitan Police. He would have 100 investigators/researchers which would break down, on average, at thirty-two individual killings per separate investigation officer. Each unsolved atrocity would be re-visited and a separate customised Report would be written up, independent of all other killings. Individual Reports would then be presented to each relevant family.

We knew that Sir Hugh Orde meant well but dealing with the dark, murky forces that once ran the RUC who were now wearing different hats in the PSNI, could amount to little or no change. The shambolic Widgery investigation into Bloody Sunday, the Stalker/Stevens' Inquiries, etc., delayed trials, the reluctance to prosecute soldiers/RUC officers, etc., are well documented. Add in the reluctance of the British to release documents relating to certain controversies and it all pointed to one thing, blatant guilt and potential organised cover-up.

The British give the impression that justice was being done but ultimately, the respective revelations were too embarrassing for the reputation of their government on the international stage. That usually results in certain investigations being closed down unexpectedly, frustrated, stalled or specific Reports not being published at all.

The Cover-up Continues

With Dave Cox, the new man in from London, propped up by a big budget, our expectations were high for a successful outcome and the answers to questions we had been asking repeatedly since 1976. Dave Cox was about to enter the Northern Ireland political snake pit.

One morning out of the blue in 2006, I got a phone call from a number I didn't recognise. 'Good morning Mr Reavey, Dave Cox here from the HET. I'm here at Ardmore Station in Newry and I was wondering if you could pop in for a chat', the caller said at the other end of the phone. I told him that if he wanted to meet me, it would be best for him to call to the house in Whitecross. In typical English form, if somewhat unusual speak for Northern Ireland, he replied, 'Great, I'll get a couple of the local Bobbies to run me out to your place.'

Days later, he called to our house, accompanied by Phil James who would later head up what was known as 'The White Team' which oversaw the atrocities carried out by the Glenanne Gang, and Kim Bowen who took notes. My brother Seamus and sister Colleen joined us. 'The White Team' was unique in that it was based outside the Northern Ireland jurisdiction at a secret location in England, because in the murky world of Northern Ireland, many previous investigations of this nature were either compromised, sabotaged and eventually halted. One only has to look at the original Bloody Sunday Inquiry and the Stalker investigation!

We sat down at the table, had a cup of tea and engaged in small talk before we got down to re-visiting the events of 4 January 1976. Dave, a qualified lawyer, told us he had worked for the MET in London for thirty years and had assisted John Stevens in his ill-fated investigation of shoot-to-kill atrocities in Northern Ireland. He was aware of what had gone on in the six counties and the dishonesty the RUC engaged in when it came to protecting their own.

Several minutes into our chat, I told Dave that this was the last chance for us to get answers even though I still had the names in my head of the suspects that my Father passed to me on his deathbed. I asked Dave, 'are you in a position to tell me who killed Brian, John Martin and Anthony?'

'Yes I do know, having read the files, but it's much too early in the process to reveal who carried out the killings.'

'Well before I engage with you Mr Cox, it would give me a bit of confidence to know that we were both on the same page.'

I suggested that I write down the names of the people who I suspected and that he do likewise on separate sheets. I then suggested we both hand our pages to Kim Bowen and she can confirm or deny if we have the same people. I wrote down four names on a page and Dave wrote down the names that he had and we handed them to Kim. She looked at the two pages and then said, 'all the names on both sheets are identical'. When I heard what she had to say, I thought, 'at long last I can sit down with someone I trust. He knows where I'm coming from and neither of us have anything to hide.' I wanted to get everything off my chest now as I knew things that I couldn't pass to an RUC or PSNI officer.

I re-stated the events of Sunday 4 and 5 January 1976. Dave was not aware that the car driven by me was the first on the scene from the Whitecross side when the Kingsmills massacre occurred. I briefly told him about visiting the morgue in Newry that evening to bring home the remains of Brian and John Martin

I told him about our Mother being verbally and physically abused by British soldiers and as I relayed that horrible story in somewhat graphic form, Dave put his pen down and stopped me in my tracks. He said, 'Eugene, please. This account of what happened will be written down and will be in the archives for ever more.' I couldn't work out if he didn't believe me or if the details were so disgusting, they would make unpleasant reading.

I continued on with my story and he stopped me a second time. He said, 'take a break and think about what you are saying'. All of a sudden I began to wonder if Dave didn't want to hear what I was saying or if he wanted a different truth contained in my testimony. I had been under a lot of stress at the time and was working on a short fuse.

The Cover-up Continues

At that point, Fr Con Malone arrived at the back door and I invited him in. After some pleasantries, I suggested to Con that he take Dave into the front room and recall his version of events which he duly did.

Dave returned to the kitchen with a tear in his eye and said, 'Eugene, I want to apologise for not believing you. This gentleman [Con] has just confirmed everything you have been telling us.' Con had told him verbatim everything I had told him earlier about what happened to my Mother.

Dave Cox then said, 'take me over to your Mother's house'. Con and myself took him to the house and when we reached the door, I introduced Dave to my Mother and they embraced before we stepped inside.

'Mrs Reavey, I want to apologise to you for the murder of your sons and the failure of any government or security force personnel to call around and enquire about your well-being ... I also want to confirm to you that your sons were completely innocent victims and had no connection to any paramilitary group. Furthermore, I want to apologise to you for the appalling treatment and harassment handed out to you and your family by members of the security forces.'

The apology was most welcome and to hear from a British state official that Brian, John Martin and Anthony had no connection to paramilitary activity was a weight off her shoulders, even though she always knew that fact.

She told Dave that she was very hurt and upset when she would read things in the papers or when the security forces told her that the lads wouldn't have been killed unless there was a valid reason. Dave was clearly moved by my Mother's comments and her emotional tone.

He seemed really bothered by what he heard and that was significant considering in his thirty years as a policeman, he regularly had to call to houses with very bad news. My Mother, being the hospitable woman that she was, disappeared for a few minutes and returned with tea and a tray full of goodies.

As she did, Dave looked bewildered at the row of ten

flickering candles on the hearth of the fire in memory of those we had lost, were in hospital and surprisingly, those who murdered her sons.

Dave Cox remarked that he wasn't used to getting tea in any house he called to in England and was somewhat taken aback at the hospitality being offered by my Mother. We sipped the tea, ate the cake and as Dave was leaving, he said to my Mother, 'Mrs Reavey, I will not leave any stone unturned until we are able to give you a Report and tell you the circumstances surrounding your sons' deaths.'

In my opinion, if Dave Cox hadn't done one other thing for the HET, the fact that he put my Mother's mind at ease was the best thing he did in his entire life. It was also a major moment for my Mother. I could sense straight away that she was less tense, more relaxed and as the months rolled on, I could see a greater sense of contentment in her daily life.

We returned to my house and re-lived the events of 4 January 1976. Later that evening, we took Dave, Phil and Kim on a local tour. We took them to Mitchell's farm in nearby Glenanne, the site where the Kingsmills massacre occurred, the graveyard at Ballymoyer, the route that the killers took to make their escape and the place where one of the burned-out get-away cars was found.

By the time Dave, Phil and Kim left that evening, they had a much better grasp of the events on 4 January as well as a more detailed understanding of the local lie of the land, both physically and politically. They thanked us for our hospitality and co-operation. They assured us that once they wrote up their Report, which would also contain the information they knew and we didn't, it would be forwarded on to us. The apology issued by Dave Cox to my Mother was followed up on 10 April 2006 with a written-version which we appreciated.

Ten days or so later, I got a call from the HET office. They wanted me to meet their investigators Peter Smith and Kim Bowen at Sprucefield PSNI Centre just outside Belfast. I met them and we discussed, what could be best described as items on the periphery to the Inquiry such as the extortion of money from me by Jimmy Craig, the threats from Davy Payne and the death of Adam Lambert, etc.

I also told them about my difficulties with the 715 Certs and my time in prison, my engagement with Tucker Lyttle of the UDA, the Paisley comments, the failure of the RUC to answer letters, the Billy Wright issues in Portadown and my ongoing problems with Willie Frazer.

After many phone calls with Dave Cox and his team where they sought information, the HET Reavey Killings interim Report was delivered to us on 30 January 2010. The seventy-page Report set out in clear understandable English, the chronology of events as they happened that night.

While we were familiar with those events anyway, the Report went a step further in so much as it detailed the RUC officers who attended the crime scene, the discrepancies in various statements regarding who was where at particular times and interestingly, how the guns used in the killings were central to other murders elsewhere in mid-Ulster.

A senior RUC officer, Harry Breen, appeared to be up to his eyes in collusion with the UVF. The Pat Finucane Centre prepared a document on behalf of the Centre for Civil and Human Rights at Notre Dame Law School, Indiana USA whose Report was published in 2006. That Report confirmed what the HET investigation revealed – Chief Inspector Breen was involved in the purchasing of weapons from RUC colleague Billy McBride and selling them on to the Mid-Ulster UVF in Portadown. The weapons were made at the home of former British army Lt Col Edward James Augustus Howard ('Peter') 'Basil' Brush. That's a lot of names for one man!

The money received for the guns was paid to the South Down Orange Welfare Group. The home-made SMG was also used at the Rock Bar in Granemore Keady where Mick McGrath was shot in the stomach. According to the HET Report, the first recorded use of the SMG was the killing of the Reavey brothers in Whitecross, Armagh.

There were other issues in the Report that didn't make sense. Timings on the movements of RUC officers didn't tally with what we knew and the details contained in previous statements. Another matter that came to light surrounded the car used in the killings. The Austin 1100, registration 7343 LZ, was stolen from Little Barrack Street, Armagh City on Friday 2 January 1976. The owner of the car, Samuel McLoughlin, reported his stolen vehicle to the RUC in Armagh City the next morning 3 January. However, the Report says the theft wasn't logged by the RUC until the following day 4 January with no time of entry. Samuel McLoughlin was not informed about the whereabouts of the car until 19 January 1976 even though the RUC would have been aware of its location on 4 January.

The Report added that Detective Constable William Poots, scene of crime officer, did not record the time of his arrival at the Reavey house or his time of departure. This all seemed to be very shoddy and unprofessional. If not either, it was certainly unusual. The HET Report focused on the removal of the burned-out Austin 1100 car which had been found at nearby Ballygorman on the Newry to Armagh main road. Hugo Cowan, who operated a local vehicle recovery service, got a message from the RUC in Bessbrook to remove the car. Strangely, nobody in the RUC felt it necessary to preserve the scene where the car had been burned out.

To make matters more inexplicable, an RUC policeman telephoned Newry fire station and requested their people to extinguish the burning car at Ballygorman. When the same RUC policeman was asked by the HET people about who told him where the car was located, he replied, 'nobody. I had a premonition. God told me.'

A separate RUC officer who was present when the car at Ballygorman was towed away, told Hugo that he would be around to his place the next day to take fingerprints and photographs. With the car burned to a cinder, the chances of getting fingerprints were zero. Hugo kept the car for thirty years and nobody ever called to take photographs or fingerprints!

The Cover-up Continues

When the HET approached RUC personnel in Newry, Bessbrook and Newtownhamilton for exhibits and records of the circumstances surrounding the killings, they were shocked to discover that no items of evidence or incident/log books existed in the three stations!

Daily log books in a police station record every single complaint from the public ranging from a missing cat, dangerous driving, a fallen tree on a busy road to unsocial behaviour by young fellas with too much to drink, etc. It's standard practice all over the world – except in Northern Ireland – where, during the Troubles, reality regularly turned into a mirage when it came to policing.

With the controversial Reavey killings claiming three lives in the middle of an ongoing war, the absence of daily record books in 1976 was nothing short of amazing in light of all the killings that had occurred in South Armagh since the outbreak of the Troubles.

No explanation was given for this extraordinary disappearance of log books and the RUC policemen, who were queried by the HET, had no answers. The HET people could not believe what they were witnessing, but for us this was very much everyday par for the course when the spotlight was on the RUC.

One of the great flaws of the HET Report was the terms of its engagement at the outset. The HET team could not investigate suspects unless they had new evidence. They could not get new evidence unless they were allowed to question suspects.

UVF operatives in mid-Ulster had been advised of these parameters by their pals in the RUC and didn't co-operate. It was a bit like a Catch 22 situation for the HET researchers. They couldn't do one thing without the freedom to do the other. Not surprisingly, the RUC gave as little co-operation that they could possibly get away with.

Another thing that caught our attention in the Report was the reference to Detective Constable David Gray. DC Gray was English and was seconded to nearby Newry Station at the latter end of 1975. At face value, this was a strange posting as the general feedback we had been hearing was that no policeman in Britain would voluntarily seek to go to a part of the UK where they automatically became targets. In South Armagh, that danger was amplified more so.

DC Gray told the HET that he took a statement from our Anthony in Daisy Hill Hospital at 12.15 p.m. on 7 January 1976. I'm 100 per cent sure that he did not. He also told the HET that he took a statement from me at 12.45 p.m. on the same day at an over-crowded Ballymoyer cemetery.

If he drove to Ballymoyer, he would not have met me at 12.45 p.m. There were hundreds of cars parked on either side of the road for the double funerals. In fact, he would have to be leaving Newry at 12.15 p.m. to be in Ballymoyer at 12.45 p.m.

If he came by helicopter, he still wouldn't have met me by 12.45 p.m. as such an arrival would have been outstanding and memorable. It never happened. It was bad enough that he lied but with the benefit of hindsight, his very presence in the Newry/South Armagh area at the time, was highly suspicious.

When the Reavey killings took place, DC Gray took my brother Oliver to Bertie Hamilton's house for questioning. He only seemed to be interested in what Oliver knew, i.e. did he see any cars, or anybody running away from the scene? He did not ask questions about what actually happened in the house when the killings occurred. He seemed more curious over what happened on the periphery. It struck us that he was more concerned about the movements and positioning of UVF, RUC, British army and Glenanne gang personnel at the time of the killings.

By early March 1976, DC Gray was back in England and never seen in our area again. His arrival and departure seemed strange in so much as his time in Newry coincided with the events of early January 1976 but once they happened and were investigated, he returned home.

The HET tried to contact DC Gray for a chat through the London Metropolitan Police pensions branch and received no reply. Former RUC officer Trevor Cartmill, who I had strong words with in our house on the night of the killings, was also a

The Cover-up Continues

person of interest to the HET. Like DC Gray, the HET tried to contact Cartmill through the PSNI pensions branch and he too refused to engage with the investigators.

After four decades of asking endless questions about the mysterious DC Gray, I learned in late 2023 from a police source that I know, that DC Gray was in Newry RUC station for very suspicious activity which was significant in the investigation into the deaths of our Brian, John Martin and Anthony.

My credible police source informed me that statements taken by DC Gray from Anthony and myself contained forged signatures. DC Gray lied repeatedly about his movements in the first week of January 1976. I learned that DC Gray did not get permission from Daisy Hill Hospital staff to interview Anthony and the statement drawn up was a verbatim account of a TV interview he gave the night previously from his hospital bed.

The Reavey family are in no doubt that DC Gray was sent to Newry from London as part of the British military intelligence plot to work with the UVF in the murder of Brian, John Martin and Anthony and then construct a cover-up to mislead the subsequent investigation. DC Gray died in 2006.

As for Trevor Cartmill, all the HET wanted to know was what were his movements on the night of the killings. Cartmill said in the past that he came to the Reavey house with Constable Bell. However, in a separate interview, Bell said that he arrived at the house with a different police colleague. Bell's version of events and timings didn't concur with those of Cartmill. Somebody wasn't telling the truth.

The HET Report also said alas, 'there is no record of any person being arrested or interviewed with these murders'. One didn't have to be a genius to see that the RUC, British army and wider security forces had colluded with the UVF and the Glenanne gang in the Reavey-O'Dowd killings. It also went on to say that Detective Sergeant Gerry McCann was one of the very few RUC officers to have gained the confidence of the Reavey family. He told the HET Report that, 'there was no way the Reaveys were involved in any paramilitary activities whatsoever'.

DS McCann told the Report that he 'did not know why the Reaveys were targeted' but added that 'it wouldn't take much' and cited possibilities from 'baseless rumour to vengefully fabricate intelligence'. McCann also believed that 'there was much disinformation, speculative and fabricated intelligence about which hindered investigations'.

The Report also stated that Lily Shields and RUC officer Laurence McClure were charged with the offence of withholding information in connection with the attack on Donnelly's Bar in Silverbridge Armagh on 19 December 1975. Charges relating to the bombing of the Rock Bar at Granemore, Keady, in June 1976 were also lumped in together. During their police interview, McClure and Shields admitted a 'limited' involvement in the attack and actually drove the attackers away. The charge against them was not proceeded with and was marked as a *Nolle Prosequi* [unwilling to pursue] on 8 April 1981. The Latin term is usually used in court when the prosecution, i.e. the state or DPP, opts not to pursue the case. Laurence McClure received a suspended sentence for his involvement in the Rock Bar explosion.

What caught the attention of many in this case were the comments made in court by the Lord Chief Justice Lowry:[2]

> All of the accused have admitted their offences ... in one case, the mortal danger of their service ... was needed and was justified to rid the land of the pestilence that has been in existence.

These were extraordinary comments from a judge. He all but said the RUC in question were right in their motives to murder and prevent republican paramilitaries pursuing their objectives. The only problem in this case was, the people who were targeted were completely innocent! Was it any wonder Catholics had no confidence in the law? McClure, Shields, and co., were being protected by the British state. If there was ever an example of collusion with the endorsement of the establishment, this was it.

The HET Report also referred to suspicious activity that occurred at Kingsmills crossroads, on the night of the Reavey killings. Seamus, my brother, told the HET that John Joe

McGrath had informed him days after the killings, that he (John) had been stopped by the RUC at a Vehicle Check Point or as it's known in police terms, a VCP. He had been stopped ten minutes before the shootings as he was en route to Ballymoyer which meant he would have had to drive past our house. The VCP must not have been authorised as if it was, the Glenanne UVF gang would not have been in the place ten minutes later. When Seamus passed this information on to me within a week of the killings, I went to Bessbrook and informed the RUC. Inexplicitly, John Joe McGrath was never interviewed by the police and unfortunately is now deceased.

Eugene Malone was a farmer who lived down the road from us at Drumherriff just off the Kingsmills crossroads. On the night of 4 January 1976, Eugene was feeding his cattle in what is known locally as Malone's meadow, when the shootings occurred. Eugene heard the bursts of gunfire and blessed himself. He thought that the shooting was taking place at nearby Hamilton's house. He then heard a getaway car taking off at top speed and revving its way towards Kingsmills crossroads, a journey of one minute. At the same time, he could see flashing white lights at Kingsmills crossroads not far from the top of his lane. As far as he was concerned, the flashing lights were a signal to the getaway car that the road ahead was clear for its escape. Within seconds of the getaway car making its way towards Kingsmills crossroads, according to Eugene, the VCP was gone.

Shortly afterwards, Patsy McKeown from nearby Glenanne and his wife, who were driving from Newry via Kingsmills towards Whitecross, noticed our Anthony crawling along the side of the road, shortly after the shooting. Unaware of the shootings, they didn't stop because they didn't think anything was wrong. What was interesting about their story was, the checkpoint that had been in place fifteen minutes previously, was now gone. This was all the more amazing as Brian and John Martin were now dead and the provision of checkpoints in the aftermath of a shooting would have been standard police practice.

When Patsy McKeown told me, I again went to the RUC

station in Bessbrook and passed on this information. It was not followed up by the RUC for inclusion in their book of evidence. As far as I know, no book of evidence was ever compiled. The Historical Enquiries Team of researchers were unable to find any material from police or army records to assist in determining the specific presence of a VCP. The Report said, 'an official VCP in such a location at the time of the attack should have deterred any paramilitary activity.

'The fact that no VCP existed is indicative that security personnel were acting in concert with the attackers. This was an important line of inquiry that was never identified and cannot now be followed up.'

The HET Report into the Reavey killings was damning of the RUC and the British army for colluding with the Glenanne UVF gang. Normal police procedures such as follow-up investigations were not adhered to and a culture of cover-up prevailed. This all combined to create the unthinkable outcome where a police force, a state army and loyalist terrorists worked together to murder innocent Catholics.

The Report says that no RUC records exist about any members of the Reavey family before the attack. Much to our amazement, the Report said there were allegations made by Willie Frazer that 'the [Reavey] Family were involved in illegal Vehicle Check Points'. If anybody can produce proof of this, please report us to the PSNI.

The Report went on to say, 'The fact that some individuals refuse to acknowledge the wrong they done is a matter of regret.'

It says the dual membership of the Glenanne gang and the security forces practised by some of those involved, could have resulted in flawed intelligence passing from one group to the next.

The HET Report repeatedly states that Brian, John Martin, Anthony and the Reavey family were entirely innocent. It praised the Reavey family for engaging with the HET in good faith and said the harassment suffered by us was 'disgraceful'.

An inclusion of note in the Report relates to the death of Anthony in Daisy Hill Hospital, twenty-six days after the killing of Brian and John Martin, refers to a suspicious action by the coroner, Noel Anderson, in the official record arising from the inquest into the cause of his death.

It says, 'As a result of submissions put forward on behalf of the Reavey Family to the Coroner, the initial recording of 'Died from natural causes' was replaced with an 'Open verdict' on 2 February 1977.

'This action by the Coroner in replacing a verdict is most uncommon and has not been noted in any other of the cases reviewed by the HET.'

This change in verdict came as a shock to us. We were not informed and we only learned of the amendment at least thirty years after it occurred. This left a lot of unanswered questions.

Why did the coroner not include 'Open verdict' when he originally wrote the Report? More to the point, what happened that made him change his mind? Did the robust challenge by our determined junior barrister Éilis McDermott make him realise he was making an incorrect call? The difference between 'Died of natural causes' and 'Open verdict' was highly significant for us. By writing 'Open verdict', the death is deemed to be suspicious in the absence of other facts. By writing 'Died of natural causes', the British were in the clear and the Reavey family could not chase them for justice and compensation arising from Anthony's death.

We don't know to this day what brought about the change in the verdict but we can only speculate that the coroner came under pressure to write 'Died of natural causes' and was later motivated by a guilty conscience to change the wording to 'Open verdict'. We eventually received a copy of the coroner's certificate which included his amended verdict and observational notes. The Report ran to seven pages. Bizarrely, two and a half pages of the Report were redacted or blacked out – why? It appeared to me it all smacked of an elaborate plan to deceive us and manipulate the message that went out to the wider public, which suited the British agenda.

Not surprisingly, Willie Frazer of FAIR, got his speak in

shortly after we received the customised Reavey Report. He called on the HET to clear all UDR soldiers murdered in South Armagh from any suspicion of paramilitary involvement. He went on to say, 'The HET have angered and hurt victims with their partisan and unprofessional comments ... They have joined the chorus of hand-wringing apologists who row up to sing the praises of the Reavey family.'

Why was Frazer so determined to defend the UDR and have a go at us? The other question was, how did Willie get access to a Report that was exclusively for the eyes and ears of the Reavey family only? Who in the British security machine gave him access?

The Historical Enquiries Team promised so much and in the end delivered very little that was new to us. Its remit and terms of reference were limited although to their credit, they confirmed a lot of suspicions we had on various activities. As we looked forward to the publication of the over-arching HET Report in the hope that something revealing would emerge from the White Team, things were happening behind the scenes.

Sir Hugh Orde announced in April 2009 that he was stepping down as chief constable of the PSNI to become President of the Association of Chief Police Officers, a job, which on the face of it, was less murky and would be more likely to give him many nights of decent sleep. Orde was replaced by Matt Baggott who, it seemed, surrounded himself with certain men who were long-serving members of the RUC. Once Baggott replaced Orde, we were hearing that changes were afoot.

Either Dave Cox and his team were uncovering details that (a) certain people didn't want published, (b) somebody somewhere in the chain didn't feel he was doing his job competently or else (c) complaints were being made from 'certain' victims' groups that the HET wasn't going far enough.

Loyalists were fearful of Dave as he was coming across details that threatened to blow the lid off the murky working arrangements they had with the RUC, UDR and British security forces. Republicans were no fans of Dave either. Their compromised members who were working as double agents were vulnerable to being 'outed' while senior PSNI staff who were once in the RUC, were nervous as Dave came across shocking details on what some of them got up to.

Whatever the reasons, dark forces were at play behind the scenes and Dave Cox was stood down from his role in September 2013. He received that news while on holidays in Greece. Dave told me that the powers that be didn't even wait for him to return so that they could call him in to their office for a confidential chat. It was my view that Dave was blatantly shafted. He joined that infamous Roll of Honour that included John Stalker and John Stevens who all had one thing in common namely, their findings had the potential to destroy the reputation of police men and women and British security personnel in Northern Ireland and would leave the British government with lots of embarrassing questions to answer on the international stage.

The HET was closed down at the end of 2014 with 'budget cuts' being cited as the reason. It left many people asking why it was set up in the first place if it wasn't going to be properly funded to the end of its mission?

Correspondence I have seen shows that Steve Morris, who was a senior member of Dave Cox's investigation team, submitted an affidavit as part of an application to the High Court in Belfast on 30 January 2015 for a judicial review into the decision to close down the HET. The application for a judicial review of the decision to halt the HET enquiries was taken by the family of Patrick Barnard (13). The young schoolboy was one of four people, including James McCaughey (13), killed in a bomb blast at the Hillcrest Bar in Dungannon, Co. Tyrone on St Patrick's Day in 1976. At issue, was the planned publication of the report written up by the White Team which would contain the findings from all the individual reports combined, dealing with alleged collusion. The affidavit makes it quite clear in repeated clauses that a Report would be the end product of the enquiries.

In clause 4 of the sworn statement it says, '... from day one,

I had tacit approval from the Chief Constable of the PSNI [Hugh Orde] and the Director of the HET, that my cases would involve the maximum disclosure possible.'

Clause 6 states, '… it was accepted by myself and the Director of the HET, Dave Cox, that in order to deal with the areas of linking cases and to effectively inform the families of the context of their case to the fullest potential, an over-arching Report was an absolute necessity.'

However, according to the affidavit, 'A letter was received from the ACC [Assistant Chief Constable] Drew Harris on 12 June 2014 clearly stating that there would be no thematic review as this was not the purpose of the HET and that there was a recourse implication.' A recourse implication could see costly compensation payments issued by the British if successfully contested in the courts.

Drew Harris went on to be Commissioner of An Garda Síochána in the Republic of Ireland. If he was correct in his letter of 12 June 2014, that begs the question, why was the White Team, as part of the HET, established as far back as 2005?

As far as I am concerned, Drew Harris has some questions to answer to clear the air even if the queries are nothing more than harmless human curiosity. Harris joined the RUC in 1983. Many of his colleagues, before and after that time, were suspected of engaging with loyalists when it came to targeting members of the nationalist community. This was stated by John Weir in his *Sunday Times* interview. Was Harris aware of these associations? We don't know at this time.

Drew Harris' father, Alwyn (51) a highly respected member of the RUC, was killed by an IRA car bomb in October 1989 in Lisburn. According to *Lost Lives*, Fr Denis Faul said that 'Superintendent Harris was exactly the kind of officer on whom a trustworthy police force could be built'.[2]

I and many others who suffered at the hands of the Glenanne gang are not convinced that the HET enquiries were closed down due to budget cuts. It had all the hallmarks of an investigation that was getting too close to the political bone. Any official

Report that would confirm collusion between certain members of the RUC, British army, etc. and loyalist terrorists would and should shock the world. Therefore, a Report had to be stopped in its tracks before it was too late – that was the viewpoint of John Stalker and John Stevens whose previous efforts to expose police and army skulduggery came to a controversial stop. Stalker, like Dave Cox, was forced out of the police for no other reason than simply doing his job to the best of his ability.

A report in the *Belfast Telegraph* in January 2022, revealed what many of us suspected when we learned that the HET was closing down. In the *Belfast Telegraph* piece referring to a BBC NI TV documentary marking twenty years of the PSNI, former chief constable Sir Hugh Orde indicated that the Historical Enquiries Team was closed down because it was about to start investigating serving politicians involved in paramilitary activity.[3]

Hugh Orde was also quoted as saying, 'Had I been the chief when that [HMIC] Report was received I'd have called a press conference ... and I'd have thrown the Report in the bin on public television and said, 'That's all very interesting but I'm going to keep going because I think the families of victims are far more important ... It was the only original idea I had in policing. I was hugely disappointed and angry when it was closed down for the reasons it was closed down.'[4]

The *Belfast Telegraph* also quoted Kenny Donaldson on 9 September 2015, a spokesman for Innocent Victims United who said 'Sir Hugh Orde's comments chime with previous information he obtained from a former senior HET investigator.

'We were advised that the senior HET Investigator had sought to interview Martin McGuinness over the [IRA] Enniskillen Poppy Day Bomb massacre [in 1987] but that he was told that this couldn't happen, that the NIO said 'this would not be a good idea'. The shenanigans and hypocrisy that permeated everyday life in Northern Ireland, showed no signs of ending.

One item of note for me was that before the HET team arrived in South Armagh in 2006, every time I was stopped at a police checkpoint, I was treated as a suspect. Once the HET came to town, that practice stopped.

The cancellation of the HET enquiries dashed our hopes of getting more answers. While it was a disappointing setback, we had wheels turning elsewhere which were well in motion before the HET enquiries got underway.

Paisley says 'No, No'

ONE DAY IN 2003, I received a phone call from Ferghal Shiels, a solicitor with Madden & Finucane in Castle Street, Belfast. This was the legal practice that was started by Pat Finucane before he was shot dead in February 1989 by the UDA/UFF with the assistance of their pals in the British security forces.

Ferghal said that his office was putting a case together that would go to the European Court of Human Rights. He said the killings of our lads fitted the criteria for the proposed action. He called up to see me in Whitecross and I signed the forms on behalf of my Mother to commence the action. The case being put forward was in my Mother's name, *Sarah Reavey V United Kingdom*. It focused on Article 2 of the Convention on Human Rights which states that everyone's right to life should be protected by law. Other failures were included in the application. These included the all-important application that 'there had been no adequate investigation into allegations of collusion and/or involvement by security forces in the shooting of her three sons, nor any effective remedy for the same.'

We had intended to travel to Strasbourg for the verdict and awaited notification. But when the court issued its verdict we were informed in writing of the decision on 27 November 2007. We won our case – the court ruled that there had been a violation of Article 2 of the convention due to a lack of independence by the RUC during the initial stage of the investigation in 1999. It was a renewed investigation arising from the John Weir statement to the *Sunday Times*. The victory in the European Court was a major confidence boost for us. The fact that the RUC was ruled as not being independent vindicated our calls for answers to the questions we had been asking since 1976, namely, an acknowledgement that the British state and its various security agencies had colluded with loyalist terrorists to kill the Reavey brothers. We took the view that if we could achieve victory in the European Court, we could do the same elsewhere as a crucial legal precedent had now been set. Follow-up court actions would be high on our list of priorities in the coming years, assuming we could collate the exact information we sought from the PSNI.

In the meantime, I had written to British Prime Minister Tony Blair. I reminded him that the PSNI and numerous secretaries of state had failed to co-operate with the Barron Inquiry. I asked him to address the issues we were seeking answers on in relation to the activities of the Glenanne gang and the scurrilous remarks made about me in the House of Commons. The letter was copied to Peter Hain, Secretary of State for Northern Ireland, Dermot Ahern, Minister for Foreign Affairs in Dublin and my solicitor Rory McShane.

A copy of the exact letter was subsequently sent to An Taoiseach Bertie Ahern, the Chief Constable Hugh Orde, Ian Paisley Senior and Nuala O'Loan, the Police Ombudsman. Tony Blair, through a sub-ordinate called E. Adams, wrote back saying a Minister in the Northern Ireland office would reply to me. An official from Peter Hain's office subsequently got in touch and said the issues were being looked into. Nuala O'Loan replied and asked one of her senior detectives to consider the matter. One of her people subsequently visited me and took notes but nothing emerged as a result of that either.

Taoiseach Bertie Ahern also replied and a follow-up meeting was arranged. Apart from him raising the matter with the British PM, there wasn't a lot he could do. Not surprisingly, I received no reply from Ian Paisley Senior.

Even though my correspondence generated some publicity in the newspapers, which in turn applied some heat on the above officials, my blitz of letters failed to move the issue on 'one' notch.

AROUND THIS TIME, WE were hearing rumours of a revolt within Ian Paisley's DUP. The deal that Paisley did with his life-long enemies, Sinn Féin, at St Andrews Scotland in October 2006 to establish a new administration at Stormont had created a political earthquake within the Democratic Unionist Party. Many of its ultra-conservative members were asking themselves if the resistance they had shown towards republicans on behalf of their loyal voters and the lengths they went to defend the Party in the previous four decades had been a complete waste of time?

Paisley going into office with Martin McGuinness was, in their opinion, like 'God' doing a deal with the 'devil'. As they saw it, the only person who gained was the 'devil'. For them, it amounted to a complete sell-out. Grassroots members whose DNA was anti-Sinn Féin from birth were absolutely furious and as they now saw it, Paisley didn't care because he was about to become 'top dog' in the Stormont Executive.

Hardliners like Jim Allister who was loyal to Paisley, left the DUP in disgust and set up the TUV, the Traditional Unionist Voice, to work against what he saw were repeated concessions being made to republicans. The DUP was in disarray behind the scenes, even though out front all appeared to be business as usual.

Paisley had marched his followers behind him for four decades. But now, *he* was at the top and they felt like fools. The fire and brimstone bible-thumping DUP leader who said 'NO, NO, NO' to every positive political initiative since the 1950s had done a spectacular u-turn and his faithful supporters were furious. There would have to be consequences. Likewise, there was extraordinary turmoil within the ranks of the Free Presbyterian Church, the religious institution he set up in 1951 and was its unchallenged head every year ever since. The flock who had defended Paisley to the last for over fifty years, couldn't believe what was happening.

Talk of hostile rebellion was emerging and the wagons were circling around Paisley. The ultimatum was becoming clear, namely, 'step down or be voted out'. In January 2008, Paisley's time as leader of the Free Presbyterian Church came to a humiliating end and he was forced to quit. The low-profile Ron Johnstone replaced him. One can only imagine the anger, rage and sense of betrayal within the church over Paisley's perceived hypocrisy. Six months later, his time as leader of the DUP, the party he founded in 1971, was over.

He had been First Minister of Northern Ireland for eleven months. The most outstanding pillar of unionist resistance and bigotry had fallen. The man who encouraged his sectarian supporters to attack innocent Catholics at Burntollet Bridge in 1969 and thus 'formally' commenced the Troubles, had 'lost' his booming voice in the space of six months. Two years later, Paisley was appointed as Lord Bannside to the British House of Lords but by then his authority was gone.

This was the same man who held rallies to 'Smash Sinn Féin' and reportedly allowed his car to transport the guns that were used in the killing of eighteen-year-old Catholic barman Peter Ward in Malvern Street Belfast on 27 June 1966.[1]

Ian Paisley, the man, who many people say, did more than anyone else to prolong the Troubles that cost so many lives, left a twisted trail of anger, injury, generational hurt and sectarian hatred, was now redundant. Northern Ireland was changing.

This development may have caused chaos within the DUP but I was no further on in trying to get Ian Paisley to withdraw the remarks he made in the House of Commons. Peter Robinson succeeded Paisley as leader of the DUP and I felt I had nothing to lose if I presented my case to him. Robinson, it seems, was looking ahead and could see that the demographics of Northern Ireland were changing and the evolving dynamics were working against unionism. He started making soundings towards Catholic voters and hinted on occasions that they would benefit greatly by giving their votes to the DUP rather than Sinn Féin.

I felt now was the time to talk to Robinson so that he could clear up unfinished business from the Paisley era. After all, if Peter Robinson could fix this issue, he would be sending out a positive signal to nationalists that he was someone they could do business with.

I knew Protestant man Raymond McCord whose son, Raymond junior, was shot dead by the UVF in 1997. Raymond and I might have been from the opposite side of the political divide but we had one thing in common, we both wanted answers from the UVF. I got to know Raymond through various victims support groups and one night at an event in Queens University Belfast, we got chatting and formed a lasting friendship. Raymond knew Peter Robinson and was willing to help when I told him I needed to speak in person with the new leader of the DUP. A meeting was arranged and I met Mr Robinson at his constituency office in east Belfast.

One of my lasting memories of the meeting was that Peter Robinson's assistants checked under my car when I parked outside his office. I was accompanied to the meeting by Raymond who sat in on the discussion. Peter Robinson told me he was fully aware of my story. He had read reports where the then chief constable, Sir Ronnie Flanagan, confirmed that I was an innocent man with no involvement in the Kingsmills massacre. I showed him my customised HET Report which stated in black and white that I had no association whatsoever with Kingsmills and had been badly wronged arising from the comments made in the House of Commons by his predecessor, Ian Paisley.

As the conversation rolled on, I began to feel that the Peter Robinson I was speaking to was a more flexible and engaging person to the one I had been seeing repeatedly on my TV screen since the 1970s. He struck me as a man who was genuinely interested in my difficulty and showed no sign of resistance knowing that I was from the nationalist heartland of South Armagh. He was clearly a pragmatic politician whose tough persona in the media was different to the man in reality and quickly impressed me as a man one could do business with.

Having presented my case, he asked me, 'so Eugene, what can I help you with?'

I told him I had two problems and he might be able to help. The first one was the document that Paisley used in the House of Commons to defame me and the others mentioned. I reminded him that Sir Ronnie Flanagan told me the document was not of RUC origin. The second query was, could he arrange for Ian Paisley to meet me in person so that we could discuss the matter further and have the Record in the House of Commons corrected?

Without hesitation, he said, 'as far as the document goes, I was present when it was handed over to Dr Paisley.' I asked him who handed over the document?

'He's a neighbour of your own', he replied.

I asked him if it was Willie Frazer?

He didn't say a word but nodded in agreement.

'Are you sure? Can I take that as gospel?' I asked.

He nodded in agreement again.

We talked at length about Willie and his changing loyalties within unionism. I got the impression that Peter was not a fan of his. I asked him if he was prepared to repeat what he just said in a court of Law?

He replied by saying words to the effect, 'that would all depend on my relationship with the House of Paisley at that particular time. Presently, I think Eugene you would have a better chance of speaking to Paisley on this issue than I would.' I sensed, rightly or wrongly, that all was not well between the Robinson and Paisley factions within the DUP arising from the recent rebellion.

That was, more or less, the end of the meeting. As we parted, he said, 'don't be afraid to contact me again if I can be of any help.' I was pleased with the meeting. It gave me a sense of relief that the new leader of the DUP understood my predicament, even though I was no further on.

A line from Susan McKay's book *Northern Protestants: An unsettled People* was an eye-opener on what we had to endure when dealing with the Frazer family.[2] Willie's mother, Peggy Frazer said, 'My father used to say, "I'll tell you one thing – there's none of them [Catholics] any good only dead ones … The sweeter they are, the worse they are".'

As Peggy Frazer displayed sectarian hatred for her neighbours, we were facing another crisis.

Raised Hopes amid Family Loss

On Saturday 27 July 2013, I went to Croke Park in Dublin to see a double-header. Cavan took on London while Cork played Galway in a Round 4 qualifier match. At half-time during the first game, I got an unexpected call from my sister Eileen who told me that our eighty-nine-year-old Mother Sarah, who everyone knew as Sadie, had taken a turn for the worse and she suggested that I go home as quick as possible. I gave my car keys to my son Anthony and got the train to Newry. My brother Frank picked me up at the train station and brought me to Daisy Hill Hospital. My Mother recognised me and squeezed my hand.

However, the news wasn't encouraging. I was told that our Mother's body was slowly closing down. We maintained an all-night vigil, taking turns to keep Sadie company. On Monday 29 July, our Mother passed away at 7.30 p.m. We were all there when she left this world. We were shattered. Sadie kept us all together as a close-knit family through good times and bad. Like a typical Irish Mother of her generation, she worked morning, noon and night washing, cleaning, feeding and giving us the best guidance she could for our own respective lives.

Despite the killing of our Brian, John Martin and Anthony, she never uttered a negative or critical word in her life. She always saw good in people and believed in the power of prayer. Her wake was huge and that didn't surprise us. Her funeral mass took place at Carrickananney church where she had been a member of the choir for sixty years. Our Mother was buried on Wednesday 31 July at Ballymoyer, next to our Dad Jimmy, and the three boys. Her funeral was covered by several newspapers and even made TV news. A new emptiness had entered our lives.

For all of the Reavey family, our Mother's death marked the end of a special era. Losing a mother is horrible and it took all of us a very long time to adjust to life without her. Our Mother's sister, Aunt Winnie, died later in the year on 29 October when she passed away in Queen's New York. Five weeks later, our Mother's other sister Rose Ellen Sheeran who lived in Camlough, died at the age of ninety-three – our Mother's generation was disappearing.

AROUND THIS TIME, BELFAST-based firm KRW Law headed by Kevin Winters, called a meeting of families whose loved ones died in suspicious circumstances during the Troubles. The shocking contents of the incomplete HET Reports had been well circulated by this time highlighting the skulduggery the Glenanne gang and British security forces got up to during the 1970s.

Arising from the contents in Anne Cadwallader's must-read book *Lethal Allies: British Collusion in Ireland* which exposed previously unpublished HET details about the close relationship between the Glenanne UVF gang and the British security forces, Kevin felt the time was right to initiate what's known in legal terms as a Class Action. This is where court proceedings are taken on behalf of numerous people in one overall case.

The meeting was called on Wednesday 9 April 2014 at the Ryandale Hotel in The Moy, Co. Tyrone. Numerous families who suffered at the hands of the Glenanne gang showed up. It was conducted by solicitors Kevin Winters, Peter Corrigan, Niall Murphy and Darragh Mackin. Also present were Anne Cadwallader and Alan Bracknell of The Pat Finucane Centre.

The families of the victims of Glenanne gang had long been discussing our options. The Pat Finucane Centre had informed us in the past that going down the legal route was fraught with danger.

Firstly, there was the amount of information on atrocities available to us and whether what we had was sufficient to prove beyond reasonable doubt that our respective cases were justified. Then there was the issue of legal costs and who was going to pay to secure justice in the courts? Also the issue of the statute of limitations whereby such legal action could be thrown out of court because the atrocities had happened so far back in time, the evidence presented in such a case might be deemed unreliable, incomplete and crucial witnesses might no longer be alive.

At the same time, the feeling was that the batch of new evidence that had come to light arising from the HET investigations and the contents of Anne Cadwallader's book would be sufficient grounds for us to take a legal action. Kevin Winters took the view that there was enough information in the HET Reports to warrant a legal High Court civil action against the British Ministry of Defence, the PSNI and the Northern Ireland Office for malfeasance in public office, i.e., collusion. The aim of the action was for the MoD, RUC and NIO to be held publicly liable for their direct and indirect involvement in the murder and attempted murder of over one hundred individuals in the Glenanne series of killings. The action would also ask for specific discovery applications in the pursuance of information.

The proposed action would centre around Article 2 of the European Convention on Human Rights where a precedent had already been established in the *McKerr V United Kingdom* case as ruled on 4 April 2000 which deals with the legal obligation to protect life. This was a precedent my Mother Sadie had relied on previously, in bringing a case before the European Court of Human Rights.

Kevin said, with emphasis, that it was regrettable that solicitors had to get involved to seek justice for members of the public who, day after day, were up against an uncooperative British state which did everything in its power to frustrate the pursuit of justice. There was overwhelming support for the proposal. There was even better news when he said that in the event of free legal aid being denied, he would take the case *pro-bono* which meant his office would not charge any fees because he believed the cause was worthy.

On foot of this, we as a collective group initiated the process of civil proceedings making it clear that in light of what emerged in the HET Reports, there were now sufficient grounds to take legal action against the British state and its various agencies.

Our timing was significant as the new Lord Chief Justice for Northern Ireland, Sir Declan Morgan, happened to be three months into the job. It seems Justice Morgan had enough of the constant demands from affected families who had been calling year in, year out, to have legacy issues sorted once and for all. The issue wasn't going away and he indicated in very clear terms that if anybody in authority was going to address the problem, it would be him.

I applied for legal aid. My application was rejected.

When the legal team analysed each of the families' HET reports it became clear that there was a consistent thread – a promise to initiate a thematic investigation. This promise was in almost every Glenanne gang HET report to establish if there were links to all the atrocities carried out by the UVF unit. The proposal was relayed to the Oireachtas when the HET gave a presentation in Dublin as to the benefits of its investigation.

The officer tasked with the HET Glenanne investigation was a former Metropolitan Police officer Steve Morris. With Steve Morris' investigation ninety per cent complete, for reasons unbeknown to us, a decision was taken by those in the upper echelons of the British establishment to discontinue the thematic investigation without further notice. This pronouncement, would at its heart, seek to derail the last avenue of truth for the families who suffered from Glenanne gang atrocities. Even though it did not surprise us, it was a decision we were not prepared to accept.

My lawyer Darragh Mackin, now with Phoenix Law, took the view that the decision was both contrary to our human rights and unlawful in that the police had acted inappropriately in seeking to sabotage our investigation into the truth. Thus began what would later be described as an 'unprecedented' legal challenge. We adopted a wider strategic approach in introducing evidence from each of the Glenanne series of cases to relay to the court the enormity and scale of the mass murder which the PSNI and British establishment were seeking to cover up.

In the weeks leading up to May 2015, our lawyers Darragh Mackin and Peter Corrigan travelled to London to meet with our Senior Counsel Danny Friedman of Matrix Chambers to prepare the case. Whilst there, they decided to reach out to the former head of the investigation, Steve Morris. What was to come, was beyond the realms of our imagination.

Steve Morris signed and swore a witness statement with our lawyers which would turn the case on its head forever. His statement personified why the HET investigation was necessary and could not be denied. He confirmed that there was collusion in ninety-five per cent of the cases. The over-arching Report to the families should be completed, he concluded.

On 7 May 2015, we embarked on our High Court action en masse. By our side was Steve Morris. As we gathered in a large court room called QB2 at the end of the great hall in the Belfast High Court, we entered in our hundreds. Families packed in to the public gallery, the media area, the jury seats, the lawyers' benches with the remainder standing shoulder to shoulder with doors unable to close. As Justice Seamus Treacy entered to commence the case, he uttered the unforgettable words, 'we are going to need a bigger court'.

With the decision reserved until summer 2017, Lord Morgan, who was also president of the Northern Ireland Coroners' Courts, decided to hold what was billed as a Legacy Engagement Event at the Hilton hotel in Belfast on 12 February 2016. He was joined by Lord Justice Weir and Justice Colton, a prominent coroner. Addressing the many affected families, Lord Morgan said, 'the purpose of today's event is to hear what you have to say about how best to ensure that all of the legacy cases are progressed as expeditiously as possible through the inquest system.' He also told the gathering that while he was president of the coroners' service, he had no control over its budget and said it was under-resourced and over-burdened with its existing work load. He made it clear, that provided the resources were in place, additional coroners would be appointed and if all state agencies co-operated fully, it should be possible to hear all the legacy cases within five years.

He added that Justice Colton, the incoming presiding

coroner, would review and manage the 724 outstanding cases. Justice Colton would see all materials in un-redacted form and would do all he could to ensure that the families are provided with the information to which they are entitled.

Lord Morgan told those in attendance that he was so determined to address these issues, he had spoken to the secretary of state for Northern Ireland, the Minister for Justice, the First and Deputy First Ministers, the NI Attorney-General and the international human rights community.

A new dedicated Legacy Inquest Unit would need to be established as a matter of urgency. Lord Morgan concluded that he was fully committed to doing all in his power to bring these legacy cases to a conclusion and providing the answers that nationalist and a small number of unionist families had waited so long for.

He finished his presentation by saying, 'you have been subjected to a series of disappointments and I do not want you to suffer another false dawn if that can be avoided.'

I sensed that, at long last, people in the upper echelons of the establishment were finally listening to us. We were on the cusp of getting the answers we had craved for so long. All of the people in the audience were impressed with the approach being taken by Lord Morgan. He sounded genuinely committed to getting answers and he came across as someone who felt the families who suffered the loss of loved ones in controversial circumstances had been given the run-around by the British state for too many years.

The next step in the process was for the Northern Ireland Executive to approve funding of £10 million for the inquests into these controversial killings to proceed. This seemed like a straight forward procedure as a £150 million budget for dealing with legacy issues had already been approved at the Stormont House talks in 2015. It also felt to us that all that had to be done was for the £10 million application to be made, it would be approved and on we'd move forward with getting the answers we had sought. That was our perception but when push came to shove, things didn't work out as expected.

Raised Hopes amid Family Loss

Like so many occasions in the past, we waited and waited. The application never made it on to the cabinet agenda. We later learned that the First Minister of Northern Ireland Arlene Foster didn't see the issue of inquests the same way as Lord Chief Justice Declan Morgan.

Arlene Foster's father, John Kelly, was shot at by the IRA in 1979. According to *The Irish Times*, she took the view that Lord Morgan's quest to secure funding was flawed because, as she saw it, it focused on killings where allegedly, the British state was involved and completely overlooked murders carried out by republican paramilitaries. As Arlene saw it, the proposed process lacked balance. Sinn Féin, overall, was conspicuous by its silence.

The failure to approve the £10 million budget was met with outrage. Here we were on the verge of getting answers and a roadblock had been placed in our way yet again. The families affected were not going to lie down quietly and after many meetings, a court action was subsequently taken against the First Minister Mrs Arlene Foster. The case was taken in the name of Mrs Brigid Hughes whose innocent husband Anthony, just happened to be driving his car through the wrong place at the wrong time when the SAS ambushed an IRA unit at Loughgall RUC barracks, Co. Armagh in May 1987 killing nine men in total. The case got in to court in March 2018 and according to *The Irish Times* of 8 March 2018, Brigid Hughes' lawyer alleged that Arlene Foster blocked a Department of Justice document from being sent to the NI Executive.

The Irish Times reported that Mrs Foster's lawyer told the court that his client 'behaved impeccably in preventing an under-cooked paper going forward at that stage. He added, 'she had been focused on balancing the limited £150 million budget for dealing with all outstanding legacy issues.' The High Court in Belfast ruled that the decision taken by the First Minister Mrs Foster was unlawful. Judge Sir Paul Girvan told the court that the decision of the DUP leader not to proceed was 'procedurally flawed'.

The court was told by lawyers for Mrs Hughes that Arlene

Foster prevented the paper from going on to the Executive agenda for 'political reasons'.[1] The judge decided that it was now up to the incumbent secretary of state for Northern Ireland, Karen Bradley, to make additional funds available to address these issues. A dedicated department to speed up the process of hearing inquests into some of the Troubles' most controversial deaths with a budget of £55 million was given the go-ahead in February 2019, almost three years after the Lord Chief Justice Declan Morgan ruled that he wanted legacy cases to be investigated once and for all.

For us, the quest for truth and justice appeared to be no nearer to a conclusion. Every twelve months, more and more witnesses who were central to these atrocities, were dying. The British and their allies, were playing the long game.

In the meantime, the long-awaited date of Friday 28 July 2017 rolled around. Mr Justice Seamus Treacy entered the court to read out his ninety-four-page ruling. In summary, he found that the failure to investigate the Glenanne series of cases was unlawful. He stated that 'The unfairness here is extreme' and that the position by the PSNI had 'completely undermined the confidence of the families whose concerns are not only still unresolved but compounded by the effects of the decisions taken.'

In remarking upon his concerns as to what appeared to be an intensive campaign to retreat from their human rights obligations, the judge stated, 'There is a real risk that this will fuel in the minds of the families the fear that the state has resiled from its public commitments because it is not genuinely committed to addressing the unresolved concerns that the families have of state involvement.'

Here was the court saying in 2017, forty-one years or so after the controversial killings in the mid-Ulster area, that the treatment of the families by the British state was appalling. I never thought I would ever hear this rhetoric in a British court. However, despite the court confirming what we always suspected, the PSNI announced that they would not accept the court's decision and sought to appeal the ruling. Lord Chief Justice Declan

Morgan would chair the appeal proceedings. On 5 July 2019, he decided that the HET investigation should not have stopped, itself a serious reprimand to the PSNI.[2]

With the PSNI getting the proverbial kicking in the court and having nowhere to turn to evade what everybody knew; the Chief Constable Simon Byrne was left with no option but to draw up terms of reference for an investigation into the Glenanne series of killings to be added to Jon Boutcher's 'Operation Kenova'. As it was, Jon Boutcher was already busy investigating the lifetimes of Freddie Scappaticci, the top IRA man who passed everything he knew about republican activities on to the British and allegedly contributed to many deaths that could have been prevented.

While we were getting more frustrated with each blockage put in place by the British, other families were not giving up the fight either. One particular legal action was to finally reveal the key players in the infamous Glenanne gang who brought so much misery to many innocent families on both sides of the border. Not only did the case reveal who was in the gang, it exposed the extraordinary number of RUC police officers and members of the Ulster Defence Regiment who engaged in blatant murder thus defying all the principles of their respective professions and the organisations they worked for.

GLENANNE GANG NAMES REVEALED

ON 16 AUGUST 1976, a no-warning UVF car bomb exploded outside The Step Inn pub in Keady, Co. Armagh. The blast killed thirty-two-year-old nurse and mother of three children Betty McDonald. Her husband owned the pub. Twenty-two-year-old plumber Gerard McGleenan, who happened to be standing outside his home on the opposite side of the street, was also killed in the explosion. Nobody was brought to justice.

It later came to my attention from a source within the HET that the bomb which exploded in Keady was originally intended for Renaghan's Bar in Clontibret, Co. Monaghan. But that mission had to be aborted when it emerged that somebody had tipped off the gardaí, resulting in numerous checkpoints around the village on the night.

RUC officer John Weir, who was on a reconnaissance mission to check out the route and get-away roads from Clontibret, was stopped at a checkpoint outside the village by a garda. Weir produced his RUC ID and was sent back to Northern Ireland.

While that bomb was being constructed in a garage at Laurence McClure's house in Glenanne, an unusual phenomenon was underway. RUC Special Branch was engaging in reconnaissance at the homes of UVF members McClure and James Mitchell. MI5, which looks after internal British security, was keeping an eye on special branch while MI6, which deals with external threats to British security, was monitoring the activities of MI5. This was proof, if proof was needed, that the British knew exactly what was going on but again turned a blind eye and a deaf ear. My source in the HET, Steve Morris, said this was the worst case of collusion that they had come across in the course of their investigation.

Roll on the years, thirty-nine to be exact and in light of the HET findings, the McDonald family made a submission to the Belfast coroner's court in 2015. In their papers to the coroner, the McDonald family sought an investigation into the circumstances of Betty's death, something that an inquest would not have the power to authorise.

However, in their submission, the McDonalds went further than any other family who suffered loss arising from the activities of the Glenanne gang. A list of persons compiled by solicitor Darragh Mackin was presented to the court by Leslie Thomas, QC. It contained the names of key people in the UVF Glenanne gang who were involved in various controversial murders. They all had one thing in common – they were either members of the RUC, the UDR, the MoD, police or the territorial army.

The list, as presented to the court, was structured as follows: Certain names have been omitted here for legal reasons.

Annex 1

NAME	JOB	ATTACKS INVOLVED IN
Bertie Frazer	UDR	Seán Farmer & Colm McCartney
Billy McBride	Constable in RUC	Seán Charles McDonnell (Weir affidavit, p. 27); also involved in the manufacture of weapons
David Kane	UDR member 1971–1973	Fred McLoughlin (Eagle Bar), Seán O'Hagan, Felix Clancy, Robert McCullough (Clancy's Bar)
David Wilson	RUC	The Rock Bar
Derek McFarland	UDR	Marion Rafferty, Thomas Mitchell, Traynor's Bar, Grew family
Edward Tate Sinclair	RUC reservist	Traynor's Bar, Brannigan's Bar, Cosy Corner Bar, bomb made on Sinclair's farm for Annaghmore petrol garage bombing (Oct 1974), Clancy's Bar (Molloy, his farm) used for Paul McNeice, attempted murder, Grew family, Denis Mullen, Peter & Jane McKearney

Garfield Beattie	Territorial [army]	Denis Mullen, Peter & Jane McKearney, Fred McLoughlin (Eagle Bar), Patrick McNeice, Clancy's Bar, Hillcrest Bombing
Person A. Cannot be named for Legal reasons.	RUC	Tully's Bar, Rock Bar, Betty McDonald, The kidnapping of Fr Hugh Murphy
Harris Boyle	Part-time UDR member	Devlin murders, Miami Showband massacre.
James McDowell	UDR member	Miami Showband massacre.
James Mitchell	RUC reservist	Reavey brothers, Tully's Bar. His farm was used in a number of attacks.
John Weir	RUC, SPG	A number of attacks including Tully's Bar, Betty McDonald, William Strathearn, and Renaghans Bar.
Joseph Lutton	Part-time RUC	Fred McLoughlin (Eagle Bar) and Clancy's Bar.
Laurence McClure	RUC officer	Hughes Bar and McArdle's Bar (Weir affidavit), Colm McCartney & Seán Farmer, Michael & Patsy Donnelly and Trevor Brecknell, Reavey brothers, Patrick Mone, Tully's Bar, Rock Bar, Betty McDonald and Three Star Inn, Castleblayney.
Lawrence Tate	UDR Member	Confessed to Non-Fatal Explosion, Killyliss Bombing.
Robert McConnell	UDR officer	Hughes Bar and McArdle's Bar (Weir affidavit), John Francis Green, Colm McCartney & Seán Farmer, Michael & Patsy Donnelly and Trevor Brecknell, Reavey brothers, Patrick Mone, Dublin-Monaghan Bombings and Thomas McNamee.

GLENANNE GANG NAMES REVEALED

Name	Role	Attack involved in
Robin Jackson	UDR until 04-03-'74, and arguably special branch agent (Weir affidavit)	Patrick Campbell murder, Miami Showband massacre, Charles McDonnell, Traynor's Bar, Bleary Darts Club, Michael & Patsy Donnelly and Trevor Brecknell, Kay's Tavern, Joe Campbell, William Strathearn, O'Dowd killings, attempted murder Thomas Tolland, attempted murder Lilly O'Hara, James McKeeveney and Martin McVeigh.
Thomas Crozier	UDR member	Miami Showband massacre.
Wesley Somerville	Part-time UDR member	Brannigan's Bar, Devlin murders, the Miami Showband Massacre.
William Hanna	UDR Sergeant and Weapons instructor	Dublin and Monaghan Bombings.
William Leonard	Private in UDR in May 1974	Devlin murders, Killen's pub, O'Neill's Pub, Quinn's Bar, Platers Hill, 25 Orpheus Drive, and Robbery of CIE Bus.
William McCaughey	RUC, SPG Officer	Rock Bar, William Strathearn, Reavey Brothers and Tully's Bar.
William Corrigan	Former UDR Member	Traynor's Bar, Cosy Corner Bar, Clancy's Bar, Grew family, Denis Mullen, Pat Molloy and Jack Wylie.
Annex 2		
NAME		**ATTACK INVOLVED IN**
Albert Herron		Brannigan's Bar (Molloy HET, pp. 20–21), Cosy Corner Bar, Clancy's Bar, Grew family.
Bill Marchant		Dublin-Monaghan bombings
David Payne		Dublin-Monaghan bombings
Garnet Busby		O'Neill's Bar, Quinn's Bar, Peter & Jane McKearney, Tully's Bar, Patrick Barnard killing.
Henry Liggett		Patrick McNeice

John Somerville		20 March 1973 – hi-jacking and burning a CIE bus in Aughnacloy, 3 April 1973 – bombing Patrick Devlin's house, Dungannon, November 1974 — Pat Falls, Aughamullan, 31 July 1975 – Miami Showband, Buskhill, 17 March 1976 Hillcrest Bar Bombing.
Lily Shields		Michael & Patsy Donnelly and Trevor Brecknell, Reavey brothers.
Robert Kerr		William Strathearn
Ronald Hanlon		Fred McLoughlin
Sammy Whitten		Tully's Bar, Peter Woolsey, Dublin and Monaghan Bombings
Shilly Silcock		Michael & Patsy Donnelly and Trevor Brecknell, Margaret Hale, Martin McVeigh, Seán Farmer and Colm McCartney
William Parr		Fred McLoughlin

JUDGE TREACY READ THE list silently and as he worked his way through the names, he appeared to be shocked that members of the British security forces were named as participants, directly and indirectly, in the long line of murders presented before him.

He said words to the effect that what he read was 'deeply disturbing' and adjourned proceedings until a ruling was issued in the British Supreme Court hearing on the Batang Kali Massacre of 1948 in Malaysia. In that particular episode of British soldiers behaving badly, twenty-four locals were shot dead and their villages burned to the ground by Scots Guards. By the end of the conflict in 1960, 226 locals were hanged by the British. Sixty-five years on, their respective families were also looking for answers.

Just to show that suffering Catholics in Northern Ireland were not the only ones having axes to grind with the Brits, the Supreme Court ruled that 'The [British] Government is not obliged to hold a public inquiry into the 1940s killings of 24 Malayan villagers by a British army patrol – even though it may have been a war crime – because the atrocity occurred too long ago.'[1]

The majority decision by the UK's highest court basically said that the duty to investigate such crimes could only be considered if the application was made ten years before 1966 when the right of individual petition to the European court of human rights was introduced.

Judge Treacy, did not give any indication as to when the hearing would re-sit. To this day, we are still waiting to get back in to court. Justice delayed was justice denied – AGAIN! Leslie Thomas, QC, who was geared up for an impressive victory in court, looked like somebody who had received a kick in the tummy. It looked as if defeat had been forced on him while in the jaws of victory.

As we continued to face mounting barriers in search of answers, so too were other families. A case being taken by a family from Dungannon would lead to yet another British state investigation. Could this be the one to get us the answers we had searched for since 1976?

The Long Search for Truth Continues

Patrick Barnard was a thirteen-year-old boy who, like so many innocent people during the Troubles, just happened to be in the wrong place at the wrong time. On 17 March 1976 as he walked without a care in the world past the Hillcrest Bar in Dungannon, Co. Tyrone, a UVF bomb exploded. Patrick died the next day. His thirteen-year-old friend James McCaughey also died as a result of the blast as did Andrew Small (62) and Joseph Kelly, aged 57.

We now know that the Glenanne gang were responsible. UVF gunman and gang member, Garnet James Busby, was convicted in 1981 of fourteen offences including the Hillcrest Bar bombing and the killing of Peter and Jane McKearney in Moy, Co. Tyrone in 1975.

The judge made no recommendation as to how long he should serve because he was convinced that 'the convicted man was remorseful.' The same judge, who sentenced Busby to six life sentences, went on to say, 'on charges of murder, I have no alternative but to sentence you to life imprisonment and the only matter that I have to decide is whether you should be confined for a certain period ... However, I feel you no longer pose any problem to the public.'[1]

Following the controversial disbandment of the HET, the families of those who died at the hands of the Glenanne gang had an expectation that the much-anticipated over-arching Report would finally reveal all the circumstances surrounding the killings of their loved ones.

As the HET final Report was not now going to be published, solicitors for Eddie Barnard, a brother of Patrick, wrote to both the chief constable of the PSNI, Sir Matt Baggott and the HET asking for confirmation that the Hillcrest Bar investigation had been linked to all other analysis of the Historical Enquiries Analytical Database (HEAD).

The chief constable 'concluded that there would be no investigative benefit to be derived from preparing such a report and that such reports were not used in contemporary policing practice in the United Kingdom in the conduct of murder investigations'.

At that time, the work of the HET had been suspended, and, in January 2015, was taken over by the Legacy Investigations Branch (LIB) of the PSNI. The establishment of the LIB, was in my opinion, a farce. We were told it would continue the work commenced by the HET. The big difference though was that senior PSNI/RUC personnel would be the filters and of course would not be independent. So far, the LIB has yet to publish a Report.

The main argument being put forward by Eddie Barnard in his letter to the PSNI was that his family had been given a 'legitimate expectation' that the entire HET investigation, including the over-arching Report, would be completed. Now they felt they had been deceived.

With the Barnard family facing familiar brick walls, the matter ended up in court where an application for a judicial review was made. In November 2017, Justice Seamus Treacy said the repeated representations made to the families of the Hillcrest victims and to the PFC by the HET, created a substantive legitimate expectation. He declared that the failure or refusal on the part of the HET to complete and publish an over-arching thematic Report regarding the linked Glenanne gang cases was unlawful and in breach of Article 2 (Right to Life) of the European Court of Human Rights.

He then made an Order of *Mandamus* – a Latin legal term – to compel the PSNI to honour its original commitment in public to provide an over-arching Report into the Glenanne gang group of cases. In other words, his message was clear, provide the final Report or there will be legal consequences.

The chief constable of the PSNI appealed this ruling and in

his subsequent judgement, the Lord Chief Justice Sir Declan Morgan upheld most of the points featured in Justice Treacy's original findings. Lord Morgan went on to say that the Order of *Mandamus* was not appropriate in this context implying – in my opinion – that independence in its findings could not be guaranteed. He added that the chief constable of the PSNI should appoint independent officers to investigate a range of killings where the police had not acted thoroughly in their respective investigations.

'Operation Kenova' was established in 2016 to investigate what senior IRA man and informer Freddie Scappaticci and his pals got up to during the Troubles. 'Operation Kenova' would also include the conduct of the Glenanne Gang amongst other atrocities. It would have a budget of £35 million and would be headed up by Jon Boutcher, a former chief constable of Bedfordshire Police.

When I heard this, I thought, 'Oh no, here we go again'. Another inquiry whereby the British are trying to give the impression that they are doing something to quell the anger of victims' families but in fact they are not. After Stalker, Stevens, the HET, this mysterious unit known as the LIB (Legacy Investigations Branch) and countless RUC investigations that went absolutely nowhere, what was the point of 'Kenova'?

Solicitor Darragh Mackin now of *Phoenix Law* took on most of these cases. The majority of those who suffered at the hands of the Glenanne Gang opted to go with him as he was fully familiar with our issues and demands. I wasn't optimistic about 'Operation Kenova' but Darragh Mackin assured me that Jon Boutcher was genuine. The only problem was that John Stalker, John Stevens and Dave Cox were also genuine but were muzzled by uncooperative security services. 'So how was Jon Boutcher going to be any different?' I wondered.

Sometime after 'Operation Kenova' was launched, I got a call from Jon Boutcher. He wanted to see me for a chat. I wasn't in the mood, as I was still deflated after the Dave Cox debacle. We chatted on the phone and I agreed to meet him at my house in Whitecross as I felt all I had to lose was time. He called to my home some days later in a Range Rover accompanied by several policemen. He came into the house on his own and we hit it off straight away. Every question I asked him, he answered politely. I also told him that we had been down this road many times before.

In reply, he said that he had powers that allowed him to go further than any of his predecessors.

Those overseeing his investigation included former Police Ombudsman Nuala O'Loan, John Miller, the former Deputy Commissioner of Intelligence & Counter terrorism with the New York Police Department, Kathleen O'Toole, the former Chief of Police in Boston Massachusetts and Iain Livingstone, the Chief constable for Police Scotland to name some in a long list of highly credible and respectable figures in global law and order. With so many impressive heavyweights to answer to, Jon Boutcher has been left with a job whereby he will have to deliver all the unpleasant gory details, good, bad or otherwise. Failing that, a lot of reputations will be on the line.

When the 'who's who' of names that Jon reports to were laid out in front of me, I sensed that maybe at long last, this is the investigation we have all been waiting for. After a detailed chat about what 'Operation Kenova' could achieve and where the others failed, I took Jon for a drive along the Kingsmills Road. I showed him the seventeen commemorative names on various headstones that dot the landscape in the space of two miles. I made a point of driving him in my car ensuring his two PSNI companions travelled separately. I also took him down the road to Glenanne and showed him the infamous Mitchell's farmhouse where all these atrocities were planned. I went through the route the killers of our brothers took on that fateful night in January 1976. I also brought him to the graveyard at nearby Ballymoyer and showed him where our lads are buried.

I then took him to Tullyvallen Orange Hall where five Protestants were shot dead by republicans on 1 September 1975. We concluded our tour of fatal localities with a visit to

Ballygorman, just off the Newry/Armagh Road, where the car used in the killing of Brian, John Martin and Anthony was abandoned and burned out.

Jon said he was amazed that so many sectarian killings took place within such a short radius in a sparsely populated rural location. What really shocked him was the failure of the RUC to properly investigate them. I told him that I was now over seventy years of age and this was my last chance to engage with anybody from officialdom to get the answers I was searching for.

He told me he would appoint two dedicated officers to liaise with me for his investigation and I would hear from them in due course. Over time, they have visited me on numerous occasions to collate the information surrounding the events of 4 January 1976. The imminent publication of Jon Boutcher's findings in to the many killings and sectarian skulduggery investigated by his team will make disturbing reading for a lot of security people, assuming that is, *it gets published.*

AN EVENT IN HAMMERSMITH London on 30 January 2016 in the Irish Centre, where victims of the Troubles told their respective stories to the public, resulted in the establishment of TARP – the Truth and Reconciliation Platform. Its members include Stephen Travers, who survived the Miami Showband massacre, Alan McBride, whose wife was killed in the 1993 Shankill Road bomb, Joe Campbell whose Catholic father – a member of the RUC – was murdered by the UVF in 1977, and myself.

The creation of TARP has opened many doors for us with other groups who are aiming to achieve the same objective. One is the Glencree Centre for Peace and Reconciliation in Enniskerry, Co. Wicklow who have invited us to many functions and one event which stands out was an occasion where we received a phone call on a Friday asking us to be in Enniskerry at 9 a.m. the following Monday.

Nobody gave us a reason, but we were told that it would be in our best interests to show up at that time. Stephen and

The Long Search for Truth Continues

myself showed up at Glencree at 9 a.m. as requested. To our surprise, security was remarkably strict. As we waited inside the venue, next thing a convoy of about twenty black cars came up the driveway. It stopped and Prince Charles and Camilla Parker-Bowles stepped out. They were there to meet various families including those whose loved ones died in The Troubles. As he worked his way along the line of people there to greet him, he came to Stephen who gave him a copy of his book *The Miami Showband Massacre – A survivor's search for the truth*. He then came to me, stuck out his hand and shook mine.

As he did, I grabbed his arm with my left hand and said to him, 'you're a fine cut of a man. You're looking well for your age.' He said, 'thank you very much'. I jovially thumped Charles in the chest and said, 'yourself and myself are the same age, born in the same month and in the same year.' I pulled him in closer to me and whispered into his ear, 'I'll arm-wrestle you for a fiver'.

This must have been the first time in the history of the British Royal family that a future monarch was physically hit in the chest by a member of the public. In fairness, Prince Charles took my behaviour in the spirit it was meant, although one or two people around him looked shocked.

The Truth and Reconciliation Platform was moving along nicely, getting the message out and helping to bring disaffected Catholics and Protestants together in certain places until the Covid 19 virus arrived in 2020.

The Quest for Truth and Justice still Goes On

Since 4 January 1976, my free time has been consumed with trying to get answers about why exactly evil individuals murdered our John Martin, Brian and Anthony. Every initiative promised by successive British governments to deliver justice to the numerous families in Northern Ireland, who suffered loss from controversial killings, has raised our hopes only to be repeatedly dashed at the last minute. The British play the long game. Every inquiry gets so close and yet so far before being controversially closed down. This delays the process of justice until the next inquiry gets underway many years later. Time passes and an elder layer of bereaved people die, thus reducing the calls for further investigations.

It is quite clear that if the British continue to prolong proper inquiries, all of us who are seeking answers will eventually end up dead and the next up-and-coming generation won't have the same determination to seek answers as the oppressed generations who went before them. That may be the case for many families but I can say with certainty, it will not be the case with ours.

Since 1976, I and others who also suffered loss have, bit by bit, amassed chunks of crucial information here, documents there and have nit-picked nuggets of details from numerous written Reports, TV documentaries, newspaper cuttings, published books, witness evidence and general items of revelations that have leaked or painstakingly been extracted from an unco-operative British security system.

Several crucial and shocking details have come to light recently, which were not known to us at the time, showing that the RUC, various loyalist groups and a wide range of units within British military security all worked together to deliberately kill Catholics and nationalists.

The Quest for Truth and Justice still Goes On

IN THE SPRING OF 2022, a local Catholic man I know well called to my house and said he wanted to have a private word with me. I knew him all my life and when he called, he was clearly nervous and somewhat agitated. Before he revealed what he did, he apologised repeatedly for not approaching me many years previously. He told me he had been under threat from the UVF and it was dangerous to talk. The same man was a regular visitor to Mitchell's farm in Glenanne where he did various jobs.

On one particular occasion, he was en route to a wedding. His mode of transport was a somewhat weather-beaten and unsightly builder's van. James Mitchell offered the use of his Wartburg car so that my friend would arrive at the wedding in a dignified fashion. He was reluctant to accept the offer but James Mitchell insisted he take the car.

When he called to Mitchell's house later that evening to get the vehicle, he noticed numerous sparkling cars in the yard, a sight that he found most unusual in South Armagh, a place not noted for displays of material wealth in the 1960s. As he went to pick up the car, a number of vehicles drove into the yard and several men dressed in RUC uniforms walked into the house. It emerged that Harry Breen, who later became an RUC chief inspector and was shot dead by the IRA on the Louth/Armagh border in March 1989, was a regular visitor to the farm.

He took the car, headed home and went to the wedding the next day. When he returned the Wartburg car to Mitchell's farm twenty-four hours later, a Saturday, he couldn't find James or Lily Shields. He walked into the kitchen to return the keys and noticed a pile of notes on the table. When he placed the keys next to a plate, his curiosity got the better of him. He glanced at the notes and there in front of him was a list of names. What caught his attention were the names of the Reavey boys. As he read on, totally unaware of its significance, Lily Shields, James Mitchell's housekeeper, walked in. She told him that he shouldn't be in the kitchen and walked him to the door. He thought no more of it, got into his builder's van and drove home.

Later that night, he received a phone call from the mysterious

'Captain Black' of the UVF who told him in very threatening terms that he was to forget about the details he saw on the table that morning and not mention them to any person, Catholic or Protestant.

This somewhat belated revelation from my friend made it clear to me that the UVF, the RUC and the Glenanne gang were monitoring Catholic families in the area eight years before the shootings at our house.

It seems there was a new sense of fear amongst hardline unionists at the time in Northern Ireland over what many of them believed was a determination from south of the border to unify the island and bring Northern Ireland under Dublin rule. This was heightened after Seán Lemass made history in January 1965 when he became the first Taoiseach to travel north since partition to meet NI PM Terence O'Neill at Stormont, a meeting that was met with strong protest by Paisley, his supporters and other hard-line loyalists.

Then unionist fears intensified when the Irish government staged a massive commemoration in April 1966 to mark the fiftieth anniversary of the 1916 Rising, which re-energised many republicans about the possibility of ending British rule on the island. These events, coupled with the increasing demands by oppressed Catholics/nationalists for civil rights in housing, education, employment and societal opportunities, made many in the right-wing Protestant/unionist community feel that a push was underway within nationalism to establish a united Ireland.

In light of the fact that Paisley supporters started the fighting at Burntollet Bridge in early 1969, which led to rioting in Derry which in turn spread to Belfast. It seems that the leader of the Free Presbyterian Church had a plan to provoke Catholics/nationalists into conflict to halt the progress of the civil rights campaign.

When our John Martin and Brian were murdered on 4 January 1976, we reluctantly had to accept the unacceptable facts around their brutal killing. However, suspicion lingers to this day over the death of Anthony.

The 'official explanation' was that he suffered a brain haemorrhage that was not connected in any way to the UVF shootings. This did not make sense and is an explanation we completely dismiss. The way he was found lying on the floor, at the top of the stairs in Dolly McMahon's house in Belleeks, didn't make sense to us. The fact nobody at Daisy Hill Hospital was aware that he had been brought in by ambulance was suspicious. Also, when we entered the hospital to visit him and nobody knew what ward he was in, this raised another red flag.

When I brought this to the attention of the medical staff at Daisy Hill, they took an instant decision to transfer him upstairs to the intensive care unit for immediate treatment. The care he received in the ICU made no impact. Mr McCaul, the neurosurgeon in London, spoke to the house doctor on duty in Daisy Hill on the Sunday night and advised him to get Anthony transferred to the Royal Vic in Belfast as quickly as possible. Despite the urgency of his recommendation, it was two days before Anthony was transferred to the RVH in Belfast, a delay we believe, may have contributed to his death.

Anthony's time in Daisy Hill left us with a lot of questions. We had the height of respect for the doctors and nurses on the 'shop floor' whose care and empathy was top-class but the way senior management handled what was happening, bothered us.

We had plenty of questions but we couldn't get answers. Anthony was in the prime of his youth when he left hospital after the shootings yet – as we saw it – he died from 'natural causes' at the age of seventeen.

One of the problems with all the madness surrounding that first week was that significant things that happened were overlooked at the time but in hindsight say a lot about the sinister motives of those who killed the Reavey brothers.

As referred to earlier, the inquest into Anthony's death took place and was announced in Armagh courthouse on 28 January 1977. The outrage of Éilis McDermott, Northern Ireland's first female QC, with the finding that his death was by 'natural causes', left us all in no doubt that something was amiss here. When the HET Inquiry customised Report for the Reavey family was presented to us, it stated on page 62, 'The Pathologist, Mr Marshall at the time of his original examination stated the injuries caused by the shooting played no part in Anthony's death.' The HET analysis comment on the same page stated, 'As a result of submissions put forward on behalf of the Reavey Family to the Coroner, the initial recording of "Died from Natural Causes" was replaced with an "Open Verdict" in February 1977.

'This action by the Coroner in replacing a verdict is most uncommon and has not been noted in any other of the cases reviewed by the HET.'

This raised a number of key questions as the findings would determine the important principle of culpability and whether or not we were ultimately entitled to compensation from the British state. I should add that for us, truth and justice far surpassed any compensation.

Either the coroner and the pathologist simply got it wrong or else they succumbed to initial British military pressure. If they got it wrong, this raised questions about their competence and professionalism:

1 Why did the coroner take three days to change his opinion in light of the determined fight he put up against our barrister on his findings?
2 Was it his conscience or did the medical facts over-arch the political agenda?
3 More to the point, why was the Reavey family never informed of this change in opinion?

SURELY UNDER THE LAW, we had a right to know. I should add that we only found out thirty-one years later in 2007 when Dave Cox and his HET team discovered the altered Report.

In 2021, I managed to get hold of the official British military file on the death of Anthony. It told us what we suspected. Firstly, 90 per cent of the pages are blacked out. This, once again, begs the most repeated question in this story namely, what is in this file that the British don't want us to know? One sentence though is not redacted and its revealing detail states, '... Anthony Reavey of Greyhilla Whitecross died of a brain haemorrhage connected with wounds received during [an] attack on his home, 4th Jan.'

So here we had a pathologist and coroner saying initially he had died of natural causes when the heavily redacted British military file said his 'brain haemorrhage' *was connected* to the shooting. One position completely contradicted the other. More lies from the British.

I have regularly asked myself if individuals working for the British state entered Dolly McMahon's house in Belleeks and engaged in action that brought on Anthony's so-called 'brain haemorrhage'.

I can't prove that belief but all the factors point to sinister activity to ensure that Anthony disappeared off the stage simply because he may have spotted faces at the time of the shooting which, if identified in a court of law, could expose who was working with who on the night of the massacre at our house.

After all, if the UVF Glenanne gang and their pals in the RUC, UDR and British army had succeeded in their attack, Anthony would have died there and then in the house with John Martin and Brian. At the end of the day, their plan was to wipe out the entire Reavey family.

We, as a family, have never believed what we've been told about Anthony's death. All the lame excuses, redacted documents, incomplete investigations and endless barriers we've come up against, have left us in no doubt that the British military, in all their various forms, were central to his ultimate death.

Are we over-reacting towards the RUC, British army, the UVF, UDR, SAS, MI5 and the like? No. The recent emergence of sensitive documents that we were not supposed to see has revealed details that will shock all nationalist families in Northern Ireland who lost loved ones during the Troubles to agents of the British government and their security services. Military records are stored at Kew in south-west London. They feature millions of notes on British military policy, activity, plans, strategy, missions, armoury, under-cover operations, offensives and results of all their engagements in the various lands around the world. These details are in parallel with territories the British invaded, pillaged, destroyed, manipulated, robbed, exploited, tortured, crushed, prospered from, murdered, lied, deceived, abused, conquered and ruled, all in the name of the crown.

If one wants to know how and why the cruel British did what they did down through the centuries, getting hold of these documents is crucial. Accessing the information can be a hit-or-miss affair. It's usually more miss than hit.

Some important documents are not there, redacted or blacked out to the point that they are simply unreadable, raising the perennial question as to what was written down that the British feel necessary to hide? Others are semi-redacted to the point where the visible written information amounts to nothing new.

Then, every so often, an extraordinary document which somebody in authority overlooked, is uncovered at the bottom of an unlikely file with no redactions and reveals all one wants to know about evil British malpractice in Northern Ireland.

Ciarán MacAirt runs an operation in Belfast called *Paper Trail*. He has devoted his adult life searching for archive documents on British military activity in Northern Ireland. Down through the decades, Ciarán has dug deeper than anyone else when it comes to searching for official information on the Reavey killings. Every so often, on his many visits to Kew in London and the Public Records Office of Northern Ireland in Belfast, Ciaran gets lucky as he looks in the boxes and folders that other researchers overlook.

One day during the Covid lockdown period, Ciarán called and had some news for me. He had managed to get hold of documents written into the diary of then 3 Infantry Brigade Major, CRN Meares, that were marked 'Restricted' and 'Secret'. They were not meant for viewing by any person outside the British government security, civil and public service structure.

The files revealed details of a meeting that took place in Lurgan, Co. Armagh, the day after the Reavey killings. The eleven-page file Ciarán managed to access was a review of the security situation in Co. Armagh at the time. It revealed the close association that the British military and RUC had with the mid-Ulster UVF. Page 7 contained the following details:

STRATEGY

7. The campaign currently waged by the MID-ULSTER UVF against Catholic targets is apparently designed to provoke the PIRA by showing the outside world that they are unable to protect the Catholic population. The intention is to force PIRA in to taking severe reprisal actions against Protestants. PIRA atrocities, as this reprisal would be termed, would be used as propaganda to sway public opinion both in Ireland and the mainland against the IRA. Coming as it does, just prior to the discussion of the Northern Ireland Convention Report in WESTMINSTER on 12 Jan 76, it could be interpreted as an attempt to influence the SSNI [Secretary of State] and HMG at a crucial time. [The Convention Report was a proposal on the way forward to govern Northern Ireland]

8. In order to carry out this strategy, the MID-ULSTER UVF has apparently laid down a new 'operational policy.' In brief, indiscriminate attacks are no longer carried out; targeting must be closely controlled and directed by UVF Leaders; security must be maintained. With the acute alarm that has been caused by the KINGSMILLS murders of 5 Jan 76, the chances of wholesale indiscriminate slaughter of Catholics must re-emerge.

TARGETING

9. In the past, indiscriminate attacks based on folklore and malicious gossip were frequent. More recently, good targeting has been particularly noticeable. The bombs at DUNDALK and SILVERBRIDGE on 29 Dec 75 both exploded outside Republican Pubs which had been sourced as PIRA meeting places and drinking haunts. The bomb attack on the home of Frank TRAINOR on 14 Dec 75 is another example. His son Thomas 'Tit' TRAINOR is a well carded member of PIRA [*sic*] and IRSP. The explosion on 26 Dec 75 outside VALLELY'S pub, ADDRESS, is part of the overall strategy. It is a known Republican haunt and was last attacked on 2 Oct 75.

10. The 2 most recent attacks on 4 Jan 76 were particularly

declined and its activities now are less militant. Some of its senior members give active support and assistance to the MID-ULSTER UVF and many of its juniors are jointly members of the UVF.

6. Detailed ORBATs and personalities should be covered in unit and sub-unit briefings.

STRATEGY

7. The campaign currently waged by the MID-ULSTER UVF against Catholic targets is apparently designed to provoke the PIRA by showing the outside world that they are unable to protect the Catholic population. The intention is to force PIRA into taking severe reprisal action against Protestants. PIRA atrocities, as this reprisal would be termed, would be used as propaganda to sway public opinion both in Ireland and the mainland against the IRA. Coming, as it does, just prior to the discussion of the Northern Ireland Convention Report in WESTMINSTER on 12 Jan 76, it could be interpreted as an attempt to influence the SSNI and HMG at a crucial time.

8. In order to carry out this strategy, the MID-ULSTER UVF has apparently laid down a new 'operational policy.' In brief, indiscriminate attacks are no longer carried out; targetting must be against extremist Republican personalities and haunts only; 'operations' must be closely controlled and directed by UVF Leaders; security must be maintained. With the acute alarm that has been caused by the KINGSMILLS murders of 5 Jan 76, the chances of wholesale indiscriminate slaughter of Catholics must re-emerge.

TARGETTING

9. In the past, indiscriminate attacks based on folklore and malicious gossip were frequent. More recently, good targetting has been particularly noticeable. The bombs at DUNDALK and SILVERBRIDGE on 29 Dec 75 both exploded outside known Republican Pubs which had been sourced as PIRA meeting places and drinking haunts. The bomb attack on the home of Frank TRAINOR on 14 Dec 75 is another example. His son Thomas 'Tit' TRAINOR is a well carded member of PIRA and IRSP. The explosion on 26 Dec 75 outside VALLELEYS Pub, ARDRESS, is part of the overall strategy. It is a known Republican haunt and was last attacked on 2 Oct 75.

10. The 2 most recent attacks on 4 Jan 76 were particularly well targetted. At WHITECROSS, 3 gunmen burst into the REAVEY's home. John Martin and Brian REAVEY were both shot dead and Anthony REAVEY was wounded. The car believed used in this attack was later found burnt out at GR 013550. Two of the REAVEY family had PIRA traces and one is believed to have been involved in the murder of CPL FRAZER, 2 UDR on 30 Aug 75 at WHITECROSS. At The Slopes, near BLEARY, 3 masked gunmen burst into number 47, singled out 4 men and shot them. Declan, Barry and Joseph O'DOWD were shot dead and Bernard O'DOWD is VSI. The O'DOWD family is carded as being associates of Brendan Patrick CURRAN, who was OC of the NORTH ARMAGH Bn PIRA and is currently serving 15 years for causing explosions in LURGAN. Declan O'DOWD was interviewed by the RUC in connection with the GILFORD ambush of 1 Aug 75.

used in the attack was later found burnt out at GRO093350 [navigational spot]. Two of the REAVEY family had PIRA traces and one is believed to have been involved in the murder of CPL FRAZER, 2 UDR on 30 Aug 75 at WHITECROSS. At The Slopes near BLEARY, 3 masked gunmen burst into number 47, singled out 4 men and shot them. Declan, Barry and Joseph O'DOWD were shot dead and Bernard O'DOWD IS VSI [very seriously injured]. The O'DOWD family is carded as being associates of Brendan Patrick CURRAN, who was OC [Officer in Charge] of the NORTH ARMAGH Bn PIRA and is currently serving 15 years for causing explosions in LURGAN. Declan O'DOWD was interviewed by the RUC in connection with the GILFORD ambush of 1 Aug 75.

When I read the above, I was shocked. There it was right before my eyes at the end of section 8 that '... wholesale indiscriminate slaughter of Catholics must re-emerge'.

This was British government/army policy with one aim, namely, to kill Catholics for the sake of it. The document clearly states that the 'targeting [of Catholics] must be closely controlled and directed by UVF Leaders'. Here was the British state saying that the UVF would do their dirty work to shoot Catholics with the clear intention of provoking the IRA out of ceasefire to kill Protestants. The British would, in turn, use such killings as propaganda to turn nationalists and republicans against the IRA with a view to decreasing their support. The British clearly had a civil war scenario in their intentions.

Then, to make matters worse for us, the document says that 'Two of the Reavey Family had PIRA traces and one is believed to have been involved in the murder of CPL Frazer, 2 UDR on 30 Aug 75 at WHITECROSS'.

This was a scandalous slur against our family. None of our lads were in the IRA and had absolutely nothing to do with the killing of Bertie Frazer. To this day, I still don't know what the term 'traces' means. To make matters all the more mysterious, not one of our family was ever questioned about the killing of Bertie Frazer which raises the issue as to how or why any of the Reavey clan were implicated in his killing.

By praising the practice of 'targeting', the British clearly had a policy of shoot first and ask questions later. Innocent until proven guilty in a court of law didn't enter the equation. This was clear 'shoot-to-kill', and Catholics were the number one target.

The contents of these files made me ask myself, how many innocent people were shot dead by the British army and loyalists for being nothing more than Catholics? When the HET Report declared that 'no person was interviewed or charged in connection with these [Reavey] murders', I now know why. The British military, RUC, UDR, UVF and other loyalist paramilitary groups, etc., were all in this together. The process is known by one word, COLLUSION. It was clear that collusion with loyalist paramilitary groups was British government policy.

Another 'Secret' military document I got hold of left me in no doubt that the British military knew of UVF plans at the time and made no attempt to intervene. It appears from the 'Secret' British documents I now have in my possession that the UVF plan was to bomb our house and kill all of us. It stated:

> The UVF bomb attack forecast for WHITECROSS has materialised as a shooting attack. A bomb was put in at a RC [Roman Catholic] pub at CAMLOUGH instead ... They [the UVF] are also anxious to get 37 kills in competition with the South Armagh PIRA who already have many mines on target ... The UVF etc will be delighted to continue the blood letting they enjoy so much.

The use of the word 'instead' revealed all we needed to know. The bomb was intended for our house but was diverted to Camlough. Had this bomb exploded in our house, the UVF would have moved significantly closer to their target of thirty-seven kills. Had the bomb gone off at our house on the night previous, our entire family could have been wiped out.

Another British military document which is heavily redacted states:

> ... It is likely that the REAVEY and O'DOWD murders were coordinated attacks and this data serves to confirm the diversity of links the mid-Ulster UVF enjoy throughout H, J and K [RUC] divisions.

The Quest for Truth and Justice still Goes On

H Division-based in Armagh – of the RUC at the time covered Armagh City, Gough, Markethill, Keady Loughgall, Middletown, Tandragee, Bessbrook, Crossmaglen, Forkhill, Newtownhamilton and Warrenpoint.

J Division RUC – in Portadown covered Lurgan, Moira, Craigavon, Banbridge, Dromore, Dromara, Gilford, Rathfriland and Portadown itself.

K Division RUC – in Cookstown had responsibility for Coagh, Moneymore, Pomeroy, Stewartstown, Dungannon, Aughnacloy, Ballygawley, Benburb, Caledon, Coalisland and Moy.

In other military pages I possess referring to the Reavey-O'Dowd killings, the British army documents state, 'In both cases [Reavey and O'Dowds], the targeting was excellent'.

So here we had a British army document stating in clear black and white that the UVF group had support and approval from a significant element within the RUC across three policing divisions in mid-Ulster, and to make matters worse, the military who were supposed to be keeping the peace, wanted us dead. And they were portraying themselves as the peacekeepers.

This information is appearing in public for the first time here and has not been published in any of the Stalker, Stevens or HET inquiries which leads one to ask, why? The British knew what the UVF plans were and not only turned a blind eye, but encouraged their execution. While we and others always suspected widespread collusion, now, all these years later, we have evidence about the relationship between the British security forces, the RUC and the UVF.

Another document which has raised suspicions relates to the Kingsmills massacre. It states:

> 2 cars [are] thought to have been involved, BLACK AUSTIN CAMBRIDGE and also a RED HILLMAN AVENGER.

How could this be known? Who said these cars were involved and who exactly witnessed their presence? We were never told who owned these cars and over a process of elimination, the RUC and if requested, the gardaí, could have located these vehicles, did a forensic examination and identified them. It just required someone to check the registration of all Black Austin Cambridge as well as Red Hillman Avenger cars in NI/Republic and question the respective owners. It didn't happen.

Ciarán MacAirt of *Paper Trail* in his analysis of these documents says that on 11 January 1976, the driver of a car stopped by 2 UDR unit in Whitecross was on the list of suspects for the Kingsmills massacre. He is named on one of the documents but his identity is redacted. According to Ciarán, the Royal Scots Brigade reported that RUC Special Branch was 'Not interested but suggest we screen him to show interest and support for 2 UDR.' It is obvious that somebody was being protected and that special branch was misleading the 2 UDR Regiment.

Ciarán also discovered something that – metaphorically speaking – floored us when it fully sank in. He found information revealing the British had imposed an eighty-four-year embargo or blockage on the release of their files relating to the Reavey killings. Think about that. The files on the killings of John Martin, Brian and Anthony have been locked away for eighty-four years. That means it will be the year 2061 when they are released. I will be long gone, and so will my generation of Reaveys. Our children will be in their seventies and eighties and even at that time, the British judge of the day in 2061 will still have the option to extend the embargo for a further period of decades if so requested by legal counsel for the crown.

This embargo means we are unlikely to know the whole truth about the British involvement in the killings of John Martin, Brian and Anthony. The revelation about the locked up files until 2061 also indicates that the UK security services were central to these and other murders.

We only learned of the moratorium through Ciarán's dedicated work in searching for hidden files. The British didn't have the decency to inform us, which says something about their malicious motives and the conniving, immoral, devious way they operate.

So many unanswered questions remain about the so-called

The Quest for Truth and Justice still Goes On

RUC 'investigation' into the Reavey and Kingsmills killings. As we continue to get our minds around the revelations from Ciarán MacAirt, there is widespread speculation about the conduct of British army Capt. Robert Nairac in South Armagh. It's now widely believed that Nairac had a direct role to play in numerous atrocities in Northern Ireland during his time there. One might ask why and what is the evidence? More to the point, why is Nairac relevant to my story?

It should not be forgotten when this book is put down that as far as the British parliament and public were concerned at that time, I set up the Kingsmills massacre. Of course, that is *completely untrue* but that's what Ian Paisley Senior announced into the record of the House of Commons.

I feel obliged to explore the role that Robert Nairac played in contributing to the defamation of my name, that of our family and to expose the constant supply of lies spewed out by the British to protect their officers. After all, I was blamed in the House of Commons for a massacre I had no hand, act or part in.

Nairac was a treble agent. He was in the British military on a Monday, the UVF on a Tuesday and the IRA on a Wednesday, etc., sometimes he was in all three at the same time. He infiltrated both sides and convinced loyalists and republicans simultaneously that he was on 'their' side. We now know, that it was our old 'friend' Frank Kitson who wrote as far back in the 1960s that:

> SAS squadrons are particularly well suited and equipped for counter-revolutionary operations ... in order to carry out the following tasks:
>
> Liaison with, and organisation of friendly guerrilla forces operating against the common enemy.[1]

Colonel Mike Dewar of the British army said as much when he contributed to the RTÉ TV programme *Today Tonight*, which was broadcast on 18 May 1995. He told reporter Brendan O'Brien, 'we regarded the Protestants [paramilitaries] as they weren't a threat to us, the security forces, as useful and if you like, I'll sign up to the phrase, they were friendly forces, they were extremely helpful, they provided information about the IRA.'

If ever one required evidence that the British worked closely with the UVF, this was it.

It seems the British intention in early 1976 was to deliberately provoke the IRA out of ceasefire and force them to go fully in to battle against the UVF. Such a scenario would have created the next best thing to an all-out civil war, deplete their respective numbers and the old British game of divide and conquer would have worked to perfection. Kitson and his criminal tactics were alive and well.

To suggest that a British soldier set up a massacre where ten Protestants were killed by their own protecting army sounds ridiculous to some. Surely the British wouldn't kill Protestants, the very people that are loyal to the UK? No?

Well, two revelations by Alan Black, who survived the massacre, are telling. One night I paid a visit to Alan Black at his home in nearby Bessbrook. It was many years after the abduction of Robert Nairac in May 1977 from The Three Steps Inn pub in Dromintee. Alan recalled that on the Monday evening – two nights after Robert Nairac was killed in 1977 – he sat down in his sitting room to watch the tea-time news on television. His wife had just brought in his dinner on a tray and returned to the small kitchen. Just at that moment, Robert Nairac's image appeared on the TV screen. In an instant, Alan dropped his tray and shouted to his wife, 'get in here quick. There's the bastard that shouted the orders [to shoot] at Kingsmills'.

As far as Alan Black was concerned, Captain Robert Nairac was central to the Kingsmills massacre. Alan Black, it should be remembered, was shot eighteen times. On the basis of British intent, he, just like the remaining members of the O'Dowd family, Stephen Travers and Des Lee in the Miami Showband massacre, should not have survived but miraculously, they did.

When I heard what Alan said, I wasn't surprised. Rumours had been swirling around South Armagh for months after the Kingsmills massacre. There were other features that pointed to British army and RUC collusion to kill those in the red Ford mini-bus that wet January night. A number of factors on the night just didn't add up.

Following the convoy of cars making its way from Whitecross to Newry, were local men Jim Malone and his brother Barry. They had been in the Reavey cortege that came upon the Kingsmills massacre. When their particular car was forced to do a u-turn on the blocked road, instead of following on with the other vehicles which turned left at the nearby crossroads, they opted to return home to Whitecross and alert their families to the shootings that happened at Kingsmills.

Shortly afterwards, Jim and Barry decided to visit their sister Marie and inform her of the killings. Marie lived on the Drumherriff Road in Whitecross, where the Reavey cortege turned left, having been told to do a u-turn earlier. As they made their way to Marie's house, they passed an RUC land rover that was parked in Eugene Malone's laneway on the right-hand side. The presence of the land rover was highly significant.

What was an RUC land rover doing parked in a laneway quarter of a mile away from the massacre at a time when no police were present at the site where the killings actually took place? This leads one to ask, did the RUC have a role in the killings?

To compound the Nairac involvement, details of the inquest into the Kingsmills massacre appeared in *The Belfast News Letter* on Tuesday, 23 May 2017. A forty-year delay for an inquest into such a high-profile tragedy was enough to raise suspicious eyebrows, but the *News Letter* quoted Alan Black's contribution to the hearing and it compounded what many suspected.

It stated, 'Kingsmills survivor Alan Black said the leader of the gunmen spoke with an English accent leading to speculation that it could have been Nairac, who sometimes operated in an undercover role.'

The inquest was told that an army officer known as MoD Witness 2 who was operations officer of the 1st Battalion Royal Scots at Bessbrook rejected claims that Nairac was in the area.

The *News Letter* quoted him as saying, '… Nairac could not

have been involved in this incident; that he was not even in Northern Ireland at this stage'. This was a complete contradiction of what John Weir told Liam Clarke in the *Sunday Times* on 7 February 1999 and what British special military intelligence agent Fred Holroyd is quoted in *Lost Lives* where he clearly states that Nairac passed on a photograph of John Francis Green to him shortly after Robert McConnell [UDR] and Harris Boyle [UVF] killed him on 10 January 1975.

I was stopped at numerous checkpoints by Robert Nairac in the weeks and months after the Reavey killings. Nairac died locally in 1977, so British denials that he wasn't in the six counties during that period are not convincing.

We now know that Nairac was involved in the organisation of the Miami Showband massacre on 31 July 1975. The investigative journalist Duncan Campbell – formerly of *The Guardian* – wrote on his site that Nairac was in Northern Ireland one year previous in 1974. As usual, just like so many other British military officials, MoD Witness 2 had a bad memory.

The belief that Nairac was at Kingsmills has been completely rejected by the British military who, as we all know, are experts in the art of telling lies. One thing though is certain, it was highly unlikely that republican gunmen in South Armagh spoke with English accents. Another mysterious and controversial revelation to come out at the inquest related to local man Charlie Hughes.

According to the BBC News website on 23 May 2017, Hughes was never questioned by the RUC despite the fact that he was the first person on the scene of the killings on 5 January 1976. He stayed at the site of the massacre that night until 8.30 p.m., three hours after the shootings. Despite informing numerous RUC officers that evening of what he saw, Charlie told me that they failed to show up for several subsequent appointments to take a statement from him. It was only forty years after the atrocity that he eventually gave a statement to the police ombudsman's office. Why was there a forty-year delay and why did the RUC feel that what he saw was not important in the compilation of evidence?

The reader can draw their own conclusions.

On the evening of 5 January 1976, Gerry and Ann McKeown from Newry, and originally from Whitecross, came upon the Kingsmills massacre from the Bessbrook side within minutes of the shootings and comforted a very bloody Alan Black as he clung on for life in complete agony. They told me that they too were not interviewed by the RUC despite witnessing the immediate chaos in the aftermath of the killings. Gerry and Ann lived 100 yards from the RUC station in Newry and even though the police noted their presence, officers never found the time to take their statements. Those who were the first on the scene of the massacre, including myself, were not interviewed either.

One of the great tell-tale revelations about the Kingsmills massacre emerged in May 2017. A woman, Esther McConville from Bessbrook, who lost her son John in the massacre, was a long-time employee at the local British army base and was there on the day the atrocity happened. She revealingly told the inquest into the killings that back in 1978 she was serving breakfast one morning to the commanding officer at the officers' mess in Bessbrook Mill. She asked an officer why were there no soldiers patrolling the roads when the Reavey family left Whitecross for Daisy Hill Hospital to retrieve the coffins containing the bodies of John Martin and Brian.

The officer with an upper-class English accent said as he read the morning newspaper, 'there was an O.B. in place'. As referred to in the inquest, many years later in conversation with a journalist, she referred to the O.B. and the reporter explained its significance to her. An O.B. means *Out of Bounds*. These comments meant that if the British army was on a mission or planning a major operation, the area would be inaccessible to members of the wider military, the RUC and the public until after the event took place. For an O.B. to be in operation, at the area around where the massacre took place, meant that the British planned an operation where they had total control.

Not only that, it would have been impossible for the gunmen to get in and escape from the area without being stopped at

British army checkpoints which were omnipresent in the area at this time.

In light of the Reavey-O'Dowd killings the day before, it would have been very brazen IRA people who would have entered the area with the intention of carrying out an atrocity considering the heavy presence of British military personnel in the locality. Yet for these two hours, they were able to come in and get out as if there were no British military personnel in the area or so it seemed.

To put that in simplistic terms, elements within the British security services would have needed to work closely with certain members of the IRA to facilitate the Kingsmills massacre. Does this explain why, at 4 p.m. on Monday 5 January 1976, all army helicopters, vehicles and personnel effectively disappeared into thin air around the Whitecross/Kingsmills area, having saturated the locality with soldiers during the previous twenty-two hours?

The officer told Esther McConville that all soldiers had been ordered to remain in barracks on the day of the Kingsmills massacre. The existence of such O.B. operations or 'frozen' areas, was confirmed by British intelligence officer Fred Holroyd on the RTÉ TV programme *Today Tonight* on 18 May 1995. When challenged about this, MoD Witness 2 told the inquest, 'I can categorically state that this was not the case'.

MoD Witness 2 went on to say, 'The maximum number of soldiers were on the ground due to escalating sectarian attacks; three Catholics were killed at a Silverbridge bar attack the month before Kingsmills and a pub in Camlough had been bombed only days beforehand.' He added, 'there was a build up to 'the Reavey incident' at Whitecross the night before Kingsmills when three Catholic brothers were fatally shot by loyalists.'[2] He said it was his understanding that a wake had been planned for the Reavey brothers on the evening of 5 January 1976 and that 'Republican sympathisers' were expected to attend.

Major Ron Brotherton told the inquest that, 'the Catholic family [Reaveys] were known by the security forces to be republican sympathisers.'

This was yet *another blatant lie* but was proof that the British would say absolutely anything to justify their position and indefensible actions. The question begs, if the Reaveys were up to their eyes in republican activity, why were we never questioned, arrested, charged, prosecuted and convicted during our entire life time? Because of comments like this, we have to live side-by side with our Protestant neighbours, many of whom look at us with a sense of suspicion.

Even the families of those who died at Kingsmills are suspicious about the British. The *Sunday World* newspaper carried a story on 10 August 2023 featuring Tania Smith and Karen Armstrong, whose brother John McConville was killed at Kingsmills. In quoting the two women, it reported, 'We got the impression the [British] authorities just want the Kingsmills massacre to be put to bed and forgotten about.' The piece by journalist Hugh Jordan added that 'Tania and Karen ... are convinced the [British] authorities have something to hide.'[3]

The piece also quoted Karen Armstrong, who quizzed the PSNI about the police investigation into Kingsmills. It said, 'I managed to get an interview with a very senior officer, and I asked him straight out, "Why wasn't Kingsmills investigated?"'

'He threw his head in his hands and said, 'because they [the British] were afraid.'[4]

If ever though there was proof that the British army played a major role in the Kingsmill massacre, it lies in the fact that despite repeated calls since 1976 for an inquest, it was May 2016 when it finally got underway. The families of those who died had to wait for an inexcusable eight years until its publication in April 2024.

The British put every roadblock possible in the way to prevent the inquest from taking place, which begs the question, why?

It was brought to my attention following the publication of the Inquest that the British applied for a number of Public Interest Immunity Certs to prevent certain sensitive information from getting into the public domain, a development that has raised much alarm locally and within the legal profession!

The Killing of the Reavey Brothers

Having written to solicitor Kevin Winters of KRW Law (Belfast) in the summer of 2024, correspondence sent to me in reply on 12 September 2024 confirmed everything we suspected all along.

The reply from Kevin Winters stated:

> Kingsmills Massacre.
>
> We act on behalf of the family of John McConville who was murdered by the IRA at Kingsmills in January 1976. We also act for Alan Black, the sole survivor of the attack.
>
> We represented them at the inquest into the killings. Through the duration of proceedings, no fewer than seven applications for Public Interest Immunity (PII) were made by the Crown solicitor's office on behalf of the engaged State agencies.
>
> The applications were contested and opposed but all of them were granted by the Presiding Coroner. Many of the applications related to the identities of suspects including deceased suspects who were assigned cipher status to prevent their full identities being revealed.
>
> PII applications are usually made when there are matters of National Security engaged. That could mean the existence of an alleged State agent/informant or other matters of intelligence. Our clients believe the content of the material subjected to PII may point to the existence of agents implicated in the atrocity. They also believe the truth of what happened in Kingsmills lies within the content of that material.
>
> The issue will be re-visited by way of ongoing high court civil proceedings against the State together with the out workings of a pending PONI (Police Ombudsman of Northern Ireland) investigation.

What this all meant in simple terms was that the British asked for the protection of the courts to ensure that certain information that the Ministry of Defence possessed about the massacre was not presented to the inquest.

To put that another way, the British were clearly involved in the Kingsmills massacre, and they don't want the public to know that their military played a part in the deliberate killing of ten innocent Protestants. Of course, the British can prove us all wrong by making the contents of the documents public, but they won't.

In the meantime, the families of Alan Black, who survived the massacre and John McConville, who was killed, have called repeatedly through their solicitors, KRW Law in Belfast, for a public inquiry into the 1976 massacre. After all these years, the British are refusing to grant that request, proof, if ever proof was needed, that the British have something of significance to hide, leading one to believe, based on all of the above, that they had a significant role in the massacre. From what I know, the British follow-up plan after Kingsmills was to assist the UVF in killing Catholic schoolchildren in nearby Belleeks primary school on the day after the Kingsmills massacre.

This, it was hoped by the British, would provoke the IRA out of ceasefire. The British, who felt the IRA was a spent force by then, would resume its war with the republicans and would defeat them within a matter of months. This would be seen in the wider world as a military victory for the British and a humiliation for the IRA. Things however, did not turn out that way. The UVF felt that the optics of killing Catholic schoolchildren in nearby Belleeks was a mission too far and didn't proceed with the attack.

ELSEWHERE, MY QUEST TO have the Ian Paisley comments in the House of Commons corrected took an unexpected turn in London in 2020. For many years, I had lobbied a number of politicians to have the Paisley matter addressed. While they all had sympathy for my situation, the matter could only be raised at an appropriate sitting, such are the rules in the House of Commons.

The only option to correct something in *Hansard* that is inaccurate is for the relative speaker to stand up in the House and state that he/she wishes to correct something previously said that may have misled the public. In my case, Ian Paisley Senior made it clear that he was not going to do such a thing, so the best option for me was for someone else to make a statement, contradicting or questioning the remarks that are already on the record.

Conor McGinn was a Labour MP for St Helens North at the time, which is close to Liverpool. He is also a native of Camlough, South Armagh and is well versed in what happened at Kingsmills. On 11 November, a parliamentary committee heard statements on the possibility of holding an Inquiry into certain controversial killings in Northern Ireland.

During numerous individual contributions on various atrocities, Conor stood up and referred to the Reavey killings. He told the committee that 'whatever the motivation behind [Paisley] making that allegation, it caused incredible pain and it was and is completely and utterly false ... Eugene Reavey had no involvement whatsoever in Kingsmills and I think it's right the record is corrected here today.'

Minister Robin Walker, Conservative MP for Worcester, responded shortly afterwards and said, '... I thank the honourable member for St Helens North in particular for the important intervention he has made on this matter and note that the PSNI's Historical Enquiries Team found no wrongdoing whatsoever by Eugene Reavey in the incident that he raises.'

At long last, the *Hansard* record had been amended to state in clear terms that I played no part in the Kingsmills massacre. A massive weight had been taken off my shoulders and the wider Reavey family. We are forever grateful to Conor McGinn and Colm Eastwood, who made it possible. The comments were widely reported in the Northern Ireland newspapers and now nobody could point a finger in my direction.

Since 2012, I, on behalf of the Reavey family, have been involved in legal actions against the British Ministry of Defence and the chief constable of the PSNI. These include a civil action against the Ministry of Defence and the PSNI. As things stand, we have been told we cannot proceed with our action until the conclusion of the 'Operation Kenova' investigation.

The Quest for Truth and Justice still Goes On

Some might find it hard to believe that all these years after the killings at our house, we are still in battle with the British in our ongoing quest for truth and justice.

Willie Frazer, who set up FAIR (Families Acting For Innocent Relatives), died on 28 June 2019, aged fifty-eight, from cancer. It is our understanding that Willie, a former member of the ruthless Red Hand Commandos, had a grudge against the Reavey family over the murder of his father Bertie on 30 August 1975 at Ballymoyer, Whitecross.[5]

Bertie, a dedicated Orangeman, was named in court documents as one of the Glenanne gang members who, seven days previously on 23 August, were implicated in the killing of two GAA men, Seán Farmer and Colm McCartney, at Altnamackin as they returned home from the Dublin *V* Derry All-Ireland semi-final in Croke Park. Willie inaccurately took the view that the Reavey brothers were involved in the killing of his father. Of course, we had no connection to Bertie's or anyone else's death, but unfortunately, Willie blamed us.

Many years after our lads died in January 1976, a number of Protestant locals came to me and said that Willie had boasted that he was a get-away driver in the Reavey murders. At the time, we didn't know whether to believe this or not as Willie was a notorious liar and fantasist. He was also fifteen at the time.

However, the PSNI provided evidence to Edward Barnard's 2017 application for a judicial review into the killing of his brother Patrick at the Hillcrest Bar that contains documentation stating that a Mr Frazer *was* involved in the Reavey murders.

We subsequently learned from BBC NI that the Reavey killings were not the only ones that Willie Frazer contributed to. Broadcast journalist Mandy McAuley reported on 8 October 2019 that Willie was the main distributor of weapons for Ulster Resistance, which was set up by Dr Ian Paisley.

The BBC *Spotlight* programme reported that the weapons distributed by Mr Frazer contributed to the deaths of over seventy people. Mr Frazer made these claims himself to the

361

BBC shortly before his death. They were backed up by multiple sources, including infamous UFF Brigadier Johnny 'Mad Dog' Adair who headed up C Company in the lower Shankill Road area of Belfast.

The Royal Ulster Constabulary confirmed to me in a letter from Sam Harkness of the RUC on 14 August 2001, that 'a person believed to have an association with a loyalist paramilitary organisation' accused me of driving Malachy McParland to the site of the Kingsmills massacre, which was also *a blatant lie*. That same allegation was repeated verbatim by Willie's friend, Ian Paisley Senior, in the House of Commons, which left us in no doubt about its source.

After all these years, the quest for answers by the Reaveys and many other families rumbles on. Some cases are being settled out of court with the British offering miserable sums of money with a built-in caveat that litigants should take what they are offered, otherwise the proposed legislation to re-visit legacy investigations could result in them getting nothing at all.

Plans by the Tory Government to introduce a Legacy Act would have resulted in no future investigations into past atrocities taking place. The Tories in London took the attitude that it was time to draw a line in the sand and let bygones be bygones, regardless of who murdered who.

The decision to introduce a Legacy Act had the unusual effect of uniting people on both sides of the divide in Northern Ireland – itself a rare occurrence – who feel they will be denied justice from a heartless and uncaring government in London that will go to any length to protect its reputation.

In the meantime, a new Labour government has been elected in the UK, and is promising to abolish the Legacy Act. At time of writing, all we can do is wait and see.

Knowing how the wheels of justice turn with the British, I won't be surprised if portions of the highly anticipated 'Operation Kenova' never see the light of day. Lots of people in the British security chain have too much to lose if all the truthful and shocking details of various atrocities emerge. That, unfortunately, has been the reality of life for so many families since the British launched 'Operation Banner' on the streets of Northern Ireland back in 1969.

Many people have asked why I put this story into book form? The blatant lies from the British and their constant rejection of questions have made me more determined to highlight the unjust way that we and others have been treated for being nothing more than Irish Catholics and asking logical questions. Great support, from Róisín, our children, my wider family and friends, has kept me going. For many years, Róisín encouraged me to put my thoughts and life experience down on paper to highlight the endless lies and lack of co-operation we, and others like us, have had to endure from the British authorities.

This story is a reminder to all around us and those yet unborn of the hell we have had to go through as part of a British plot to turn Catholics and Protestants in South Armagh against each other. As I said before, if Civil Rights had been granted and the 1966 killings never took place, would 3,500 or so people have lost their lives in the subsequent years?

At least the guns are now silent and the children of today, on both sides, can live what many people might say is a 'normal life' even if reconciliation remains difficult in certain areas. I can now look out the window of my house and watch my grandchildren happily playing GAA games across the road knowing that they are growing up in a safer society than the one we found ourselves plunged into back in the early 1970s.

The Irish traditions and Christian values that my parents passed on to me are being passed on to them. Hopefully the Ireland they will grow up in, will be a much more progressive one than the place that went before them.

In the meantime, the Reavey family unveiled a special memorial at our family home in January 2016. It features three photographic images of John Martin, Brian and Anthony imprinted into marble and inserted on the wall at the front gate of the house where the shootings took place on 4 January 1976. It will remain in place long after the current generation of

Reaveys have passed on to the next life, ensuring their deaths will remain in the memory of locals for ever more.

There are currently seventeen names on headstones along a three-mile stretch of the road that runs past our house. They are a stark reminder to those living in and beyond South Armagh, and in particular, the blinkered civil servants in Whitehall London, that although the Troubles in Northern Ireland are over, the battle for truth and justice, for so many families, still goes on.

Endnotes

Sectarian tensions start to boil
1. *The Troubles*, Thames Television in association with MacDonald Futura Publishers, 1980, pp. 124, 1980.
2. https://www.rte.ie/archives/2019/0726 /1065362-broadcast-by-an-taoiseach/
3. *Lost Lives*, Vol. 1, Chris Thornton, Seamus Kelters, Brian Feeney, David McKittrick, Mainstream Publishing, 1999, p. 57.
4. *Ibid.*
5. *The Poisonous Legacy of Colonialism*, The Pat Finucane Centre, www.patfinucanecentre.org
6. *Kitson's Irish War: Mastermind of the Dirty War in Ireland*, David Burke, Mercier Press, p. 33. 2023.

Crouzon's Syndrome Comes to our door
1. *A State in Denial*, Margaret Urwin, Mercier Press, 2016, p. 110.

Mystery surrounds local killing
1. *Secret Hero*, John Parker, Metro Books, 2004, p. 112
2. *The Miami Showband Massacre*, Stephen Travers and Neil Fetherston Haugh, Hachette Books Ireland, 2007, p. 100.
3. *Lethal Allies*, Anne Cadwallader, Mercier Press, 2013, p. 112.
4. *Sunday World*, Hugh Jordan, 25 February 2018.
5. *Bear in Mind These Dead*, Susan McKay, Faber and Faber, 2008, p. 74.
6. *Lethal Allies*, p. 135.
7. *Ibid.*, p. 137.
8. *Ibid.*

Welcome to South Armagh
1. *Secret Operations of the SAS*, Mike Ryan, MBI Publishing Company, St Paul, MN, 2003, p. 108, p. 11.

British Brutality in Ballymoyer
1. *Majella O'Hare*, Fr Denis Faul & Fr Raymond Murray, published (locally) September 1976.
2. *Ibid.*
3. *Ibid*
4. *Ibid*
5. *Ibid*

Building an empire
1 'Daughter of republican Máire Drumm seeks answers to murder 40 years on', *Irish News*, John Monaghan, 26 October 2016.

Better to let sleeping dogs lie
1. *The Life of Sir Basil Brooke*, Dr Sam Logan, Book Guild Publishing, 2018, p. 50.

The Hungers Strikes hit home
1. *The Irish Hunger Strike*, Tom Collins, White Island Book Company, 1986, p. 484.

The Collusion Intensifies
1. *The Dirty War*, Martin Dillon, Hutchinson Books London, 1988, p. 456.

He calls himself Doctor Death
1. 'Foiled plot would have equipped UVF and UDA', *Belfast Telegraph* online, 30 September 2015.

Brits signal desire to leave
1. 'Loughlin Maginn: Family of man shot dead by UDA settle claim against police and MoD', *Belfast Live* online, Maurice Fitzmaurice, 16 September 2022.
2. 'Loyalist Killer Sentenced in Catholic Murders', *Catholic World News* Feature, 11 December 1998.
3. Loughlin Maginn, *Lost Lives*, p. 1176.
4. Peter Brooke. *Irish Times* obituary online, 20 May 2003.

Talks about talks
1. *Lost Lives*, Vol. 1, Chris Thornton, Seamus Kelters, David McVea, Brian Feeney and David McKittrick, Mainstream Publishing, 1999, p. 28.
2. *Ibid.*

Paisley puts our lives in danger
1. 'Call for Paisley to withdraw allegations', *The Armagh-Down Observer*, 4 February 1999.

The collusion cat escapes from the bag
1. 'Colleagues and politicians pay tribute to journalist Liam Clarke', *Irish Times*, Gerry Moriarty, 27 December 2015.
2. http://news.bbc.co.uk/1/hi/northern_ireland/3333919.stm

There's a new Sheriff in Town
1. *Lethal Allies*, p. 291.
2. 'Glenanne Gang bomber named accomplices, Court told', *Belfast Telegraph* online, Alan Erwin, 22 November, 2016.
3. *Lethal Allies*, p. 333.
4. *Ibid.*, p. 193
5. John Weir statement, *Sunday Times*, Liam Clarke, 7 February 1999.
6. *Ibid.*

Endnotes

Garda file goes missing
1. (1st) Barron Report: Conclusions, *Irish Times*, 11 December, 2003.
2. 'Garda apology for investigation into atrocity demanded', Seán McCartaigh, *Irish Examiner*, 5 April 2007.

The cover-up continues
1. *Lethal Allies*, pp. 17, 306.
2. *Ibid*.
3. *Lost Lives*, Vol. 1, p. 1181.
4. 'Ex-chief Constable Sir Hugh Orde says the Historical Enquiries Team was closed down because it was about to start investigating serving politicians from both sides involved in terrorism', *Belfast Telegraph*, Phillip Bradfield, 25 January 2022.

Paisley says No, No, No
1. 'War of words', Hugh Jordan, *Sunday World*, 16 October 2011.
2. *Northern Protestants: An unsettled people*, Susan McKay, Blackstaff Press, 2000, p. 187.

Raised hopes and family loss
1. 'Delay in dealing with Troubles killings "impacting on human rights"', *Irish Times*, Alan Erwin, 8 March 2018.
2. Glenanne gang: Court of Appeal rules investigation must be held. https://www.bbc.com/news/uk-northern-ireland-48883185 5 July 2019

Glenanne Gang names revealed
1. 'Relatives lose fight for Inquiry into 1948 Batang Kali "massacre"', *The Guardian* online, Owen Bowcott, 25 November 2015.

The Long Search for Truth continues
1. *Lethal Allies*, p. 171.

The quest for truth and justice still goes on
1. Appendix to *Frank Kitson's Army Land Operation Manual* (Vol 3. MoD), 29 August 1969.
2. https://www.judiciaryni.uk/files/judiciaryni/202404/%5B2024%5D%20NI Coroner% 2021.pdf
3. 'UDA Rebels to start up rival gang', Steven Moore, *Sunday World*, 5 August 2012.
4. 'Family's Agony: Sisters of Kingsmills massacre victims believe atrocity was "allowed to happen"', *Sunday World*, Hugh Jordan, 10 August 2023.

Bibliography

Burke, D. *Kitson's Irish War: Mastermind of the Dirty War in Ireland*, Mercier Press, Cork 2023.

Cadwallader, A. *Lethal Allies*, Mercier Press, Cork 2013.

Collins, T. *The Irish Hunger Strike*, White Island Book Company, Dublin 1986.

Dillon, Martin, *The Dirty War*, Arrow; New edition, London 1991.

Dixon, P. O'Kane, E. *Northern Ireland since 1969*, Document 20. Peter Brooke's Whitbread speech, Routledge Publishing, 11 February 2011.

Downing, T. (Editor) *The Troubles*: Thames Television in association with MacDonald Futura Publishers, London 1980.

Logan, Sam. *The Life of Sir Basil Brooke*, Book Guild Publishing, 2018. Leicestershire.

The Pat Finucane Centre. *The Poisonous Legacy of Colonialism*, www.patfinucanecentre.org

McKay, S. *Bear in Mind These Dead*, Faber and Faber, London 2008.

—— *Northern Protestants: An unsettled people*, Blackstaff Press, Belfast 2000.

McKittrick, D. Feeney, B. Kelters., S. Thornton, C. *Lost Lives*, Mainstream Publishing, Edinburgh 1999. Vol. 1.

Murray, R. & Faul, D. *Majella O'Hare*, published locally, September 1976.

Parker, J. *Secret Hero*, John Parker, Metro Books, London, 2004.

Travers, S. and Fetherston-Haugh, N. *The Miami Showband Massacre*, Hachette Books Ireland, Dublin 2007.

Ryan, M. *Secret Operations of the SAS*, MBI Publishing Company, St Paul, MN USA 2003.

Urwin, M. *A State in Denial*, Margaret Urwin, Mercier Press, Cork 2016.

INDEX

A

Abbey Grammar School 17, 18
Abbey Primary School 17
Adair, Johnny 'Mad Dog' 235, 362
Adams, Gerry 169, 170, 256
Ahern, Bertie 312
Ahoghill 159, 273, 286
Allister, Jim 313
Altnamackin 52, 124, 282, 286, 361
Anderson, Coroner Noel 155, 156, 157, 305
Andrews, Irene 207
Annaghmore 327
Antrim 47, 158, 159, 263, 273, 286
Armagh City 154, 298, 349
Armagh Gaol 169
Armstrong, Corp. Ian 31
Armstrong, Gary 274, 278, 287
Armstrong, Karen 357
Atkins, Humphrey 172
Aughamullan 330
Aughnacloy 330, 349

B

Baggott, Matt 306, 332
Ball, Julian 'Tony' 164
Ballydougan 9, 59, 70, 87
Ballygawley 230, 349
Ballygorman 298, 336
Ballylane Road 44, 54
Ballymoyer 15, 16, 17, 51, 53, 62, 74, 90, 91, 92, 93, 94, 99, 115, 116, 136, 143, 144, 145, 149, 166, 175, 296, 300, 303, 317, 335, 361

Ballymurphy 29, 31, 122, 147
Banbridge 37, 38, 42, 43, 46, 47, 284, 349
Barbour, Davy 60
Barbour, Nora 60
Barnard, Edward 285, 332, 333, 361
Barnard, Patrick 307, 329, 332, 361
Barron Inquiry 280, 289, 290, 312
Barron, Judge Henry 39, 281, 289
Barron Report 289
Bartholomew, Frederick 50
Batang Kali Massacre 330
Bates, Robert 'Basher' 235
Battle of the Bogside 24, 29
Beattie, Emily 21
Beattie, Garfield 53, 285, 328
Belfast 13, 14, 18, 23, 24, 25, 26, 27, 29, 30, 31, 40, 57, 58, 67, 70, 76, 110, 112, 114, 134, 135, 139, 147, 151, 153, 155, 156, 158, 160, 163, 169, 171, 176, 177, 182, 189, 191, 193, 194, 197, 198, 200, 201, 202, 203, 205, 206, 207, 209, 210, 211, 214, 216, 220, 222, 225, 226, 227, 228, 229, 231, 232, 234, 235, 237, 238, 239, 240, 241, 244, 246, 247, 248, 250, 252, 256, 257, 259, 268, 270, 273, 277, 285, 296, 307, 309, 311, 314, 315, 318, 321, 323, 326, 340, 341, 344, 353, 358, 359, 362
Bellaghy 50, 177, 191
Bell, Const. 301

Belleeks 35, 37, 106, 107, 128, 130, 133, 141, 169, 179, 182, 183, 184, 186, 189, 275, 285, 341, 343, 359
Bell, Johnny 53, 54
Bell, Raymond 134, 136
Bell's Eggs 134, 136, 152
Benagh 37, 39
Benburb 349
Bennett, Joe 220
Bernard, Patrick 332
Bessbrook 14, 16, 26, 42, 57, 60, 64, 75, 77, 83, 84, 85, 88, 91, 95, 96, 97, 99, 102, 105, 112, 115, 122, 123, 127, 130, 138, 141, 149, 162, 174, 216, 234, 298, 299, 303, 304, 349, 352, 353, 355
Best, Don 103
Bingham, John 220, 221
Black, Alan 84, 85, 102, 104, 148, 263, 352, 353, 355, 358, 359
Black, Capt. 204, 205, 207, 208, 209, 235, 340
Blair, Tony 312
Bloody Sunday 30, 122, 140, 147, 253, 292, 293
Blundell, James 155
Bogside 24, 25, 29, 31, 178
Boutcher, Jon 325, 334, 335, 336
Bowen, Kim 293, 294, 296
Boyd, Frank 202
Boyle, Edward 72
Boyle, Harris 48, 49, 328, 354
Bracknell, Alan 318
Bradley, Karen 324
Brannigan's Bar 327, 329
Brecknell, Alan 284
Brecknell, Trevor 55, 284, 285, 328, 329, 330
Breen, Harry 158, 287, 297, 339
Brooke, Basil 167, 168, 196
Brooke, Peter 253, 254
Brotheron, Ron 356
Browne, Andrew Neville 252
Brown, Judge 105
Brush, Lt Col 297
Bryans, John 84, 95
Buchanan, Const. Raymond 105
Burntollet 24, 314, 340
Busby, Garnet James 285, 329, 332
Buskhill 47, 49, 330
Byrne, Gerry 77, 78, 98
Byrne, Simon 325

C

Cadwallader, Anne 50, 318, 319
Caledon 21, 22, 167, 349
Camlough 47, 59, 60, 61, 62, 64, 67, 70, 79, 99, 103, 114, 121, 132, 137, 141, 165, 173, 177, 178, 184, 185, 267, 318, 348, 356, 360
Campbell, Alice 60, 68, 69, 71, 92, 93, 144, 146, 147, 148
Campbell, Jim 222
Campbell, Joe 158, 329, 336
Campbell, Mrs Margaret 42, 43
Campbell, Patrick 42, 329
Carlisle, Const. Norman 105
Carrickananney 14, 15, 35, 60, 119, 234, 317
Carrickasticken 143
Carrickgollogly 128, 130
Carroll, Briege 36, 185, 194, 203, 204, 230
Cartmill, Trevor 65, 300, 301
Cassidy, Dr Seamus 264, 265
Castleblayney 50, 273, 277, 328
Castlereagh 216, 218, 277, 278
Castlewellan 136
Cavan 255, 317
Chambers, Robert 83, 95
Chancellor's Road 177

Chapman, Reggie 60, 83, 96
Chapman, Walter 60, 83, 96
Charlemont 285
Civil Rights 21, 22, 24, 25, 32,
    86, 257, 340, 363
Civil Rights Association 22
Clancy, Felix 327
Clancy's Bar 327, 328, 329
Clarke, Liam 272, 273, 274,
    275, 276, 354
Cleary, Peter 133, 163
Clontibret 326
Clough 136
Coagh 349
Coalisland 349
Coleraine 208
Collusion 150, 223, 225, 252,
    275, 283, 288, 297, 302, 307,
    309, 311, 319, 321, 326, 348,
    349, 352
Colton, Justice 321, 322
Conway, Cardinal William 91,
    115
Cook Report 225, 228, 232,
    239, 240, 246
Cook, Roger 225, 226, 228, 229
Cookstown 18, 19, 349
Cooper, Ivan 24
Corlatt Drive 100, 102, 104,
    105, 107, 109, 114, 115, 116,
    139
Corrigan, Peter 318, 320
Corrigan, William 53, 329
Cortamlet 50
Cosgrave, Liam 46, 134
Cosy Corner Bar 327, 329
Cotton, Michael John 43
Courtbane 31
Cowan, Hugo 298
Cox, Dave 292, 293, 294, 295,
    296, 297, 306, 307, 308, 309,
    334, 342
Coyle, Maurice 276
Craigavon 228, 241, 349

Craig, James (Jimmy) 153, 168,
    182, 197, 198, 199, 200, 201,
    202, 203, 204, 206, 207, 208,
    210, 211, 212, 214, 215, 217,
    218, 219, 220, 221, 222, 225,
    226, 227, 228, 229, 231, 232,
    233, 234, 235, 236, 238, 239,
    240, 241, 243, 244, 245, 246,
    248, 250, 259, 297
Crampton, Colin 283
Creggandufff 126
Crossgar 134, 136, 139, 152
Crossmaglen 27, 28, 50, 125,
    126, 152, 162, 230, 258, 268,
    279, 349
Crouzon's Syndrome 35, 40,
    110
Crozier, Thomas 329
Crumlin Road 153, 241, 245,
    247, 272
Cullaville 68
Cully, Const. George 64
Cullyhanna 55, 127
Cunningham, Imelda 59, 60
Curran, Brendan Patrick 347
Currie, Austin 22, 24, 53
Curry, Frankie 235
Cushendall 158

D

Daisy Hill Hospital 39, 55, 60,
    63, 64, 65, 68, 69, 70, 77, 78,
    85, 88, 89, 92, 97, 100, 101,
    103, 104, 107, 108, 109, 110,
    132, 144, 148, 155, 157, 174,
    178, 184, 258, 287, 300, 301,
    304, 317, 341, 355
Davies, Col Philip 95
Democratic Unionist Party
    (DUP) 172, 221, 262, 263,
    267, 268, 269, 312, 313, 314,
    315, 316, 323
Derry 22, 23, 24, 25, 26, 27, 29,
    31, 32, 33, 50, 51, 58, 87, 140,

147, 159, 177, 178, 188, 191, 208, 247, 253, 340, 361
Devine, Micky 191
Devlin, Matt 192
Devlin murders 328, 329
Devlin, Paddy 24
Devlin, Patrick 330
Dewar, Col Mike 351
Dobson, Lorraine 284
Doherty, Kieran 191
Donaghmore 42
Donaldson, Const. Sam 27
Donaldson, Kenny 309
Donnelly, Michael 55, 285, 328, 330
Donnelly, Patrick 55, 285
Donnelly, Patsy 328, 329, 330
Donnelly's Bar 55, 56, 279, 280, 285, 302
Down, County 26, 32, 37, 42, 47, 49, 50, 70, 134, 136, 195, 213, 218, 239, 252, 286, 287, 344
Downpatrick 136
Doyle's pub 60, 96
Dromara 349
Dromore 218, 349
Drumherriff 15, 16, 36, 68, 71, 84, 93, 94, 97, 98, 117, 119, 136, 183, 303, 353
Drumhoney 16, 36
Drumilly 26
Drumintee 162
Drumm, Jimmy 182
Drumm, Máire 152, 153, 182
Drumnahuncheon 166
Dublin 13, 25, 31, 32, 44, 45, 46, 47, 48, 50, 55, 59, 83, 96, 151, 159, 161, 163, 171, 232, 253, 255, 256, 273, 278, 280, 281, 289, 291, 312, 317, 320, 340, 361
Dublin and Monaghan Bombings 159, 161, 163, 289, 329, 330

Duddy, Brendan 191
Dundalk 27, 36, 55, 58, 133, 143, 151, 251, 255, 279, 345
Dundrum 229, 239
Dungannon 21, 49, 53, 170, 264, 307, 330, 331, 332, 349
Dungiven 188, 248
Dungormley 51

E

Eagle Bar 285, 327, 328
Eastwood, Colm 360
Elliott, Kinnear 101, 102
Enniskillen 229, 231, 246, 309
European Convention on Human Rights 319
European Court of Human Rights 311, 312, 319, 333
Extortion money 197, 204, 209, 211, 213, 216, 218, 220, 226, 227, 228, 229, 232, 237, 244, 249, 251, 256, 297

F

Falls, Pat 330
Falls Road 27, 29, 112
Families Acting for Innocent Relatives (FAIR) 282, 305, 361
Farmer, Seán 286, 327, 328, 330, 361
Farmer, Seán [John P.] 50, 51, 52
Faul, Fr Denis 170, 171, 183, 308
Fee, David 'Artie' 198, 201, 202, 203, 204, 206, 208, 218, 219, 222, 225, 234, 236, 237, 244, 259
Feeley, Frank 82
Fermanagh 87, 167, 171, 172, 173, 174
Ferris, Brendan 268, 269
Finnegan, Killian 130

Finnegan, Lily 121
Finnegan's Corner 136
Finnegan, Ted 92
Fitt, Gerry 24
Flanagan, Chief Constable Ronnie 265, 268, 269, 270, 283, 315
Forces Research Unit (FRU) 10
Forkhill 56, 133, 143, 162, 268, 349
Forrester's Hall 15
Foster, Arlene 323
Frazer, Peggy 316
Frazer, Robert 'Bertie' 51, 52, 54, 282, 327, 347, 361
Frazer, Willie 52, 54, 282, 297, 304, 305, 316, 361
Freeburn, Robert 84, 86, 94
Free Presbyterian Church 134, 263, 269, 313, 340
Friedman, Danny 321

G

Gaelic Athletic Association (GAA) 10, 11, 15, 17, 18, 25, 26, 36, 38, 51, 64, 87, 90, 149, 159, 175, 213, 216, 239, 243, 266, 279, 282, 286, 361, 363
Garda Síochána 290, 291, 308
Geraghty, Tony 49
Gibson, Justice Maurice 150
Gilford 59, 70, 75, 91, 349
Girvan, Paul 323
Glasgow 19, 20, 230, 246
Glenanne 18, 43, 44, 54, 75, 83, 96, 106, 255, 268, 276, 278, 280, 281, 284, 285, 286, 288, 289, 290, 293, 296, 300, 301, 303, 304, 308, 312, 318, 319, 320, 324, 325, 326, 327, 332, 333, 334, 335, 339, 340, 343, 361
Glencree Centre 336

Gordon, Dr Derek 110, 111, 112
Gosford Castle 44
Gough 349
Granemore 138, 297, 302
Grant, Micky John 68
Gray, David 299, 300, 301
Greenisland 211, 244
Green, John Francis 163, 277, 328, 354
Gregg, John 235
Grew family 327, 329
Greyhilla 15, 16, 26, 114, 157, 343
Grove Housing Association 194, 195, 197, 199, 200, 204
Guiding Star Temperance Orange Lodge 52

H

Hackballscross 31
Hain, Peter 312
Hale, Margaret 330
Hamilton, Bertie 66, 300
Hamilton, Margaret 66, 74
Hanlon, Ronald 330
Hanna, Billy 278
Hanna, William 329
Harkin, Greg 267
Harkness, Sam 362
Harris, Alwyn 308
Harris, Drew 308
Harte, Bill 76
H-Blocks 172, 173, 180, 194, 214, 260
Heath, Edward 31, 34
Henry, David 285
Herbert, Michael Francis 43
Hermon, John 233
Herron, Albert 329
Herron, William 52
Hillcrest 307, 328, 330, 332, 333, 361
Hilltown 136, 213

373

Historical Enquiries Analytical Database (HEAD) 333
Historical Enquiries Team (HET) 52, 285, 292, 293, 296, 297, 298, 299, 300, 301, 302, 304, 305, 306, 307, 308, 309, 310, 315, 318, 319, 320, 321, 325, 326, 332, 333, 334, 342, 348, 349, 360
Holroyd, Fred 354, 356
Hughes' Bar 46
Hughes, Brigid 323
Hughes, Charlie 354
Hughes, Francis 169, 177, 191
Hughes, Fr Peter 39, 62, 63, 64, 74, 76, 90, 91, 94, 96, 99, 102, 103, 107, 108, 109, 110, 115, 122, 123, 130, 139, 140, 141, 146, 148
Hughes, Richard 84
Hulme, Shirley 133
Hume, John 24
Hunger strikes 152, 168, 169, 170, 171, 172, 173, 174, 175, 176, 177, 178, 179, 180, 181, 182, 183, 184, 185, 188, 189, 191, 192, 193
Hurson, Martin 191

I

INLA 161, 169, 178, 188, 191, 197, 260
Inquests 33, 38, 154, 155, 157, 158, 253, 305, 321, 327, 341, 353, 354, 355, 356, 357, 358
Inquiries 292, 338
IRA 11, 27, 28, 29, 31, 32, 38, 42, 43, 46, 47, 48, 49, 50, 51, 52, 53, 54, 57, 58, 59, 83, 87, 95, 96, 104, 119, 124, 126, 129, 132, 133, 134, 137, 138, 141, 143, 145, 147, 149, 152, 160, 161, 162, 163, 165, 166, 167, 168, 169, 170, 171, 172, 173, 175, 176, 177, 178, 179, 180, 181, 184, 189, 191, 192, 197, 199, 208, 220, 221, 228, 232, 233, 244, 249, 252, 255, 256, 257, 258, 261, 262, 263, 264, 272, 273, 274, 275, 277, 278, 279, 280, 281, 282, 308, 309, 323, 325, 334, 339, 345, 347, 351, 352, 356, 358, 359

J

Jackson, Robin 42, 43, 49, 105, 106, 235, 274, 277, 278, 279, 329
Jameson, Richard 258
James, Phil 293, 296
Johnson, John 52
Johnstone, Ron 313
Jonesborough 162
Justice for the Forgotten 289, 291

K

Kane, Dalzell 285
Kane, David 327
Kay's Tavern 55, 151
Keady 36, 51, 138, 150, 151, 278, 297, 302, 326, 349
Keenan, Johanna 284
Kelly, Joseph 332
Kelly, Terry 112, 113
Kennon, Hugh 92, 145
Kennon, Mrs 17
Kerr, Robert 330
Kielty, Jack 239, 240
Kilcoo 136
Killen's pub 329
Kingscourt 255
Kingsmills 19, 57, 65, 72, 75, 77, 78, 79, 80, 82, 83, 84, 86, 87, 94, 95, 96, 97, 98, 99, 100, 101, 102, 103, 106, 119, 120, 121, 129, 136, 143, 166, 258, 261, 262, 263, 264, 265, 268,

269, 270, 273, 282, 294, 296,
302, 303, 315, 335, 345, 349,
350, 351, 352, 353, 354, 355,
356, 357, 358, 359, 360, 362
Kitson, Brig. Frank 29, 30, 32,
147, 351, 352
KRW 318, 358, 359

L

Lambert, Adam 230, 231, 246, 297
Largey, Hughie 125, 126
Laurelvale 258, 259
Lavery, Michael 241
Lee, Des 352
Legacy Act 362
Legacy Investigations Branch (LIB) 333, 334
Lemass, Seán 25, 340
Lemmon, Joseph 83, 96
Lenny, Bishop Francis 91, 92
Leonard, William 329
Lewis, Brendan 267
Lies 11, 33, 49, 263, 264, 266, 270, 343, 351, 354, 363
Liggett, Henry Garfield 286, 329
Limavady 247
Lindsay, John 39
Lisburn 100, 185, 233, 236, 252, 308
Little, Noel 238
Livingstone, Iain 335
London 10, 13, 14, 25, 26, 30, 32, 33, 34, 41, 44, 48, 54, 57, 66, 67, 71, 72, 76, 84, 109, 135, 149, 152, 170, 171, 172, 176, 177, 181, 182, 184, 186, 189, 214, 228, 229, 232, 253, 254, 258, 263, 268, 274, 281, 283, 292, 293, 300, 301, 317, 320, 336, 341, 343, 344, 359, 362, 364
Loughbrickland 214

Loughgall 285, 323, 349
Lough Inn pub 60
Loughran, Peter John 16
Loughran, Seán 90, 247
Loughry College 18
Louth 31, 55, 133, 152, 163, 170, 251, 339
Lowry, Justice 302
Lundy, Samuel 'Cliffy' 166
Lurgan 9, 75, 105, 274, 277, 278, 344, 347, 349
Lutton, Joseph Norman 285, 328
Lynch, Jack 25, 31
Lynch, Kevin 183, 188, 189
Lynch, Paddy 227
Lynch, Tommy 235, 237
Lyttle, Tommy 'Tucker' 222, 223, 225, 237, 248, 252, 297

M

MacAirt, Ciarán 344, 350, 351
Mackin, Darragh 318, 320, 327, 334
Magee, Hughie 58
Maghaberry 259
Magilligan 247
Maginn, Loughlin 223, 252, 253
Maginn, Maureen 253
Maguire, Frank 171
Mallon, John 46
Mallon, Seamus 23, 82, 175, 267
Malone, Ann 67
Malone, Barry 97, 146, 353
Malone, Bernie 67
Malone, Eugene 98, 303, 353
Malone, Fr Con 54, 63, 64, 67, 70, 76, 78, 83, 90, 91, 112, 113, 114, 115, 123, 128, 295
Malone, Jim 97, 353
Malvern Arms 18
Marchant, Bill 329

375

Markethill 14, 15, 23, 44, 57, 103, 175, 238, 259, 277, 349
Marshall, Thomas K. 156, 342
Matilda, Gould 257
Mayobridge 37, 39, 136, 264
Maytown 100
Maze/Long Kesh 142, 167, 170, 171, 191, 260
McAleavey, John 86
McBride, Alan 336
McBride, Const. Billy 39, 287, 297, 327
McCabe, Philip 264
McCammond, Bob 127, 128, 134, 135
McCann, Charlie 211, 212, 244
McCann, DS Gerry 56, 288, 301
McCartney, Colm 50, 51, 52, 286, 327, 328, 330, 361
McCaughey, James 307, 332
McCaughey, William [Billy] 274, 275, 284, 285, 286, 329
McCaul, Mr 341
McClinton, Kenny 235
McClorey, Annie 74
McClure 279, 302
McClure, Laurence 52, 278, 279, 285, 286, 302, 326, 328
McColl, Ian 109
McConnell, Robert 52, 132, 277, 279, 280, 285, 328, 354
McConville, Esther 355, 356
McConville, John 83, 96, 357, 358, 359
McCoo, Sammy 279
McCord, Raymond 314
McCormick, Terry 163
McCoy, Brian 49
McCreesh, Raymond 141, 142, 169, 173, 177, 178, 182, 184
McCullagh, Geoffrey 252
McCullough, Joe 124
McCullough, Robert 327

McDermott, Éilis 154, 156, 305, 341
McDonald, Betty 151, 326, 327, 328
McDonald, Jackie 203, 204, 207, 259
McDonald, Malachi 151
McDonnell, Charles 327, 329
McDonnell, Gerard 38
McDonnell, Joe 191
McDonnell, Seán Charles 37, 38, 39, 327
McDowell, James 328
McElwee, Thomas 191
McEntee, Patrick 290, 291
McFarland, Derek 327
McGeown, Pat 192
McGinn, Conor 360
McGleenan, Gerard 151, 326
McGrath, John Joe 302, 303
McGrath, Mick 138, 286, 287, 297
McGuinness, Danny 142
McGuinness, Martin 169, 256, 309, 313
McGuinness, Phelim 59, 143
McGuinness, Robbie 58, 74, 143
McHale, Kathleen [nee Reavey] 15, 26, 57, 66, 69, 71, 76, 335
McHale, Pat 66, 71
McKay, Kevin 202
McKeag, Stephen 'Top Gun' 235
McKearney, Jane 285, 327, 328, 329, 332
McKearney, Peter 285, 329, 332
McKee, James 52
McKeeveney, James 329
McKee, William 52
McKenna, Kirsty 258
McKenna, Paul 258
McKeown, Ann 41, 67, 355
McKeown, Bernie 67

McKeown, Gerry 67, 68, 116, 355
McKeown, Laurence 192
McKeown, Patsy 62, 303
McKeown, Peter 58
McLogan, P.J. 69, 74, 90
McLoughlin, Frederick 285, 327, 328, 330
McLoughlin, Samuel 298
McMahon, Dolly 107, 341, 343
McManus, Frank 24
McManus, Seamus 264
McMichael, John 197, 232, 233, 245, 248
McNamee, Brendan 154, 157
McNamee, Thomas 279, 328
McNeice, Patrick 285, 328, 329
McNeice, Paul 327
McParland, Malachy 362
McShane, Rory 24, 141, 142, 224, 241, 259, 268, 312
McVeigh, Martin 329, 330
McVerry, Dr Michael 38
McWhirter, James 83, 96
Meaklim, William 50, 279
Meares, CRN 344
Meehan, Paul 202
Meigh 73
MI5 Security Service 10, 43, 45, 326, 343
MI6 Secret Service 10, 43, 45, 326
Miami Showband 47, 49, 50, 105, 147, 151, 159, 161, 163, 328, 329, 330, 336, 337, 352, 354
Middletown 349
Millar, Const. Roy 27
Millar, Frankie 200, 225
Miller, John 335
Ministry of Defence (MoD) 11, 149, 255, 319, 327, 353, 354, 356, 358, 360
Mitchell, Ian 278, 285, 286

Mitchell, James 54, 277, 278, 279, 281, 286, 289, 290, 326, 328, 339
Mitchell, Johnny 279
Mitchell, Thomas 327
Moira 349
Molloy, Pat 329
Monaghan 14, 45, 46, 50, 52, 95, 122, 151, 159, 161, 163, 167, 273, 277, 278, 289, 290, 291, 326
Mone, Patrick 328
Moneymore 349
Moorcroft, Const. Tom 276, 277
Moore, Tom 85
Morgan, Justice Declan 320, 321, 322, 323, 324, 334
Morrison, Danny 173, 192
Morris, Steve 307, 320, 321, 326
Mountnorris 64, 165, 258
Mowhan 44, 276
Moy 50, 53, 285, 318, 332, 349
Moygashel 42
MRF (Mobile Reaction Force) 10
Mullen, Denis 53, 285, 327, 328, 329
Mullen, Edith Dorothy 286
Mullen, Jerome 82
Murder Triangle 49, 50
Murphy, Arthur 28
Murphy, Cyril 63, 98
Murphy, Fr Hugh 328
Murphy, Jessie 63, 64
Murphy, Lenny 197, 235
Murphy, Malachy 98
Murphy, Mary (nee Quinn) 36, 39, 132, 185, 190
Murphy, Mickey 265
Murphy, Niall 318
Murphy, Thomas 'Slab' 275

N

Nairac, Robert 47, 133, 159, 161, 162, 163, 164, 255, 280, 351, 352, 353, 354
Newry 14, 17, 18, 24, 25, 26, 31, 37, 38, 39, 46, 47, 49, 50, 54, 55, 58, 59, 60, 63, 65, 66, 67, 68, 69, 70, 73, 74, 77, 78, 81, 83, 85, 86, 97, 98, 99, 100, 101, 103, 105, 107, 114, 122, 125, 132, 136, 139, 141, 142, 148, 152, 154, 157, 174, 177, 178, 183, 206, 215, 224, 234, 242, 246, 251, 266, 267, 282, 293, 294, 298, 299, 300, 301, 303, 317, 336, 353, 355
Newtowncloghoge 58, 152
Newtownhamilton 14, 20, 50, 51, 63, 70, 95, 101, 107, 124, 125, 132, 133, 139, 246, 279, 280, 299, 349
Newtown Hatcheries 20
New York 21, 67, 83, 176, 179, 180, 181, 193, 235, 318, 335
NIHE 142, 205, 206, 210, 211, 227, 229, 241
Nixon, Maud 96
Nixon, Rev. Robert 85, 96
Northern Ireland Office (NIO) 309, 319
Northland Street 206, 240

O

O'Connor, Paul 284
O'Donnell, John 86
O'Dowd, Barry 59, 60, 76
O'Dowd, Declan 76
O'Dowd Family 9, 71, 75, 91, 347, 348, 352
O'Dowd, Joe 76
Ó Fiaich, Tomás 183
O'Hanlon, Angela 20, 62, 63, 71
O'Hanlon, Paddy 24, 82
O'Hanlon, Patrick 62
O'Hara, Lilly 329
O'Hara, Patsy 169, 178
O'Hare, Agnes 37
O'Hare, Jim 143, 145, 146, 147, 149
O'Hare, Majella 143, 145, 146, 147, 148, 149, 150, 151
O'Hare, Mary 117, 148, 149
O'Hare, Michael 99
O'Kane, Paul 234
Oldham, Jeanette 262
O'Loan, Nuala 312, 335
Omagh 261, 263, 264
O'Neill, Charlie 98
O'Neill, Hubert 33
O'Neill, Kevin 132
O'Neill, Paddy 139, 140, 141
O'Neill's Pub 329
O'Neill, Terence 26, 340
Operation Banner 363
Operation Kenova 325, 334, 335, 360, 362
Orange Order 52, 53, 124, 167, 220, 231, 286
O'Rawe, Richard 192
Orde, Hugh 283, 288, 292, 306, 308, 309, 312
O'Toole, Fran 49

P

Paisley, Ian 24, 26, 54, 134, 172, 221, 238, 261, 262, 263, 264, 265, 266, 267, 268, 269, 270, 272, 274, 282, 297, 311, 312, 313, 314, 315, 316, 340, 351, 359, 360, 361, 362
Paisley, Ian, jr 269
Parachute Regiment 32, 33, 136, 137, 140, 142, 148, 253
Parr, William 53, 285, 330
Pat Finucane Centre (PFC) 282, 284, 297, 318, 333

Payne, Davy 235, 236, 237, 238, 239, 250, 259, 278, 297, 329
People's Democracy 23
PIRA 264, 345, 347, 348
Platers Hill 329
Poland, John 277
Police Service of Northern Ireland (PSNI) 10, 253, 283, 284, 288, 289, 290, 292, 294, 296, 301, 304, 306, 307, 308, 309, 312, 319, 320, 324, 325, 332, 333, 334, 335, 357, 360, 361
Pomeroy 349
PONI (Police Ombudsman of Northern Ireland) 358
Poots, William 298
Portadown 18, 39, 47, 49, 57, 75, 119, 124, 125, 126, 127, 134, 226, 238, 258, 276, 288, 297, 349
Porter, Joe 165
Poultry Husbandry 19, 20
Powell, Francis 138
Poyntzpass 103, 213, 264
Priest Bush Road 15, 98, 126
Prince Charles 337
Prior, Jim 192
Protection money 196, 198, 199, 200, 202, 203, 217, 220, 235, 239, 258
Public Interest Immunity (PII) 357, 358

Q

Quinn, Gary Martin 252
Quinn, Gerry 213
Quinn, John 189
Quinn, Laurence 189
Quinn, Mary 188
Quinn, Mrs Katie 77, 128, 130, 131, 132, 141, 142, 170, 171, 179, 182, 183, 184, 185, 186, 187, 188, 189, 190, 191, 192, 193
Quinn, Paddy 139, 141, 142, 168, 170, 171, 178, 179, 180, 182, 183, 184, 185, 186, 187, 188, 189, 190, 191, 192, 193
Quinn, Philomena 183
Quinn's Bar 329
Quinn, Seamie 151

R

Rafferty, Ciaran 268
Rafferty, Marion 327
Rainey, Victor 244
Rathfriland 252, 349
Ravenhill 270
Reagan, Ronald 180
Reavey, Aisling 123, 247
Reavey, Aisling 47
Reavey, Anthony 13, 16, 26, 57, 58, 61, 62, 63, 69, 70, 72, 75, 81, 85, 88, 89, 94, 97, 100, 101, 102, 104, 105, 106, 107, 108, 109, 110, 111, 112, 113, 114, 115, 116, 118, 119, 120, 121, 124, 142, 144, 148, 149, 154, 155, 156, 157, 158, 165, 188, 204, 216, 234, 247, 250, 261, 284, 287, 294, 295, 300, 301, 303, 304, 305, 317, 323, 336, 338, 340, 341, 342, 343, 346, 350, 363
Reavey, Anthony, Jr 317
Reavey, Brian 13, 16, 25, 57, 59, 60, 61, 62, 63, 65, 68, 69, 71, 72, 75, 77, 78, 81, 82, 86, 88, 89, 90, 92, 93, 94, 97, 103, 114, 116, 118, 119, 120, 121, 124, 142, 144, 148, 149, 154, 156, 157, 165, 204, 216, 234, 250, 262, 284, 294, 295, 301, 303, 304, 305, 317, 336, 338, 340, 343, 346, 350, 355, 363
Reavey Brothers 9, 96, 142, 152, 194, 195, 200, 207, 210, 213,

215, 217, 219, 225, 229, 231, 234, 241, 246, 249, 250, 251, 252, 259, 280, 288, 297, 311, 328, 329, 330, 341, 356, 361
Reavey Brothers (Contractors) Ltd 142, 152, 194, 195, 200, 210, 215, 217, 219, 229, 231, 234, 241, 250, 251, 252
Reavey, Catriona 39, 40, 41, 42, 84, 110, 121, 123, 139, 140, 247
Reavey, Colleen 16, 26, 57, 61, 71, 144, 293
Reavey, Eileen 57, 67, 71, 93, 103, 110, 113, 317
Reavey, Eugene, jr 266
Reavey, Fergal 247
Reavey, Frank 26, 35, 40, 57, 65, 74, 91, 102, 142, 196, 197, 201, 204, 205, 208, 209, 223, 224, 317
Reavey, Jimmy 13, 14, 16, 26, 57, 60, 61, 67, 69, 70, 73, 74, 75, 76, 79, 86, 92, 101, 103, 104, 111, 112, 113, 114, 115, 116, 118, 119, 139, 142, 144, 174, 175, 317
Reavey, John Martin 13, 16, 25, 36, 57, 60, 61, 62, 63, 65, 69, 75, 77, 78, 81, 82, 86, 88, 89, 90, 92, 93, 94, 97, 103, 114, 115, 116, 118, 119, 120, 121, 124, 142, 144, 148, 149, 154, 156, 157, 165, 204, 216, 234, 250, 261, 262, 284, 294, 295, 301, 303, 304, 305, 317, 336, 338, 340, 343, 346, 350, 355, 363
Reavey, Kathleen 109
Reavey, Kevin 64, 90
Reavey, killings 72, 158, 275, 284, 285, 299, 300, 302, 304, 344, 346, 347, 348, 350, 354, 360, 361
Reavey, Laura 247
Reavey, Marie 102
Reavey/O'Dowd killings 151, 159, 161, 163, 165, 275, 280, 301, 328, 349, 356
Reavey, Oliver 16, 26, 30, 57, 61, 62, 63, 66, 74, 90, 91, 92, 106, 108, 112, 113, 142, 151, 219, 223, 224, 300
Reavey, Patsy 14, 71
Reavey, Paul 16, 26, 57, 65
Reavey, Róisín (nee Quinn) 35, 36, 39, 40, 41, 55, 64, 71, 77, 79, 84, 111, 112, 121, 123, 127, 128, 129, 130, 132, 135, 139, 143, 160, 168, 169, 170, 179, 180, 181, 182, 215, 216, 224, 227, 237, 238, 243, 247, 249, 251, 263, 265, 266, 363
Reaveys 59, 64, 65, 71, 90, 94, 100, 101, 102, 103, 104, 107, 115, 117, 118, 143, 155, 158
Reavey, Sadie [nee Loughran] 15, 16, 17, 19, 20, 26, 38, 57, 59, 60, 61, 64, 67, 74, 79, 80, 81, 82, 88, 101, 103, 104, 106, 108, 109, 110, 112, 113, 114, 115, 130, 132, 139, 141, 151, 152, 166, 169, 175, 181, 182, 187, 190, 217, 258, 294, 295, 296, 311, 317, 318, 319, 326
Reavey, Sarah 247, 266, 311
Reavey, Seamus 26, 57, 64, 68, 69, 72, 73, 74, 76, 79, 81, 91, 100, 102, 106, 108, 113, 142, 144, 146, 212, 222, 223, 224, 259, 284, 293, 302
Reavey, Seán 90
Reavey, Teresa 68, 74, 93, 101, 102
Reavey, Una 16, 26, 57, 61, 112, 145, 258
Red Hand Commando 43, 55, 56

Rees, Merlyn 45
Republican Action Force 53, 87
Robb, Alec 103, 175
Robinson, Mervyn 178
Robinson, Peter 314, 315, 316
Rock Bar 138, 278, 297, 302, 327, 328, 329
Rodgers, Charlie 277
Rooney, Jack 55
Ross Poultry 47, 54, 57, 121, 124, 126, 127, 128, 134, 135, 281
Rossville Street 32
Rowland, Martin 165
Royal Black Preceptory 96, 286
Royal Ulster Constabulary (RUC) 9, 10, 24, 27, 28, 29, 31, 32, 39, 42, 43, 50, 51, 52, 55, 56, 60, 62, 64, 65, 66, 70, 72, 75, 78, 98, 99, 104, 105, 106, 127, 129, 130, 138, 139, 141, 147, 149, 151, 154, 155, 158, 159, 161, 165, 173, 175, 176, 178, 183, 184, 185, 190, 205, 208, 209, 215, 216, 217, 218, 219, 223, 224, 226, 233, 234, 238, 239, 241, 246, 247, 249, 250, 251, 252, 253, 256, 259, 261, 265, 267, 268, 269, 271, 272, 273, 274, 275, 276, 277, 278, 279, 280, 281, 284, 285, 286, 287, 288, 289, 292, 293, 294, 297, 298, 299, 300, 301, 302, 303, 304, 306, 307, 308, 309, 311, 315, 319, 323, 325, 326, 327, 328, 329, 333, 334, 336, 338, 339, 340, 343, 345, 347, 348, 349, 350, 351, 352, 353, 354, 355, 362
Royal Victoria Hospital 103
Royal Victoria Hospital (RVH) 40, 57, 110, 113, 155, 158, 189, 191, 341
Rush, John 230

S

Sands, Bobby 168, 169, 171, 172, 173, 174, 176, 177, 182, 183
Sandy Row 199
SAS 10, 44, 52, 95, 133, 134, 152, 164, 323, 343, 351
Savage, Lillian 58, 89, 92, 106, 107, 113, 116
Sayers, Eddie 226, 228, 246, 272
Scappaticci, Freddie 325, 334
Scott, Bobby 74
Scott, Isaac 37, 39
Scott, William 278
Scullion, John 257
SDLP 23, 53, 82, 175, 207, 267, 268
Seawright, George 231, 232
Shankar-Naryan, Dr 69
Shankill 18, 151, 197, 206, 207, 220, 223, 225, 229, 232, 235, 240, 248, 336, 362
Sheeran, Nora 96
Sheeran, Rose Ellen 61, 62, 64, 67, 318
Shields, Lily 279, 285, 289, 290, 302, 330, 339
Shiels, Ferghal 311
Shore Road 194, 195, 196, 197, 198, 199, 200, 201, 202, 203, 204, 205, 206, 208, 209
Silcock, Phillip 52, 279, 330
Silverbridge 27, 55, 151, 162, 279, 280, 285, 302, 345, 356
Sinclair, Edward Tate 327
Sinn Féin 21, 152, 173, 177, 182, 254, 267, 272, 312, 313, 314, 323
Small, Andrew 332
Small, Vincie 73
Smith, Andrew David 252

Smith, Peter 296
Smith, Tania 357
Smyth, DC William David 69
Somerville, John 330
Somerville, Wesley 42, 48, 49, 329
South Armagh 9, 10, 11, 13, 14, 17, 18, 19, 20, 21, 25, 26, 27, 28, 31, 32, 36, 38, 41, 49, 50, 53, 55, 56, 58, 66, 68, 70, 76, 80, 83, 84, 87, 88, 92, 94, 95, 96, 99, 100, 114, 122, 123, 124, 125, 126, 127, 129, 133, 134, 142, 143, 148, 150, 161, 162, 164, 169, 173, 174, 175, 177, 178, 182, 186, 195, 197, 200, 213, 225, 238, 239, 247, 249, 251, 252, 255, 261, 262, 264, 268, 270, 272, 275, 276, 277, 279, 286, 299, 300, 306, 309, 315, 339, 348, 351, 352, 354, 360, 364
South Down Orange Welfare Group 297
Special Patrol Group (SPG) 274, 276, 277, 278, 328, 329
Spence, Gusty 17, 257
Springfield Road 27
Sprucefield 214, 296
Stagg, Frank 152
Stalker, John 292, 293, 307, 309, 334, 349
Step Inn pub 151, 326
Stevens Inquiry 283
Stevens, John 293, 307, 309, 334, 349
Stewart, Dr Joe 63, 64, 66, 69, 76, 107, 117
Stewartstown 349
St Killian's GAA 17, 71, 89, 90, 92, 102, 149
Stone, Michael 235
Stormont 22, 23, 34, 167, 168, 312, 313, 322, 340

Strathearn, William 159, 273, 275, 286, 328, 329, 330
Stronge, James 167, 168
Stronge, Norman 167, 168
Stroud, Michael 124, 125, 126
Sunningdale Agreement 44

T

Taggart, Dr Allister 158
Tandragee 258, 259, 349
Tate, Lawrence 328
Tax 715 Cert 195, 198, 199, 210, 213, 214, 218, 226, 228, 234, 241, 250, 297
Taylor, John 286
Territorial army 328
Tessier, Dr Paul 40, 41
Thatcher, Mgt 171, 172, 173, 176, 180, 189, 192, 254
Thomas, Leslie 327, 331
Thornton, Harry 27, 28, 29, 31
Three Star Inn 328
Three Steps pub 162, 352
Tickell, Brig. Marston 28
Tiger's Bay 194, 198, 209
Tolland, Thomas 329
Toner, Pat 268
Topping, Rev. Robert 94
Traditional Unionist Voice (TUV) 313
Trainor, Frank 345
Trainor, Thomas 345
Travers, Stephen 48, 49, 147, 336, 352
Traynor's Bar 327, 329
Treacy, Judge 321, 324, 330, 331, 333, 334
Trinity College 255
Truth and Reconciliation Platform (TARP) 336, 337
Tullyah 15, 16, 70, 78, 98, 178, 287
Tullydonnell 27
Tully's Bar 37, 285, 328, 329,

330
Tullyvallen 52, 87, 124, 132, 261, 264, 279, 280, 335
Tyrie, Andy 222
Tyrone 18, 21, 42, 49, 50, 53, 87, 151, 167, 170, 171, 172, 173, 174, 230, 285, 307, 318, 332

U

Ulster Central Intelligence Agency (UCIA) 49
Ulster Defence Association (UDA) 42, 43, 45, 56, 152, 153, 182, 193, 197, 203, 204, 205, 207, 209, 210, 211, 213, 216, 220, 221, 222, 223, 225, 226, 227, 228, 229, 230, 231, 232, 233, 234, 235, 240, 244, 245, 248, 249, 252, 253, 272 280, 297, 311
Ulster Defence Regiment (UDR) 10, 27, 32, 37, 42, 43, 50, 51, 52, 54, 75, 97, 132, 145, 161, 165, 166, 208, 215, 252, 253, 255, 267, 273, 277, 278, 280, 282, 285, 286, 287, 289, 306, 325, 327, 328, 329, 343, 347, 348, 350, 354
Ulster Freedom Fighters (UFF) 42, 43, 56, 152, 197, 204, 205, 207, 209, 225, 235, 240, 252, 256, 311, 362
Ulster Resistance Movement 238, 361
Ulster Volunteer Force (UVF) 9, 17, 31, 39, 43, 45, 46, 48, 49, 50, 52, 53, 54, 56, 72, 75, 85, 106, 150, 151, 158, 161, 165, 175, 197, 199, 204, 215, 220, 221, 222, 225, 231, 235, 238, 239, 249, 256, 257, 258, 265, 270, 273, 274, 275, 277, 279, 280, 281, 282, 285, 286, 288, 297, 299, 300, 301, 303, 304, 314, 315, 318, 320, 326, 327, 332, 336, 339, 340, 341, 343, 345, 347, 348, 349, 351, 352, 354, 359
Urwin, Margaret 289

V

Vallely's 345
Vehicle Check Point (VCP) 287, 303, 304

W

Wahab, Dr 68
Walker, Robert 83, 96
Walker, Robin 360
Walsh, Donal 275
Ward, Peter 18, 314
Warrenpoint 57, 349
Waters, Hugh 55
Watson, Joe 51, 52
Weir, John 246, 272, 273, 274, 275, 276, 280, 281, 286, 308, 311, 326, 327, 328, 329, 354
Weir, Lord Justice 321
West, Harry 172, 173
Wharton, Kenneth 83, 95
White, Agnes 68
Whitecross 9, 13, 14, 15, 16, 17, 18, 19, 20, 21, 25, 26, 35, 36, 37, 39, 41, 50, 51, 54, 57, 58, 63, 66, 67, 68, 70, 71, 72, 74, 75, 77, 78, 82, 83, 85, 86, 87, 89, 90, 91, 92, 94, 96, 97, 98, 99, 100, 102, 103, 104, 105, 106, 107, 109, 114, 116, 117, 118, 123, 124, 126, 136, 138, 139, 141, 143, 144, 148, 149, 151, 157, 160, 196, 203, 204, 207, 213, 216, 219, 230, 255, 258, 262, 279, 281, 287, 293, 294, 297, 303, 311, 335, 343, 346, 347, 348, 350, 353, 355, 356, 361

Whitehall 32, 33, 170, 214, 364
White, John 'Coco' 207
Whiterock Road 227
Whitten, James 286, 330
Whittington hospital 26, 57, 109
Widgery, Chief Justice 32, 33, 292
Wilford, Col Derek 31
Williamson, Derek 284, 287, 288
Williams, Pte Michael 150
Wilson, David 278, 285, 286, 327
Wilson, Paddy 207
Winters, Kevin 318, 319, 358
Woodvale 220, 229, 235
Woolsey, Peter 330
Wren, Larry 45
Wright, Billy (King Rat) 235, 258, 259, 297
Wylie, Jack 329

Y

Young, Stuart 279